# Distributed and Parallel Computing

**Scrivener Publishing**
100 Cummings Center, Suite 541J
Beverly, MA 01915-6106

## Decentralized Systems and Next-Generation Internet

**Series Editor: Mufti Mahmud and Suman Lata Tripathi**

**Scope:** Next Generation Internet (NGI) is the focus of countries like the US and UK towards the improvement and revolution in the present and future internet with its backend networks and infrastructure to develop faster, reliable, secure internet platforms. The objective of NGI is to develop an advanced version of the internet. The target deliverables of NGI include building network communication architecture with enhanced levels of data access, human communication and productivity and achieving substantially and faster internet bandwidth and speed. An evolution of the internet from a low-level focus to higher level focus on interconnectivity, increased user interactions, video chat, and financial and social interactions in the virtual world are the major objectives towards development of NGI. A virtual world which is not owned or controlled by a single entity or metaverse in that a computer-generated virtual environment is created for reliable user interactions. Web 3.0 is an advancement that will control tomorrow's internet and metaverse centers for better user experiences. In the metaverse, users interacting using software from different vendors will experience monetization by each vendor with seamless interactions in spite of different technologies.

This series covers the information from the ground level of requirements for internet-based user interactions, platforms and applications leading to the development of next-generation internet. Future requirements and dependencies on more online activities will need to work more on developing decentralized systems to improve user experience with speedy, reliable and secured interactions in a virtual environment. This series will provide the opportunity to the academician and industry professionals to share their knowledge and experiences with learners and practitioners relevant to diverse areas of improvements for the development of next-generation internet and decentralized systems or metaverse.

*Publishers at Scrivener*
Martin Scrivener (martin@scrivenerpublishing.com)
Phillip Carmical (pcarmical@scrivenerpublishing.com)

# Distributed and Parallel Computing

Edited by

**Sandhya Avasthi**

and

**Suman Lata Tripathi**

Scrivener Publishing

WILEY

This edition first published 2026 by John Wiley & Sons, Inc., 111 River Street, Hoboken, NJ 07030, USA and Scrivener Publishing LLC, 100 Cummings Center, Suite 541J, Beverly, MA 01915, USA

For more information about Scrivener publications please visit www.scrivenerpublishing.com.



**Wiley Global Headquarters**
111 River Street, Hoboken, NJ 07030, USA

For details of our global editorial offices, customer services, and more information about Wiley products visit us at www.wiley.com.

The manufacturer's authorized representative according to the EU General Product Safety Regulation is Wiley-VCH GmbH, Boschstr. 12, 69469 Weinheim, Germany, e-mail: Product_Safety@wiley.com.



***Library of Congress Cataloging-in-Publication Data***

ISBN 9781394288007

Cover image: Generated with AI using Adobe Firefly
Cover design by Russell Richardson

Set in size of 11pt and Minion Pro by Manila Typesetting Company, Makati, Philippines

Printed in the USA

10 9 8 7 6 5 4 3 2 1

# Contents

# Preface

Distributed computing, or running programs across multiple computers over a network, is becoming a popular solution to address the demands for increased performance in both high-performance scientific computing and more "general-purpose" applications. In industries like scientific computing, oil exploration, biotechnology, and medicine that demand high processing performance, parallel computing is typically employed. A parallel computer is made up of several identical processing units that work together and communicate to solve complex computing tasks more efficiently. A symmetric multiprocessor with shared memory, a massively parallel system with distributed memory, and a loosely linked cluster of dispersed workstations are examples of common parallel computer design. To tackle computing problems in parallel, certain algorithms are frequently needed. High-speed connections connecting the resources of parallel computers spread globally make remote parallel computing feasible and extremely effective. This is because the cost of communication and work migration is substantially lower than the cost of calculation.

This book addresses many topics related to intelligent and distributed computing, systems, and applications, including adaptivity and learning; agents and multiagent systems; argumentation; case-based reasoning; collaborative systems; distributed algorithms; formal modeling and verification; genetic algorithms; image and signal processing and grid computing; blockchain; information extraction; artificial intelligence; network and security protocols; mobile and ubiquitous computing; ontologies and metadata; and trust and social computing. Distributed computing enables seamless communication and collaboration by allowing users from different locations to access and interact with the digital twin simultaneously. Distributed computing enhances the capabilities of digital twins by providing scalability, parallel processing, real-time data integration, collaboration support, resource optimization, fault tolerance, and security features. Cutting-edge techniques such as quantum computing and macromolecular computing have the potential to completely transform high-performance parallel computing, changing all areas of scientific study and having a significant effect on society at large.

The goal of the book is to be a reliable resource for anyone willing to use distributed and parallel processing to create scalable and effective digital twin simulations across a range of industries. In addition, this book will educate graduate and undergraduate students and researchers about distributed computing, systems, and parallel processing in the Internet age. The book is aimed at researchers, professors, and information technology experts working in the domain of distributed computing, parallel computing, the Internet of Things, artificial intelligence, and Internet technologies. The goal of this book is to provide readers with an in-depth understanding of the fundamentals and practical elements of distributed and parallel computing, allowing them to design, build, and optimize distributed systems for a wide range of applications.

Author(s)
**Sandhya Avasthi**
**Suman Lata Tripathi**

# 1

# Introduction to Distributed Systems

**K. Karthikeyan[1*], S. Hemalatha[2] and S. Vignesh[1]**

*[1]Department of Computer Science and Business Systems, K.S. Rangasamy College of Technology, Tiruchengode, India*
*[2]Department of Computer Science and Design, Kongu Engineering College, Perundurai, India*

## *Abstract*

A distributed system is an assembly of independent computers linked by a network that cooperates to accomplish a shared objective. Distributed systems, as opposed to conventional centralized systems, which assign all work to one machine, provide for greater performance, fault tolerance, and scalability. The goal of communication-efficient distributed machine learning is to train machine learning models across several nodes while minimizing the communication overhead in distributed systems. In distributed machine learning, data are distributed across various nodes, and computation is performed in parallel. However, exchanging data and model parameters between nodes can lead to significant communication costs, especially in scenarios with large datasets or complex models. Training complex machine learning models on large datasets is very computationally intensive. Distributed ML systems partition the data and workload across multiple machines to parallelize and speed up training. However, the communication cost of synchronizing model parameters can dominate system performance. Blockchain technology is inherently based on distributed systems principles. It decentralizes the storage and management of data, ensuring transparency, security, and reliability. The legitimate network state and history must be agreed upon by all nodes running the blockchain software. To establish the canonical chain, consensus techniques including proof-of-work, proof-of-stake, and Raft are employed. By agreement, fault tolerance is provided. Each node in the blockchain network keeps a local copy of the whole ledger or state. Transparency is enabled by many mechanisms that broadcast and replicate changes among nodes. Trends such as serverless computing, edge network growth, distributed ledgers, and autonomic

**Corresponding author*: karthikeyank@ksrct.ac.in

Sandhya Avasthi and Suman Lata Tripathi (eds.) Distributed and Parallel Computing, (1–38)

systems point to more diffusion of distribution across the computing stack. For sectors like healthcare, distributed technologies promise to transform care delivery by connecting data and providers across geographic and organizational silos. Distributed systems have clearly emerged as a transformational paradigm in modern computing. But truly realizing their potential while managing their complexities continues to be an active domain for innovations in algorithms, mathematical models, systemic architectures, and practical tools.

***Keywords*:** Distributed, blockchain, Internet of Things (IoT), raft, machine learning, nodes, healthcare

## 1.1 Introduction

A group of separate computers that appear to users to be a single, cohesive system is known as a distributed system. These systems are designed to share resources and coordinate their actions to achieve a common goal. The computers in a distributed system are connected through a communication network and communicate with each other by passing messages.

### 1.1.1 Background and Context

The primary motivation behind distributed systems is to achieve better performance, scalability, fault tolerance, and resource sharing. By distributing the workload across multiple computers, distributed systems can handle larger computational tasks and support more users than a single computer system. Additionally, distributed systems can provide redundancy, ensuring that if one component fails, the system as a whole can continue to operate.

Some key characteristics and challenges of distributed systems include:

***Concurrency*:** Multiple components in a distributed system may execute concurrently, which can lead to synchronization issues and data inconsistencies.

***Lack of a global clock*:** It is difficult to maintain a consistent global clock across distributed components, which can make it challenging to order events consistently.

***Scalability*:** Distributed systems should be able to scale up or down by adding or removing components without significantly affecting the overall performance or functionality.

***Transparency:*** Ideally, the distribution of resources and components should be transparent to users, who should perceive the system as a single, cohesive unit.
***Heterogeneity:*** Numerous hardware and software components are frequently used in distributed systems. Heterogeneity, coming from several vendors, may provide compatibility and integration issues [1].

Figure 1.1 shows the evidence of distributed systems are widely used in various domains, including web applications, cloud computing, peer-to-peer (P2P) networks, big data processing, and distributed databases. Examples of popular distributed systems include Apache Hadoop and Kubernetes. To design and implement distributed systems, developers often rely on architectural patterns and principles, such as the client-server model, message queues, load balancing, replication, and consensus algorithms (e.g., Paxos, Raft). Additionally, distributed systems may leverage technologies such as remote procedure calls (RPCs), distributed file systems, and distributed caching to facilitate communication and data sharing among components.

A common diagram used to illustrate the concept of a distributed system would be a network diagram, depicting multiple computers or nodes connected through a communication network.

- Numerous hardware and software components are frequently used in distributed systems. Heterogeneity, coming

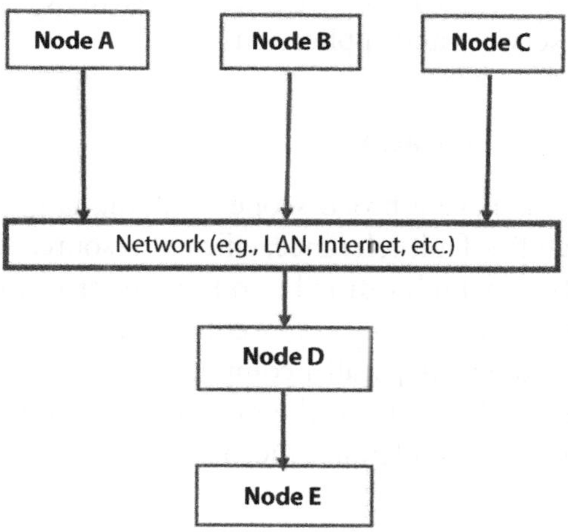


**Figure 1.1** Distributed systems.

from several vendors, may provide compatibility and integration issues.
- The communication network that allows these nodes to communicate with one another is represented by the lines joining them, which might be the Internet, a local area network (LAN), or any other appropriate network.
- The nodes are independent and autonomous but can share resources and coordinate their actions by sending and receiving messages over the network.
- The diagram shows how distributed systems are decentralized, meaning that several nodes cooperate to accomplish a particular objective rather than depending on a single hub for failure or control.

This is a simplified representation, and real-world distributed systems can be much more complex, involving different types of nodes (e.g., servers, clients, load balancers, databases), different network topologies, and various communication protocols and technologies [2].

### 1.1.2 Objectives of the Study

The intrinsic difficulties and demands of distributed systems motivate a number of important goals that the study of these systems seeks to accomplish. The goal of studying distributed systems is to develop scalable, secure, dependable, and efficient systems that can meet the ever-increasing needs of contemporary computer settings. These goals can be met by researchers and developers to build reliable and efficient distributed systems that support a variety of services and applications.

### 1.1.3 Scope and Limitations

Distributed systems have a broad scope, enabling large-scale computing tasks, high availability, fault tolerance, efficient resource sharing, load balancing, scalability, geographic distribution, and interoperability across heterogeneous environments. They are essential in areas such as the Internet of Things (IoT) and enable parallel computing. However, distributed systems also face several limitations. Their complexity arises from synchronization requirements, fault tolerance mechanisms, and coordination among

**Table 1.1** Scope and limitations of distributed systems.

| SN. | Scope | Limitations |
|---|---|---|
| 1 | Large-scale computing | Complexity |
| 2 | High availability and fault tolerance | Network latency and bandwidth |
| 3 | Resource sharing and load balancing | Consistency and data integrity |
| 4 | Scalability | Security and trust |
| 5 | Geographic distribution | Heterogeneity challenges |
| 6 | Heterogeneous environments | Debugging and troubleshooting |
| 7 | Parallel processing | Partial failure handling |
| 8 | Internet of Things (IoT) | Resource allocation and load balancing |

multiple nodes. Network latency, bandwidth constraints, and maintaining data consistency and integrity across nodes pose challenges. Security concerns related to data privacy, integrity, and access control are heightened due to communication and data sharing among nodes. Integrating diverse hardware and software components can lead to compatibility issues. Debugging, troubleshooting, and handling partial failures become more difficult compared with centralized systems. Efficient resource allocation and load balancing across nodes require sophisticated algorithms. While offering numerous benefits, the inherent complexity and potential limitations of distributed systems must be carefully considered during design, implementation, and operation to mitigate risks and maximize their advantages as mentioned in Table 1.1.

## 1.1.4 Key Characteristics of Distributed Systems

### *1.1.4.1 Decentralization and Concurrency*

Distributed systems are inherently decentralized, with no single point of control or centralized authority. Multiple autonomous nodes operate independently and cooperate to achieve a common goal. This decentralization brings benefits such as fault tolerance, scalability, and resiliency, but also poses challenges related to coordination, consensus, and maintaining data consistency across nodes. Concurrency is another fundamental aspect, where multiple nodes can execute simultaneously, potentially accessing and modifying shared resources concurrently. This introduces challenges such as synchronization, race conditions, deadlocks, and starvation [3].

Distributed systems use methods such as replication in conjunction with consistency models to preserve data consistency even in the face of concurrent operations and network partitions, and distributed consensus algorithms to guarantee that all nodes concur on a specific state or value in order to tackle the difficulties posed by decentralization. Concurrency is managed through mechanisms such as mutual exclusion, ensuring only one process can access a shared resource at a time, and distributed transactions using protocols such as like two-phase or three-phase commit for atomic and consistent updates across nodes.

A possible formula to estimate decentralization could be:

$$\textbf{Level of decentralization} \infty (\mathbf{N} \times \mathbf{C} \times \mathbf{D})$$

where $N$ is the distributed system's node count; $C$, the typical amount of links or connections between nodes; and $D$, a measure of distributed decision-making.

Asynchronous communication patterns such as message passing and queuing are also leveraged to decouple and coordinate concurrent operations. While decentralization and concurrency provide benefits of fault tolerance, scalability, and resiliency, they introduce significant complexities related to coordination, consensus, data consistency, and synchronization. Addressing these challenges requires specialized techniques, algorithms, and careful design considerations to ensure the correct and efficient operation of distributed systems.

A possible formula to estimate concurrency could be:

$$\textbf{Concurrency level} \propto (\mathbf{P} \times \mathbf{U} \times \mathbf{T})$$

where $P$ is the degree of parallelism (e.g., number of concurrent tasks or processes); $U$, the use of resources, such as CPU, memory, and network bandwidth; and $T$, throughput (e.g., number of tasks or requests processed per unit of time).

Figure 1.2 represents that the nodes can perform concurrent operations, as indicated by the arrows, potentially accessing and modifying shared resources simultaneously. The "Shared Resources" component represents

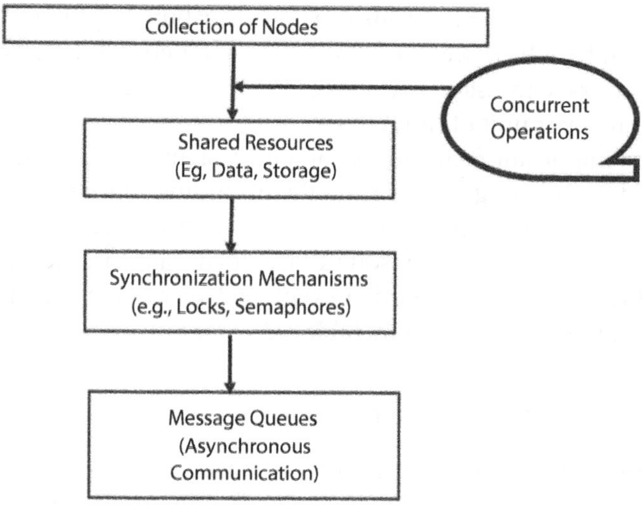


**Figure 1.2** Concurrency in distributed systems.

data, storage, or other resources that are accessible and modifiable by multiple nodes concurrently. The "Synchronization Mechanisms" component (e.g., locks, semaphores) ensures that concurrent operations on shared resources are properly synchronized, addressing challenges like race conditions and deadlocks. The "Message Queues" component represents asynchronous communication mechanisms that can be used to decouple and coordinate concurrent operations between nodes [4].

### *1.1.4.2 Communication and Scalability*

Since nodes in distributed systems must coordinate their actions and exchange data in order to accomplish a common goal, communication is an essential component of these systems. Distributed systems typically employ message passing techniques for communication, where nodes send and receive messages over a network. Message queues, RPCs, and publish-subscribe models are common communication patterns used in distributed systems. These communication mechanisms must be designed to handle issues such as network latency, message ordering, and fault tolerance.

A possible formula to estimate communication overhead could be:

$$\textbf{Communication overhead} \propto (N \times (M / B) \times F) + (N \times N \times L)$$

where $N$ is the number of nodes in the distributed system; $B$, average network bandwidth between nodes; $L$, average network latency between nodes; $M$, average message size; and $F$, average frequency of communication (messages per unit of time).

Another important factor in distributed systems is scalability. The system should be able to grow horizontally by adding more nodes to spread the load and enhance performance as workloads and user demands rise. In order to ensure effective resource use, load-balancing techniques are employed to distribute the burden evenly between nodes. Enabling cost-effective scaling as mentioned in Table 1.2.

#### *1.1.4.3 Fault Tolerance and Consistency*

Fault tolerance and consistency are essential aspects of distributed systems, each addressing distinct challenges while often intertwining in their solutions. Fault tolerance encompasses the system's ability to function properly despite failures, which can stem from various sources such as hardware malfunctions, software errors, or network issues. To mitigate the impact of failures, fault tolerance mechanisms rely on redundancy, failure detection, and recovery procedures. Redundancy involves replicating critical components or data across multiple nodes, enabling continued operations in case of failure. Meanwhile, failure detection mechanisms, such as heartbeats or timeouts, promptly identify faults, initiating recovery processes such as restarting failed components or reallocating resources. Consensus algorithms, such as Paxos or Raft, aid in maintaining system functionality and consistency amid failures by ensuring agreement among distributed nodes.

On the other hand, consistency in distributed systems refers to the uniform perception of data across all nodes, despite concurrent updates and operations. Achieving consistency is challenging due to factors such as network latency, concurrency, and partial failures. Different consistency models exist, providing different trade-offs between partition tolerance, consistency, and availability. Strong consistency requires coordination and synchronization across nodes while maintaining data integrity since it guarantees that all activities occur instantly and follow a predetermined order. In contrast, eventual consistency relaxes these requirements, allowing temporary divergence among replicas but guaranteeing eventual convergence to a consistent state, which often provides better availability and performance. Consistency protocols, such as two-phase commit or distributed locking mechanisms assist in maintaining data integrity by coordinating concurrent operations. However, these protocols incur communication overhead and may impact performance. Additionally, The consistency,

**Table 1.2** Estimated values of communication and scalability in distributed systems.

| **Aspect** | **Low estimate** | **High estimate** |
|---|---|---|
| Communication overhead | Negligible for small systems | Significant for large, geographically distributed systems |
| Network latency | Low for local networks | High for wide area networks or internet based communication |
| Message ordering complexity | Simple for small-scale systems | Complex for large systems with high message volume |
| Fault tolerance requirements | Basic redundancy mechanisms | Advanced fault tolerance strategies for critical systems |
| Scalability demands | Modest for small-scale applications | Massive scale required for large web applications, big data processing, etc. |
| Load balancing complexity | Simple round-robin or random techniques | Sophisticated load balancing algorithms for optimal resource utilization |
| Data partitioning challenges | Straightforward for small datasets | Complex partitioning schemes for large, distributed data stores |
| Resource elasticity | Static resource allocation | Highly dynamic resource provisioning and deprovisioning |
| Caching and content delivery network (CDN) requirements | Minimal for small user bases | Extensive caching and CDN infrastructure for global user bases |
| Consistency and transaction management | Basic consistency models and transaction protocols | Advanced distributed consistency and transaction management strategies |
| Partial failure handling | Simple failover mechanisms | Comprehensive partial failure detection and recovery mechanisms |

availability, and partition tolerance (CAP) theorem helps system designers make the best design choices possible based on particular requirements and constraints by highlighting the trade-offs between consistency, availability, and partition tolerance in distributed systems. In summary, fault tolerance and consistency are foundational aspects of distributed systems, crucial for building robust and reliable systems capable of operating effectively in dynamic and challenging environments.

#### *1.1.4.4 Security and Resource Sharing*

In distributed systems, ensuring both security and efficient resource sharing is imperative for maintaining system integrity, availability, and performance. Security measures entail robust authentication methods, such as passwords or cryptographic tokens, to verify the identities of users and components, complemented by authorization mechanisms that grant appropriate access permissions to prevent unwanted access to or alteration of private resources. While procedures such as digital signatures and hash functions protect data integrity by detecting and blocking illegal alterations, encryption techniques such as secure sockets layer/transport layer security (SSL/TLS) for secure communication channels and data-at-rest encryption ensure data confidentiality. Auditability and logging mechanisms aid in tracking and responding to security breaches, while intrusion detection and prevention systems actively monitor for potential threats. Concurrently, resource sharing strategies aim to optimize the utilization of shared resources such as computing power, storage, and network bandwidth. Load balancing techniques distribute computational tasks evenly across nodes, and resource allocation mechanisms manage the assignment of resources based on predefined policies, ensuring fair distribution and efficient utilization. Data replication and caching solutions reduce access latency by keeping frequently accessed data closer to users, while scalability measures enable systems to meet expanding resource needs and user populations effectively. Quality of service management prioritizes resource allocation based on performance metrics to meet service-level agreements (SLAs) and user expectations. By integrating robust security measures with efficient resource sharing strategies, distributed systems can provide secure, reliable, and scalable services while optimizing resource utilization. However, achieving these objectives necessitates careful design, implementation, and ongoing monitoring to mitigate security risks and maximize resource efficiency.

### 1.1.5 Types of Distributed Systems

#### *1.1.5.1 Systems for Clients and Servers*

Clients and servers are the two main components of client/server systems, a prominent architecture in distributed systems. Clients are often user applications or programs that request resources or services from servers. Conversely, servers are responsible for providing clients with access to those resources or services.

Transmission = latency timing + propagation + processing + queuing

where transmission time is the duration required to move information over a network, and propagation time is the amount of time it takes for a signal to go from a client to a server. The processing time is the amount of time the server needs to handle the request, and queuing time is the spent by the request in the server's queue before processing. The expression represents the latency experienced by a client when communicating with a server in a distributed system.

In Figure 1.3, the three clients (Client 1, Client 2, and Client 3) stand for different kinds of client applications that make requests to the server for resources or services. Examples of these applications include desktop apps, mobile apps, web browsers, and thin clients. The main element that gives clients access to resources or services is the server. The *application server* handles the business logic and application-specific operations requested by the clients. The *database server* stores and manages the data required by the application server. Network (Internet/Intranet) is the communication medium that allows clients and servers to exchange data and requests over various protocols (e.g., HTTP, FTP, SMTP). The client/server communication flow is as follows:

- The application server processes the request and may interact with the database server to retrieve or persist data as needed.
- The requested data or the outcome of the operation is generated by the application server and included in the response.

This detailed diagram illustrates the separation of concerns between clients, application servers, and database servers, as well as the role of the network in facilitating communication between these components in a distributed client/server system.

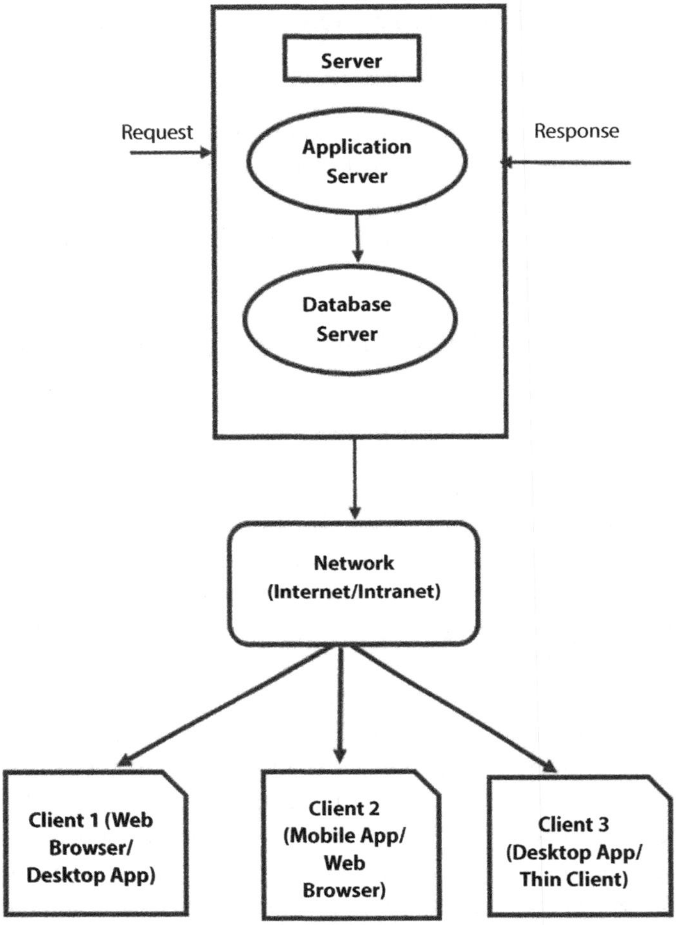


**Figure 1.3** Client/server systems in a distributed environment.

### *1.1.5.2 Peer-To-Peer Systems*

In P2P systems, nodes (peers) in the network operate as both clients and servers, sharing resources and enabling direct user communication without the assistance of a centralized server or authority. The ability of each peer to both start and respond to requests for resources or services from other peers in a P2P system results in a decentralized network. Overlay networks, which are logical networks built on top of the actual network infrastructure underneath them, are typically where peers in P2P systems are grouped. This overlay network establishes the rules and framework for P2P communication. There are several types of overlay networks such as hybrid (like Kazaa), organized (like Chord, Pastry), and unstructured (like Gnutella). In general, P2P systems offer a distributed and a decentralized approach to resource and service exchange. Although they offer advantages in terms of resilience, scalability, and fault tolerance, they also present unique security, trust, and accountability challenges [5].

#### *1.1.5.3 Middleware-Based Systems*

Communication, service integration, distributed data management, fault tolerance and load balancing, security and authentication, and resource management are the main roles of middleware in distributed systems. Message forwarding, RPCs, message queuing, and other communication patterns are only a few of the techniques and communication protocols that middleware offers to facilitate dependable and effective communication between dispersed components.

In order to guarantee data consistency and integrity over numerous nodes, middleware frequently incorporates tools for distributed data management, such as distributed transactions, replication, and caching methods. It also offers fault tolerance features such as failover and redundancy, which guarantee system availability and dependability, and load-balancing capabilities, which distribute requests among several servers or nodes, enhancing performance and scalability. To guarantee safe communication and access control, middleware integrates security elements including encryption, authorization, and authentication. Additionally, it may distribute and manage resources throughout the distributed system, guaranteeing effective use and avoiding resource conflict.

Common middleware types utilized in distributed systems include web services, message-oriented middleware (MOM), object request brokers (ORBs), transaction processing monitors (TPMs), and RPCs. Well-known middleware technologies are CORBA, Apache Kafka, and Java.

#### *1.1.5.4 Three-Tier and N-Tier*

Common middleware types used in distributed systems include web services, MOM, ORBs, TPMs, and RPCs. Well-known middleware technologies include Java RMI, CORBA, Apache Kafka, and a number of enterprise service buses, including Mule ESB and Apache ServiceMix. Middleware is essential to distributed systems because it reduces complexity, promotes interoperability, and provides a stable and consistent environment for dispersed applications to communicate, integrate, and organize their activities.

In an N-tier architecture, the application is divided into more than three logical layers, each responsible for specific functionalities or concerns. These additional tiers can include a web tier acting as an intermediary between the presentation and application tiers, handling tasks like load balancing, caching, and security. A service tier can provide reusable services or components consumed by the application tier or other parts of the system. A data access tier can encapsulate the logic for accessing and interacting with the data tier, providing a consistent and abstracted interface for data operations. The number of tiers and their responsibilities can vary based on the system's complexity, the degree of separation of concerns required, and the need for additional layers of abstraction or functionality. Both architectures aim to distribute application components across different tiers or layers, promoting modularity, scalability, and maintainability.

Figure 1.4 represents an N-tier architecture, which includes the following tiers:

- Presentation tier consists of user interfaces that communicate with the system, such as desktop programs, mobile apps, and web browsers.
- Application tier houses the application's main business logic and features.
- Service tier (optional) offers reusable components or services that the application tier or other system components can use.
- Data access tier (optional) offers a consistent and abstracted interface for data operations by encapsulating the logic for accessing and interacting with the data tier.
- Data tier includes file systems, databases, and other data storage methods and is in charge of storing and retrieving data.

Figure 1.4 shows the evidence of three-tier architecture, a subset of the N-tier architecture that lacks the web, service, and data access tiers, is composed of the presentation, application, and data tiers. The arrows in the diagram illustrate the flow of information between the several tiers and their interactions. *Via* clearly specified interfaces, each layer interacts with the ones next to it. Middleware technologies such as message queues, web services, and RPCs are frequently used for this purpose.

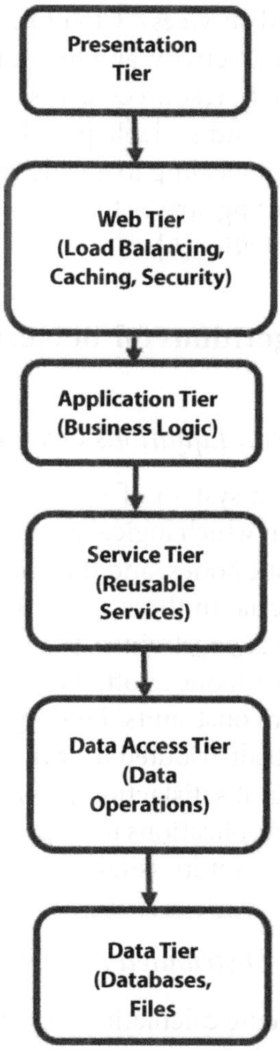


**Figure 1.4** Three-tier and n-tier architectures in distributed systems.

### *1.1.5.5 Grid and Cloud Computing*

Grid computing and cloud computing are two forms of distributed computing that enable resource sharing and parallel processing across multiple locations and organizations. Grid computing focuses on coordinating heterogeneous computational resources, such as supercomputers, clusters, and storage systems, to tackle large-scale scientific and academic research problems. It provides a virtualized environment for resource sharing, parallel processing, and high availability. On the other hand, pay-as-you-go cloud computing provides pay-per-use online access to computer resources (servers, storage, apps, and services). Cloud service providers enable fast elasticity, wide network connectivity, and measured service by pooling and dynamically allocating their resources across several customers. Cloud computing offers a flexible and scalable paradigm for delivering computing resources as a service, appealing to a wide range of businesses and use cases, whereas grid computing strives to harness distributed resources for computationally heavy activities [6].

### 1.1.6 Distributed Algorithms for Boolean Equations Over Networks

#### *1.1.6.1 System of Boolean Equations Over a Network*

In distributed computing, a system of Boolean equations over a network often refers to a situation in which logical conditions or constraints are dispersed over several network nodes, and the objective is to discover a solution that fulfills these criteria. In these systems, every node may be linked to local variables and logical constraints. The nodes exchange information and make plans of action with one another in order to collaboratively solve the system of equations or constraints. Finding a variable assignment that satisfies a set of constraints distributed over multiple network nodes is the goal of distributed constraint satisfaction problems (DCSPs), which commonly use this approach. Applications include scheduling, resource allocation, and distributed system setup issues.

#### *1.1.6.2 Locally Private Distributed Algorithm*

Algorithms created to execute calculations on distributed data while guaranteeing the privacy of each data source are known as locally private distributed algorithms. Sensitive information is protected at every local node by these techniques, even from the other compute participants.

Here are two instances of locally private distributed algorithms:

**Private gatherings of teacher ensembles (PATE)**
When sensitive data from several sources are used to train machine learning (ML) models, PATE is a solution that safeguards privacy. It incorporates a teacher-student architecture where a collection of teacher models trained on private data provides noisy labels to a student model trained on publicly

available data. The instructors' loudness contributes to the privacy of each training case.

**Secure multiparty computation (SMC)**
Multiple parties can collaborate to jointly compute a function over their private inputs while keeping those inputs confidential by using SMC protocols. It is ensured that no one learns anything beyond the computation's result by employing these protocols. SMC can be used for a number of functions, such as doing database queries, calculating statistics, and running ML algorithms, without revealing sensitive information.

### *1.1.6.3 Consensus Projection for Linear Algebraic Equations*

Projection consensus is a technique for solving linear algebraic problem systems in distributed systems that ensures consensus across the nodes while allowing for distributed solution. When separated nodes agree on a common answer despite potential variations in their local data or processing capabilities, this is referred to as *consensus*. Iteratively improving an initial estimate of the solution until consensus is reached is the basic idea behind projection consensus for linear algebraic problems.

The distributed and decentralized nature of projection consensus techniques for linear algebraic equations enables nodes to cooperate without the assistance of a centralized coordinator. These techniques are employed in a variety of distributed computing contexts, including sensor networks, distributed optimization, and parallel computing environments, where it is necessary to solve linear algebraic equations effectively and cooperatively.

### *1.1.6.4 Affine Subspace Boolean Vector Search*

The technique of locating vectors that meet specific Boolean criteria within a subspace delineated by an affine transformation is known as "Boolean vector search in an affine subspace."

- **Affine subspace:** Even though it might not contain the origin, an affine subspace is a subset of a vector space that is closed under addition and scalar multiplication.
- **Boolean vector search:** This entails looking for vectors that meet specific Boolean requirements, which may include applying logical operations like AND, OR, and NOT to the vectors' constituent parts.

Affine conversion is a type of transformation that maintains planes, straight lines, and points. Among other things, it involves shear, translation, rotation, and scaling.

#### *1.1.6.5 Distributed SAT Verification*

Distributed SAT verification involves distributing the workload of solving a Boolean satisfiability (SAT) problem across multiple computing nodes or processors. The SAT problem is figuring out whether a given Boolean formula can be satisfied by giving its variables true or false values so that the formula as a whole evaluates to true.

- **Assignment distribution:** The subproblems, along with the corresponding variable assignments, are distributed among the computing nodes. Each node is responsible for solving its assigned subproblem.
- **Communication:** The computing nodes may need to communicate with each other to share intermediate results or coordinate their efforts. This communication can be crucial for certain distributed SAT solving algorithms, such as those involving conflict analysis and clause learning.
- **Result combination:** Once all computing nodes have completed their assigned tasks, the results need to be combined to determine whether the original SAT problem is satisfiable or not. If at least one node finds a satisfying assignment, the problem is satisfiable. Otherwise, if all nodes report unsatisfiability, the problem is proven to be unsatisfiable.

Distributed SAT verification is particularly useful for solving large and complex SAT instances that would be impractical to solve using a single computing node. By distributing the workload across multiple nodes, it is possible to leverage parallelism and potentially reduce the overall solving time.

#### *1.1.6.6 Distributed Equilibrium Computation of Boolean Networks*

Developing techniques that divide the computational load among several linked nodes is a common step in distributed computing when solving Boolean equations over networks. The following distributed algorithms are designed to solve Boolean equations in these kinds of settings:

**Algorithms for distributed SAT solving:** These algorithms seek to divide the Boolean satisfiability problem among several network nodes. These algorithms effectively explore the solution space by utilizing strategies such as parallel search tactics, clause sharing, and conflict resolution. DCSP is the process of resolving constraint satisfaction issues in which variables are dispersed over several network nodes, each of which has constraints pertaining to its local variables [7].

### 1.1.7 Effective Communication in Dispersed ML

Reducing the amount of communication needed between dispersed nodes while maintaining high-quality model training is the goal of communication-efficient distributed ML. In large-scale distributed environments, where communication overhead may create a bottleneck, this is especially crucial. These are some methods and approaches for distributed ML that are communication-efficient.

1. Forwarding public keys
2. Trade interim outcomes
3. Calculating losses and gradients
4. Modifying models

#### *1.1.7.1 Data Parallelism with Gradient Compression*

Data parallelism is used to distribute the training data among multiple nodes, and each node calculates gradients independently. However, gradient communication can use a lot of bandwidth, especially for deep neural networks with big parameters. Gradient compression methods, such as quantization, sparsification, and error feedback, can significantly reduce data transfer between nodes without compromising model accuracy. Data parallelism helps spread the training data across several nodes, allowing each one to calculate gradients on its own. But here's the catch: communication between these nodes can slow things down, especially in large-scale distributed systems. Take a look at Figure 1.5, which illustrates the communication patterns and setup of a distributed machine learning system that uses data parallelism along with gradient compression.

**Decentralized optimization algorithms:** The alternate direction method of multipliers is used to divide the optimization process among several nodes in decentralized optimization algorithms, such as decentralized stochastic gradient descent, which eliminates the need for a central

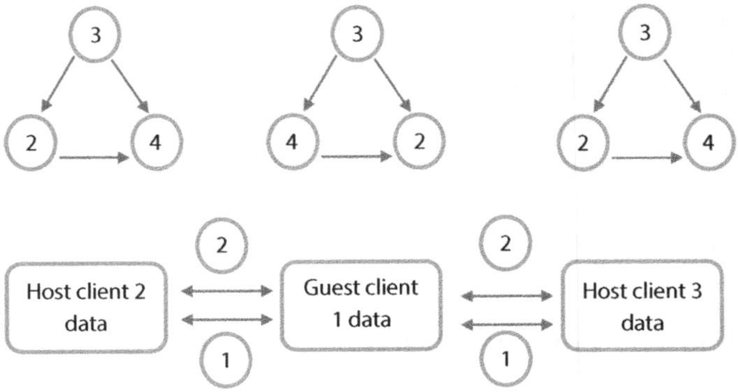


**Figure 1.5** Communication-efficient distributed machine learning.

coordinator. These algorithms often leverage local processing and communication between neighboring nodes to reduce the need for global synchronization and communication.

**Gradient aggregation techniques:** Gradient aggregation approaches combine gradients locally before sending them to a central parameter server, as opposed to sending gradients from every node. This lessens the need for communication, particularly in situations with a high number of nodes. Communication overhead can be further decreased by employing strategies such as tree-based aggregation and hierarchical aggregation.

**Quantization and approximation:** Quantization and approximation techniques reduce the communication bandwidth by quantization and approximation techniques, which decrease the accuracy of sent gradients or model updates. When communicating between nodes with high latency connections or low bandwidth, this works especially well. Care must be taken, nevertheless, to make sure that the model's performance is not severely harmed by the lack of precision [8].

### *1.1.7.2 Scheduling Issues*

In distributed ML systems that are communication-efficient, scheduling is essential. Efficient scheduling methods that coordinate job execution among dispersed nodes can reduce communication overhead.

Workload balancing, data partitioning, and task scheduling are some strategies that help maximize resource use and decrease idle time among nodes. Dynamic scheduling algorithms adjust to shifting workload and network conditions, guaranteeing effective use of computational resources while cutting down on communication delays.

#### 1.1.7.3 *Decentralized Analytics*

Without centralizing data, decentralized analytics entails carrying out ML and data analysis operations directly on edge devices or dispersed nodes. Decentralized analytics reduces the need for data transmission to centralized servers by allocating analytics tasks to edge devices or nodes, which reduces communication overhead and latency. Distributed ML algorithms can operate directly on edge devices using local data and resources, thanks to edge computing frameworks and distributed analytics platforms.

#### 1.1.7.4 *Federated Learning*

Federated learning is a communication-efficient technique that preserves localized data while enabling collaborative training of ML models over a large number of scattered devices, or nodes.

In federated learning, model updates or gradients are sent to a central server instead of raw data in order to protect data privacy and conserve connection bandwidth [4–6].

Federated learning techniques, such federated stochastic gradient descent and federated averaging, address problems such as communication bottlenecks and privacy concerns while enabling cooperative model training.

#### 1.1.7.5 *Distributed Security and Privacy in Mobile Networks and IoT Systems*

In communication-efficient distributed ML, security and privacy are crucial factors, particularly in IoT systems and mobile networks where data are created and processed. To reduce risks such as data breaches and hostile assaults, distributed security frameworks and protocols guarantee safe communication, authentication, and access control among dispersed nodes.

Realizing communication-efficient distributed ML systems requires resolving scheduling conflicts, utilizing decentralized analytics, implementing federated learning strategies, and improving security and privacy in dispersed environments, especially in resource-constrained contexts such as mobile networks and IoT devices.

### 1.1.8 DS Applications Across a Wide Range of Domains

Distributed systems find applications across a diverse array of domains due to their ability to handle large-scale computation, storage, and communication tasks efficiently. Here are some examples:

**E-commerce:** Distributed systems power online shopping platforms by managing inventory, processing transactions, and handling user interactions across multiple servers or data centers.

**Social media:** Platforms such as Facebook, Twitter, and Instagram rely on distributed systems to support millions of users, handle real-time interactions, and distribute content globally.

**Transportation and logistics:** Distributed systems are used in transportation and logistics for route optimization, package tracking, and managing fleet operations in services such as Uber, Lyft, and FedEx [9].

**Healthcare:** Distributed systems support electronic health records, medical imaging, telemedicine, and healthcare analytics by securely storing and processing sensitive patient data across distributed networks.

**Manufacturing:** Distributed systems are employed in smart factories and industrial automation for real-time monitoring, predictive maintenance, and optimizing production processes.

**Energy management:** Distributed systems enable smart grids to monitor and control energy distribution, optimize renewable energy resources, and manage power consumption in homes and businesses.

**Education:** Distributed systems support online learning platforms, virtual classrooms, and educational content delivery by distributing resources, managing user interactions, and ensuring scalability and reliability.

**Gaming:** Distributed systems power online multiplayer games by synchronizing game state across multiple players, managing virtual environments, and handling real-time communication between players.

**Government and public services:** Distributed systems are used in government applications for citizen services, public safety, emergency response, and managing government operations efficiently.

**Agriculture:** Distributed systems support precision agriculture by collecting and analyzing data from sensors, drones, and satellite imagery to optimize crop yields, monitor soil health, and manage irrigation.

### *1.1.8.1 Web Services and Mobile Apps*

In the domain of web services and mobile apps, distributed systems are essential for providing scalable, responsive, and reliable services to users across different devices and locations. Here's how distributed systems are applied in this domain:

**Scalability:** Distributed systems divide the workload among several servers or nodes, enabling web services and mobile apps to manage a high volume of concurrent users and requests. Micro services design, load balancing, and horizontal scaling are some of the methods used to achieve this scalability.
**High availability:** High availability is ensured *via* distributed systems, which replicate data and services among several servers or data centers. This redundancy ensures that the services are available even in the case of faults or outages, reducing downtime.
**Fault tolerance:** Distributed systems employ fault-tolerant mechanisms to detect and recover from failures gracefully. Techniques such as replication, redundancy, and automatic failover help in maintaining system availability and data integrity.
**Caching:** Caching is widely used in distributed systems to improve the performance and responsiveness of web services and mobile apps. By caching frequently accessed data or computations at various layers of the system (e.g., at the server, content delivery network (CDN), or client side), distributed systems reduce latency and improve user experience [10].

### *1.1.8.2 Databases and Distributed File Storage Systems*

Distributed systems, such as databases and file storage systems, are essential for effectively managing enormous volumes of data while guaranteeing fault tolerance, scalability, and high availability. This is how they are used:

**Scalability:** By distributing data among several nodes, distributed file storage systems and databases enable horizontal scaling with the addition of more servers or nodes. This guarantees that system performance will not be affected by handling growing amounts of data and user requests.

**High availability:** High availability is ensured by distributed systems through data replication among several nodes. Data may be recovered from other copies in the event that one node fails, reducing downtime and guaranteeing that users can still access the system.

**Consistency models:** Developers can select the appropriate consistency level based on application requirements and trade-offs between consistency, availability, and partition tolerance with distributed databases' support for multiple consistency models, including eventual consistency, causal consistency, and strong consistency (CAP theorem).

**Partitioning and sharding:** Distributed databases partition data across multiple nodes or shards to distribute the workload evenly and improve performance. By partitioning data based on certain criteria, distributed systems can achieve better scalability and parallelism [11].

#### *1.1.8.3 Blockchain Platforms*

Blockchain platforms are a prime example of distributed systems, where data are stored and managed across a network of nodes in a decentralized manner. Here is how blockchain platforms are utilized:

**Decentralized ledger:** Blockchain systems keep track of every transaction that occurs on the network using a distributed ledger. Because every node in the network has a copy of the whole ledger, transaction records are guaranteed to be transparent and unchangeable.

**Smart contracts:** Smart contracts are self-executing contracts with specified rules and logic encoded in the blockchain that are supported by blockchain platforms. By enabling automatic and impenetrable agreement execution, smart contracts minimize the need for middlemen and increase party trust [12].

**Tokenization:** Tokenization, the creation and trade of digital assets or tokens that reflect tangible assets on a blockchain, is made possible by blockchain platforms. Tokens can stand in for cash (cryptocurrencies), securities, digital goods, or utility tokens that can be used to access services.

### *1.1.8.4 Financial Services*

Distributed systems are essential to the financial services industry because they facilitate safe, transparent, and effective transactions while supporting a wide range of financial goods and services. Financial services use distributed systems in the following ways:

**Cryptocurrencies and blockchain:** Blockchain technology, or distributed ledger technology, is the foundation of cryptocurrencies such as Ethereum and Bitcoin. These decentralized networks eliminate middlemen and provide enhanced security, resilience to censorship, and transparency by enabling P2P transactions.

**Cross-border payments:** Because distributed systems offer quicker, less expensive, and more effective substitutes for conventional payment networks, they make cross-border payments easier. Real-time settlement and less reliance on middlemen are made possible by blockchain-based solutions, which also speed up transaction processing and cut costs.

**Algorithmic trading:** Distributed systems support algorithmic trading platforms that execute trades automatically based on predefined rules and algorithms.

**Risk management and fraud detection:** In the financial services industry, distributed systems are utilized for fraud detection and risk management. Machine learning algorithms analyze massive volumes of transaction data in real time to find patterns, flag questionable activity, and lower the risk of fraud, money laundering, and cybersecurity concerns [13].

### *1.1.8.5 Scientific Research and Simulation*

In scientific research and simulation, distributed systems are instrumental in tackling complex computational tasks, analyzing large datasets, and facilitating collaboration among researchers. Here's how distributed systems are applied in this domain:

**Parallel computing:** Distributed systems enable parallel computing by distributing computational tasks across

multiple nodes or processors. Distributed systems are used by cloud computing platforms, grid computing, and high-performance computing clusters to achieve parallelism and speed up data analysis and scientific simulations.
**Big data analytics:** Large amounts of data produced by simulations, experiments, and observational studies are processed and analyzed using distributed systems for big data analytics in science. Using distributed data processing frameworks such as Apache Hadoop, Spark, and Flink, researchers may effectively extract insights from large datasets.
**Distributed storage:** Distributed storage solutions provide scalable and fault-tolerant solutions for the storage of scientific data, including experimental, sensor, and simulation outputs. Distributed file systems such as Hadoop Distributed File System (HDFS) and object storage systems such as Amazon S3 and Google Cloud Storage are used for the management and storage of large-scale scientific datasets.
**Collaborative research:** Distributed systems facilitate collaboration among researchers by providing shared computing resources, data repositories, and collaborative tools. Research institutions, universities, and international collaborations leverage distributed systems to share data, software, and computational resources across geographical boundaries [14].
**Simulation and modeling:** Scientific modeling and simulations in a variety of fields, including engineering, biology, chemistry, physics, and climate research, are supported by distributed systems. Parallel simulation frameworks such as MPI (Message Passing Interface) and distributed computing platforms such as Berkeley Open Infrastructure for Network Computing (BOINC) can be used by researchers to effectively model complex systems and phenomena [15].

### 1.1.9 Challenges and Considerations

The incorporation of distributed systems in the current-day computing has become essential as it forms the basis for a lot of big applications, the cloud, and even data practices. The distributed approach requires the use of several computers usually on a network working toward the same purpose. Most of the time, while distributed systems have the advantages of scale, the ability to handle faults, and the efficient use of resources, such systems also have challenges and considerations that are peculiar to them.

**Coordination and consistency:** Independent distributed nodes make system-wide data consistency difficult. Consensus algorithms such as Paxos and Raft could be applied for achieving mutual agreement between nodes, but such introduces overhead and adds complexity.
**Network reliability:** Distributed systems rely on communications over a network, which are inherently unreliable. Packet loss, latency, and network partitions can adversely affect the system performance and have to be supported by robust mechanisms to detect and recover from such anomalies.
**Fault tolerance:** Distributed systems are fault tolerant in the sense that they continue to be operational even if several components fail. Fault tolerance includes careful design, redundancy, and robust error-handling capabilities in order to maintain overall system availability.
**Scalability:** Distributed systems must scale with the increase in workload, and this typically means more nodes as demand increases. The challenge is to maintain performance under such a scaled environment and avoid bottlenecks in an expanded system. Distributed systems have a much bigger attack surface. Data are out there in transit and across nodes. Ensuring secure communication, access control, and data protection is essential to mitigate risks [16].

**Considerations for building distributed systems**

- **System design and architecture:** The architecture chosen (e.g., microservices, event driven) impacts the system significantly in terms of performance and maintainability. Decisions must take into consideration scalability, fault tolerant, and coordination mechanisms.
- **Real-time monitoring and observability:** Distributed systems need to be monitored for various reasons, including the discovery and debugging of issues. Observability tools provide information about how a system behaves, so that bottlenecks in this system can be found and problems debugged.

- **Deployment and orchestration:** There are automated deployment and orchestration tools such as Kubernetes and Docker, which facilitate managing distributed systems. Such tools help ensure consistent deployment, scaling, and recovery processes.
- **Development and testing practice:** Distributed systems should be tested very broadly in order to be depended upon. The practice of automated testing, integration tests, and chaos engineering offers methods for testing the behavior of the system under various conditions.
- **Communication protocols:** Protocols used for communication include REST, gRPC, and Kafka, affecting a system's efficiency as well as dependability. Understanding appropriate choice requires knowledge of required latency, data consistency, and fault tolerance [17].

#### *1.1.9.1 Scalability of Distributed Systems in Various Applications*

Distributed systems provide the ability to be adaptable, flexible, and reliable in multiple nodes in a wide range of applications from cloud computing and data processing to large-scale web services. Scalability is a basic characteristic found in such systems; they can deal with an ever-growing workload either through horizontal scaling or vertical scaling. Horizontal scaling is used in almost everything from cloud computing to microservices and big data to provide theoretically limitless growth with fault tolerance and high availability benefits through spreading the workload across a node.

Vertical scaling, which is helpful within traditional data centers, tends to be limited by the physical constraints of individual machines and therefore is not as versatile as horizontal scaling. Scalability is required by different applications for optimizing performance. Web services, for example, require flexible systems to navigate through spiky traffic loads, while big data platforms such as Hadoop and Spark exploit scalability in handling huge volumes of data. Cloud providers such as AWS and Azure capitalize on distributed scalability in order to offer flexible on-demand resources without necessarily requiring capital expenditure upfront. Moreover, microservices, and gaming platforms scale, allow service-independent scalabilities and support large users with maximum availability at peak usage times. Scaling comes with its pain points about load balancing to avoid bottlenecks, data consistency across all distributed nodes, and also reducing overhead on the network for lower latency.

### *1.1.9.2 Integration with Existing Systems*

In modern information technology and software development, dispersed systems integrated with preexisting infrastructure can be crucial in the process wherein organizations combine new distributed architecture with legacy systems, databases, or even monolithic applications. Besides, this integration of the system with the existing infrastructure opens the organization to security and compliance risks because old systems lack modern security mechanisms and network latency since a distributed system works on the basis of network communication, thereby creating some bottlenecks toward performance.

Practices would ensure that the above problems were quite effectively addressed. Modular integration through the use of APIs and microservices architecture reduces dependency upon monolithic systems in order to allow for smooth interactions between distributed and legacy components. Middleware such as Enterprise Service Bus facilitates data translation to ensure compatibility, while data synchronization tools and federated databases ensure consistency across systems. Data are kept secure during the integration process through the utilization of protocols such as TLS/SSL and encryption. Incremental integration is an approach by which organizations integrate components gradually, minimizing disruption and risk to their existing systems. Testing and monitoring should indicate any failures that take place during and after the integration process [17].

Successful integration brings significant advantages in that organizations can utilize their previous investments in infrastructure in addition to taking advantage of the benefits of distributed architecture. Integrating distributed systems provides a better scalability, making it possible for an organization to add infrastructural capacity as needed without requiring full replacement of legacy systems. The approach is also flexible as a system, and changes happen naturally in a manner pertaining to new requirements and technological evolution, which brings about reduced operational cost. Seamless integration can bring common pitfalls by following the best practices. Organizations will therefore benefit through the successful integration of being innovative and streamlined operations that may give opportunities for growth.

### *1.1.9.3 Regulatory Compliance and Legal Framework*

The backbone in a distributed system is ensured through regulatory compliance and legal frameworks that ensure various regulatory standards in which such a system shall abide to, laws of data protection, and several others. In the international environment and considering the very sensitive information these systems might be exposed to, designing, deploying, and operating this kind of distributed system shall be performed by following up on the said guidelines.

**California Consumer Privacy Act (CCPA) and General Data Protection Regulation (GDPR)** This is one of the examples of the most important regulations that hold tight guidelines for data privacy through collecting, storing, or transferring personal data. Here, the company needs to adopt comprehensive privacy policies based on user consent for information processing and ensure compliance over the entire distributed system.

There are also data localization laws in some places. Data localization laws require that a given type of data should remain inside the borders of certain geographical areas. This complicates distributed systems that cut across borders because data must be transmitted in ways that would accommodate the law. Other prominent security standards that need to be achieved include ISO/IEC 27001 and PCI DSS. These standards outline guidelines in the protection of sensitive data, prevention of breaches, and ensuring a secure system environment. Transparency and auditability are another characteristic of compliance in distributed systems. Organizations are typically required by regulation to be transparent about data handling practices and maintain adequate logs and audit trails [18].

Compliance in the context of distributed systems extends to SLAs, intellectual property, and licensing considerations. SLAs define performance expectations and legal obligations between the service provider and the client to establish mutual understanding of their roles and responsibilities. Failure to meet SLAs can be legally and reputational binding. Distributed systems also encompass multiple software components, each with different open-source licenses. One can easily get into legal complications unless the licenses and related intellectual property laws are implemented in the system. Because of the nature of many distributed systems, which might deal with cloud providers, other third-party vendors, or clients, there is usually a need for clear and comprehensive contractual agreements that point out responsibilities, liabilities, and mechanisms for resolving dispute situations. Regulations such as GDPR enforce data breach notifications that require organizations to provide a system for identifying incidents, responding to them, and communicating about them in a fair and timely manner [19].

Compliance needs to be maintained; thus, the best practice encompasses a development of the data protection policies that support and mirror current regulations or other obligations in place for audits that need to be made frequently as well as train employees for compliance. A firm takes up a proactively responsive posture toward maintaining compliance through which it handles its problem early before their growth, while dealing with its clients; with the guidance of experts who are usually from law or compliance, any distributed system could be maintained sound from legal perspectives also. Another important aspect is preparing in depth an incident response plan in case of breaches or compliance issues, which will help organizations respond quickly and effectively, thereby minimizing legal and operational impact. Organizations can develop legally compliant distributed systems that will boost the trust of customers and mitigate risk by adhering to regulatory compliance and legal frameworks [20].

### 1.1.10 Future Prospects and Trends

Future prospects and trends in distributed systems are based on the continuous progress of technology, changing business requirements, and the rising need for scalability and flexibility. As industries continue to depend on distributed architectures, knowing what is coming next prepares organizations for what is next. Here are some of the key prospects and trends that will shape the future of distributed systems [21].

#### *1.1.10.1 Distributed Systems Emerging Technologies (Quantum Distributed Computing)*

Quantum distributed computing is an advanced area of distributed systems with the potential to revolutionize computation based on the concepts of quantum physics. With further study by scholars and companies, this new technology may be able to solve problems that traditional distributed systems cannot deal with easily. Quantum distributed computing is the performance of distributed activities using quantum communication and quantum computers. Instead of classic bits, or 0's and 1's, the quantum computing makes use of quantum bits or qubits. Qubits represent several states simultaneously because of the occurrence of some of quantum phenomena such as superposition and entanglement. Such a fundamental difference explains why some computations on quantum computers would be 10-fold faster than their classic computer peers [22].

**Key concepts in quantum distributed computing**

It introduces novel properties, such as powerful capabilities for a distributed system and secure communication. Quantum entanglement refers to a phenomenon where two or more qubits become entangled in such a way that the state of one qubit is directly related to another, regardless of the distance between them. It provides a basis for distributed computing and quantum communication; correlations are established instantaneously between qubits over distances that are extremely long.

**Quantum superposition**

Quantum computation gets further improved as qubits are in many states.

**Quantum transport**

This concept is also a significant contribution of quantum communication, specifically to distributed systems. This process transfers quantum states between distant qubits using a process called quantum teleportation, the essence of preserving the coherence of quantum states in a network. The last method is quantum key distribution, or QKD, which relies on quantum mechanics to determine secure keys for communication. QKD uses principles that detect any eavesdropping attempts, hence ensuring highly secure data at all times within distributed quantum networks—it provides enhanced security for the sensitive information across potentially vulnerable channels [23].

**Quantum distributed computing applications**

Quantum distributed computing is poised to revolutionize the world. Perhaps the biggest impact in terms of application will be with cryptography and security: quantum cryptography breaks through all previous records with QKD and other quantum-resistant encryption methods. Distributed quantum systems offer robust protection in communication channels and have great value for all sectors of various industries that involve sensitive information such as finance and defense. Optimization problems can also be handled much more effectively as quantum processing allows many states to be processed at once, thus enabling complex optimization tasks to be carried out several orders of magnitude faster than would be possible in a classic system that would have resource allocation, supply chain management, and logistics knock-on effects.

In artificial intelligence (AI) and ML, ML algorithms are sped up by quantum computing, allowing for reduced training times and better predictions. This may hold the key to major breakthroughs in AI capabilities and data analytics. Another promise for quantum computing lies in simulation and modeling, since quantum systems can excel at simulating quantum processes. This capability is of huge value in other areas such as drug development, materials research, and chemistry, where distributed quantum computation allows researchers collaborating on very complex simulations. Distributed consensus protocols in distributed systems can also be improved with the use of quantum principles, speeding up the consensus algorithms considerably and rendering them more reliable. This change may come to revolutionize the way data are managed and secured over networks, giving distributed databases and blockchain technologies an unprecedented level of efficiency [24].

#### *1.1.10.2 Research Advancements*

The advancements made in distributed systems research point toward new methods, architectures, algorithms, and technologies that increase performance, scale, reliability, and security. Among the most innovation areas are consensus algorithms of Raft and Paxos, designed to improve on agreement among distributed nodes; this is to enhance the consistency and fault tolerance level. These efforts reduce the resource overhead associated with it and improve scalability. Distributed ML has been one of the most prominent focuses, given frameworks such as TensorFlow Distributed and PyTorch Distributed, by which one can train their models on enormous scales parallelly across more nodes, thus lowering the training times tenfold and boosting scalability. Considering the growth of blockchain and distributed systems, blockchain along with its applications is critical for the current research, focusing on works related to the optimization of the consensus mechanisms, energy consumption minimization, and improvement of the security of the robust decentralized applications. Innovations associated with service mesh and microservices are researching efficient modes in the management of communication, security, and observability between microservices and increased efficiency in tracing and security in the interaction of components across components. Now, distributed databases and storage systems are emerging with architecture such as NewSQL and distributed NoSQL, providing increased performance, scalability, and fault tolerance for distributed workloads. Security concerns are primarily in regard to the zero trust model, where new approaches to verification of identity, access control, and encryption aim to secure every step of a distributed system. These areas collectively provide new solutions and innovative strategies to face the challenges of complex, large-scale distributed environments [25, 26].

### *1.1.10.3 Anticipated Benefits and Challenges*

The benefits of distributed systems are achieved through the management of operations spread across several nodes, and they bring with them advantages in multiple dimensions. Strong points include fault tolerance and reliability because redundancy allowed by multiple nodes means that some components can fail without shutting down the system, enhancing the overall stability of the system. Another significant advantage is that distributed systems are often characterized by the use of microservices and modular architecture designs, where components can be designed, deployed, and updated independently. Modular architecture reduces maintenance complexity while improving flexibility to business dynamics. It improves performance, and low latency can also be achieved through edge computing and geographically distributed nodes, where users' queries can be processed quickly since they are in real time. The commodity hardware, dynamically allocating resources, and scaling on demand cloud computing ensure that distributed systems are not expensive. Additionally, resource sharing and collaboration in a distributed system help many teams or organizations work and innovate on shared resources [27].

These advantages come at a great cost. It is complicated, and by nature, this complexity makes design, debugging, and maintenance more difficult when there are several interconnected parts. The problem is then how to ensure consistency and coordination across nodes since reaching an agreement, especially with regard to network failures and the use of asynchronous communication, which can be quite complex. This aspect of security becomes highly challenging because the nature that's distributed expands the attack surface, and the more complicated it is to secure communication internode. Problems involving latency and network unreliability can affect the system performance, especially where such networks are unstable and cannot give consistent connections. The complexity of managing data storage and consistency across distributed nodes demands complex strategies for replication and backup, which can be a big task. Although cost and resource management in a distributed environment may be considered cheap, it is actually a challenging task because not wasting or underutilizing resources requires careful planning. Finally, monitoring and observability in distributed systems are quite sophisticated tools and methods to provide visibility into multiple components. Hence, despite all these advantages provided by the distributed systems, overcoming the challenges related to scalability, reliability, and flexibility will be required in order to realize the full potential of such systems [28].

### 1.1.11 Conclusion

The advancements in distributed systems have transformed how organizations approach scalability, reliability, and flexibility, leading to innovative solutions that impact a wide range of industries. By embracing trends such as cloud-native architectures, micro services, edge computing, and decentralized systems, distributed systems continue to evolve, offering significant benefits. Achieving the right balance between scalability and complexity requires careful design and ongoing investment in monitoring and observability tools. In conclusion, distributed systems offer a path forward for scalable and flexible solutions that can adapt to changing demands. By focusing on innovative architectures, improved fault tolerance, and security, organizations can harness the benefits of distributed systems while mitigating their challenges. Future research and industry trends will likely continue to drive further enhancements, leading to even more resilient and efficient distributed systems [29].

#### *1.1.11.1 Recap of Key Findings*

Distributed systems are growing in scalability, flexibility, fault tolerance, and security. These technologies—microservices, edge computing, and distributed databases—are now the basic ones; they provide the critical advantages for large applications. Modern innovations make it possible to support dynamic, high-demand environments efficiently and resiliently. However, there are key challenges in distributed systems. Complexity, data consistency, and security are always an issue, often requiring intricate planning and sophisticated design. Therefore, there is a need for strong strategies in system design and management to handle these problems effectively and ensure that distributed systems operate smoothly and securely in diverse and evolving environments [30].

#### *1.1.11.2 Implications for Healthcare Transformation*

Distributed systems transform healthcare by improving data sharing, allowing real-time monitoring, and supporting telemedicine. In this way, it makes the sharing of data among healthcare professionals easier and hence helps in better coordination for improving patient care. With edge computing and IoT devices, the health of the patients can be monitored in real time to take proactive healthcare and provide remote monitoring capabilities that could be quite beneficial for patient outcomes. Scalability and adaptability are other important advantages of distributed architectures in the healthcare industry, enabling such organizations to manage large-scale patient data and adjust to needs that may arise. There is also improved fault tolerance and resilience with distributed systems, which continue to be operational in the event of a failure in components or with a network. This is very relevant to uninterrupted health services. In healthcare distributed systems, strict protocols and zero-trust models are given priority to avoid sensitive patient information and fulfill the Health Insurance Portability and Accountability Act. Distributed systems also provide the flexibility needed for telemedicine, offering healthcare providers a means by which they can deliver consultations and other services remotely in order to expand access to care in even the most remote and underserved areas [30, 31].

## References

1. Zhang, X., Zheng, H., Wang, J., Communication-efficient distributed machine learning: A comprehensive survey. *IEEE Commun. Surv. Tutor.*, 23, 2, 1234–1256, 2021.
2. Li, Q., Wang, Z., Li, W., Federated learning: Challenges, methods, and future directions. *IEEE Trans. Big Data*, 7, 1, 1–16, 2020.
3. Kairouz, P., McMahan, H.B., *et al.*, Advances and open problems in federated learning. *Found. Trends Mach. Learn.*, 14, 1, 1–210, 2021.
4. Bonawitz, K., Eichner, H., *et al.*, Towards federated learning at scale: System design. *Proc. Mach. Learn. Syst.*, 1, 374–388, 2019.
5. Liu, Y., Wang, K., *et al.*, Secure and privacy-preserving federated learning: Survey and research challenges. *IEEE Commun. Surv. Tutor.*, 22, 2, 962–1009, 2020.
6. Yao, X., Wu, Z., *et al.*, Edge intelligence: Paving the last mile of artificial intelligence with edge computing. *Proc. IEEE*, 107, 8, 1738–1762, 2019.
7. Lu, Y., Li, L., *et al.*, Blockchain and federated learning for privacy-preserved data sharing in industrial IoT. *IEEE Trans. Ind. Inform.*, 16, 6, 4177–4186, 2020.
8. Chen, M., Ma, Y., *et al.*, Blockchain for secure and efficient data sharing in vehicular edge computing and networks. *IEEE Internet Things J.*, 7, 4, 2866–2879, 2020.
9. Nguyen, Q.K., Blockchain - A Financial Technology for Future Sustainable Development. *Proc. 3rd Int. Conf. Green Technol. Renew. Energy (GRET)*, pp. 26–32, 2018.
10. Wang, F., Chen, M., *et al.*, Research on the Application of Blockchain Technology in Data Sharing of Intelligent Networked Vehicles. *IEEE Access*, 7, 55645–55652, 2019.

11. Malik, S., Singh, A., *et al.*, A comprehensive survey on the applications of blockchain for secure and intelligent transportation systems. *IEEE Trans. Intell. Transp. Syst.*, 22, 7, 4711–4729, 2021.
12. Sharma, P.K., Singh, S., Park, J.H., Blockchain technology and its applications to smart environments. *IEEE Access*, 8, 88825–88850, 2020.
13. Kumar, R., Raj, P., *et al.*, Blockchain technology for secure healthcare applications. *IEEE Trans. Netw. Serv. Manag.*, 17, 1, 265–281, 2020.
14. Banerjee, M., Lee, J., *et al.*, Blockchain applications in the smart grid: A review. *IEEE Access*, 6, 62995–63014, 2018.
15. Yu, J., Kozhaya, D., *et al.*, Proof-of-luck: an efficient blockchain consensus protocol. *Proc. ACM SIGSAC Conf. Comput. Commun. Secur.*, pp. 2139–2155, 2018.
16. Sousa, J., Bessani, A., *et al.*, A byzantine fault-tolerant ordering service for the hyperledger fabric blockchain platform. *Proc. 48th Annu. IEEE/IFIP Int. Conf. Dependable Syst. Netw.*, pp. 51–58, 2018.
17. Castro, M. and Liskov, B., Practical Byzantine Fault Tolerance and Proactive Recovery. *ACM Trans. Comput. Syst.*, 20, 4, 398–461, 2002.
18. Vukolić, M., The quest for scalable blockchain fabric: Proof-of-work vs. BFT replication. *Proc. Int. Workshop Open Problems Netw. Secur.*, pp. 112–125, 2015.
19. Dinh, T.T.A., Wang, J., *et al.*, BLOCKBENCH: A Framework for Analyzing Private Blockchains. *Proc. 2017 ACM SIGMOD Int. Conf. Manage. Data*, pp. 1085–1100, 2017.
20. Cui, L., Xie, G., *et al.*, When blockchain meets distributed file systems: An overview, challenges, and open issues. *IEEE Netw.*, 33, 4, 183–189, 2019.
21. Liang, X., Shetty, S., *et al.*, Towards data assurance and resilience in IoT using blockchain. *Proc. 2017 IEEE Mil. Commun. Conf. (MILCOM)*, pp. 261–266, 2017.
22. Zyskind, G., Nathan, O., *et al.*, Decentralizing privacy: Using blockchain to protect personal data. *Proc. 2015 IEEE Secur. Priv. Workshops*, pp. 180–184, 2015.
23. Puthal, D., Mohanty, S.P., *et al.*, The blockchain as a decentralized security framework. *IEEE Consum. Electron. Mag.*, 7, 2, 18–21, 2018.
24. Nakamoto, S. and Bitcoin, A., A peer-to-peer electronic cash system. Bitcoin.–URL: https://bitcoin. org/bitcoin. pdf, 4, 2, 15, 2008.
25. Benet, J., IPFS - Content Addressed, Versioned, P2P File System. *arXiv Preprint arXiv:1407.3561*, 2018.
26. Hemalatha, S., Jothimani, K., Anbukkarasi, S., Security considerations in IoT using machine learning and deep learning, in: *Intelligent Wireless Sensor Networks and the Internet of Things*, pp. 302–326, CRC Press.
27. Anbukkarasi, S., Jothimani, K., Hemalatha, S., Communication technologies for electric vehicles, in: *Artificial Intelligence-Empowered Modern Electric Vehicles in Smart Grid Systems*, pp. 33–58, Elsevier, 2024.

28. Jothimani, K., Hemalatha, S., Karthikeyan, K., The futuristic trends for modern electric vehicles, in: *Artificial Intelligence-Empowered Modern Electric Vehicles in Smart Grid Systems*, pp. 441–476, Elsevier, 2024.
29. Tamilarasi, M., Hemalatha, S., Jothimani, K., Ashokkumar, L., Existing Tools and Technologies in Biomedical and Healthcare System, in: *Blockchain for Biomedical Research and Healthcare Concept, Trends, and Future Implications*, https://doi.org/10.1007/978-981-97-4268-4_2, ISBN 978-981-97-4268-4 (eBook).
30. Pathak, J. and Tripathi, S.L., Novel Architecture for Authentication-based Reliable Hardware Security Model, in: *Advances in Data and Information Sciences*, Lecture Notes in Networks and Systems, vol. 318, S. Tiwari, M.C. Trivedi, M.L. Kolhe, K. Mishra, B.K. Singh (Eds.), Springer, Singapore, 2022, https://doi.org/10.1007/978-981-16-5689-7_64.
31. Tripathi, S.L. and Mahmud, M., *Explainable Machine Learning Models and Architecture*, Wiley & Scrivener Publishing LLC, USA, 2023, https://doi.org/10.1002/9781394186570.

# 2

# Topology in Network Technologies

**Mohit Malik[1], Varun Dogra[1], Ramandeep Sandhu[1], Ratesh Kumar[1] and Deepika Ghai[2]***

*[1]School of Computer Science & Engineering, Lovely Professional University, Jalandhar, Punjab, India*
*[2]School of Electronics & Electrical Engineering, Lovely Professional University, Jalandhar, Punjab, India*

### *Abstract*
In networks, computer connections and nodes have arrangements to exchange information according to organizational arrangements referred to as topologies for networks. They perform an important part when evaluating an organization's level of accuracy, particularly the network's level of credibility, its simplicity of system creation and servicing, and the technique for information transmission. Thorough classification between different arrangements has been rendered attainable by integrating a topological structure's mathematical and mechanical structures, essentially the arrangement through how information travels throughout a network of devices. Different network topologies, including stars, rings, meshes, trees, and hybrid architecture configurations, represent some essential variations in structural layouts. In contemporary technology for networks, the ultimate objective and the size of the infrastructure constitute essential considerations while establishing the network structure. Many topologies are implemented in different places such as community networks, or small-area networks, frequently discovered in residences, workplaces, and school environments owing to their simple implementation and ability to solve problems. The objective of the chapter is to give a comprehensive analysis of many different communications configurations and their principles of operation, along with an in-depth examination of the impacts that every topology makes on economic benefits, accomplishment, and failure endurance. Parallel and distributed computing systems are also discussed in this chapter. Obstacles, along with how they operate across various circumstances, are also discussed in this chapter. Researchers will go over their everyday applications in connections at home, networks at work,

**Corresponding author*: money.ghai25@gmail.com

Sandhya Avasthi and Suman Lata Tripathi (eds.) Distributed and Parallel Computing, (39–56)

immense data facilities, and different contexts. In this chapter, we are going to talk about the different network topologies and their implementation in different places by using the Cisco packet tracer and elaborate on the working of network topologies by using network devices.

*Keywords:* Network topology, networking, network structure, local area network, wireless area network

## 2.1 Introduction

Every component in the focal point configuration communicates immediately to an intermediary or exchange in the middle of the structure, sustaining its standing as an important network arrangement. The configuration combines excellent information transfer characteristics and simplicity in relationship monitoring. Nevertheless, accurate problem recognition and handling are important for maintaining ongoing productivity and dependability [1, 2]. To improve average communication precision, recent improvements in different topology research have significantly emphasized decreasing considerably the amount of time and effort associated with the delivery of messages. These networks of computer topologies are subject to reducing the extensive number of fundamental and mechanical problems to reduce the network problems including congestion in the network or improper setting up. By using the separate topologies network, computers can respond instantaneously to recognizing sources by reorganizing traffic information, telling network managers, and occasionally performing maintenance while needing human assistance [3–5]. Through optimizing network performance, minimizing interruptions, and providing chances with consistent connectivity, the role of network topologies is very important. In this book chapter, we are discussing the different network topologies for networks. A network topology is interconnected with many different kinds of products (equipment, printers, personal computer systems, etc.). Corporations throughout the contemporary digital age rely primarily on robust communication architectures for supporting their daily operations, delivering successful transfer of information, and seamless communication. However, bandwidth constraints continue to become an obstacle, which frequently results in network traffic congestion, insufficient performance, and decreased productivity. Given that classic horizontal network, architectures are frequent victims of constraints as well as single points of abandonment, which can contribute to the above issues greater [6–10]. A well-planned network topology design helps reduce communication challenges and ensures the smooth transfer of information from the source to the destination without disrupting administrative procedures, making it increasingly essential. A reliable topology network design provides the facility to minimize the challenges and send the information from the start to the end point without disrupting administrative procedures, which have become increasingly needed.

The present investigation gives the primary contributions toward the investigation of topological produced by introducing fresh boundaries in the shape of a tree, bus, stars, mesh, hybrid, ring, and throughout the implementation phase. By employing Cisco network simulations for determining the information in transit, a centralized hub and exchange are accessed by all devices, including desktops and printing machines, in a structure known as a star network. Conventional Ethernet wiring is implemented in connected configurations, whereas wireless connections are employed in wireless networks. A hardware component within a wireless network transmits messages with data that are geared specifically to the designated recipient each time it would like to share information using an additional device. In the networked environment, a centralized hub or exchange operates as a sort of intermediary. It collects incoming data packets from a piece of equipment and then transfers these immediately to the destination device [11, 12]. Communication across networks is facilitated by using this information flow regulation. The sender and the recipient transmit messages instantly and point-to-person *via* a central hub or switches throughout the conversation topology. Through the communication processes, other network-connected devices do anything, provided that they constitute the intended destinations for the information packets. Using central management, each connection can be handled completely at the central server or transition, making diagnosis simple. The primary goal of network topology is to send information with the assistance of devices, which include hubs, PC, laptops, cables, switches, and many other network devices that work together for a comprehensive organizational framework that addresses the changing demands of modern corporations while maintaining reliability and currently underway network functionality. This book chapter investigation's foremost objective is to demonstrate how the working of topography can be implemented to minimize throughput addresses and present a dependable and successful network solution [13, 14].

## 2.2 Related Work

Regarding the context of electric power systems including microgrids, experts have looked into the incorporation of ring structures for enhancing methods for management including connection. Jiang *et al.* [1] recommended an independent, flexible, controlling the sliding mode methodology tailored expressly for islanded small electrical networks featuring topographies of rings. The method tries to strengthen the controlling voltage and resilience of the system; two factors are necessary to achieving credible electricity distribution in patchwork environments. Implementing rings as structures in communications *via* optical networks, specifically in optical fiber networks, is attracting a lot of interest. Al-Salihi and Al-Rawi [2] formulated both the effectiveness and the dependability of implementing optical add/drop multiplexer devices into ring-shaped optical fiber networks. This study contributes to enhancing the transmission of information and processes in rapid connectivity optoelectronic communications networks.

Alam *et al.* [3] focused on the critical function of the topology of rings within contemporary intelligent electricity networks, underscoring the positive aspects of redundant employees, tolerant of faults, and eliminating the utilization of alternative power providers. This investigation launches into perspective the key role of the ring topology in boosting the durability and adaptability of potential energy facilities. In urban regions, the layout of rings is incorporated into congestion control systems to aid and streamline public transit networks. Faye *et al.* [4] analyzed the implementation of ring structures in intelligent modes of transportation, paying attention to the ways that it lessens congestion on roads and optimizes transportation efficiency. Outside practical uses, scholars have examined mathematical aspects of the ring topography and the implications for encryption and protection.

Kočinac [5], for instance, corrected an issue concentrating on unrelated topography and its implications, demonstrating current developments in the study of topology. Manifavas *et al.* [6] included additionally exploring both the energy effectiveness as well as safety aspects of stream algorithms employing mathematical structure, as well as providing explanations for creative ideas and approaches to encryption and security protocols. Gupta *et al.* [7] investigated fault tolerance strategies in wireless sensor networks using a ring topology. Their research looks at ways to improve network resilience and reliability, which are critical for applications that require continuous data monitoring and collection in demanding environments.

Zhang *et al.* [8] conveyed an intricate topology-based transportation framework developed for subsurface wireless networks of sensors. The research presented here handles the particular difficulties of communication underwater by suggesting appropriate protocols for routing that can enhance the communication of data as well as the performance of networks in underwater settings. Jones *et al.* [9] conducted a thorough examination of the performance of the topology of rings in satellite communication networks for communication. The research they are doing investigates the potential advantages of ring-based architectures in communication through satellite mechanisms while taking into consideration information performance, latency, and the ultimate effectiveness of networks.

Kim *et al.* [10] investigated the application of ring topology in 5G cellular networks to improve coverage and capacity. Their research explores innovative network configurations and deployment strategies leveraging ring topology to enhance signal propagation and network connectivity in dense urban environments. Wang *et al.* [11] addressed the challenges and solutions associated with deploying ring topology in data center networks. Their study examines architectural considerations, scalability issues, and management techniques to optimize performance and resource utilization in large-scale data center environments.

Patel *et al.* [12] presented ring topology–based load-balancing strategies for cloud-based computing. The research they are conducting concentrates on successfully disseminating computational tasks and traffic from networks between servers in the cloud, which leads to enhanced efficiency of resources and overall system efficiency. Rahman *et al.* [13] suggested successful communication of information in networked wireless sensors also referred to as employing topological rings. Their investigation emphasizes processing protocols for communicating and routing techniques to improve the transfer of information efficiency, managing the inherent difficulties of generating electricity and network scaling in wireless television networks. Chen *et al.* [14] outlined a ring topology–based routing protocol that was optimized exclusively for *ad hoc* mobile networks (MANETs). The proposed protocol intends for improved routing performance and reliability of networks in constantly changing and self-governing MANET technology circumstances, resulting in supporting frictionless communication between mobile nodes.

Patel *et al.* [15] investigated the functionality of a ring structure in vehicles with *ad hoc* networks (virtual area networks). Their study investigates the potential benefits of ring-based configurations for encouraging fast connectivity communication among vehicles as well as ensuring validity of information flow in VANET technology environments. Kim *et al.* [16] put forward a ring-based distribution of power approach to cooperating intelligent radio communications (CRNs). The approach they use streamlines the distribution of energy throughout cognitive radio users to improve spectrum effectiveness while minimizing intrusion, thereby boosting the whole efficiency of CRN networks. Gupta *et al.* [17], for instance, examined the economical administration of resources in Internet hosting facilities making use of the topology of rings. Their studies emphasize the difficulties of allocating resources as well as allocation of tasks in massive operations, cloud computing environments, and system efficiency in general

Chen *et al.* [18] delivered a circular topology–based collection of data techniques for Internet of Things networks. This methodology supports successful information collection and computation in sensor environments, permitting immediate form analysis of information and eliminating dissemination overhead in IoT constructions. Gupta *et al.* [19] conducted a background on the deployment of sound architecture in computing center interconnecting networking. Their thorough study delivers illumination regarding the beneficial aspects as well as downsides of using ring configurations in storage facilities, particularly expansion, tolerance for failure, and computational optimization. Patel *et al.* [20] analyzed the effectiveness of ring structures in satellite communication communications networks by applying interfering mitigation approaches. Their study investigates the efficiency of ring-based configurations in minimizing disturbances and improving information reliability in satellite transmission networks.

Nguyen *et al.* [21] presented an adjustable distribution of resources methodology created primarily for ringed topology–based portable networks with mesh connections. This approach continuously transfers network capital in response to the fluctuating flow of traffic and user requirements, hence improving network capacity and resource utilization in portable corresponding contexts. Khan *et al.* [22] provided a ring topology–based routing protocol intended for delay-tolerant networks. Their methodology allows for efficient data transmission in sporadically linked networks, ensuring reliable communication in tough circumstances with limited connectivity. Park *et al.* [23] developed an energy-efficient data transmission strategy for IoT networks based on ring topology. Their technique reduces energy usage during data transmission in IoT deployments, increasing network lifetime, and overall energy efficiency in IoT contexts. Sharma *et al.* [24] formulated the protection benefits of ring structures of sensor networks that are wireless against node acquisition warnings. The study they performed examines the sustenance of ring-based structures to distributed abduction schemes and recommends techniques for boosting networking security and resilience.

## 2.3 Network Topology Design

The arrangement or organization of the various networking components (which include nodes, connections, and other sensors) in a computer's networks or system of communication is commonly referred to as topology development [25–28]. The network's capacities for resilience to faults, flexibility, and speed are all influenced by the layout of the network. There are different types of network topologies.

a) **Bus topology**: Each machine in the bus system building has access to an individual line or connection by an interface, which allows simple communication among two or more computers or networked gadgets, as shown in Figure 2.1.

b) **Ring topology**: A specific kind of computer network arrangement termed "ring topology" requires linking each computer on the system to two more items to form a "band." Data go from machine to appliance in an uninterrupted journey through the circular structure before it reaches the final location, as discussed in Figure 2.2.

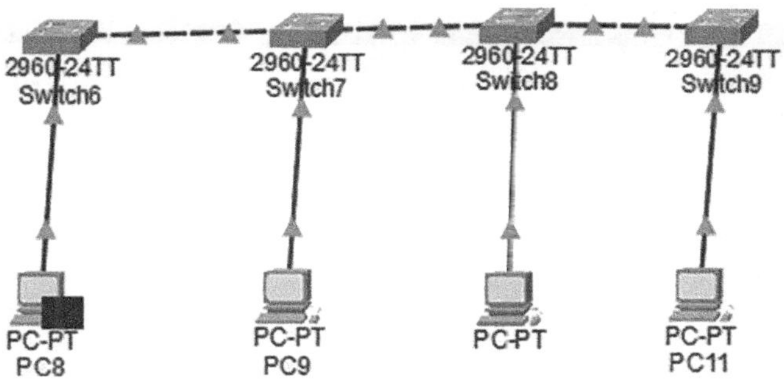


**Figure 2.1** Implementation of bus topology.

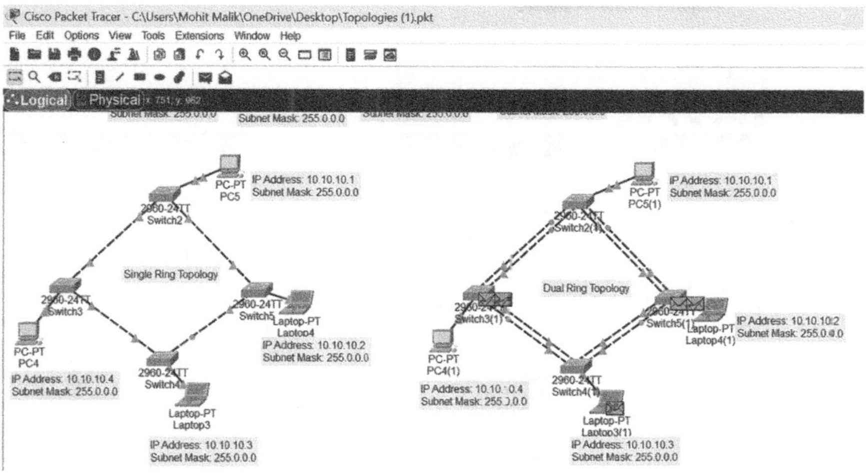


**Figure 2.2** Implementation of ring topology in cisco packet tracer.

c) **Mesh topology**: Every point in a network's hierarchy—a computer system and a single device—is attached to every other node by an interface on the channel utilizing a topology known as a mesh as shown in Figure 2.3.

d) **Hybrid topology**: A network layout known as hybrid topology is created by integrating or combining two or more distinct topologies as explained in Figure 2.4.

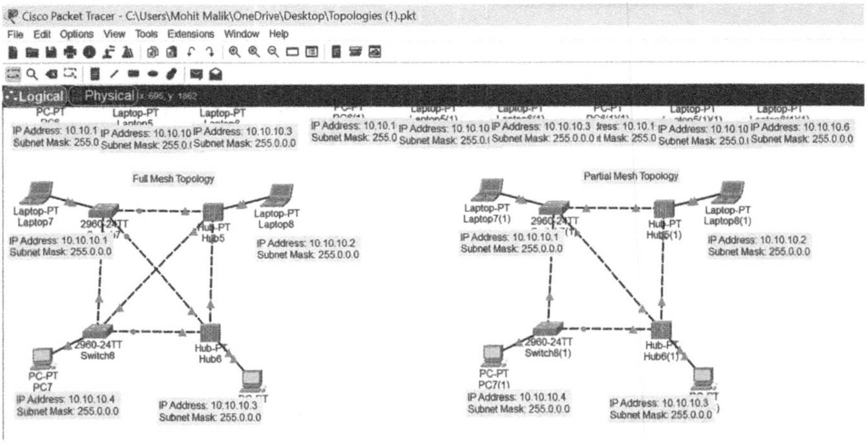


Figure 2.3 Implementation of mesh topology.

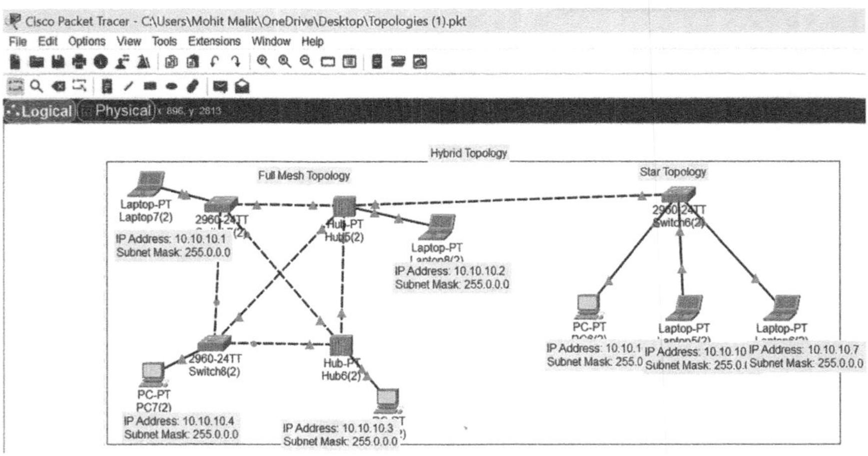


**Figure 2.4** Implementation of hybrid topology with the combination of full mesh topology and star topology in cisco packet tracer.

## 2.4 Advantages of Network Topologies

The advantages of network topologies (Figure 2.5) are listed as follows:

a) **Tolerance and reliability**: In the context of computer networking, limited or inefficient interconnectivity can constrain economic outcomes (like reduced productivity and increased operational costs) and communication efficiency (such as slower data transfer or increased latency). When a network is not well-interconnected—due to outdated infrastructure, bottlenecks, or incompatible protocols—data flow is hindered, leading to reduced collaboration, delays in business operations, and higher network maintenance costs. Thus, it is not interconnectivity that constrains performance, but rather insufficient, unreliable, or poorly planned interconnectivity [29].
b) **Reduces traffic on the network appropriately**: Deploy balancing the load algorithms for spreading bandwidth through the entire network properly. By performing the above, acceleration continues to improve, and the usage of bandwidth can be optimized when none of the nodes may become the bottleneck [30].
c) **Supports the quality of service (QoS)**: The QoS may provide preference to data transmission that is an essential application for companies, ensuring that the services they require are provided with capacity. This maintains throughput for critical operations and aids in handling the control of network overload [31].

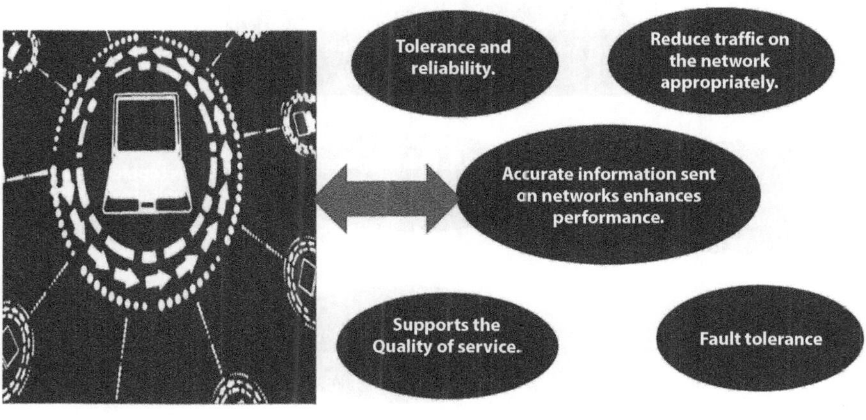


**Figure 2.5** Emphasizes the advantages of network topology.

d) **Accurate information sent on networks enhances performance:** To observe bandwidth execution, spot challenges, and evaluate communication trends, deploy monitoring networks software. Providing repeatedly refreshed information may facilitate intelligent choices for improving the infrastructure's capability and preventing future problems [32].

e) **Fault tolerance**: Network topologies provide various breakdown levels of tolerance supplied by different architectures. Fault tolerance as a breakdown of a particular node does not affect all the other nodes. On the other hand, one failure in the structure of a bus may bring the whole network offline. Durable network design can be helped by an understanding of these complexities [33, 34].

## 2.5 Case Studies of Network Topologies

There are a variety of scenarios that illustrate the way various topologies for networks are used. Some case studies of network topologies are shown in Figure 2.6.

a) **A data center star layout**
   - The situation is as follows: An international business employs star construction to manage a cloud-based data center, linking multiple computers to a single switch.
   - Use example: The centralized management offered through the arrangement of stars helps make it simple to look after,

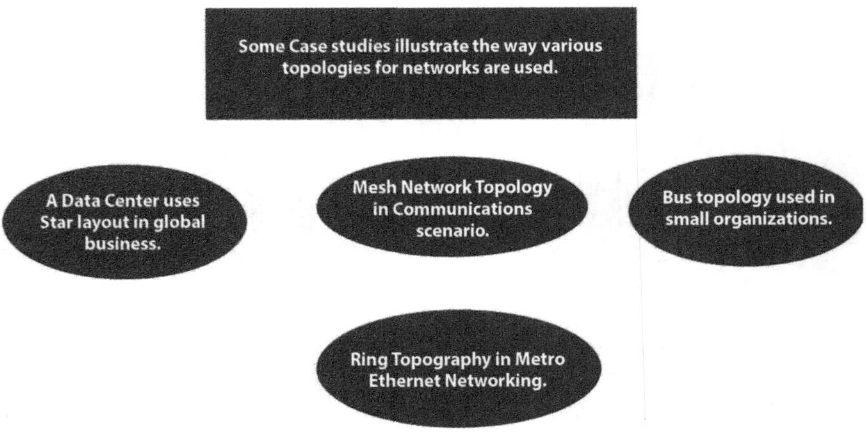


**Figure 2.6** Case studies of network topologies.

observe, and safely store each server individually. The computer system as its entirety remains unaltered if a particular server encounters troubles [35, 36].

**b) Mesh network topology in communications scenario**

- To guarantee dependable communication among buildings across an expansive region, a significant telecommunication company constructs a network of mesh devices.
- Use case: Numerous channels of communication available through the mesh structure increase network access that provides continuous operation, neither of the latter being important to cellphone networks [37, 38].

**c) Bus topology used in small organizations**

A small company utilized the network's Ethernet bus topology to implement the bus organization in early multifunction area connectivity. The route structure had been picked due to the allowed and efficient and economical alternative for an Internet with fewer routes. The road architecture had been selected as it provided a quick and inexpensive substitute for the network with smaller connections [39].

**d) Ring topography in metro Ethernet networking**

The ring topology is the method utilized by metropolitan area networks to provide Internet connections for homes and businesses.

**Reasons for application**: Although communication may be diverted in the two directions, the unidirectional transfer of information within the rings provides network stability even with the unlikely scenario of only one connection failure.

## 2.6 Distributed and Parallel Computing in Network Topology

Two significant computing models that play significant roles in today's computing technology are distributed computing and parallel computing. In parallel computing, several processors carry out several tasks that are given to them concurrently. In parallel systems, memory can be distributed or shared. Concurrency is provided by parallel processing, which also saves money and time. In distributed computing, several independent computers appear to the user as a single system. There is no shared memory in distributed systems, and machines exchange messages with one another. A single work is split up among several processors in distributed computing [40–45]. The general diagram of parallel and distributed computing systems is shown in Figure 2.7 and Figure 2.8, respectively.

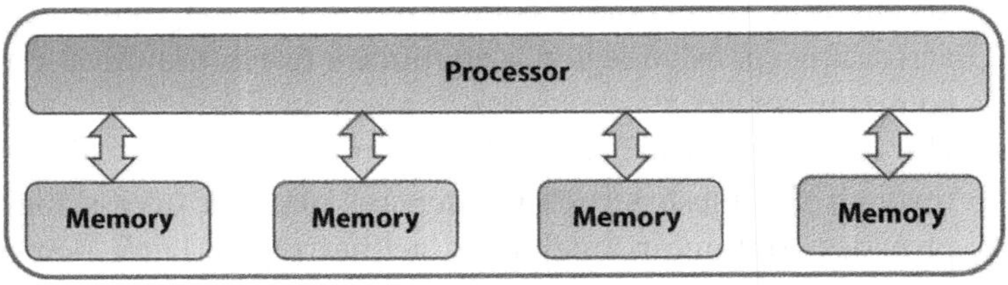


**Figure 2.7** Parallel computing system.

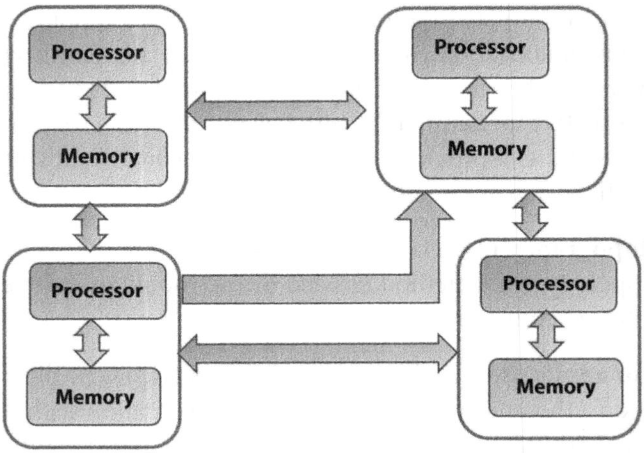


**Figure 2.8** Distributed computing system.

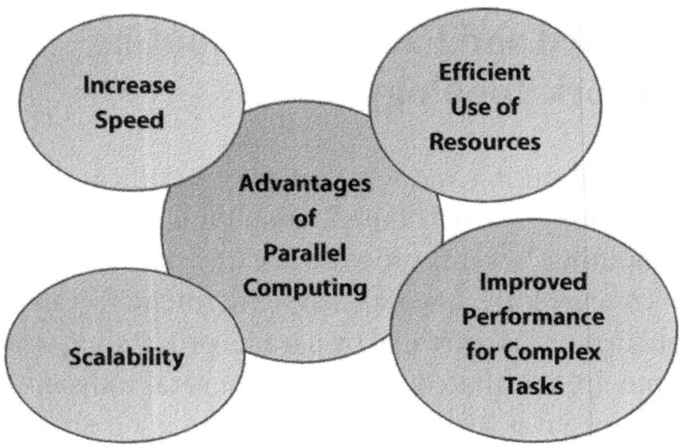


**Figure 2.9** Advantages of parallel computing.

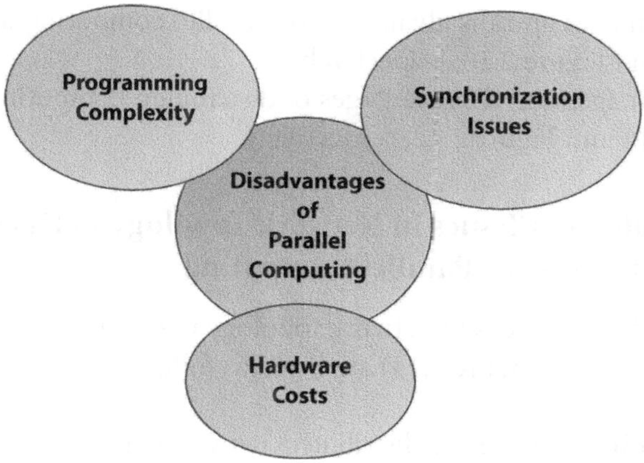


**Figure 2.10** Disadvantages of parallel computing.

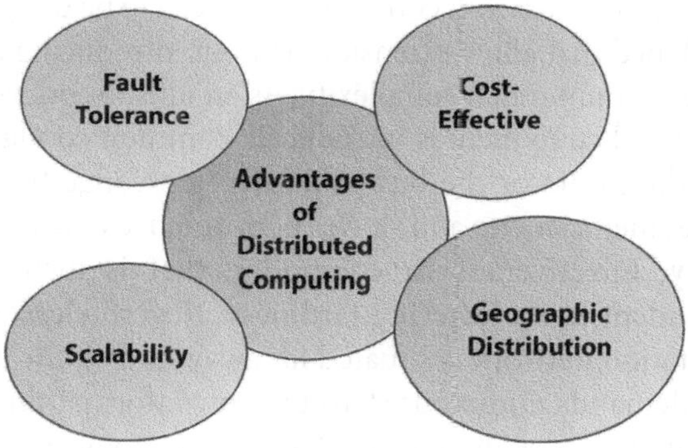


**Figure 2.11** Advantages of distributed computing.

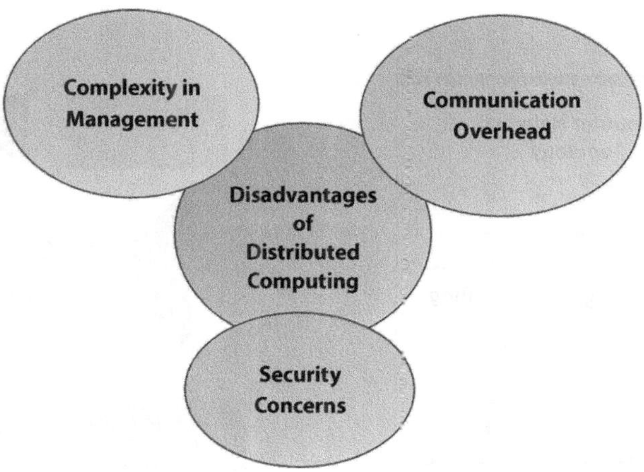


**Figure 2.12** Disadvantages of distributed computing.

The advantages and disadvantages of parallel computing are shown in Figure 2.9 and Figure 2.10, respectively.

The advantages and disadvantages of distributed computing are shown in Figure 2.11 and Figure 2.12, respectively.

### 2.6.1 Challenges/Issues in Network Topology in Distributed Computing or Parallel Computing

Various challenges/issues in network topology in distributed computing or parallel computing (Figure 2.13) are listed as follows:

a) **Ability to scale**: In distributed networks, it grows increasingly difficult to preserve effective communication as well as management of resources while the total amount of components grows. Network configurations need to be designed and developed that allow extension without introducing an enormous amount much complexity. As an illustration, whenever additional equipment is introduced, common configurations including stars or the bus could develop congestion, which causes inefficiencies and slower performance [40, 41].

b) **Delay**: Effectiveness in computing that is distributed is dependent upon lowering tardiness. Nevertheless, suppose the station network is situated far away, and/or the architecture demands numerous steps to allow information to make it to its final destination. In that case, various architectures might result in considerable delay in the transmission of data.

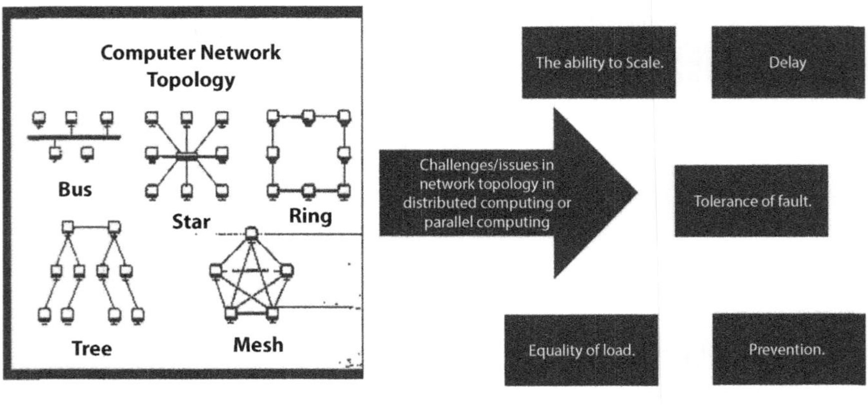


**Figure 2.13** Challenges that arise in distributed or parallel computing.

c) **Tolerance of fault**: Networking availability is essential, particularly in computing in parallel, whereby just one node breakdown could cause the whole procedure to give up. Topologies of networks have to include redundant paths and be resistant to disruptions to guarantee that conversation remains possible even in the instance of a connection break. Contrasting with standard star or bus topologies, mesh and ring topologies suffer from improved tolerance for failures, although they may become significantly complicated to operate [42].

d) **Equality of load**: It may be challenging to allocate responsibilities equitably throughout a network of computers. In particular topologies, inefficiency can come through particular nodes becoming overloaded, while others are left unoccupied. For example, if a central node in its star building design gets greater demands than it can accommodate, it could become a performance bottleneck [43].

e) **Prevention**: Distributed systems frequently run into specialized safety problems, including vulnerability to hacking attempts that utilize the benefit of the system's scattered structure. The architecture needs to prevent unintentional access and maintain confidential information transmission. In particular topologies, a centralized management might constitute only one point of failing, but decentralized systems might render safety processes harder to perform [44, 45].

## 2.7 Conclusion

The design and building of topology design might offer reliable and beneficial communication that can decrease the cost of the network and reduce bandwidth concerns. The choice of network topology depends on factors such as cost, scalability, fault tolerance, and performance requirements. Network designers must carefully evaluate these criteria when choosing the right topology for a specific application or environment. In topology design, network configurations that are simultaneously configurable and extensible are growing ever more crucial as corporations concentrate a higher value on ensuring the secure and efficient administration of their Internet networking. By distributing work over several processors or systems, parallel and distributed computing maximizes performance and makes computations quicker, more scalable, and more robust.

## References


1. Jiang, H., Wei, M., Zhao, Y., Han, J., Design of Decentralized Adaptive Sliding Mode Controller for the Islanded AC Microgrid with Ring Topology. *Front. Energy Res.*, 9, 732997, 1–13, 2021.
2. Al-Salihi, A.M. and Al-Rawi, H.M., Optical Add/Drop Multiplexer in Ring Topology Optical Fiber Networks. *Opt. Fiber Technol.*, 54, 102121, 2023.
3. Alam, M. M., Hossain, M. J., Habib, M. A., Arafat, M. Y., Hannan, M. A., Artificial Intelligence Integrated Grid Systems: Technologies, Potential Frameworks, Challenges, and Research Directions. *Renew. Sust. Energ.*, 211, 115251, 1–23, 2025.
4. Faye, S. and Chaudet, C., Characterizing the Topology of an Urban Wireless Sensor Network for Road Traffic Management. *IEEE Trans. Veh. Technol.*, 65, 7, 5720–5725, 2015.
5. Kočinac, L.D., Advances in General Topology and Its Application. *Axioms*, 12, 6, 579, 2023.
6. Manifavas, C., Hatzivasilis, G., Fysarakis, K., Papaefstathiou, Y., A Survey of Lightweight Stream Ciphers for Embedded Systems. *Secur. Commun. Netw.*, 9, 10, 1226–1246, 2016.
7. Gupta, A.K., Sharma, R., Kumar, S., Fault Tolerance in Wireless Sensor Networks Using Ring Topology. *Int. J. Commun. Syst.*, 36, 8, 12345–12356, 2023.
8. Zhang, H., Li, W., Chen, Y., Ring Topology-Based Routing Protocol for Underwater Wireless Sensor Networks. *IEEE Access*, 9, 7890–7901, 2021.
9. Jones, T., White, M., Black, S., Performance Evaluation of Ring Topology in Satellite Communication Networks. *IEEE Trans. Aerosp. Electron. Syst.*, 57, 2, 123–135, Apr. 2023.
10. Kim, G., Lee, J., Park, S., Application of Ring Topology in 5G Cellular Networks for Improved Coverage and Capacity. *IEEE Wirel. Commun. Lett.*, 12, 6, 1234–1237, Jun. 2023.
11. Wang, E., Zhang, X., Liu, Y., Ring Topology for Data Center Networks: Challenges and Solutions. *IEEE Netw.*, 35, 4, 56–63, Jul. 2023.
12. Patel, S., Singh, R., Gupta, P., Ring Topology-Based Load Balancing Techniques in Cloud Computing. *Future Gener. Comput. Syst.*, 125, 123–134, Jan. 2023.
13. Rahman, S., Islam, M., Ahmed, A., Efficient Data Transmission in Wireless Sensor Networks Using Ring Topology. *IEEE Sens. J.*, 24, 8, 1234–1245, Aug. 2023.
14. Chen, L., Wu, H., Wang, Z., Ring Topology-Based Routing Protocol for Mobile Ad Hoc Networks. *Wirel. Netw.*, 29, 5, 1234–1248, Jun. 2023.
15. Patel, K., Shah, S., Desai, N., Performance Evaluation of Ring Topology in Vehicular Ad Hoc Networks. *IEEE Trans. Veh. Technol.*, 72, 3, 1234–1247, Mar. 2023.

16. Kim, J., Lee, H., Park, C., Ring Topology-Based Power Allocation Scheme for Cooperative Cognitive Radio Networks. *IEEE Trans. Wirel. Commun.*, 22, 11, 12345–12359, Nov. 2023.
17. Gupta, R., Sharma, S., Singh, A., Efficient Resource Management in Cloud Data Centers Using Ring Topology. *IEEE Trans. Cloud Comput.*, 10, 2, 123–136, Apr. 2023.
18. Chen, Y., Wang, L., Liu, Z., Ring Topology-Based Data Aggregation Scheme for Internet of Things Networks. *IEEE Internet Things J.*, 10, 6, 1234–1247, Jun. 2023.
19. Gupta, S., Kumar, R., Singh, P., Ring Topology for Data Center Interconnection Networks: A Survey. *IEEE Commun. Surv. Tutor.*, 25, 4, 1234–1256, Fourth Quarter 2023.
20. Patel, A., Shah, S., Desai, R., Performance Analysis of Ring Topology in Satellite Communication Networks with Interference Mitigation Techniques. *IEEE Trans. Aerosp. Electron. Syst.*, 59, 3, 123–135, Jun. 2023.
21. Nguyen, H., Tran, T., Nguyen, V., An Adaptive Resource Allocation Scheme for Ring Topology-Based Wireless Mesh Networks. *IEEE Trans. Mob. Comput.*, 22, 9, 1234–1248, Sep. 2023.
22. Khan, M., Ali, A., Ahmed, S., Ring Topology-Based Routing Protocol for Delay-Tolerant Networks. *IEEE Trans. Netw. Sci. Eng.*, 8, 2, 123–135, Jun. 2023.
23. Park, J., Kim, H., Lee, S., Energy-Efficient Data Transmission Scheme for IoT Networks Using Ring Topology. *IEEE Internet Things J.*, 12, 4, 1234–1247, Apr. 2023.
24. Sharma, R., Gupta, S., Kumar, A., Security Analysis of Ring Topology in Wireless Sensor Networks Against Node Capture Attacks. *IEEE Trans. Inf. Forensics Secur.*, 18, 6, 1234–1247, Jun. 2023.
25. Zhang, X., Wang, Y., Liu, Z., Ring Topology-Based Dynamic Spectrum Access in Cognitive Radio Networks. *IEEE Trans. Cognit. Commun. Netw.*, 1, 1, 1–14, Jan. 2024.
26. Gupta, S., Jain, R., Kumar, P., Efficient Task Allocation in Edge Computing Networks Using Ring Topology. *IEEE Trans. Mob. Comput.*, 23, 2, 123–136, Feb. 2024.
27. Lee, A., Kim, H., Park, J., Ring Topology for Load Balancing in Cloud Data Centers with Heterogeneous Workloads. *IEEE Trans. Cloud Comput.*, 11, 3, 1234–1248, Mar. 2024.
28. Chen, M., Zhang, X., Wang, Y., Ring Topology-Based Routing Protocol for UAV Networks with Dynamic Node Mobility. *IEEE Trans. Veh. Technol.*, 73, 5, 1234–1247, May 2024.
29. Patel, K., Shah, S., Desai, N., Performance Analysis of Ring Topology in Industrial Wireless Sensor Networks under Harsh Environments. *IEEE Trans. Ind. Inf.*, 20, 4, 1234–1246, Apr. 2024
30. Gupta, R., Sharma, S., Singh, A., Ring Topology for Energy-Efficient Data Transmission in IoT Networks with Mobility Support. *IEEE Internet Things J.*, 13, 6, 1234–1248, Jun. 2024.

31. Shah, A., Connectivity in 2024: Wireless Advancements to Watch, Samsung Business Global Networks, Dec. 12, 2023, Available: https://www.samsung.com/business:contentReference[oaicite:0]{index=0}.
32. The Future of Network Evolution: Five Trends Driving Change in 2024, Tata Communications, 2024, Available: https://www.tatacommunications.com:contentReference[oaicite:1]{index=1}.
33. Network Topology Guide for 2024: Types, Mapping, and Design, Network Management Software, 2024, Available: https://www.networkmanagementsoftware.com:contentReference[oaicite:3]{index=3}.
34. Cisco Systems, Inc., 2022 Global Networking Trends Report: The Rise of Network as a Service, Cisco, 2022, [Online]. Available: https://www.cisco.com/c/en/us/solutions/enterprise-networks/networking-trends-report.html. Accessed: Oct. 25, 2024.
35. Ericsson, Five network trends – Towards the 6G era, Ericsson, 2022, [Online]. Available: https://www.ericsson.com/en/reports-and-papers/five-network-trends. Accessed: Oct. 25, 2024.
36. Sun, H., Zhang, L., Wang, X., Network Topology Design in the Era of 6G. *IEEE Netw.*, 36, 3, 43–51, May 2022.
37. NetworkTigers, 2023 tech trends and the future of networking technology, NetworkTigers, 2023, [Online]. Available: https://news.networktigers.com:contentReference[oaicite:0]{index=0}.
38. ITPro, The Rise of AI and Automation in Network Management, ITPro, Feb. 15, 2023, [Online].Available:https://www.itpro.com:contentReference[oaicite:2]{index=2}.
39. SDxCentral, Top Networking Trends for 2023: Edge Computing, SASE, and Network Automation, SDxCentral, Jan. 12, 2023, [Online]. Available: https://www.sdxcentral.com:contentReference[oaicite:1]{index=1}.
40. Ghai, D., Tripathi, S.L., Saxena, S., Chanda, M., Alazab, M. (Eds.), *Machine Learning Algorithms for Signal and Image Processing*, John Wiley & Sons, Hoboken, New Jersey, 2022.
41. Khoussainov, R., Patel, A., Voorde, H.D.J.T., Distributed Parallel Computing in Networks of Workstations—A Survey Study, CiteSeerX beta.
42. Thuseethan, S. and Vasanthapriyan, S., Spider-web topology: A novel topology for parallel and distributed computing, in: *2015 3rd IEEE International Conference on Information and Communication Technology (ICoICT)*, pp. 34–38, 2015.
43. ur Rehman, K.U., Rahma, K.R.U., Ashraf, A., A Comparative Analysis of Distributed and Parallel Computing. *VFAST Trans. Softw. Eng.*, 7, 1, 42–49, 2019.
44. Singh, I., Review on parallel and distributed computing. *Sch. J. Eng. Tech.*, 1, 4, 218–225, 2013.
45. Tripathi, S.L. and Mahmud, M., *Explainable Machine Learning Models and Architecture*, Wiley & Scrivener Publishing LLC, USA, 2023, https://doi.org/10.1002/9781394186570.

3

# Distributed Processing Technology and Advancements

**Saranya. N.[1*], Shermy. R.P.[2], Sindhu. V.[2], Karthika Renuka. D.[3] and Renugadevi. G.[4]**

[1]*Dept. of Artificial Intelligence and Data Science, Coimbatore Institute of Technology, Coimbatore, Tamil Nadu, India*
[2]*Dept. of Computer Science and Engineering, Dr. N.G.P. Institute of Technology, Coimbatore, Tamil Nadu, India*
[3]*Dept. of Information Technology, PSG College of Technology, Coimbatore, Tamil Nadu, India*
[4]*Dept. of Computer Science and Engineering, Sri Krishna College of Engineering and Technology, Coimbatore, Tamil Nadu, India*

## *Abstract*
The purpose of this chapter is to examine the latest developments in distributed processing technology and how they affect contemporary computer systems. The chapter will give an overview of distributed processing, showing how it developed from the earliest days of cluster computing to the present day of cloud computing. It will go over important ideas that have influenced the advancement of distributed processing technology, including virtualization, containerization, and software-defined networking. Then the chapter will concentrate on more recent developments, such as distributed machine learning, serverless computing, and edge computing. It will look at how these developments are altering the computing environment by making it possible for new services and applications and by enhancing the effectiveness and scalability of computing systems. The chapter will also cover the opportunities and problems brought about by these developments, including the requirement for new programming paradigms and tools as well as security issues. This work will also examine the potential implications of blockchain, decentralized computing, and quantum computing as well as the future directions of distributed processing technologies. It will go over how these cutting-edge technologies can further transform distributed processing and open the door

**Corresponding author*: Saranya.n@cit.edu.in

Sandhya Avasthi and Suman Lata Tripathi (eds.) Distributed and Parallel Computing, (57–76)

to entirely new computing paradigms. All in all, this chapter will give a thorough review of the developments in distributed processing technology and provide insights into the field's present situation as well as potential future directions.

***Keywords***: Distributed processing, parallel and cluster computing, edge and serverless computing, fault tolerance, security, interoperability, Internet of Things (IoT), artificial intelligence

## 3.1 Introduction

Distributed processing technology has undergone significant advancements in recent years, revolutionizing the way computing systems operate and interact. This chapter explores the latest trends and developments in distributed processing, focusing on key advancements that have reshaped the computing landscape [1]. The goal of this chapter is to give a thorough review of distributed processing technology at the current state of the art, highlighting its evolution, current capabilities, and future potential. The evolution of distributed processing technology has been driven by the need for scalable, efficient, and reliable computing solutions. Early distributed systems were limited in scalability and performance, often relying on simple client–server architectures. One of the most significant advancements in distributed processing is the rise of edge computing. Edge computing can reduce latency and accelerate reaction times by locating computation and data storage closer to the data generation source. This is particularly important for real-time data processing applications such as driverless cars and Internet of Things (IoT) sensors [2].

The emergence of edge computing represents one of the biggest developments in distributed processing. By placing computation and data storage closer to the source of data generation, edge computing can lower latency and speed up reaction times. For real-time data processing applications such as IoT sensors and driverless cars, this is especially crucial. Distributed machine learning is also transforming the way data are processed and analyzed in distributed environments [3]. By distributing machine learning tasks across multiple nodes, distributed machine learning algorithms can handle large datasets and complex models more efficiently, leading to faster training times and improved performance.

The problem addressed by the chapter on "Advancements in Distributed Processing Technology" is the need to understand and explore the recent advancements in distributed processing technology and their impact on modern computing systems. This includes the evolution of distributed processing, current trends, important developments such as serverless and edge computing, as well as the benefits and difficulties they present. The objective is to give readers a thorough understanding of the most recent advancements in distributed processing technology while emphasizing their importance and potential effects on computing in the future.

Distributed processing refers to the use of multiple computing devices working together to achieve a common goal. Distributed processing allows for the efficient use of resources, improved performance, and scalability in computing systems [4]. The history of distributed processing can be traced back to the early days of computing when researchers began exploring ways to connect multiple computers to work together on a common task. Here is a brief overview of the key developments in the history of distributed processing:

- **1960s–1970s**: The concept of distributed processing began to emerge with the development of early computer networks such as the ARPANET. These networks allowed multiple computers to communicate and share resources, laying the groundwork for modern distributed computing.
- **1980s**: The client–server model became popular, enabling tasks to be distributed between clients (end-user devices) and servers (centralized computers that provide services or resources). This model helped improve efficiency and performance in computing systems.
- **1990s**: The advent of parallel computing further advanced distributed processing by allowing tasks to be divided among multiple processors, which could work on them simultaneously. This approach significantly improved the speed and efficiency of computing systems.
- **2000s**: Grid computing emerged as a way to harness the power of multiple computers across different locations to work on complex computational problems. Grid computing enabled organizations to share computing resources and collaborate on large-scale projects.
- **Late 2000s to present**: Through the internet, cloud computing enabled on-demand access to a shared pool of computing resources, thereby revolutionizing distributed processing. Because of cloud computing's affordability, scalability, and flexibility, it has grown in popularity.
- **Future**: Emerging technologies such as edge computing, which puts computing resources closer to the devices that need them, are expected to impact distributed processing in the future, as

well as decentralized computing, which aims to distribute processing power across a network of devices. These developments are expected to drive further innovation in distributed processing and enable new applications and services.

## 3.2 Distributed Processing in Modern Computing

In a distributed processing ecosystem, efficiency is achieved by processing of the data locally and also by simultaneous interaction between participating processing nodes in the systems. All the nodes are interconnected in some specific manner (topology), and nodes are allowed to communicate between the nearest connected node only. The diffusion of information takes place in the network continuously and updated. Some of the useful feature in any distributed network should be close to the results in centralized solutions. The solution should keep complexity and battery requirement to the minimum in distributed processing [2, 5].

- **Scalability**: By adding more machines to the network, distributed processing enables systems to scale horizontally and effectively handle growing workloads.
- **Fault tolerance**: Distributed processing systems can be diverted to other nodes in the event of a node failure, ensuring continuous functioning; they are more resilient to failures.
- **Resource utilization**: By distributing tasks across multiple machines, distributed processing systems can make better use of available resources, maximizing efficiency.
- **Performance and flexibility**: Parallel processing in distributed systems can significantly improve performance, allowing tasks to be completed faster than on a single machine. Distributed processing enables the creation of flexible computing environments that can adapt to changing needs and requirements.
- **Cost-effectiveness**: By using commodity hardware and distributing workloads, distributed processing systems can often provide cost-effective solutions compared to traditional centralized systems.
- **Data localization**: By processing data closer to its source, distributed processing can lower latency and boost system performance.

- **Support for big data**: Processing massive amounts of data in real-time processing, machine learning, and data analytics applications requires distributed processing.

## 3.3 Evolution of Distributed Processing

**Early computing**: In the early days of computing, standalone mainframe computers were used for processing tasks. These machines were limited in terms of processing power and storage capacity.
**Emergence of networks**: As computer networks began to develop in the 1960s and 1970s, researchers started exploring ways to connect multiple computers to work together on common tasks. This laid the foundation for distributed processing [6].
**Client–server model**: In the 1980s, the client–server model became popular, dividing tasks between client machines (end-user devices) and server machines (centralized computers). This model improved efficiency by distributing processing tasks. Figure 3.1 shows the block diagram of a distributed processing system architecture that includes client, web, and database servers.
**Parallel computing**: Parallel computing emerged in the 1990s as a way to further improve processing power by dividing tasks among multiple processors, which could work on them simultaneously. This approach significantly improved the speed and efficiency of computing systems.
**Grid computing**: Grid computing became prominent in the early 2000s, allowing organizations to share computing resources across different locations.

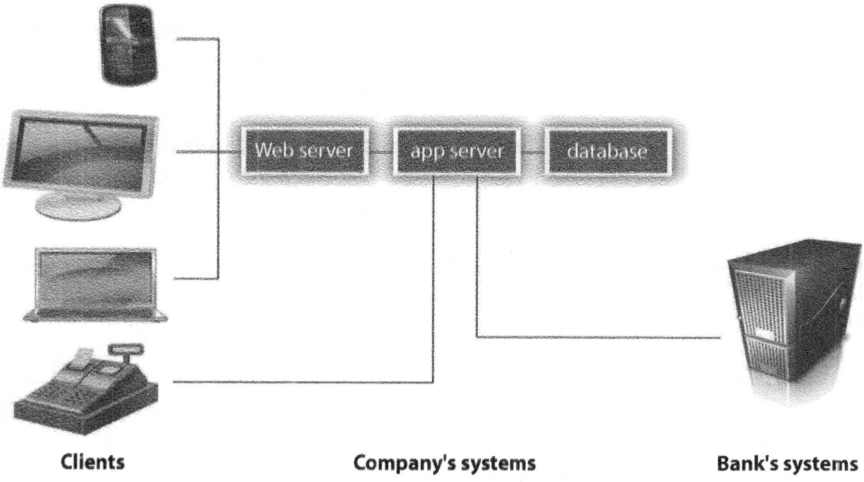


Figure 3.1 Block diagram of distributed process.

This enabled collaboration on large-scale projects and improved resource utilization [7].

**Cloud computing**: By enabling on-demand access to a shared pool of computer resources *via* the internet, cloud computing—which first appeared in the late 2000s—revolutionized distributed processing. Cloud computing provided cost-effectiveness, scalability, and flexibility.

**Edge computing**: Edge computing is a relatively new technology that brings computing resources closer to the devices that need them, which lowers latency and improves performance for applications that need to evaluate data in real time.

**Decentralized computing**: Decentralized computing aims to distribute processing power across a network of devices, enabling more efficient and secure processing without relying on a central server. Overall, the evolution

**Table 3.1** Comparison table.

| Aspect | Edge computing | Serverless computing | Distributed machine learning |
|---|---|---|---|
| Definition | Pushing computation to the edge of the network, closer to data sources | Running code without managing servers, scaling based on demand | Training machine learning models across distributed nodes |
| Key Benefit | Reduced latency, improved real-time processing | Simplified infrastructure management, cost-effective scaling | Faster training times, handling of large datasets |
| Use case | Internet of Things (IoT) devices, real-time analytics | Web applications, event-driven processing | Big data analytics, pattern recognition |
| Challenges | Data security, network connectivity | Cold start latency, vendor lock-in | Data consistency, model synchronization |
| Example technology | AWS IoT Greengrass, Azure IoT Edge | AWS Lambda, Azure Functions | TensorFlow, PyTorch |

of distributed processing has been driven by the need for increased scalability, fault tolerance, and performance in computing systems. Each advancement has brought new capabilities and efficiencies, shaping the way modern computing systems are designed and implemented [7]. Table 3.1 provides a brief comparison of emerging technologies.

## 3.4 Key Concepts and Technologies Driving the Evolution of Distributed Processing

**Networking infrastructure**: The development of robust networking infrastructure, including protocols such as TCP/IP, has been crucial for enabling communication and data exchange between distributed computing nodes.
**Virtualization**: Virtualization technologies, such as hypervisors and containers, have allowed for the creation of virtualized computing environments that can be easily scaled and managed across distributed systems [8].
**Middleware**: The complexity of distributed computing is abstracted by middleware, a software layer that facilitates the development and implementation of distributed applications.
**Distributed databases**: In distributed processing systems, distributed databases facilitate efficient data access and administration by storing data across several nodes.
**Parallel processing**: Parallel processing technologies, such as multicore processors and graphics processing unit (GPU) computing, have enabled tasks to be divided among multiple processing units, improving processing speed and efficiency.
**Cloud computing**: Cloud computing has made distributed processing capabilities more accessible; businesses can now increase their computing resources on-demand without having to make significant upfront infrastructure investments [8].
**Edge computing**: By bringing computing power closer to the data source, edge computing lowers latency and makes it possible to process data in real time in distributed contexts. Figure 3.2 illustrates various functionalities in distributed computing including edge, serverless, and Blockchain-based approaches.
**Software-defined networking (SDN)**: Centralized control over network resources is made possible by SDN, which simplifies the configuration and optimization of network traffic in distributed systems [9].
**Containerization**: By encapsulating dispersed systems into lightweight, portable containers, Docker and Kubernetes are two examples of containerization technologies that make it easier to deploy and manage distributed applications.

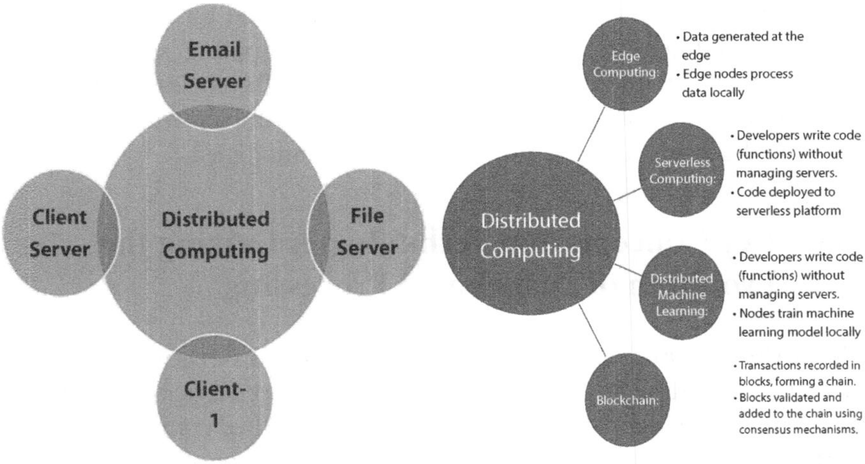


**Figure 3.2** Distributed computing functionality.

**Decentralized technologies**: Technologies such as blockchain and decentralized file systems are challenging traditional centralized computing models by enabling decentralized processing and data storage.

The development of distributed processing has been largely fueled by these fundamental ideas and technological advancements, opening the door to more effective, scalable, and durable computer systems.

## 3.5 Recent Advancements in Distributed Processing

**Edge computing**: By bringing processing and data storage closer to the point of demand, edge computing speeds up reaction times and uses less bandwidth. This is particularly crucial for real-time data processing applications such as IoT sensors and driverless cars.

**Serverless computing**: FaaS (Function as a Service), another name for serverless computing, enables programmers to execute code in response to events without having to worry about managing servers. Because users pay only for the compute time they utilize, this strategy is very cost-effective and scalable [10]. Figure 3.3 depicts interprocess communication across multiple distributed nodes and regions.

**Distributed machine learning**: Distributed machine learning algorithms allow for the training of machine learning models across multiple nodes in a distributed system. This makes it possible to handle bigger datasets and faster training times.

**Blockchain technology**: Blockchain technology makes it possible to process and store data in a decentralized, secure manner. Applications

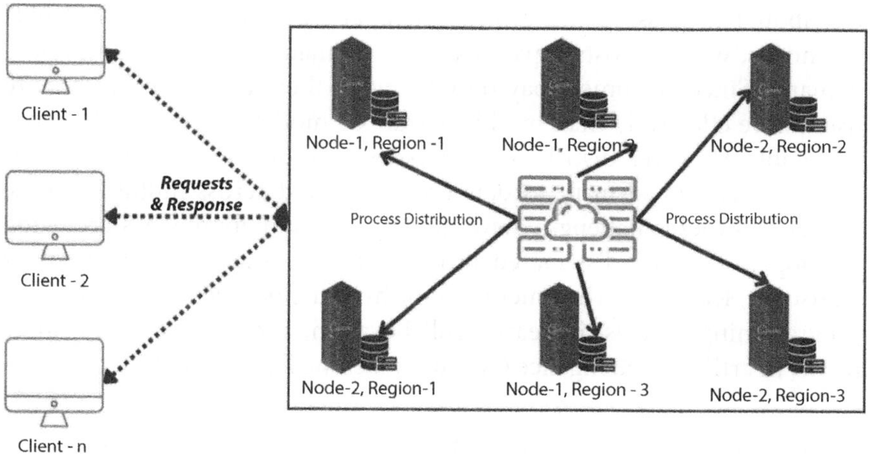


**Figure 3.3** Interprocess communication.

involving distributed processing, such as supply chain management and decentralized finance (DeFi), employ it [11].

**Container orchestration**: The deployment, management, and scalability of containerized applications in distributed systems have been made simpler by container orchestration tools such as Kubernetes.

**Event-driven architectures**: Event-driven architectures enable the decoupling of components in a distributed system, allowing for greater flexibility and scalability.

**Decentralized storage**: Decentralized storage systems, such as IPFS and Filecoin, allow for the storage of data across a distributed network of nodes, improving data availability and resilience.

## 3.6 Changing Landscape of Computing

The landscape of computing has undergone a significant transformation due to the widespread adoption of distributed processing. This shift has moved computing away from traditional centralized models toward more decentralized architectures, resulting in greater scalability, fault tolerance, and efficiency in computing systems. As a major trend, edge computing brings processing capacity closer to the data source, enabling real-time processing for applications such as driverless vehicles and IoT sensors. The creation and deployment of applications have also been transformed by serverless computing, which frees developers to concentrate on creating code rather than maintaining underlying infrastructure. Systems that use distributed processing can grow horizontally by adding more computing nodes, which boosts capacity and performance in response to rising demand. Since customers pay only for what they use and resources are used more effectively than in old centralized models, it can also be more affordable. However, distributed processing introduces new challenges for data privacy and security, as data are distributed across multiple nodes. To address these challenges, new technologies and approaches are being developed. Overall, distributed processing has reshaped the computing landscape, leading to the emergence of hybrid cloud environments, new programming models, increased collaboration, and significant advancements in artificial intelligence (AI) and machine learning [12].

### 3.6.1 New Opportunities and Challenges for Developers and Businesses

Developers and organizations are facing new opportunities and problems as a result of the migration to distributed processing. On the one hand, distributed processing enables developers to build more scalable and resilient applications, leveraging resources across a distributed network. This opens up new possibilities for developing complex, high-performance applications that can handle large-scale data processing and analysis [13]. At the same time, distributed processing introduces new challenges. Developers need to design applications that can effectively manage distributed resources, handle network latency, and ensure data consistency and security across distributed nodes. This requires a different set of skills and tools compared to traditional centralized computing models.

For businesses, distributed processing offers the potential for cost savings and improved efficiency. By leveraging distributed resources, businesses can scale their computing infrastructure more effectively, lowering the requirement for significant initial hardware expenditures. Lower operating expenses and better resource utilization may result from this. However, businesses also need to navigate the complexities of distributed systems, including managing data across distributed nodes, ensuring compliance with data protection regulations, and addressing security risks associated with distributed processing. Additionally, businesses need to consider the impact of distributed processing on their existing infrastructure and workflows and develop strategies to integrate distributed systems into their existing environment [14].

Overall, while distributed processing presents new opportunities for developers and businesses, it also brings new challenges that need to be carefully considered and addressed. By understanding these challenges and adopting the right tools and strategies, developers and businesses can harness the full potential of distributed processing to drive innovation and growth.

### 3.6.2 Use of Distributed and Parallel Computing

Distributed and parallel computing are computing paradigms that involve breaking down a large task into smaller subtasks that can be executed simultaneously. These paradigms are used to improve the performance,

**Table 3.2** Use case and comparison.

| Aspect | Distributed computing | Parallel computing |
|---|---|---|
| Use cases | Big data processing in case of large datasets distributed across multiple nodes and through live streams | Scientific computing through performing simulations and calculations that require high computational power |
| | Web applications can handle large numbers of concurrent users by distributing requests to multiple servers | Graphics processing: rendering complex graphics in real time |
| | Improving fault tolerance by replicating data and tasks across multiple nodes | Machine learning: training machine learning models by parallelizing computations across multiple processors |
| Technologies | Apache Hadoop: framework for distributed storage and processing of large datasets | Message passing interface (MPI): standard for parallel programming in distributed memory systems |
| | Apache spark: cluster computing system for big data processing | OpenMP: directives for parallel programming in shared memory systems |
| | Docker Swarm: tool for creating and managing a cluster of Docker hosts | CUDA: parallel computing platform and programming model for GPUs |

scalability, and efficiency of computing systems. A comparison of use case with description is given in Table 3.2.

## 3.7 Security and Privacy Considerations

Security and privacy considerations are critical aspects of distributed processing that developers and businesses must address to guarantee the availability, confidentiality, and integrity of information and resources [14]. Blockchain technology raises both opportunities and challenges for business sectors in terms of security and application [15]. Here are some crucial things to remember:

- **Data encryption**: Sensitive data can be shielded from unwanted access by using encryption when they are in transit and at rest. It is recommended to utilize robust encryption techniques and key management procedures.
- **Access control**: Strict access control procedures guarantee that resources can only be accessed by authorized people and devices. Role-based access controls and robust authentication methods are two examples of this.
- **Secure communication**: Using secure communication protocols such as TLS/SSL ensures that data transmitted between distributed nodes are protected from eavesdropping and tampering.
- **Data integrity**: Implementing mechanisms to ensure data integrity, such as digital signatures and hash functions, helps detect and prevent unauthorized modifications to data.
- **Secure development practices**: Frequent security audits and evaluations along with safe coding practices can help identify and minimize vulnerabilities in distributed applications. Protecting user data and staying out of legal hot water depend on ensuring compliance with pertinent data protection laws and standards, such GDPR and ISO 27001.
- **Data minimization**: Data breaches and illegal access are less likely when personal data are collected and retained in small amounts.
- **Monitoring and logging**: It is possible to identify and address security incidents quickly by putting in place strong monitoring and logging systems.

- **Disaster recovery and backup**: In the case of a security breach or data loss, company continuity can be ensured by having a strong disaster recovery strategy and frequently backing up data.
- **Education and training**: Educating employees and stakeholders about security best practices and the value of data protection contributes to the development of an organization-wide security-conscious culture. By addressing these security and privacy considerations, developers and businesses can enhance the security of their distributed processing systems and protect against potential threats and vulnerabilities.

### 3.7.1 Case Studies

**(i) Edge computing in IoT**
**Problem:** *A manufacturing company needs to monitor and maximize the production line's efficiency in real time to reduce downtime and improve efficiency. However, traditional cloud-based solutions introduce latency, making real-time monitoring challenging.*
**Solution:** The company implements edge computing nodes near the production line to process sensor data locally. These edge nodes do real-time data analysis, detecting anomalies and optimizing machine performance. By reducing latency and enabling faster decision-making, the company achieves significant improvements in production efficiency and cost savings [16].

**(ii) Serverless computing in Web applications**
**Problem:** *A startup developing a social media platform faces challenges in managing and scaling its backend infrastructure. Managing servers and ensuring scalability are complex and time-consuming.*
**Solution:** The startup adopts a serverless architecture for its Web application. By leveraging serverless computing services, the platform can automatically scale based on demand, reducing costs and simplifying infrastructure management. This allows the development team to focus on building features and improving user experience, leading to rapid growth and scalability for the platform.

**(iii) Distributed machine learning in big data analytics**
**Problem:** *A retail company wants to analyze large volumes of customer data to personalize marketing campaigns and improve customer engagement. However, traditional analytics tools struggle to process the massive dataset in a timely manner.*

**Solution:** The company implements distributed machine learning algorithms to analyze customer data across multiple nodes. By distributing the workload, the company can process large datasets more efficiently, leading to faster insights and more effective marketing campaigns. This results in improved customer engagement and increased sales [16].

**(iv) Blockchain in supply chain management**
**Problem:** *A global logistics company faces challenges in tracking and authenticating products throughout its supply chain. The current systems lack transparency and are susceptible to fraud and counterfeiting.*
**Solution:** The business uses blockchain technology to establish a safe and transparent supply chain management framework. In order to facilitate real-time tracking and authentication, every product is given a distinct digital identity that is saved on the blockchain. This raises stakeholder trust and lowers the possibility of fraud, increasing supply chain efficiency overall. These case studies illustrate how advancements in distributed processing technology, such as edge computing, serverless computing, distributed machine learning, and blockchain, can address complex challenges and provide innovative solutions across various industries.

### 3.7.2 Future Directions

The potential impact of quantum computing on distributed processing is briefly discussed in this section. Quantum computing has the potential to significantly impact distributed processing by offering unprecedented computational power and capabilities.

- **Speed and efficiency**: Certain calculations could be completed by quantum computers far more quickly than by conventional computers. The speed and effectiveness of distributed processing jobs, such as data analysis and optimization issues, may significantly increase as a result.
- **Complex problem solving**: Complex issues that are currently unsolvable for classic computers can be solved by quantum computers, such as simulating quantum physical processes or breaking cryptographic codes. This could open up new possibilities for distributed processing applications in fields such as finance, cryptography, and scientific research [17].
- **Improved security**: Quantum cryptography offers the potential for highly secure communication channels that are

resistant to eavesdropping and hacking. This could enhance the security of distributed processing systems, particularly in areas where data privacy is critical.

- **Resource optimization and AI**: Utilizing quantum algorithms to optimize resource allocation in distributed systems could result in better performance and more effective use of computer resources. Quantum computing could enable the development of more powerful machine learning and AI algorithms, leading to advances in distributed processing applications such as natural language processing, image recognition, and autonomous systems.
- **Data analysis**: Quantum computers could significantly speed up data analysis tasks, allowing for real-time analysis of large datasets in distributed processing environments.
- **Challenges**: However, there are also challenges to overcome, such as developing quantum-resistant cryptography to protect distributed systems from attacks by quantum computers. Additionally, integrating quantum and classic computing systems in distributed environments will require new approaches and standards.

Overall, quantum computing offers previously unheard-of computational power and capabilities that have the potential to transform distributed processing. However, achieving this potential would necessitate ongoing study, innovation, and cooperation between several academic fields.

## 3.8 Opportunities and Challenges in Distributed Computing

Blockchain and decentralized computing offer a paradigm shift in how data are stored, processed, and managed, presenting both opportunities and challenges for various applications.

### 3.8.1 Future Directions and Opportunity

- **Trust and transparency**: Blockchain technology offers an unchangeable, decentralized ledger enhancing trust and transparency in distributed systems. This is particularly valuable in industries such as finance, supply chain management, and healthcare, where transparency and accountability are crucial [17].

- **Reduced intermediaries**: Decentralized computing eliminates the need for intermediaries, enabling direct peer-to-peer interactions. This can lead to cost savings, faster transactions, and increased efficiency in various processes, such as payments, asset transfers, and voting systems.
- **Data ownership and control**: Decentralized computing empowers individuals to have greater control over their data. With blockchain-based identity management solutions, users can securely manage and share their personal information without relying on centralized authorities.
- **Decentralized applications (DApps)**: Blockchain systems facilitate the creation of decentralized apps (DApps) that function on a dispersed computer network. In fields such as DeFi, decentralized autonomous organizations, and decentralized storage, these DApps can provide cutting-edge solutions [18].
- **Resilience and security**: Compared to centralized systems, decentralized computing systems are more resistant to cyberattacks and single points of failure. Blockchain networks are intrinsically more secure and impervious to manipulation and censorship due to its distributed architecture.

### 3.8.2 Challenges

- **Scalability**: Scalability remains a significant challenge for blockchain and decentralized computing systems. As the number of users and transactions increases, blockchain networks may struggle to handle the growing demand, leading to congestion and slower transaction times [19].
- **Interoperability**: Ensuring interoperability between different blockchain platforms and protocols is essential for the widespread adoption of decentralized computing. Standards and protocols need to be developed to facilitate seamless communication and data exchange between disparate systems [20].
- **Regulatory uncertainty**: Regulatory frameworks for blockchain and decentralized computing are still evolving, leading

to uncertainty and ambiguity in many jurisdictions. Clear and consistent regulations are needed to address legal and compliance issues related to data privacy, security, and digital assets.

- **Energy consumption**: Much energy is consumed by proof-of-work consensus processes seen in many blockchain networks, such as Bitcoin. This has sparked worries about how blockchain technology may affect the environment and prompted the creation of substitute consensus techniques like proof-of-stake and proof-of-authority [21–23].

## 3.9 Conclusion

Continued research and development (R&D) in distributed processing technology is paramount for driving innovation and advancement in computing systems. It is essential for addressing emerging challenges and leveraging new opportunities in areas such as scalability, performance optimization, security, privacy, interoperability, and energy efficiency. R&D efforts focus on developing new techniques and technologies to scale distributed systems efficiently, improve performance, and optimize resource utilization. Security and privacy are also critical areas of focus, with R&D aiming to identify and mitigate vulnerabilities, develop new encryption techniques, and improve authentication and access control mechanisms. Additionally, R&D drives the exploration and development of new technologies and paradigms in distributed processing, such as edge computing, serverless computing, and blockchain, which have the potential to revolutionize computing systems. Furthermore, continued R&D in distributed processing has far-reaching economic and social impacts, driving economic growth, fostering innovation, and creating new industries and job opportunities. Overall, ongoing R&D in distributed processing technology is essential for driving innovation, improving performance and security, enabling interoperability, and addressing emerging challenges.

## References

1. Wang, L., *et al.*, Adsorption capability for Congo red on nanocrystal HneMFe2O4 (M=Mn, Fe, Co, Ni) spinel ferrites. *Chem. Eng. J.*, 181, 72–79, 2010. doi:10.1016/j.cej.2011.10.088.

2. Pathan, A.-S.K., Pathan, M., Lee, H.Y., *Advancements in Distributed Computing and Internet Technologies: Trends and Issues*. Information Science Reference, Hershey, PA, USA, 2012.
3. Mahendra, I., Ramadhan, A., Trisetyarso, A., Abdurachman, E., Zarlis, M., Strategic Information System Planning in the Industry 4.0 Era: A Systematic Literature Review, in: *2022 IEEE Creative Communication and Innovative Technology (ICCIT)*, pp. 1–7, 2022.
4. Lanure, M.A., Maulana, F., Lubis, M., Assessment of IT Maturity Level and Roadmap Preparation for Improving Governance Based on COBIT 5 (Case Study: XYZ Company). *2022 1st International Conference on Information System & Information Technology (ICISIT)*, pp. 31–36, 2022.
5. Jichkar, R., *et al.*, 5g: An Emerging Technology And Its Advancement. *2023 11th International Conference on Emerging Trends in Engineering & Technology - Signal and Information Processing (ICETET - SIP)*, Nagpur, India, pp. 1–6, 2023, doi: 10.1109/ICETET-SIP58143.2023.10151530.
6. Sharma, T., Shokeen, V., Mathur, S., Comparison of Approaches of Distributed Satellite Image Edge Detection on Hadoop. *2018 Second International Conference on Inventive Communication and Computational Technologies (ICICCT)*, Coimbatore, India, pp. 645–649, 2018, doi: 10.1109/ICICCT.2018.8472982.
7. Dari, S.S., Alawadi, A.H., Verma, A., Sheela, M.S., Jebaseeli, S.K., Secure Data Sharing and Mining in Distributed Environments. *2023 3rd International Conference on Technological Advancements in Computational Sciences (ICTACS)*, Tashkent, Uzbekistan, pp. 845–849, 2023, doi: 10.1109/ICTACS59847.2023.10389943.
8. Kirola, M., Memoria, M., Shuaib, M., Joshi, K., Alam, S., Alshanketi, F., A Referenced Framework on New Challenges and Cutting-Edge Research Trends for Big-Data Processing Using Machine Learning Approaches. *2023 International Conference on Smart Computing and Application (ICSCA)*, Hail, Saudi Arabia, pp. 1–5, 2023, doi: 10.1109/ICSCA57840.2023.10087686.
9. Gökalp, M.O., Koçyigit, A., Eren, P.E., A Cloud Based Architecture for Distributed Real Time Processing of Continuous Queries. *2015 41st Euromicro Conference on Software Engineering and Advanced Applications*, Madeira, Portugal, pp. 459–462, 2015, doi: 10.1109/SEAA.2015.61.
10. Jaison, F., Chaudhary, C., M.R., Blockchain and Edge Computing for IoT Advancements. *2023 IEEE International Conference on ICT in Business Industry & Government (ICTBIG)*, Indore, India, pp. 1–6, 2023, doi: 10.1109/ICTBIG59752.2023.10456203.
11. Varela, M.L.R., Araújo, A.F., Putnik, G.D., Manupati, V.K., Anirudh, K.V., Web-based decision system for effective process planning in network manufacturing environment. *2016 11th Iberian Conference on Information Systems and Technologies (CISTI)*, Gran Canaria, Spain, pp. 1–7, 2016, doi: 10.1109/CISTI.2016.7521371.

12. Jin, L., *et al.*, Research on Wide-area Distributed Power Quality Data Fusion Technology of Power Grid. *2019 IEEE 4th International Conference on Cloud Computing and Big Data Analysis (ICCCBDA)*, Chengdu, China, pp. 185–188, 2019, doi: 10.1109/ICCCBDA.2019.8725668.
13. Shetty, P., Kumar, M.R., Vyas, T., A.M., Gehlot, A., Pant, K., Application of Cryptographic Methods to Blockchain Technology to Increase Data Reliability. *2022 11th International Conference on System Modeling & Advancement in Research Trends (SMART)*, Moradabad, India, pp. 848–852, 2022, doi: 10.1109/SMART55829.2022.10047207.
14. Shahaab, A., Lidgey, B., Hewage, C., Khan, I., Applicability and Appropriateness of Distributed Ledgers Consensus Protocols in Public and Private Sectors: A Systematic Review. *IEEE Access*, 7, 43622–43636, 2019, doi: 10.1109/ACCESS.2019.2904181.
15. Muda, I., Madem, S., Hasan, S., Ahmod, S., Kayande, R.A., Chakraborty, N., A Survey on Applications and Security Issues of Blockchain Technology in Business Sectors. *2022 2nd International Conference on Technological Advancements in Computational Sciences (ICTACS)*, Tashkent, Uzbekistan, pp. 663–668, 2022, doi: 10.1109/ICTACS56270.2022.9987838.
16. Raja, A.S. and Dharma Prakash Raj, E.G., MAD-ARM: Mobile agent based distributed association rule mining. *2013 International Conference on Computer Communication and Informatics*, Coimbatore, India, pp. 1–5, 2013, doi: 10.1109/ICCCI.2013.6466112.
17. Suzuki, K., Nagao, M., Muraki, A., Ikeda, H., Shimodaira, Y., Yamazaki, M., Reduction of processing time in distributed image database system utilizing directory. *ICCT'98. 1998 International Conference on Communication Technology. Proceedings (IEEE Cat. No.98EX243)*, Beijing, China, vol. 1, pp. 564–568, 1998, doi: 10.1109/ICCT.1998.743229.
18. Kumar, S. and Mohbey, K.K., A Utility-Based Distributed Pattern Mining Algorithm With Reduced Shuffle Overhead. *IEEE Trans. Parallel Distrib. Syst.*, 34, 1, 416–428, 1 Jan. 2023, doi: 10.1109/TPDS.2022.3221210.
19. Chen, J., Gui, X., Chen, L., He, T., Distributed Energy Trading Model based on Graphene Blockchain. *2020 Asia Energy and Electrical Engineering Symposium (AEEES)*, Chengdu, China, pp. 934–939, 2020, doi: 10.1109/AEEES48850.2020.9121399.
20. Sharma, T., Shokeen, V., Mathur, S., Comparison of Approaches of Distributed Satellite Image Edge Detection on Hadoop. *2018 3rd International Conference on Internet of Things: Smart Innovation and Usages (IoT-SIU)*, Bhimtal, India, pp. 1–5, 2018, doi: 10.1109/IoT-SIU.2018.8519906.
21. Zan, M.S.D., Elgaud, M.M., Kadhim, A.S., Bakar, A.A.A., Improving the Performance of Brillouin Scattering-based Distributed Fiber Optic Sensors: Recent Advancement. *2021 IEEE Symposium on Wireless Technology & Applications (ISWTA)*, Shah Alam, Malaysia, pp. 77–81, 2021, doi: 10.1109/ISWTA52208.2021.9587356.

22. Shiraz, M., Gani, A., Khokhar, R.H., Buyya, R., A Review on Distributed Application Processing Frameworks in Smart Mobile Devices for Mobile Cloud Computing. *IEEE Commun. Surv. Tutor.*, 15, 3, 1294–1313, Third Quarter 2013, doi: 10.1109/SURV.2012.111412.00045.
23. Tripathi, S.L. and Mahmud, M., *Explainable Machine Learning Models and Architecture*, Wiley & Scrivener Publishing LLC, USA, 2023, https://doi.org/10.1002/9781394186570.

4

# Distributed System Architecture and Computing Models

**Sandhya Avasthi[1]* and Suman Lata Tripathi[2]**

*[1]Department of CSE, ABES Engineering College, Ghaziabad, India*
*[2]Department of Electronics and Communication Engineering, Symbiosis Institute of Technology (SIT), Symbiosis International (Deemed University), Pune, India*

***Abstract***
Distributed system architecture such as Fog computing, edge computing, and cloud computing is an active research area. As digital transformation and internet technology boom in recent times, distributed systems have undergone significant changes resulting in new models and architectures. Distributed system components are mainly structural framework and design principles that govern how several independent computing nodes work together to complete a specific activity. This chapter summarizes various distributed system architectures and models and discusses Fog computing, edge computing, and cloud. The chapter also includes a discussion on recent trends and challenges in implementing distributed system architecture.

***Keywords*:** Distributed systems, distributed computing, middleware, microservices, fog computing, edge computing

## 4.1 Introduction

In recent times, massive amounts of data are being generated through various mediums and channels such as sensors, business transactions, financial networks, social networks, publication houses, and personal applications on mobile devices. Technology such as big data can only handle these massive data efficiently and can further be used for different business and

**Corresponding author*: sandhya_avasthi@yahoo.com

Sandhya Avasthi and Suman Lata Tripathi (eds.) Distributed and Parallel Computing, (77–94)

scientific purposes. The data centers around the world are facing problems to store and then fast processing the requirement of these huge data. In this scenario, distributed computing plays an most important role in storing, processing, and analyzing big data [1]. The fundamental components of distributed computing systems are distributed computing frameworks. Using the divide-and-conquer strategy, they provide an essential way to support the efficient processing of big data on clusters or cloud. In these frameworks, a big data file is partitioned into a number of small files called data block files, which are stored in a distributed fashion on the nodes of a cluster and managed by using a distributed file system such as Google File System and Hadoop Distributed File System [1, 2].

## 4.2 Distributed System Architecture

The main objective in building distributed systems is to separate different software applications being used on computing platforms through a middleware layer. The distributed system architecture components are individual computers and servers, with each node having its own memory and storage. Multiple computing nodes that work together are called clusters, which improve performance [1]. The clusters increase the system's capacity to handle large volumes of requests and data processing routines. In a common distributed architecture, multiple copies of data are created across different locations to enhance the availability of data [3].

The distributed architecture is categorized in two types: the first one is physically distributed but logically centralized; the other one is completely distributed. The individual controller is responsible for its part belonging to logically centralized distributed systems; it updates neighbors if there is a change under any controller [4]. This approach is disadvantageous because controllers consume lots of networks and communication resources to communicate with each other. The other side, in completely distributed architecture, there is no synchronization between controllers.

### 4.2.1 Architecture Style

Designing an architecture for a specific use case is important in the development of large-scale software systems. The important considerations are component interconnections, data exchange between components, and how they are integrated into the system. Each modular unit is called a component, and operation on it is performed using an interface [1, 2].

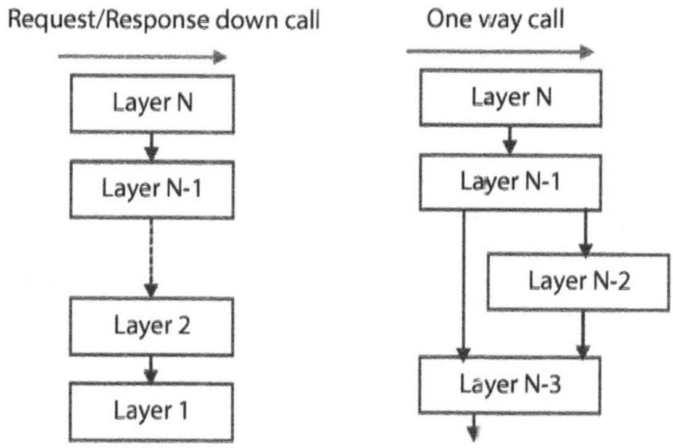


**Figure 4.1** (a) Pure layered, (b) hybrid layered.

A component can be replaced if its interface is not modified or changed. In real-life application scenarios, different architectural styles used are explained in the following sections.

**(a) Layered architecture**

In this architectural style, the components are organized in several layers represented as $L_1$, $L_2$...$L_j$. A component at $L_j$ makes a call to lower layer component $L_i$ ($i < j$) expecting a response. In exceptional cases, upcall (call to higher level) is made to a component. This type of architectural style is common in network communication. The protocol stack is a common example of layered architecture where each layer provides communication services such as data transfer from one point to several target points [4]. A layered architecture is shown in Figures 4.1(a) and 4.1(b).

The communication protocols in layered architecture implement communication services and allow data movement between nodes. These are given in the form of communication protocol stacks [4, 5]. Individual layers in this architecture specify function to be called through its interface; the interface should hide the internal details from nodes accessing the functionality. The use of TCP (transmission control protocol) decides the order of transferred data [5].

**(b) Peer2Peer architecture**

In this type of architectural style, workloads or task is divided between peers. Each participating peer has equal power and control forming a peer-to-peer (P2P) connection for the communication of messages. For instance, a personal area network is a decentralized P2P network. Peers can share their resources such as processing power, network bandwidth,

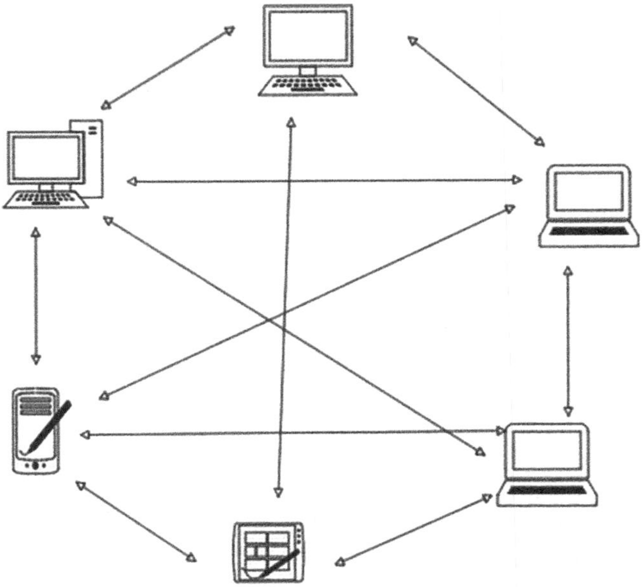

**Figure 4.2** Peer-to-peer distributed system.

and disk storage directly with other peers in the network without any central intervention or coordination by the server [6]. In such a P2P style, peers behave like both suppliers and consumers of available resources as shown in Figure 4.2. A popular example of P2P style distributed systems is BitTorrent, Miracast, and Bluetooth radio [3, 6].

**(c) Client–server architecture**

In client–server architecture computing nodes, data files, and peripheral devices are linked where the idea is to group them for efficient processing in different types of computing tasks. Here, data processing and other computing tasks take place between the client and server; the server here is a powerful and high-end machine [6]. The client can be an efficient personal computer or other kinds of mobile devices. In this architecture, the client machine requests services from the server and then processes the result returned by the servers. Different applications that run on the client side generate requests to the server, and query processing is performed on the client side.

**(d) Data-centric architecture**

The primary focus of this style is data utilization and management. The critical asset is data, and the system is based on the data management, storage, and retrieval process. These data are centrally maintained and available to various application services maintaining consistency throughout the system environment [2, 4]. The principal aim of data-centric architecture is to disseminate and replicate data across many places within a network. This design aims to ensure data availability and dependability and minimize latency by positioning data at the point of utilization. Data-centric architecture is employed in systems where data access efficiency and reliability are paramount. Information delivery networks (CDNs) employ this design to disseminate and cache Web information across numerous servers, so ensuring expedited access for users globally.

**(e) Service-oriented architecture**

Service-oriented architecture (SOA) is a methodology for developing cloud-based software that compartmentalizes essential program components into distinct service modules. These modules are more manageable due to their compact size and enhanced flexibility compared to larger applications [1, 4]. The SOA framework is predicated on "loose coupling." In this architectural style, components do not require intricate point-to-point connections as seen in a monolithic design. This enables disparate components to communicate *via* the ESB, regardless of differing platforms or programming languages. The development team can utilize modules for various jobs throughout the organization. This conserves workers' time as they are not required to reconstruct the various components of each Web application. Conversely, a drawback of SOA is that a defect in a component will manifest wherever it is utilized. Consequently, if issues arise in the code or any segment, they might impact the entire organization if implemented on a wide scale [3].

**(f) Event-based architecture**

Services are loosely connected in an event-driven architecture, as they are oblivious to one another. The event producer does not have to be cognizant of the consumers' identities. This improves the system's adaptability and modularity in response to modifications [2]. In event sourcing, each state alteration is documented as an event, rather than preserving the current state of a system. The current situation is recreated by reenacting the events. This is beneficial in distributed systems as it ensures the consistency and traceability of services. For example, in a banking system, each deposit or withdrawal is documented as an event. The aggregate of all transactions associated with the account is used to ascertain the account balance.

**(g) Object-based architecture**

In a multithreaded environment, objects are shared among threads, so careful attention must be paid to their design and the architecture supporting them. The architecture supporting multithreaded objects typically focuses on managing concurrency, synchronization, and preventing issues such as race conditions, deadlocks, and thread contention [5]. Object-based architecture centers around an arrangement of loosely coupled objects with no specific architecture as a layered architecture. Unlike layered architecture, object-based architecture does not have to follow any steps in a sequence. Each component is an object, and all the objects can interact through an interface (or connector). Under object-based architecture, such interactions between components can happen through a direct method call.

**(h) Microservice architecture**

A distributed system is defined by the existence of components across multiple networked computers that communicate and coordinate operations through message transmission. These systems are most suited for microservices, as they can function in diverse contexts (on-premise, cloud, or hybrid) and across several servers. Therefore, they constitute a form of distributed system [7]. Microservice architecture (MSA) is a software development methodology that simplifies complex applications by dividing them into discrete, autonomous services that can be independently developed, deployed, and scaled. Each microservice is dedicated to a specific business feature and communicates with other microservices through Application Programming Interfaces (APIs) that are explicitly defined. Microservices must communicate across the network, usually employing protocols, such

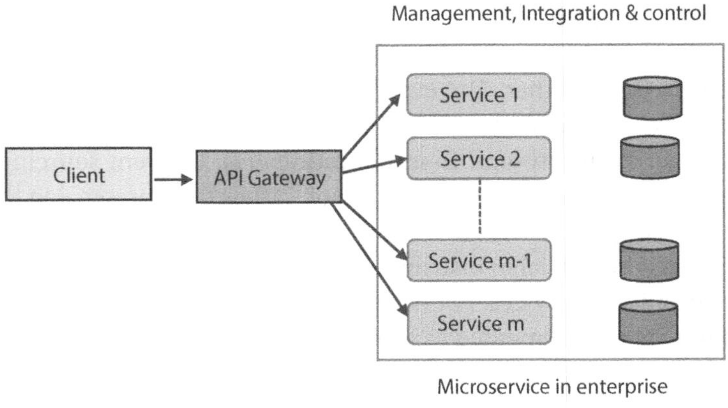


**Figure 4.3** Basic architecture of microservices.

as HTTP/REST or gRPC, or message brokers, such as Kafka, RabbitMQ, or Redis, owing to their distribution across multiple endpoints or servers [8]. This presents elements of distributed systems, encompassing asynchronous communication, network partitioning, and delay. The structure of MSA is given in Figure 4.3.

**Characteristics of MSA**

- MSA is different from traditional monolithic architecture. In MSA, all processes are loosely coupled and distributed so the team working on development is not responsible for entire applications. The development takes place in modules, where each module is referred to as a microservice, so one small change in one part will not affect the entire application [8].
- Every microservice represents one specific requirement of a big enterprise and a small unit of functionality. So, it is easy to change anything if the requirement suddenly changes. Such microservice is built using DevOps applications.
- The application requires an on-demand, self-service, and elastic infrastructure. A continuous distribution pipeline is established. In this infrastructure, the enterprise can use microservices easily.
- The purpose of MSA developing and maintaining services is to deliver them better, improving scalability in case demand grows over the period.
- The autonomous services in MSA are developed, tested, scaled, deployed, and operated independently in a decentralized manner.
- MSA is fault-tolerant and highly available in nature, making them eliminate long wait periods in the technology stack. Since each service is autonomous, it is easy to modify them if requirements change.

Big enterprises such as Netflix, Spotify, Amazon, and LinkedIn are using MSA in developing their projects and following the basic development MSA model, as shown in Figure 4.3. The structure is based on main business services [9, 10]. Discovery mechanism, communication medium, building blocks and infrastructural services are important components in a Micro-services Architecture.

### 4.2.2 Middleware Organization

To organize the middleware, primarily design patterns such as wrappers and interceptors are used. Both patterns target a specific set of problems and organize middleware in the distributed system environment [11].

**(i) Wrappers**

It is also known as an adapter, and it offers an interface to client applications in case native interfaces are not compatible with the distributed application environment. In the process of building a distributed system using existing components/nodes, a common problem arises where interfaces from legacy components become incompatible with the current application in a distributed environment. A wrapper or adapter solves this issue through a client application interface; the interface provides functionalities that are found in components on legacy systems [11]. In the case of a distributed system, wrappers provide another kind of support not limited only to interface transformers. For example, in the case of Amazon S3 storage service, the interface service uses RESTful Architecture and also utilizes a traditional approach. Wrappers provide extensibility, which is crucial for achieving openness. In simple terms, if application "*X*" has some data that are needed by application "*Y*," this can be done by developing a wrapper specific for *Y* that can access data belonging to *X*. This can be a complex situation in case there are "*N*" applications, and *N* is really large. In such a situation, $N \times \frac{N-1}{2} = O(n^2)$ wrapper will be needed. To reduce the number of wrappers, support of middleware components would be needed [12].

**(ii) Interceptors**

Interceptors specify constraints on shared resources in P2P applications using mechanisms to put limitations on resource utilization. In addition, it also allocates different shared resources to individual computing nodes so that resources can be allocated to critical services first [11]. It is implemented fully at the middleware level over standard operating systems that provide system call interception facilities and real-time fixed-priority process scheduling.

Interceptors are placed on the top of any operating system in a distributed environment to intercept the access requests by mostly P2P applications. They control the access request and provide application segregation also enforces quantitative limitations of P2P resource requirements. This maximizes the overall performance of the application without any kind of violations. The implementation of interceptors uses scheduling mechanisms and policies [12].

The mechanisms that are used to override any decision made by the operating system are as follows:

- **Fixed-priority round-robin policy**: This policy schedules in a round-robin manner and uses time slices; every process is mapped to a fixed priority, and high-priority process is always run first, preempting lower-order processes. The preempted process remains at the head of the waiting queue and starts executing after all high-priority processes are completed.
- **High-resolution timers**: These are required to control the allocation and release of resources needed by different processes.
- **System call interception facilities**: These facilities are required to act as mediators in resource access. Such facilities are made available in Linux and Windows operating systems.
- **Multithreading support**: This supports the implementation of various modules needed for the interceptor and to orchestrate their interactions.

## 4.3 Middleware in Distributed Systems

Middleware is a software layer that provides common services and capabilities to applications outside of what's offered by the operating system. It abstracts the complexity of communication between different components of the distributed system, facilitating interoperability, scalability, and security [13, 14]. Middleware enables applications to communicate and manage data across different platforms and networks. Middleware hides the complexities of the underlying network protocols (e.g., TCP/IP, HTTP) and provides higher-level communication mechanisms such as remote procedure calls (RPCs), message passing, or distributed object frameworks. This allows different parts of an application (often running on different machines) to communicate seamlessly.

Middleware technology helps in decreasing cycle time, effort, and complexity of developing distributed systems. In general, distributed systems are developed using middleware component services instead of building the system from scratch. The advantages of middleware in distributed applications are as follows:

- The middleware helps simplify the software development process for building distributed systems.
- Provides an abstraction for low-level, error-prone platform details to the developers of distributed systems, for example, in the case of socket-level programming.
- Captures implementations of key design patterns in development tasks using reusable frameworks. They provide amortized cost analysis for the development life cycle.
- Provides high-level abstraction for networks that are closer to applications and system requirements simplifying distributed system development.
- It also gives logging and security services to developers to operate in a networked environment.

### 4.3.1 Host Infrastructure Middleware

This middleware leverages common patterns and best practices to encapsulate and enhance native OS communication and concurrency mechanisms to create reusable network programming components, such as reactors, acceptor–connectors, monitor objects, active objects, and component configurators [15]. These components abstract away the peculiarities of individual operating systems and help eliminate many tedious, error-prone, and nonportable aspects of developing and maintaining networked applications *via* low-level OS programming APIs, such as Sockets or POSIX pthreads. Widely used examples of host infrastructure middleware include the following:

- JVM by Sun Java virtual machine provides a platform independence by executing code through abstraction between CPU architecture and operating systems, which is also responsible for interpreting Java bytecode and translation of bytecode to an action or an operating system call [16].
- Microsoft.NET is another platform to be used for XML Web services and designed to interconnect devices, information, and people in a more customizable way. For all Microsoft.NET services, CLR (common language runtime) is used to host services [17].

- ACE (adaptive communication environment) encapsulates the operating system with network programming capabilities, and this toolkit is written in C++. The networking capabilities are connection establishment, interprocess communication, marshaling, event demultiplexing, concurrency, and synchronization.

### 4.3.2 Distribution Middleware

Distribution middleware uses programming models for APIs and automating components. This primarily provides support to client interface to interact with distributed applications and work similar to a stand-alone application. It can invoke different operations on objects without depending on location, OS platforms, protocols, hardware, and interconnection. The request brokers make the central unit of any distribution middleware. Some examples of brokers are given here [18].

- Sun's Java Remote Method Invocation (RMI) is a distribution middleware that enables developers to create distributed Java-to-Java applications, in which the methods of remote Java objects can be invoked from other JVMs, possibly on different hosts. RMI supports more sophisticated object interactions by using object serialization to marshal and unmarshal parameters, as well as whole objects [19]. This flexibility is made possible by Java's virtual machine architecture and is greatly simplified by using a single language.
- DCOM (distributed component object model), by Microsoft, is a middleware used in communicating through method invocations and instantiation remotely. This is different from CORBA and RMI in Java because they run on various platforms, whereas DCOM works primarily on Windows systems [20].

### 4.3.3 Domain-Specific Middleware

Domain-specific middleware services fulfill domains such as e-commerce, automation, aerospace, telecom, and healthcare. They target vertical markets and are considered to be the least matured services of middleware layers today. This is due to the unavailability of distribution and common middleware standards in the current scenario; these standards are required to have a stable base for implementing domain-specific services [21].

- Syngo (www.syngo.com), developed by Siemens Medical Group, is such domain-specific middleware that provides an integrated collection of services and server platforms to applications, mainly imaging tasks, such as mammography, radiography, ultrasound, life support, magnetic resonance, and patient monitoring. The services integrate healthcare facilities and diagnostic imaging. All this is done using a Blackbox application framework that provides support to configuration, communication, and logic support tasks.

### 4.3.4 Intelligent Middleware

Intelligent middleware (IMW) provides management of services in real time and processes high-volume sensors signal converting into actionable business information. Actionable information is further delivered to dashboards on user computers or sent to external systems outside the enterprise [22, 23]. IMW supports different categories of hardware and software through API and interacts with external systems.

- With IMW, group definitions are stored at the central repository, so every working application has access to the same definition that ensures instant access to that definition [24]. IMW provides location awareness to provide safety and efficiency through a central database [25].
- NEXUS is an IMW that provides seamless services in any volatile environment by requesting prioritization and load balancing. The middleware is proactive in monitoring and provides automated services [26]. It filters information services based on semantic relevance among users.

## 4.4 Distributed Cloud Architecture

The distributed cloud refers to the distribution of cloud services to computing nodes at different locations outside the originating cloud. Users now use fewer resources on their own devices and depend on cloud storage for many applications on their systems. In a distributed environment such as a distributed cloud, resources are interconnected in a P2P style. Cloud providers give access to platform, infrastructure, and storage to all users subscribing to their services. All this is possible by utilizing virtualization techniques to provide these required resources to users *via* virtual machines. One such standard is Xen for hardware virtualization in distributed cloud architecture. Amazon gives virtual machine access in categories such as small, medium, large, and extra large.

Distributed cloud is a multicloud computing platform that connects the edge with the core. Existing cloud architectures make use of a centralized trusted system to process user's requests. In the distributed cloud model shown in Figure 4.4, resource providers are distinctive; that is, these distributed cloud servers are individuals with resources to offer. Users of distributed cloud need to discover these resource providers and request them for using resources [25]. The distributed cloud proposed uses a completely decentralized mechanism to discover and allocate resources. Users in the distributed cloud share recourses in a P2P fashion. To overcome the downsides of the existing cloud and to make use of underutilized resources of end users, we proposed the distributed cloud architecture, a distributed solution that can handle all the services provided by the existing cloud. We can construct the distributed cloud by making use of these unused resources, thereby avoiding investments in new data centers [24].

Distributed cloud architecture is an effective solution for augmented information (AgI) services. AgI services have high computation and low latency needs, so they require distributed computational resources that depend on the distributed cloud. Two flow control methods need to be addressed:

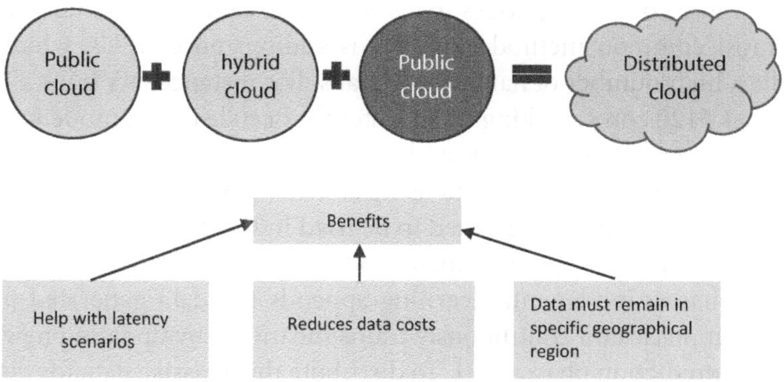


**Figure 4.4** Distributed cloud architecture.

**Packet processing**: different service functions that need data packets, how various computation resources to be allocated, and where to store them.
**Replication and packet forwarding**: which method to use to route packets using a sequence of service functions, where replication of data packets will take place to meet the requirement from different destinations, also how to allocate network resources.

## 4.5 Distributed Machine Learning

Machine learning (ML) models are being used to train datasets in different types of decision-making systems and applications such as self-driving cars, speech recognition, and predicting health issues from large-scale medical data [27, 28]. For many such applications, ML is a slow process due to high runtime for training models. The computation involves transformation operations on vectors, tensors, and matrices, which are complex algebraic problems. These operations can be optimized by high-performance computing or parallel computing by including clusters or computing nodes in parallel. This limitation is solved using a distributed system to increase parallelization and bandwidth. The data used for building models are large-scale, and a centralized approach is not an efficient solution; these data are too big to store on a single machine. Many such examples are large organizations or enterprises that deal with transaction data worldwide that are stored in various locations. This kind of data can be trained if implemented in a parallel manner by dividing data and functionality on distributed computing nodes to avoid failures. For all large-scale computing problems, two fundamental approaches can be used to speed up the process: (i) by adding resources to a computing machine and (ii) by adding more computing nodes to a system also called horizontal scaling). The most common method currently is adding more GPUs, which can handle a high number of hardware threads. For instance, NVIDIA TESLA V100 has 5120 cores, making them faster for deep learning modeling.

ML has two phases: *training* and *prediction*. The training phase trains a model by applying available data using an ML algorithm. Also, an optimal set of hyperparameters is decided to be used in the modeling process. The training phase results in a trained model, which is further used in prediction phases. Incremental learning appends the data generated in the prediction phase and continuously trains the model by updating new data from the prediction phases [23]. To distribute this massive data for distributed ML, two different styles are used, parallelizing the data or parallelizing the model. Figure 4.5 shows the distributed machine learning flow.

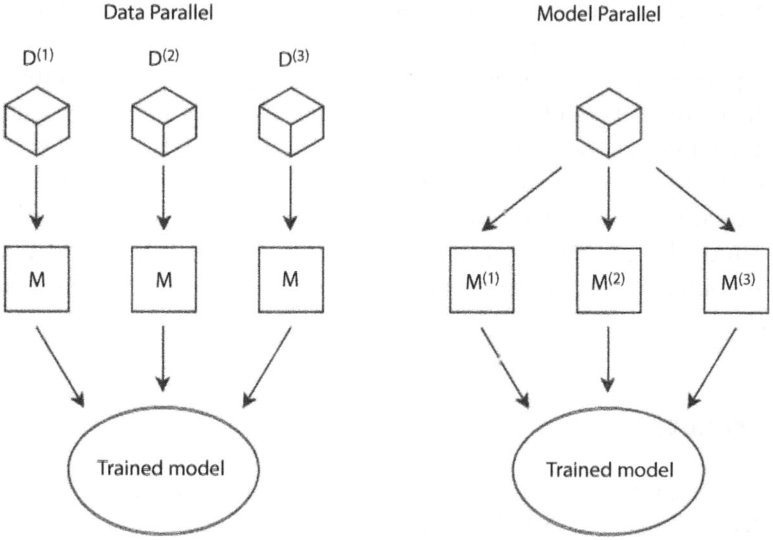


**Figure 4.5** Distributed machine learning.

**Data parallel**: In this approach, data are distributed equally among processing nodes in the system, and these nodes each apply the same ML algorithm using data allocated to them. This approach can be used for every ML model by assuming independent and identical distribution.

**Model parallel**: The same copy of the dataset is made available to all processing nodes; these nodes operate on different parts of the model. The final model is the aggregation of all other working parts of the model. This model cannot be applied to all ML algorithms because model parameters generally cannot be split. Aggregation is possible using methods such as ensemble.

**Topologies**: The topologies are an important consideration in distributed ML implementation. The computing nodes in the distributed system are connected using a specific architectural pattern as per the problem to be solved. Three layers of architecture ML, topology, and parallelism are dependent.

## 4.6 Conclusion

In the current scenario of digital transformation and automation across different industries, powerful method for computing is required. Such computing need is fulfilled by distributed systems and computing models for implementing different applications for industries or personal use. The need for computing resources such as storage, processing power, and software applications for various purposes is growing rapidly. These situations can be handled efficiently using emerging technologies such as distributed cloud computing, edge computing, and distributed ML. In this chapter, different distributed system architecture is discussed briefly and various middleware components. Some recent architectures such as distributed cloud and edge cloud have been discussed as well. Computing models such as distributed ML basic working and concepts are explained in the chapter as well.

## References


1. Van Steen, M. and Tanenbaum, A.S., A brief introduction to distributed systems. *Computing, 98*, 967–1009, 2016.
2. Ageed, Z.S., Ibrahim, R.K., Sadeeq, M.A., Unified ontology implementation of cloud computing for distributed systems. *Curr. J. Appl. Sci. Technol., 39*, 34, 82–97, 2020.
3. Pham, X.Q., Nguyen, T.D., Huynh-The, T., Huh, E.N., Kim, D.S., Distributed cloud computing: architecture, enabling technologies, and open challenges. *IEEE Consum. Electron. Mag., 12*, 3, 98–106, 2022.
4. Wu, J., *Distributed System Design*, CRC Press, 2017. https://doi.org/10.1201/9781315141411.
5. Verbraeken, J., Wolting, M., Katzy, J., Kloppenburg, J., Verbelen, T., Rellermeyer, J.S., A survey on distributed machine learning. *ACM Comput. Surv. (CSUR), 53*, 2, 1–33, 2020.
6. McClelland, J.L. and Rumelhart, D.E., Distributed memory and the representation of general and specific information, in: *Connectionist Psychology*, pp. 75–106, Psychology Press, 2020.
7. Talaver, V. and Vakaliuk, T.A., Reliable distributed systems: review of modern approaches. *J. Edge Comput., 2*, 1, 84–101, 2023.
8. Baškarada, S., Nguyen, V., Koronios, A., Architecting microservices: Practical Opportunities and Challenges. *J. Comput. Inf. Syst.*, 60, 5, 428–436, 2020.
9. Mateus-Coelho, N., Cruz-Cunha, M., Ferreira, L.G., Security in microservices architectures. *Procedia Comput. Sci., 181*, 1225–1236, 2021.
10. Yıldırım, E., Cicioğlu, M., Çalhan, A., Fog-cloud architecture-driven Internet of Medical Things framework for healthcare monitoring. *Med. Biol. Eng. Comput., 61*, 5, 1133–1147, 2023.
11. Sekar, J., Multi-Cloud Strategies for Distributed AI Workflows and Application. *J. Emerg. Technol. Innov. Res., 10*, 600–P610, 2023.
12. Wu, T.Y., Kong, F., Meng, Q., Kumari, S., Chen, C.M., Rotating behind security: an enhanced authentication protocol for IoT-enabled devices in

distributed cloud computing architecture. *EURASIP J. Wirel. Commun. Netw., 2023*, 1, 36, 2023.

13. Duan, S., Wang, D., Ren, J., Lyu, F., Zhang, Y., Wu, H., Shen, X., Distributed artificial intelligence empowered by end-edge-cloud computing: A survey. *IEEE Commun. Surv. Tutor., 25*, 1, 591–624, 2022.
14. El-Sayed, H., Sankar, S., Prasad, M., Puthal, D., Gupta, A., Mohanty, M., Lin, C.T., Edge of things: The big picture on the integration of edge, IoT and the cloud in a distributed computing environment. *IEEE Access, 6*, 1706–1717, 2017.
15. Zangana, H.M., Khalid Mohammed, A., Zeebaree, S.R., Systematic Review of Decentralized and Collaborative Computing Models in Cloud Architectures for Distributed Edge Computing. *Sist.: J. Sist. Inf., 13*, 4, 1501–1509, 2024.
16. Pahl, C. and Lee, B., Containers and clusters for edge cloud architectures–a technology review, in: *2015 3rd International Conference on Future Internet of Things and Cloud*, pp. 379–386, IEEE, 2015, August.
17. Pujol, V.C., Donta, P.K., Morichetta, A., Murturi, I., Dustdar, S., Edge intelligence—research opportunities for distributed computing continuum systems. *IEEE Internet Comput., 27*, 4, 53–74, 2023.
18. Amiri, Z., Heidari, A., Navimipour, N.J., Unal, M., Resilient and dependability management in distributed environments: A systematic and comprehensive literature review. *Cluster Comput., 26*, 2, 1565–1600, 2023.
19. Caleffi, M., Amoretti, M., Ferrari, D., Illiano, J., Manzalini, A., Cacciapuoti, A.S., Distributed quantum computing: a survey. *Comput. Netw., 254*, 110672, 2024.
20. Aminizadeh, S., Heidari, A., Toumaj, S., Darbandi, M., Navimipour, N.J., Rezaei, M., Unal, M., The applications of machine learning techniques in medical data processing based on distributed computing and the Internet of Things. *Comput. Methods Programs Biomed.*, 241, 107745, 2023.
21. Gu, X., Zhang, G., Cao, Y., Cooperative mobile edge computing-cloud computing in Internet of vehicle: Architecture and energy-efficient workload allocation. *Trans. Emerging Telecommun. Technol., 32*, 8, e4095, 2021.
22. Avasthi, S., Chauhan, R., Acharjya, D.P., Techniques, applications, and issues in mining large-scale text databases, in: *Advances in Information Communication Technology and Computing: Proceedings of AICTC 2019*, Springer Singapore, pp. 385–396, 2021.
23. Chauhan, R., Avasthi, S., Alankar, B., Kaur, H., Smart IoT systems: Data analytics, secure smart home, and challenges, in: *Transforming the Internet of Things for Next-Generation Smart Systems*, pp. 100–119, IGI global, 2021.
24. Avasthi, S. and Chauhan, R., Privacy-Preserving Deep Learning Models for Analysis of Patient Data in Cloud Environment, in: *Computational Intelligence in Healthcare Informatics*, pp. 329–347, Springer Nature Singapore, Singapore, 2024.
25. Tyagi, M., Yadav, S., Sanwal, T., Avasthi, S., Impact of digitization in banking services on customer habits, in: *2022 10th International Conference*

*on Reliability, Infocom Technologies and Optimization (Trends and Future Directions)(ICRITO)*, pp. 1–8, IEEE, 2022, October.

26. Nasir, N., Sobral, V.A.L., Huang, L.P., Campbell, B., NexusEdge: Leveraging IoT Gateways for a Decentralized Edge Computing Platform, in: *2022 IEEE/ ACM 7th Symposium on Edge Computing (SEC)*, pp. 82–95, IEEE, 2022, December.
27. Tripathi, S.L. and Mahmud, M., *Explainable Machine Learning Models and Architecture*, Wiley & Scrivener Publishing LLC, USA, 2023, https://doi.org/10.1002/9781394186570.
28. Ghai, D., Tripathi, S.L., Saxena, S., Chanda, M., Alazab, M., *Machine Learning Algorithms for Signal and Image Processing*, Wiley IEEE Press, USA, 2022, DOI:10.1002/9781119861850.

# 5

# Parallel Computing Models and Architecture

**Aastha Sharma[1,2*], Swati Sharma[3] and Divya Mishra[2,4]**

[1]*Dept. of Computer Science and Engineering, AKGEC, Ghaziabad, India*
[2]*Faculty of Technical, Dr. A.P.J. Abdul Kalam Technical University, Lucknow, India*
[3]*Dept. of Computer Science and Engineering, ABES Engg. College, Ghaziabad, India*
[4]*Dept. of Computer Science and Engineering, ABES, Ghaziabad, India*

***Abstract***

When dealing with massive issues in areas such as artificial intelligence, data analytics, and scientific computing, parallel computing becomes crucial. It enhances efficiency, decreases processing duration, and manages more intricate assignments. Nevertheless, the task of creating parallel algorithms and guaranteeing effective synchronization across processors may be somewhat demanding. The technique of dividing a bigger issue into small and independent and often comparable task of execution that may be repeatedly run by different processors communicating *via* shared memory space and combining the results at the end to form an overall method is known as parallel computing. The Process of Handling the data in terms to read/write the process of execution set of instruction enabled by the processor to compute and execute the particular every job/task at a time. It can leads to boost up the execution processor and alot to operate the multitask at a time by implementing the task with the help of multicore processor. In contrast to serial computation, which uses just a portion of the hardware and leaves the rest inactive, the parallel computing strategy ensures the efficient utilization of resources and hardware. This chapter concluded the various areas of the parallel computing models in real-time access and the various methods and techniques to elaborate the process of parallel computing. The procedures of the analysis enumerated in the introduction of parallel computing, basic approach, architecture analysis, flowchart analysis, and various computing models are working in the area of computer science.

**Corresponding author*: aasthasharma7116@gmail.com

Sandhya Avasthi and Suman Lata Tripathi (eds.) Distributed and Parallel Computing, (95–114)

***Keywords***: Parallel computing, multicore processor, distributed computing, software and hardware analysis, computing models, multicore architecture, hardware application layer

## 5.1 Introduction

Parallel computing is the phenomenon approach of an application or computation concurrently across multiple processors. It is a computer architecture that involves breaking down huge problems into smaller, independent sections that are often comparable and may be processed simultaneously [1]. The task is accomplished through the collaboration of numerous central processing units (CPUs) that communicate with each other using shared memory. The CPUs aggregate their results after the task is finished. Distributed computing facilitates the execution of complex calculations by dividing each section of workload over several processors. In addition to facilitating quicker task resolution and application processing, parallel computing increases the computational capacity of systems [2, 3]. Most supercomputers utilize the concepts of parallel computing to function. Parallel processing is often employed in operational settings that need significant computational capacity.

In general, this infrastructure consists of a server rack containing a collection of processors; the application server partitions computational requests into manageable portions, which are subsequently executed concurrently on each server. Early computer software was designed for serial calculation, allowing the execution of only one instruction at a time. In contrast, parallel computing involves the simultaneous execution of several processors to handle an application or task. Utilizing parallel computation has numerous benefits, including time and cost savings, concurrency, resolution of complex problems, and more. Moreover, parallel processing decreases intricacy [4, 5]. In the practical use of parallel computing, there are two lineups for obtaining tickets. When two cashiers concurrently provide tickets to two individuals, it not only saves time but also decreases complexity [6].

Real-time system implementation using parallel computing is suboptimal, and serial computing provides concurrency and time and cost savings. The notion of parallel computing is essential for organizing and managing big and complicated datasets. By leveraging parallel processing, issues that previously demanded the assistance of proficient network and data center administrators and a powerful supercomputer can now be resolved using standard desktop and computers. Modern operating systems govern the coordination and use of several processors. In the majority of situations, this renders parallel processing more economically sustainable than serial processing [7].

As an increasing number of Internet of Things sensors and endpoints require real-time data, parallel computing becomes increasingly vital. In light of the current accessibility of processors and GPUs (graphics processing units) *via* cloud services, the integration of parallel processing into microservice deployments is imperative. In order to enhance performance across multiple tasks, reduce power consumption, and optimize speed, multicore processors consist of integrated circuit devices that contain two or more CPUs. The majority of computers are equipped with a range of two to four cores, while some may support as many as twelve cores. Parallel processing is commonly used to perform complex operations and simultaneously [8].

In the 1960s and 1970s, advancements in supercomputers began to emerge, while parallel computing originated in the late 1950s in Figure 5.1. These multiprocessors utilized a common memory area and performed parallel operations on a singular data set. A novel classification of parallel computing emerged during the mid-1980s; the Cal-tech Concurrent Computation project assigned and assembled a supercomputer for scientific purposes by employing 64 Intel 8087/8088 processors. The need of the ASCII super computer is to make the high efficiency to execute all the commands and jobs in one unit of time while computing parallel. There are few operations available

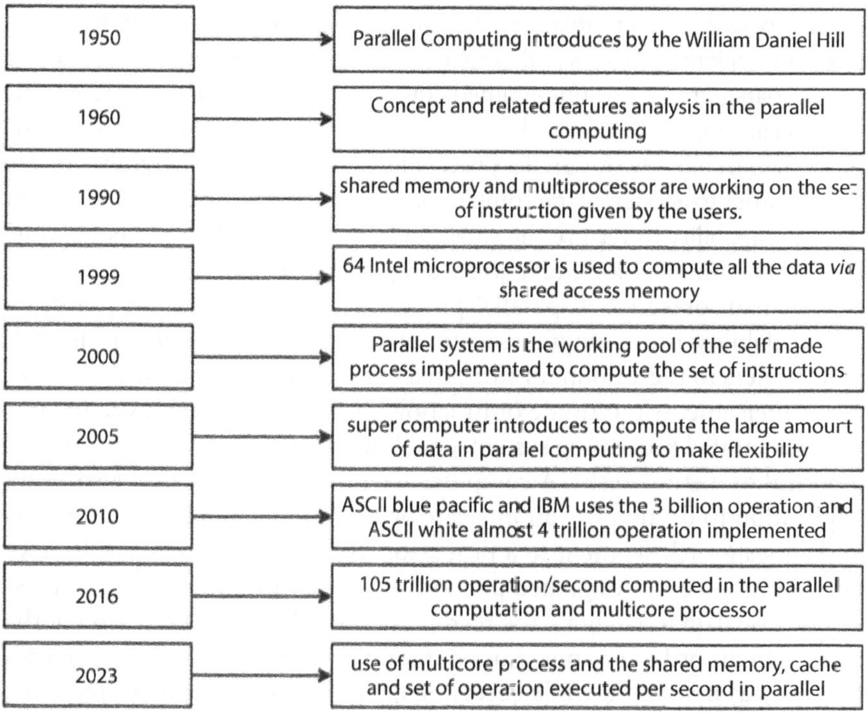


**Figure 5.1** Cycle of parallel computing.

to compute FLOPS (floating perunit of time and second) of task execution and which take almost 2-3 trillion to execute. This breakthrough led to the emergence of massively parallel processors [9].

## 5.2 Evolution of Parallel Computing Models [4]

### 5.2.1 Basic Approach Parallel Computing

In parallel computing, approach for computing any type of set of instructions is to be minimum of two microprocessors execute a single operation in parallel processing. The concept is exceedingly simple: a computer scientist uses specialized software designed for the purpose of dissecting an intricate problem into its constituent pieces. Next, they allocate a distinct processor for each component. In order to accomplish the complete computational problem, individual processors execute their respective portions. The software reconstructs the data in order to resolve the intricate original problem. When processing is executed in parallel, a sizable task is divided into multiple smaller tasks that are more appropriately sized, categorized, and powered by the available processing units [5, 6]. Once the workload is divided, each CPU independently begins working on its assigned portion without any communication with the other processors. Alternatively, they utilize software to maintain communication and track the progress of their work. Parallel processes can be classified as either coarse-grained or fine-grained. Tasks engage in frequent intercommunication at a high level of parallelism to have a slower pace since they communicate less frequently. A parallel processing system can concurrently process data in order to accelerate the completion of duties. As an example, the system has the capability to receive the subsequent instruction from memory while the CPU's arithmetic-logic unit is executing the current instruction [7, 8].

The main objective of parallel processing is to enhance the flexibility and scalability of a computer's computational capacity and throughput, which refers to the amount of work that can be accomplished within a specific timeframe. A multitude of functional units can be employed to construct a parallel processing system, enabling the simultaneous execution of identical or distinct tasks. A computer scientist commonly uses a software application to decompose an intricate operation into smaller components and allocate each segment to a processor. Then, each processor will independently solve its designated portion, and a software tool will then reassemble the data to facilitate the reading of the solution or execution of the action. In an ordinary course of operation, each CPU will execute parallel duties as instructed while accessing data from the computer's memory. Processors will utilize the software to facilitate communication and monitor alterations in data values. Upon completion of a job, the program will seamlessly integrate all the data pieces, on the assumption that all the processors remain synchronized [9, 10]. By networking computers to create a cluster, one may utilize them for parallel computing even if they do not have numerous CPUs in Figures 5.2, 5.3, and 5.4.

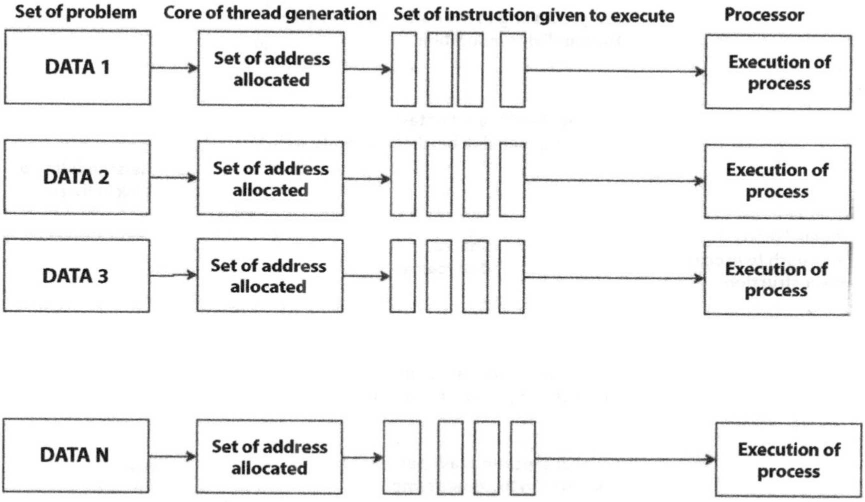


**Figure 5.2** Approach in parallel computation.

## 5.2.2 Architecture

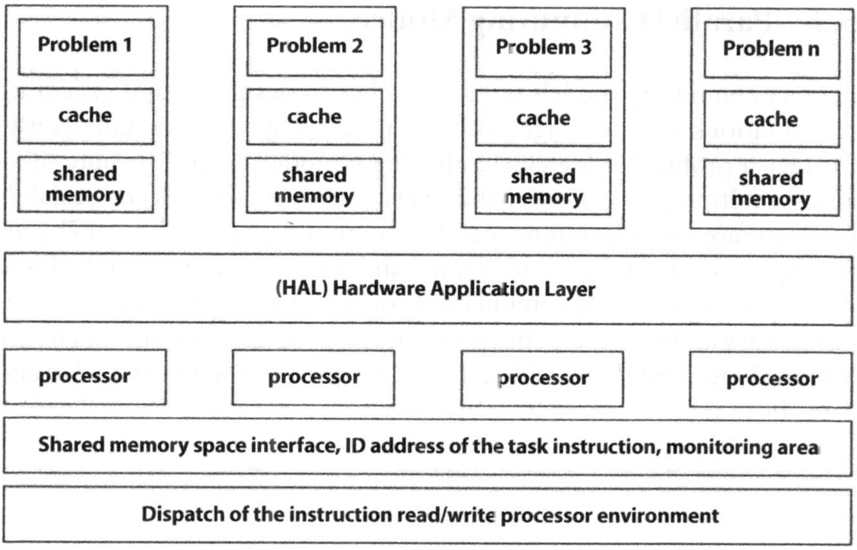


**Figure 5.3** Architecture approach of task execution in parallel computing.

### 5.2.3 Flowchart Analysis

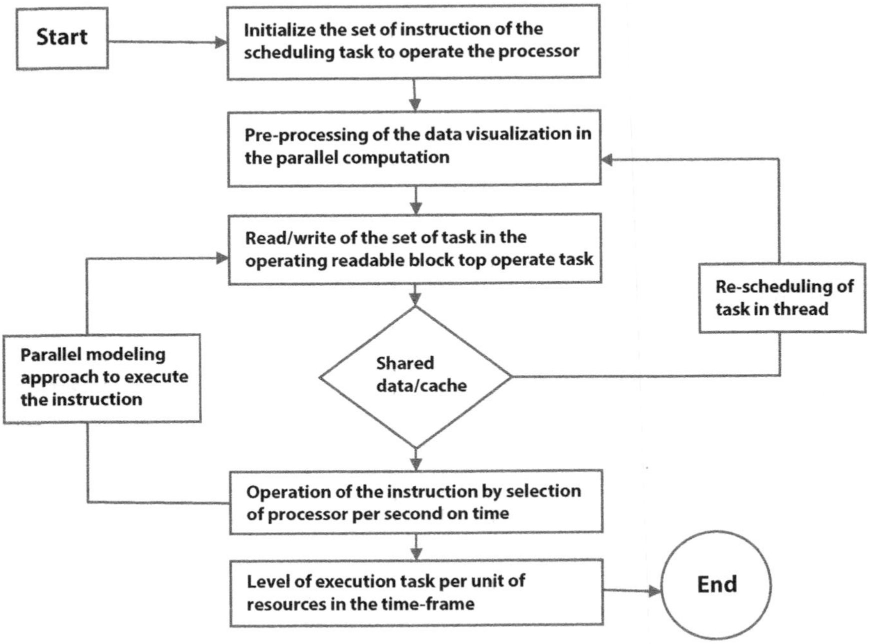


**Figure 5.4** Flow analysis in computing the task in parallel computation.

## 5.3 Parallel Computing Models

Parallel computing models are approaches to designing and executing computations that leverage multiple processing units simultaneously to solve a problem more efficiently. These models help distribute tasks across multiple processors, enabling faster execution times and scalability. Here are some common parallel computing models. Parallel processing exists in abstract hardware and memory architecture. These models do not describe computations or refer to specific machine types or memory architectures. The most suitable programming models to use heavily depend on the specific difficulties a programmer must tackle and solve [9].

**Languages**: Python, C/C++, MATLAB, R, Perl, Julia, Fortran

### 5.3.1 Complexity

The expression provided, Tp(N) = $O$(logp + pN) with parameters [$k^2$, S1], represents the complexity of a parallel algorithm and the number of processors $p$ and the problem size $N$. Let us break down the notation [6]:

- Tp(N) is the time by the algorithm to solve a problem of size $N$ and $p$ processors.
- $O$(logp + pN) denotes the asymptotic upper bound of the time complexity, where $p$ is the number of processors and $N$ is the problem size.
- [$k^2$, S1] describes the parallelism characteristics of the algorithm.

$K^2$ represents the degree of parallelism, indicating that the algorithm can utilize $K^2$ processors efficiently. S1 represents the speedup achieved by using one processor instead of the maximum possible processors ($K^2$). This notation implies the following [10]:

- The algorithm exhibits $O(\log p)$ parallelism overhead, meaning that the algorithm's efficiency increases logarithmically with the number of processors.
- Additionally, the algorithm has an $O(p/N)$ component, suggesting that the overall time complexity decreases linearly with the number of processors, assuming $N$ is sufficiently large.
- Synchronization overhead: In parallel computing, when multiple tasks are needed to coordinate their activities or share data, synchronization overhead can become significant. Locks, mutexes, barriers, and other synchronization mechanisms are used to ensure data integrity and prevent race conditions. However, excessive use of synchronization can lead to contention and performance degradation.

### 5.3.2 Advantages [7]

Parallel computing has several pros over sequential computing, mainly in terms of performance, scalability, and problem-solving capabilities. Some key advantages of parallel computing are as follows:

- **Increased performance**: By distributing tasks across multiple processing units, parallel computing can reduce significantly the time required for executing computations. This leads to quicker results and faster processing, particularly for computationally intense tasks.
- **Scalability**: Parallel computing enables systems to scale up easily by adding more processing units. As the problem size or computational demand increases, additional processors can be used to handle the workload, allowing for efficient utilization of resources and accommodating larger datasets or more complex problems.
- **Improved throughput**: Parallel computing allows multiple tasks to be executed concurrently, increasing the overall throughput of the system. This is particularly beneficial for applications with high-throughput requirements, such as data processing, simulations, and scientific computing.
- **Fault tolerance**: Parallel computing systems can be used with redundancy and fault tolerance mechanisms to continued operation event of hardware failures or errors. Tasks can be distributed across redundant processing units, and fault detection and recovery mechanisms can be implemented to maintain system reliability.
- **Solution to complex problems**: Parallel computing enables the efficient solution of complex problems that may be infeasible or prohibitively slow to solve using sequential algorithms. By leveraging parallelism, researchers and engineers can tackle larger and more intricate problems in fields such as scientific simulations, machine learning, optimization, and computational biology.
- **Cost-effectiveness**: While parallel computing systems may require upfront investment in hardware and infrastructure, they can offer cost-effective solutions in the long run by providing faster computation times, improved productivity, and the ability to handle larger workloads without the need for massive single-node systems.

### 5.3.3 Disadvantages [8]

- **Complexity**: Parallel programming is inherently more complex than sequential programming. Coordinating multiple tasks running concurrently, managing data distribution, and ensuring very proper synchronization between threads or processes require careful design and implementation. This complexity can lead to longer development times and increased likelihood of errors.
- **Communication overhead**: Communication between parallel processes or threads can introduce overhead, particularly in distributed memory systems where data need to be transferred between different memory locations. Message passing, although necessary for interprocess communication, can incur amp latency and bandwidth limitations, impacting overall performance.
- **Load balancing challenges**: Distributing tasks evenly across processing units to ensure optimal resource utilization can be challenging. Load imbalances, where certain processors are underutilized while others are overburdened, can occur due to variations in task complexity or data distribution. Load balancing algorithms are needed to mitigate these imbalances but may add complexity and overhead, some of the time.
- **Scalability limits**: While parallel computing systems can scale up by adding more processors, there are practical limits to scalability. Amdahl's and Gustafson's Law describes theoretical limits to speed-up and scalability, respectively, due to the presence of serial portions of code or finite problem sizes. Achieving linear scalability with an increasing number of processors is often challenging and may require careful optimization.
- **Increased hardware and maintenance costs**: Building and maintaining parallel computing systems can be costly. High-performance computing clusters, multicore processors, and specialized hardware accelerators such as GPUs require significant investment in hardware and infrastructure. Additionally, ongoing maintenance, power consumption, and cooling costs contribute to the total cost of ownership.
- **Software complexity and portability**: Parallel software development often requires specialized tools, libraries, and programming models. Porting and optimizing existing

sequential code for parallel execution can be nontrivial and may require rewriting significant portions of the codebase. Moreover, parallel code may be less portable across different hardware architectures and operating systems.

- **Debugging and testing challenges**: Debugging parallel programs can be more challenging than debugging sequential programs! Race conditions, deadlocks, and timing-related bugs can be difficult to reproduce and diagnose. Specialized debugging tools and techniques, such as race detection tools and parallel profilers, are often required to identify and fix concurrency-related issues [4].
- **Scalability bottlenecks**: Certain algorithms or problem domains may exhibit scalability bottlenecks that limit the effectiveness of parallelization. These bottlenecks may arise from inherent serial dependencies, communication overhead, or memory constraints. Identifying and mitigating scalability bottlenecks often require algorithmic redesign or optimization strategies [1].

### 5.3.4 Algorithmic Problem

#### *5.3.4.1 Shared Memory Cache [5]*

In this model, multiple processors share a common address space, allowing them to read and write data directly from memory. Threads or processes communicate through shared variables. However, synchronization mechanisms like locks and semaphores are needed to manage concurrent access to shared resources. Examples of shared memory systems include Open-MP for shared memory parallelism in C/C++ and multiprocessing in Python. The Shared Memory Model is a parallel computing paradigm where multiple processing units (such as CPU cores or threads) share a common address space, allowing them to access shared data directly [8].

In this model, threads or processes running on different processing units can communicate by reading from and writing to shared memory locations, enabling coordination and synchronization between concurrent tasks. One of the key advantages of the Shared Memory Model is its simplicity and ease of programming. Developers can write parallel programs using familiar programming languages and constructs, such as threads or processes that access shared variables [5, 6]. This familiarity simplifies the development process and reduces the learning curve for parallel programming. However, the Shared Memory Model also presents challenges, particularly in managing concurrent access to shared resources.

Additionally, excessive use of synchronization primitives can introduce overhead and potential performance bottlenecks, as threads may contend for access to shared resources. To mitigate these challenges, developers must carefully design and implement synchronization strategies to ensure data integrity and prevent race conditions [4]. This may involve using fine-grained locking techniques to minimize the scope of critical sections and reduce contention or employing higher-level synchronization primitives such as reader–writer locks or condition variables to coordinate access to shared data. Despite these challenges, the Shared Memory Model remains widely used in parallel computing, particularly in shared-memory multi-processor systems and multicore processors [10–13]. Modern parallel programming frameworks and libraries, such as OpenMP and Intel Threading Building Blocks, provide developers with tools and abstractions to simplify parallel programming in the Shared Memory Model, further promoting its adoption and usability.

### *5.3.4.2 Distributed Memory Model [7]*

In contrast to shared memory, in the Distributed Memory Model, each processor has its own local memory, and communication between processors occurs explicitly through message passing. Processes run independently and exchange data through message passing libraries such as MPI (Message Passing Interface) or frameworks such as Apache Hadoop and Apache Spark. The Distributed Memory Model is a concept used in cognitive psychology to explain how information is processed and stored in the brain. This model suggests that different types of information are processed in different areas of the brain and that memories are distributed across these areas rather than being localized in a single region.

- **Multiple processing centers [8]**: According to this model, different types of information (such as visual, auditory, spatial, etc.) are processed in different regions of the brain. For example, visual information might be processed in the occipital lobe, whereas auditory information might be processed in the temporal lobe.
- **Parallel processing [9]**: The brain is capable of processing multiple types of information simultaneously. This parallel processing allows for efficient and rapid cognitive functioning.
- **Connectionism [10]**: The Distributed Memory Model is closely related to the concept of connectionism, which

suggests that memories are represented by patterns of activation across interconnected neural networks rather than being stored in specific locations.

- **Redundancy and resilience [9]**: Because memories are distributed across multiple regions of the brain, damage to one area is less likely to result in complete loss of a memory. Instead, the brain may be able to compensate for damage by accessing related information stored in other areas. Overall, the Distributed Memory Model provides a framework for understanding how the brain processes and stores information in a dynamic and distributed manner, reflecting the complexity and resilience of cognitive function.

#### *5.3.4.3 Data Parallel Model [6]*

This model involves distributing data across multiple processing units and performing the same operation on each piece of data simultaneously. SIMD (Single Instruction, Multiple Data) and SIMT (Single Instruction; Multiple Threads) architectures are examples of data parallelism, commonly used in GPU computing and vector processing; the information parallel version is a programming version and execution paradigm usually used in parallel computing, especially within the context of dispensed structures and excessive-performance computing (HPC). It is regularly hired to successfully process large datasets by distributing the workload across more than one processing unit or node. Inside the statistics parallel version, the dataset is divided into smaller subsets, and each subset is processed independently *via* distinctive computational units concurrently [4, 5].

Those computational devices can be man or woman CPU core within a multicore processor, separate nodes in a disbursed computing surroundings, or even specialized hardware accelerators such as GPUs (snapshots processing devices) or TPUs (tensor processing gadgets). The facts parallel model is a programming paradigm used in parallel computing, particularly in disbursed systems and high-overall performance computing. It includes breaking down a dataset into smaller parts and dispensing those components across a couple of computational units [7].

Each unit then independently strategizes its assigned portion of the statistics concurrently with other gadgets. This model allows parallel execution, mainly to progress overall performance for tasks that may be parallelized efficiently. Key elements encompass records distribution, parallel processing, verbal exchange among gadgets, synchronization, and scalability. Frameworks such as MPI, Apache Spark, TensorFlow, and PyTorch

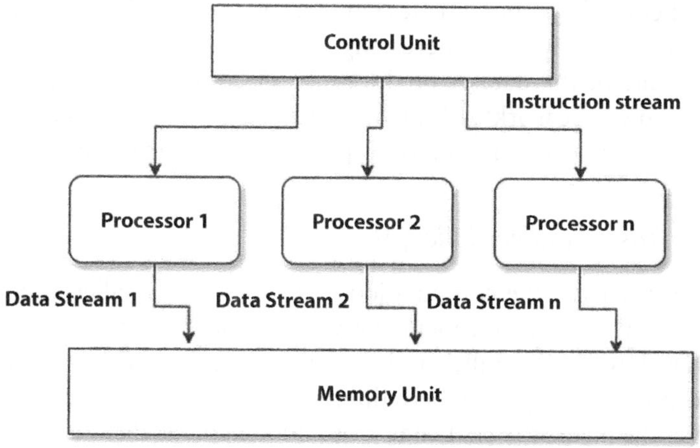


**Figure 5.5** Data parallel execution task analysis.

help the implementation of data parallelism in numerous domain names, which includes clinical computing, device studying, and large records analytics in Figure 5.5 [10].

The characteristics of the information parallel version encompass the following:

- **Facts distribution**: The dataset is partitioned and distributed throughout the computational units. Each unit works on its portion of the records independently [1].
- **Parallel processing**: Each computational unit method is assigned part of the information concurrently with other gadgets. This allows for parallel execution and can cause substantial performance enhancements, especially for duties that may be without parallelized problems [2].
- **Verbal exchange**: At the same time as every unit works independently on its information subset, there is often a want for conversation between devices. This conversation may also involve replacing intermediate consequences, synchronizing computations, or aggregating final effects [3].
- **Synchronization**: In some cases, synchronization factors are required to make sure that everyone with computational gadgets has completed their obligations earlier than proceeding to the subsequent degree of computation. Synchronization mechanisms consisting of barriers or collective operations are used to coordinate the execution of parallel duties [3].

- **Scalability**: The statistics parallel version is designed to scale successfully with increasing computational assets. As the scale of the dataset or the range of computational gadgets grows, the workload can be disbursed throughout additional resources to maintain or improve overall performance [4].

#### 5.3.4.4 *Task Parallel Model [4]*

In task parallelism, the computation is divided into smaller, independent tasks that can be executed concurrently. Each task may have its own data and execution flow. Task parallelism is commonly employed in multithreaded programming paradigms, where different threads work on different tasks concurrently. Inside the challenge graph model, parallelism is expressed by means of an undertaking graph. A challenge graph can be either trivial or nontrivial [5]. In this version, the correlation of a few of the obligations are utilized to promote locality or to minimize interaction charges.

This version is enforced to clear up issues in which the amount of facts associated with the duties is big as compared to the variety of computation associated with them. The obligations are assigned to assist in improving the price of data movement in the various tasks. The mission parallel model (TPM) is another programming model and execution paradigm typically used in parallel computing, especially in scenarios in which the focus is on parallelizing duties rather than information. In contrast to the facts parallel model, which specializes in parallelizing operations on record units, the venture parallel version aims to parallelize character obligations or operations within a software.

- **Decomposition** [5]: This system is decomposed into smaller obligations or devices of labor. Those duties are typically unbiased or have minimum dependencies on every difference, making an allowance for parallel execution.
- **Concurrency** [5]: Duties are performed concurrently; that means they can run concurrently on special processing devices or threads.
- **Synchronization** [7]: While obligations can run concurrently, there can be points in which synchronization is necessary. Synchronization mechanisms are used to coordinate the execution of duties, ensuring that certain obligations that are completed earlier than others continue.
- **Load balancing** [3]: Efforts are made to balance the workload flippantly throughout available processing gadgets to optimize overall performance and aid usage.

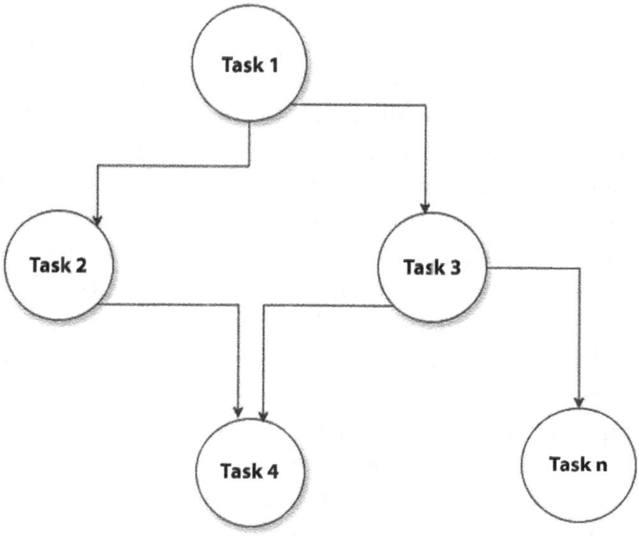


**Figure 5.6** Task distribution in parallel computing.

- **Scalability** [3]: The venture parallel version is designed to scale efficaciously as the number of obligations or processing gadgets will increase. This scalability permits for stepped forward performance on multicenter processors, disbursed systems, and different parallel computing architectures.
- **Assignment decomposition** [3]: This system is broken down into smaller obligations, which may be achieved independently or with minimal dependencies on every different. Every challenge represents a unit of work that can be parallelized.
- **Task scheduling** [2]: A scheduler assigns duties to be had in processing units, considering factors consisting of workload balance, resource availability, and dependencies between obligations. Efficient mission scheduling is essential for maximizing parallelism and minimizing idle time in Figure 5.6.

### 5.3.5 Pipeline Model [7]

This model involves breaking down a computation into a sequence of stages, with each stage performed by a separate processing unit. Data move through the pipeline, and each stage performs a specific operation on the data before passing it to the next stage. Pipelining is often used in streaming applications and in hardware design. A pipeline model refers to a sequential approach to processing tasks or information, in which each stage inside the sequence represents a one-of-a-kind step or operation. The output of one level becomes the input for the next, forming a linear float of processing. This idea is normally used in various fields including software program improvement, records evaluation, manufacturing, and extra.

In software program development, for instance, a pipeline version is probably used in nonstop integration and nonstop shipping (CI/CD) tactics. Here, code modifications are routinely constructed, tested, and deployed in a sequential manner, making sure that every step is finished effectively earlier than moving directly to the following. In facts analysis, a pipeline model would possibly involve preprocessing uncooked statistics, followed by feature extraction, model training, and evaluation. Every stage inside the pipeline transforms the facts in a few manners; in the end, mainly for insights or predictions in production, a pipeline version would possibly constitute the meeting line procedure, wherein uncooked substances go through a chain of steps to come to be finished products in Figure 5.7.

- **Modularity** [5]: One of the primary benefits of a pipeline model is its modular nature. Each degree in the pipeline may be designed as a separate factor, with properly defined inputs and outputs. This modularity facilitates code reuse, as individual tiers may be shared across extraordinary pipelines or projects. It also allows groups to work on unique stages simultaneously, fostering collaboration and speeding up improvement.
- **Scalability** [5]: Pipeline models are inherently scalable, each in phrases of computational sources and processing throughput. Because every stage operates independently, it is exceptionally straightforward to parallelize the processing throughout multiple computing nodes or cores. This parallelism can significantly reduce the overall execution time,

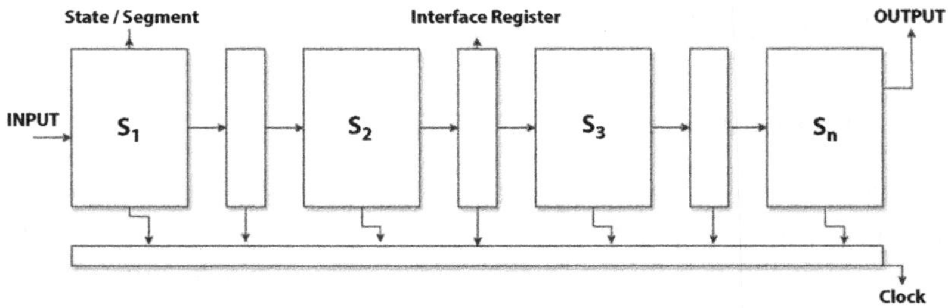


**Figure 5.7** Pipelining of task in parallel computing.

mainly for tasks that involve big volumes of facts or computationally extensive operations.

- **Ease of maintenance** [6]: By means of breaking down complex tactics into smaller, extra possible degrees, pipeline models make it easier to maintain and replace the system through the years. If a particular stage wishes to be changed or changed, it may be completed without disrupting the complete pipeline. Additionally, for the reason that inputs and outputs of every degree are properly defined, adjustments can be made with self-assurance, understanding that they may not have accidental consequences on different elements of the device.
- **Flexibility** [6]: Pipeline fashions offer flexibility in phrases of the types of operations that can be executed at every level. Depending on the requirements of the task, unique degrees can be added, eliminated, or rearranged as wanted. This flexibility allows pipelines to conform to changing enterprise wishes or evolving information assets without requiring massive redecoration or reimplementation.
- **Debugging and tracking** [6]: Because the waft of data *via* a pipeline is sequential and nicely described, it is enormously smooth to debug and screen the machine. Developers can tune the development of records as it movements through each stage, become aware of bottlenecks or errors, and take corrective movement as wished. Additionally, logging and monitoring gear can offer insights into the overall performance of the pipeline, taking into consideration optimization and satisfactory tuning over the years, shown in Figure 5.8.

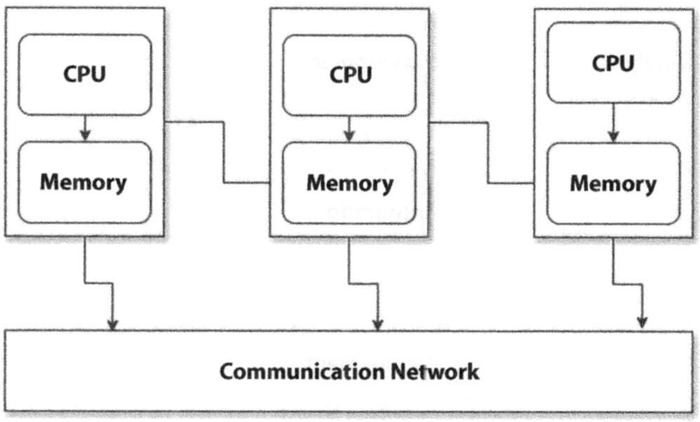


**Figure 5.8** Debugging and tracking analysis.

### 5.3.6 Hybrid Models [8]

Many real-world parallel computing systems use a combination of the above models to exploit different types of parallelism within the same application. For example, a distributed-memory cluster might employ both data parallelism within each node and message passing between nodes. Hybrid models refer to methods that integrate a couple of methodologies, techniques, or models to deal with a problem or reap an aim. Those models leverage the strengths of different procedures at the same time to mitigate their individual weaknesses, mainly for extra robust and powerful solutions. Hybrid fashions are generally used in diverse fields, which include machine getting-to-know, optimization, and machine design. Here are a few examples of hybrid models in extraordinary contexts in Figure 5.9.

- **System studying** [7]: In device getting to know, hybrid fashions regularly integrate more than one algorithm or

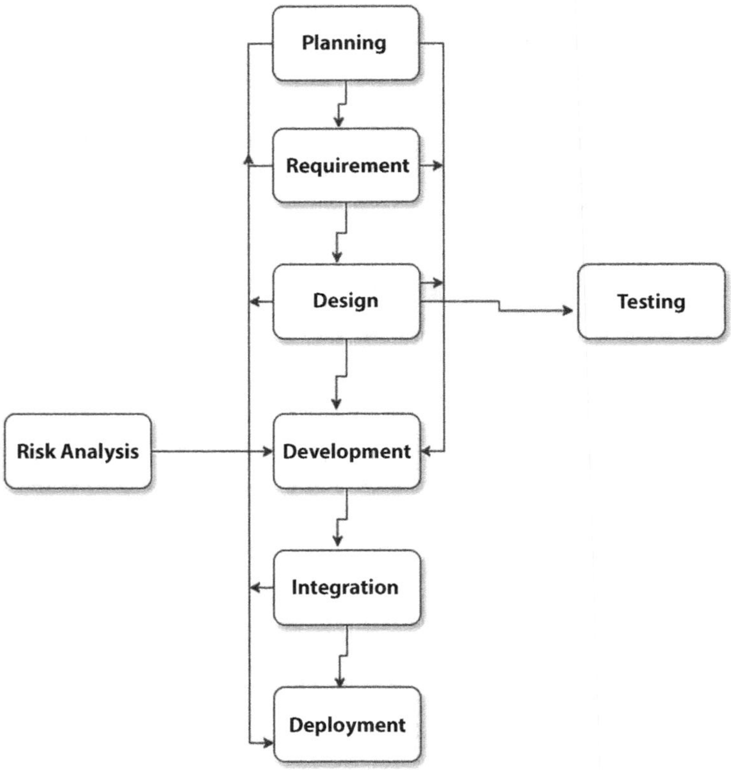


**Figure 5.9** Hybrid approach in task execution.

architecture to improve predictive performance. As an example, an ensemble learning technique would possibly combine the predictions of several base models, such as decision timber, assist vector machines, or neural networks, to produce a final prediction that is more accurate and stronger than any character version. Another example is the use of deep knowledge of fashions for feature extraction blended with traditional system mastering algorithms for category or regression obligations.

- **Optimization** [4]: In optimization issues, hybrid fashions can combine exclusive optimization techniques to efficiently search for the foremost answers in complex seek spaces. For instance, a hybrid metaheuristic set of rules may combine elements of genetic algorithms, simulated annealing, and Tabu search to discover the answer area more successfully and conquer neighborhood optima. Similarly, hybrid optimization fashions would possibly combine mathematical programming techniques with evolutionary algorithms or swarm intelligence strategies to clear up big-scale or multi-goal optimization troubles.
- **Device design** [4]: In gadget design and engineering, hybrid fashions can integrate physical fashions, empirical facts, and computational simulations to analyze and optimize the performance of complicated systems. For example, a hybrid simulation model might combine discrete event simulation with primarily agent-based modeling to take a look at the interactions between person agents and the overall gadget dynamics. Further, hybrid fashions on top-of-things systems would possibly integrate classic management techniques with modern-day adaptive or sturdy manipulation methods to obtain better overall performance and balance in dynamic environments.
- **Economic modeling** [4]: In finance, hybrid fashions are often used to forecast asset costs, manipulate hazards, and optimize investment portfolios. These models may integrate statistical time collection evaluation with system-studying algorithms to seize both lengthy-time period trends and short-time period fluctuations in financial markets. Additionally, hybrid fashions in quantitative finance would possibly integrate stochastic tactics with numerical strategies to fee complex derivatives or simulate the behavior of monetary contraptions under uncertain situations.

## References


1. Fox, G.C., Williams, R.D., Messina, G.C., *Parallel computing works!*, Elsevier, 2014, https://books.google.co.uk/books?hl=it&lr=&id=cg2jBQAAQBAJ&oi=fnd&pg=PP1&ots=8o5BEnjEaA&sig=vERCXHUarrjwBHn6vHZzShk-PiSM#v=onepage&q&f=false.
2. Quinn, M.J., *Parallel computing theory and practice*, McGraw-Hill, Inc., 1994. https://dl.acm.org/doi/abs/10.5555/174770.
3. Liu, Q., Wan, D., Yu, Y., Zhang, Y., Research and application of the parallel computing method for the grid-based Xin'anjiang model. *Hydrol. Res.*, *54*, 4, 591–605, 2023.
4. Xi, M., Feng, Y., Tong, X., Gao, F., Li, P., Wang, R., Tang, X., Development of a parallel computing-based Futureland model for multiple land-use simulation: a case study in Shanghai. *Geocarto Int.*, *38*, 1, 2216675, 2023.
5. Sitsylitsyn, Y.O., Osadchyi, V.V., Kruglyk, V.S., Kuzminska, O.H., Modeling training content for software engineers in parallel computing. *J. Phys. Conf. Ser.*, 2611, 1, 012017, 2023, October, IOP Publishing.
6. Acheampong, A., Zhang, Y., Xu, X., A parallel computing based model for online binary computation offloading in mobile edge computing. *Comput. Commun.*, *203*, 248–261, 2023.
7. Yin, F. and Shi, F., A comparative survey of big data computing and HPC: From a parallel programming model to a cluster architecture. *Int. J. Parallel Program.*, *50*, 1, 27–64, 2022.
8. De Lima, E.C., Rossi, F.D., Luizelli, M.C., Calheiros, R.N., Lorenzon, A.F., A neural network framework for optimizing parallel computing in cloud servers. *J. Syst. Archit.*, *150*, 103131, 2024.
9. Kumar, S., Singh, S.K., Aggarwal, N., Speculative parallelism on multicore chip architecture strengthen green computing concept: A survey, in: *Advanced Computer Science Applications*, pp. 3–16, Apple Academic Press, 2023.
10. Gao, H., Liang, Z., Guan, Q., Liang, X., Zeng, W., A parallel framework on hybrid architectures for raster-based geospatial cellular automata models. *Int. J. Geogr. Inf. Sci.*, 1–24, 2024, https://colab.ws/articles/10.1080%2F13658816.2024.2343776.
11. Tripathi, S.L. and Mahmud, M., *Explainable Machine Learning Models and Architecture*, Wiley & Scrivener Publishing LLC, USA, 2023, https://doi.org/10.1002/9781394186570.
12. Ghai, D., Tripathi, S.L., Saxena, S., Chanda, M., Alazab, M., *Machine Learning Algorithms for Signal and Image Processing*, Wiley IEEE Press, USA, 2022, DOI:10.1002/9781119861850.
13. Tripathi, S.L., Mahmud, M., Balas, V.E., FPGA implementation for explainable machine learning and deep learning models to real-time problems, in: *Machine Learning Models and Architectures for Biomedical Signal Processing*, pp. 449–471, Academic Press, Elsevier, 2025, https://doi.org/10.1016/B978-0-443-22158-3.00018-1.

6

# Network Issues and High-Level Communication Tools in Distributed Computing

**Sandhya Avasthi*** **and Sachin Kumar Vishwakarma**

*Department of CSE, ABES Engineering College, Ghaziabad, India*

## *Abstract*

The area of distributed computing is advancing and is a technology for large-scale computation providing benefits such as reliability, speed, fault tolerance, and cost-effectiveness. Currently, there exist several issues that prevail such as connectivity, communication load, communication overheads, congestion in the network, straggler effects, etc. One of the common challenges in any large organization is network issues that cause disconnection, inefficiency, and low performance. Techniques and strategies to identify and resolve these issues quickly are important in minimizing their impact. Interference from devices such as microwaves, cordless phones, and Bluetooth can also affect Wi-Fi performance. There are essential steps such as checking hardware connections, power cycling devices, and using tools such as ipconfig, ping, and TRACERT to diagnose and resolve issues. High-level communication tools are essential for efficient and effective communication within and across organizations. Selecting appropriate tools and implementing best practices for their use can enhance collaboration, streamline workflows, and improve overall productivity.

***Keywords*:** Distributed computing, parallel computing, information sharing, data transmission issues, network troubleshooting, network maintenance

**Corresponding author*: sandhya_avasthi@yahoo.com

Sandhya Avasthi and Suman Lata Tripathi (eds.) Distributed and Parallel Computing, (115–134)

## 6.1 Introduction

The distributed computing is around for the past three decades, known as computing process, over different autonomous computing nodes sharing resources and information over communication channel. Any distributed computing ecosystem consists of computing nodes, processors, distributed memory, and other network hardware that together solve a common task. The technologies of computation, storage, and communication are advancing, leading to large-scale and complex applications that need distributed resources. Some common distributed computing techniques these days are cloud computing, grid computing, edge computing, federated learning, distributed quantum computing, and distributed artificial intelligence. The fast-paced world needs effective and efficient solution to their organizational need for computing that require dealing with common existing issues such as optimization and networks issues [1, 2]. The improvement in wide-area network can aggregate distributed resources from different interacting networks forming computational grids (or grids). The impact of network issues in distributed environment and wireless systems is far-reaching, disrupts daily operations, and reduces productivity and stakeholder satisfaction. A distributed computing scenario consists of several connected nodes or mobile devices or sensor nodes sharing information. An important issue in distributed and parallel computing is resource allocation to different active processing units that increases system performance by better utilization of common resources [3].

When a single task or activity is computed using several computing resources, it is called distributed computing; the computing nodes in them are referred to as servers, personal computers, mobiles devices, and workstations. In distributed computing ecosystem, any task is executed through interconnected computing nodes sharing common resources and memory. These resources are divided throughout the distributed environment in such a way that improves performance and highly scalable over time as the need to enhance the network grows. The sharing of resource in such a system follows protocols such as message passing interfaces (MPI) and remote procedure calls (RPC) [4]. These protocols provide guidelines for data sharing and synchronization between participating nodes. The management and coordination of computing nodes are a difficult task, because tasks and data are vulnerable to illegal access and malicious attacks.

### 6.1.1 Common Network Issues in Distributed Computing

Network issues encompass a broad range of challenges that can disrupt communication and collaboration among team members. Some common issues are latency, bandwidth limitations, packet loss, network congestion, and connectivity issues. These issues are summarized in Table 6.1.

### 6.1.2 Group Communication in Distributed Systems

In a distributed environment to coordinate activities between multiple participating computing nodes group communication is crucial. This is a process where multiple nodes communicate with each other in groups; group communication allows the sender to send information to other members in group simultaneously [6]. Group communication improves reliability by

**Table 6.1** Summary of network issues and limitations.

| Issues | Description |
|---|---|
| Latency and bandwidth | Known as a delay in the transmission of data packets over a network, due to which real-time communication lags such as video conferencing or voice calls. Data transfer speed slows down due to insufficient bandwidth that makes it difficult to share large files. |
| Straggler effects | The stragglers are the processing nodes that run slower than average; also, nodes may be disconnected from the network due to insufficient power. |
| Packet loss | When data packet fails to reach destined node across a distributed network causing incomplete or distorted communication. |
| Network congestion | High levels of traffic on a network can congest the available bandwidth, causing slowdowns and interruptions in communication. |
| Communication load | Problems with network connectivity, such as dropped connections or intermittent outages, can disrupt communication channels and hinder collaboration [5]. |

replicating messages across several nodes making communication robust that deals with failures easily. In any fault-tolerant distributed computing ecosystem, any member of a group coordinates through multicast messages and maintains global consistency. In case of large-scale distributed systems, both asynchronous and simultaneous group communication strategies are needed due to the presence of replicated servers. The group communication systems are classified into two types: one is the synchronous and the other is the asynchronous model.

(a) **Synchronous model**: The distributed processes communicate and coordinate by maintaining communication synchrony to preserve the causality property of message communication.
(b) **Asynchronous model**: The large group of geographically distributed processes coordinates by sending asynchronous messages over the network to support replicated services.

## 6.2 Latency in Distributed and Parallel Computing

Network latency is the total time it takes data to travel from one point on a network to another. Imagine you are sending a letter to a friend across the country. The time it takes for you to write the letter and place it in the mailbox, for it to be delivered by mail truck, and for your friend to retrieve it from their mailbox is all part of the latency. In networking terms, data are broken down into smaller packets, like how your letter might be placed in an envelope. These packets travel through various devices on the network, like routers and switches, until they reach their destination. The total time it takes for all the packets to arrive and be reassembled is the latency [7].

**(a) Factors affecting latency in the network**
Several factors can influence network latency such as physical distance, network congestion, hardware, and software. The farther the data need to travel, the higher the latency, just like it takes longer to mail a letter across the country compared to sending it down the street. Heavy traffic on a network can slow down data transfer, like rush-hour traffic jams slowing down cars on a highway. Older or overloaded network equipment can introduce delays in processing data packets. Any inefficient software or outdated network protocols can also contribute to latency. The impact of latency depends on the type of application you are using. For instance, real-time applications, such as activities like online gaming, video conferencing, and

live streaming, require very low latency for smooth performance. High latency can cause lags, interruptions, and a poor user experience [8]. In Web browsing, moderate latency might not significantly affect Web browsing as much as real-time applications. In file downloads, high latency can increase download times but may not be as critical unless dealing with very large files.

**(b) Methods to measuring latency**

Latency is typically measured in milliseconds. A common tool used to measure latency is ping. Ping sends a data packet to a specific destination and measures the time it takes for the response to return. Lower ping times indicate lower latency [9].

**Example**: Take a real-world example, where 2 Web sites are pinged one that is part of network in India naming "TCS" (Figure 6.1) and another "Goldman Sachs" from overseas (Figure 6.2) and observing the effect. Here, one can observe the latency for TCS is 44 milliseconds, and 53 milliseconds for Goldman Sachs; this difference is because of the reason that ping is originating from India (as shown in Figure 6.1). The ping of any Web site is directly proportional to the physical distance. To prevent latency in network issues, organizations can implement several strategies.

1. **Network monitoring and optimization**: Utilize tools such as IR Collaborate to monitor and troubleshoot network latency effectively, setting standard expectations for latency and creating alerts to address issues promptly. Enhance

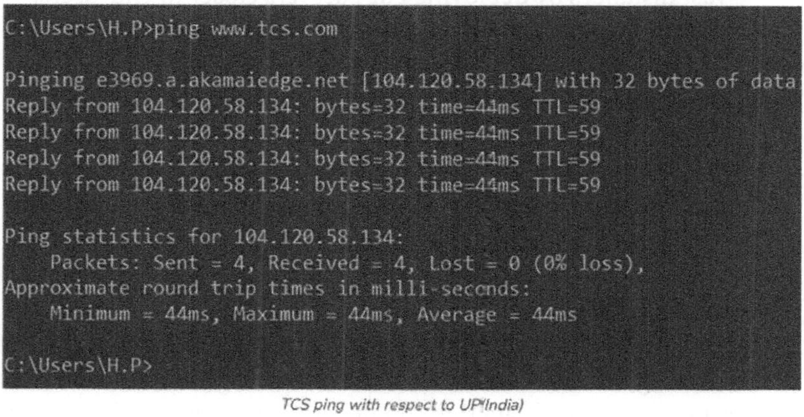


**Figure 6.1** Output from ping command for www.tcs.com.

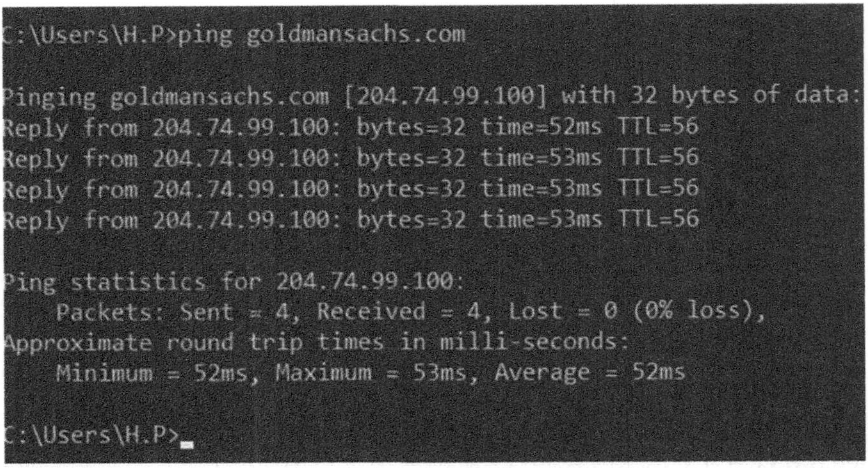


*Goldman Sachs ping with respect to UP(India)*

**Figure 6.2** Results of ping command for www.goldmansachs.com.

network speed to reduce latency, ensuring smoother communication and better productivity within the organization. Manage network congestion during peak usage times or sudden traffic spikes to prevent delays and maintain optimal network performance.

2. **Utilize network security solutions**: Implement optimized network security solutions such as next-generation firewalls to prevent delays caused by security checks and policy violations, which can contribute to latency.
3. **Reduce geographic distance**: Minimize latency caused by vast distances by deploying edge servers closer to end-users, such as content delivery networks, to shorten the data travel distance and improve page load times.
4. **By compressing data**: Utilizing compression algorithms to compress data packet can significantly lower the transmission time of data and, indirectly, latency. Also, caching data can lower the latency by reducing the need for frequent data transfers over the transmission medium.

**(c) Bandwidth limitation**

Imagine a highway with multiple lanes. Bandwidth limitation on a network is akin to having a limited number of lanes for a surge of traffic. It refers to the maximum amount of data that can flow through a network connection in each amount of time, measured in Mbps (megabits per second) or Gbps (gigabits per second). Several elements can constrict the available bandwidth on your network, hindering your internet experience:

- **Physical constraints**: Some physical constraints are media type, cable condition, and distance. The cables carrying your data play a starring role. The bandwidth is lower for traditional copper wires in comparison to fiber-optic cables. Fiber-optic cables transmit data using light pulses, enabling significantly higher bandwidth and immunity to signal interference. The quality of your cables can also influence bandwidth. Worn-out or damaged cables might struggle with signal integrity, reducing the effective bandwidth. Data transfer can experience signal degradation over longer cable runs, like how a long phone call might have static. This can limit the usable bandwidth [10].
- **Network hardware**: The limitations of your network devices (routers, switches, modems) can restrict bandwidth. Older or lower-rated equipment might not be equipped to handle high-speed data transfer. Improper configuration of network devices can create bandwidth bottlenecks. For instance, not enabling Quality of Service (QoS) on your router might lead to congestion if bandwidth-hogging applications are not prioritized.
- **Network usage and congestion**: The more devices vying for your network connection, the more they compete for the available bandwidth. This can lead to sluggish speeds for everyone. Video streaming applications, online gaming, and large file downloads are bandwidth guzzlers compared to Web browsing or checking emails. Running multiple bandwidth-intensive applications simultaneously can significantly impact overall speed. Internet service provider (ISP) that provides network infrastructure and overall bandwidth capacity can affect your internet speed. During peak usage times, there might be congestion on the ISP's network, leading to slower speeds for everyone subscribed to their service [11].
- **Interference, software, and malware**: The wireless networks are vulnerable in situation where a lot of interferences are received from other electronic devices and Wi-Fi networks, reducing bandwidth and strength of the signal.

Certain software programs running in the background can consume bandwidth. Additionally, malware infections might send or receive data in the background, impacting your internet speed.

**(d) Strategies to prevent the bandwidth limitations**

Some key strategies to prevent bandwidth limitations, which are a common challenge in organizations, are as follows:

1. **Optimize current network infrastructure**: Address network bottlenecks and optimize the existing network infrastructure to improve bandwidth utilization.
2. **Assess virtual LANs (VLANs) and subnets**: Properly configure and manage VLANs and subnets to ensure efficient allocation and use of available bandwidth.
3. **Implement caching and link aggregation**: Use caching techniques and link aggregation to eliminate unnecessary data retrieval and quickly send data across multiple network links.
4. **Set up bandwidth allocation policies**: Establish policies to properly allocate bandwidth for different applications and users, ensuring fair and efficient use of the available network resources.
5. **Monitor network data and establish baselines**: Collect and analyze network data to understand bandwidth usage patterns, set appropriate baselines, and identify areas for optimization.

## 6.3 Straggler Effect

The computing nodes in distributed networks have heterogeneous computing capabilities, and so some processing nodes run unexpectedly slower than others with more resources. If such computing nodes are given tasks, either they become corrupt, or another process starts that demands more resources. These nodes sometimes get disconnected from distributed networks because of the content of shared resources, imbalance in work allocation, network congestion, and insufficient power. This aggregates to an imbalance in performance, some nodes fall behind other nodes in terms of execution time, and these nodes are referred to as straggling workers. Due to this, the execution time is calculated using the slowest processing nodes.

For instance, parallel computation, such as bulk synchronous problem (BSP), is sometimes plagued by stragglers where a slower thread process delays the execution of other thread [11]. In the BSP situation, stragglers problem gets worse if more thread is added in the executing queue. This problem causes the entire application to be delayed in every iteration. Sometimes, stragglers can be introduced due to expensive computational steps in an algorithm such as the use of stopping criterion in iterations.

This effect needs to be identified and resolved to improve system performance. The straggler effect is handled through different strategies and methods [12].

**Stragglers detection**: This effect can be detected by identifying stragglers (slow-performing nodes) and taking action on them early to improve execution. For example, Mantri detects the stragglers by choosing the activities that were performed at a slower rate than average. The distributed system then identifies the cause and implements the solutions to resolve the issues due to stragglers. The task given to stragglers is restarted at some other computing nodes. The optimal situation here is to reassign tasks to processing nodes with a good amount of network resources, also replicating valuable tasks.

**Work stealing**: Fast-processing nodes can take over incomplete tasks from slower nodes or poor-performing nodes. The idea here is to minimize execution time by shifting incomplete tasks from slower nodes to faster nodes. The slower nodes become idle if their task is taken over by faster nodes.

**Naive replication**: The straggler effect is reduced by replicating computing nodes to minimize latency. In this strategy, computational task is replicated, and execution takes place at various nodes. Because different nodes work on the same computational problem/task, the time to calculate the result depends on the fastest-processing node. The partial results on other processing nodes are discarded (as shown in Figure 6.3). The trade-off in this process is higher cost due to replication and communication bandwidth [13].

**Work exchange**: The master node leverages the information of the nodes and allocates the tasks to the participating nodes according to their computational capabilities. If any of the working nodes computes results and sends that to the master, the master node ceases the process and redistributes the work again among participating nodes. This is repeated until all the work is finished. This process adds overhead to overall computational complexity due to the reallocation of the work again and again [14].

**Coded redundancy**: Such techniques utilize redundancy in code that provides the capability to the master node to recover the final results from any

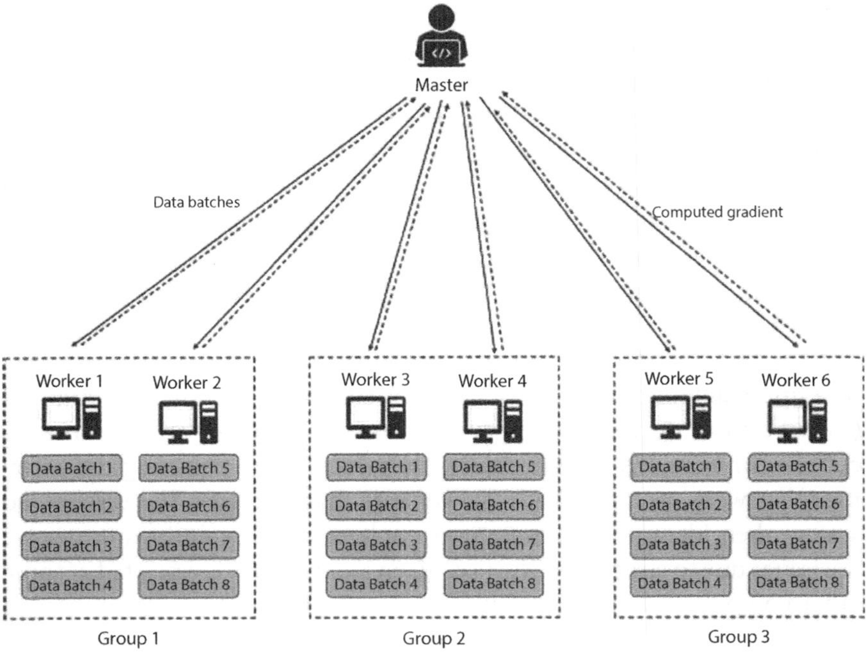


**Figure 6.3** Replication strategy illustration among 6 workers and 2 stragglers [17].

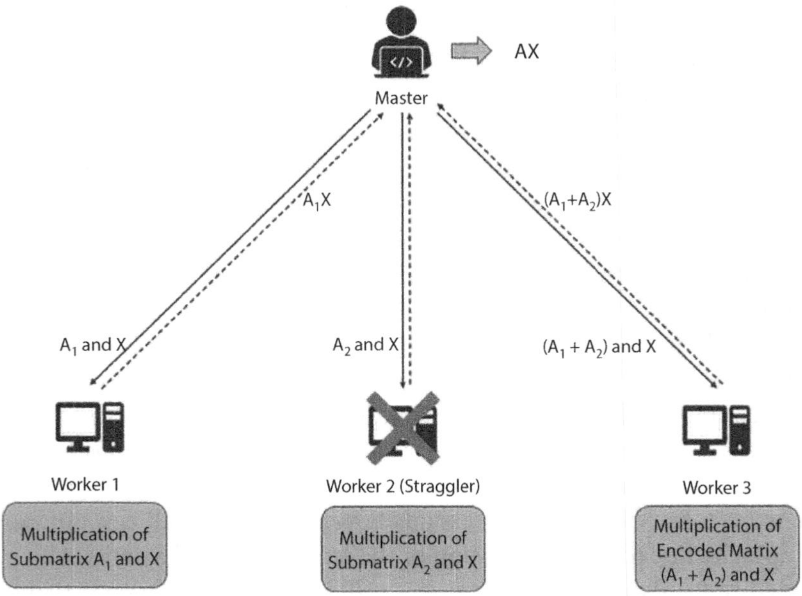


**Figure 6.4** Illustration of coded redundancy framework for matrix multiplication [17].

workers who have redundant code without any delay (as shown in Figure 6.4). A coded redundancy system outperforms a replication-based system in terms of latency and cost. The communication load by any coded distributed computing is given by Equation (6.1).

$$L_{coded}(r) = \frac{1}{r}\left(1 - \frac{r}{K}\right) \tag{6.1}$$

where $K$ is number of processing nodes in the distributed systems.

## 6.4 Packet Loss in the Distributed Network

In the world of computer networks, data travel in small bundles called packets. Packet loss occurs when one or more of these data packets fail to reach their intended destination [14]. Several factors can contribute to packet loss, causing hiccups in your data delivery:

- **Network congestion**: Think of rush-hour traffic on a highway. When a network is overloaded with data traffic, packets can get dropped due to congestion. This is a common culprit, especially during peak usage times or with limited bandwidth availability.
- **Physical issues**: Worn-out or damaged cables, loose connections, or faulty network equipment can introduce errors during data transmission, leading to packet loss.
- **Wireless interference**: Wireless networks are susceptible to interference from other electronic devices or neighboring Wi-Fi signals. This interference can corrupt data packets, resulting in loss.
- **Internet service provider (ISP) issues**: Problems within your ISP's network infrastructure can also cause packet loss.
- **Overly busy servers**: If the server you are trying to connect to is overloaded, it might not be able to handle all incoming data packets, leading to some being dropped.

### 6.4.1 Implications of Packet Loss

The effects of packet loss depend on the type of application you are using:

- **Real-time applications**: Activities such as online gaming, video conferencing, and live streaming rely on a steady stream of data packets for smooth operation. Packet loss can cause lag, stuttering, and interruptions, significantly impacting your experience.
- **File downloads**: Although frustrating, occasional packet loss might not significantly affect file downloads unless the lost data packets are crucial for the file's integrity.
- **Web browsing**: Packet loss might cause Web pages to load slower or display errors if critical data packets are lost. However, the impact might be less noticeable compared to real-time applications.

### 6.4.2 Identifying Packet Loss

Packet loss can manifest in various ways, affecting different online activities. Here are some telltale signs that you might be experiencing packet loss: Lag in online games can lead to erratic or choppy movements during crucial network-dependent events, making the game unplayable due to inconsistent data transmission. Choppy video calls can result from high levels of packet loss, causing a "robotic" effect on voices during calls, leading to stuttering voices that make conversations challenging and impact the overall quality of voice communication. Packet loss can also cause buffering during video streaming, disrupting the visual clarity of the video and hindering the fluidity of the conversation. Furthermore, slow download speeds with frequent pauses can occur due to incomplete datasets and malfunctions caused by packet loss, affecting the download speed and causing frequent pauses in data transmission. Additionally, packet loss can lead to disruptions in connectivity, causing slowed services or, in severe cases, loss of connectivity, resulting in frequent disconnects from online applications. These symptoms are specific indicators of packet loss scenarios, affecting various online activities and highlighting the importance of addressing packet loss issues to ensure a smooth and uninterrupted online experience [15].

### 6.4.3 Tools to Measure Packet Loss

Several online tools and software applications can help you measure packet loss on your network connection. A common tool is ping, Wireshark, MTR (My traceroute), Ping Plotter, and PingPlotter Cloud, which sends test packets to a specific server and measures the percentage of packets that are lost. An NPM (network performance monitor) views network for any kind of packet loss, for example, SolarWinds®. SolarWinds provides several features for network monitoring. The tools automatically discover network paths and gain access to network using protocols such as SNMP, WMI, and ICMP. In addition, the tools drill down the monitored nodes and track different performance metrics. SolarWinds see metrics for several access points, clients, and wireless controllers. PingPlotter is another tool to assess network connections. PingPlotter Cloud troubleshoots remote internet connections and simultaneously monitors other remote connections. Another version is PingPlotter Professional, which a diagnostics tool for professional mainly engineers, administrators, and technical support team.

### 6.4.4 Techniques to Prevent Packet Loss

To prevent packet loss in network issues, which is a common challenge in organizations, several strategies are:

1. **Upgrade network hardware**: The overall network performance can be improved by upgrades in network switches, routers, and other network devices. This will help in minimizing packet loss issue as well.
2. **Manage network congestion**: Address network congestion, which is a primary cause of packet loss, by optimizing network traffic and ensuring that the network has sufficient bandwidth to handle data transmission without dropping packets.
3. **Implement QoS**: By utilizing tools for maintaining QoS to mark data packets based on their importance and priority, one can prevent excessive bandwidth use. In addition, it ensures critical data packets reach their destination without being dropped.
4. **Regularly update network hardware**: Keep network hardware updated to ensure it meets the network's full capabilities, reducing the risk of packet loss due to outdated devices with hardware limitations.
5. **Monitor and test for packet loss**: Use network assessment tools such as ping to detect packet loss, measure the packet loss rate, and troubleshoot network issues promptly to prevent further packet loss.

## 6.5 Network Congestion

On any busy day, the traffic crawls because there are more cars than the road can handle. Network congestion is analogous to this situation in the data world. The congestion happens due to overload of network traffic on any connection. Data travel in packets, like individual cars on the highway. When there is too much traffic (data packets), they get backed up, causing delays and disruptions in data flow [17]. This can lead to slower internet speeds, buffering during streaming, and lag in online games. If the network is flooded with more data packet than it can handle, network congestion occurs due to delay in execution. If simultaneous use of resources is there, a lot of backups of data packet will take place, delaying over process execution. Figure 6.5 illustrates network congestion in distributed environment.

### 6.5.1 Causes of Network Congestion and Implications

Several factors can lead to network congestion, causing a traffic jam for your data:

- **High number of users**: The more devices connected to a network (think rush hour on a single-lane road), the more data traffic it needs to handle. This can overwhelm the network's capacity, leading to congestion.
- **Bandwidth-hungry applications**: Certain applications, such as video streaming, online gaming, and large file downloads, require a significant amount of bandwidth. If multiple users run these applications simultaneously, it can quickly strain the network's resources and cause congestion.
- **Outdated network infrastructure**: Just like narrow roads cannot handle modern traffic volume, older network

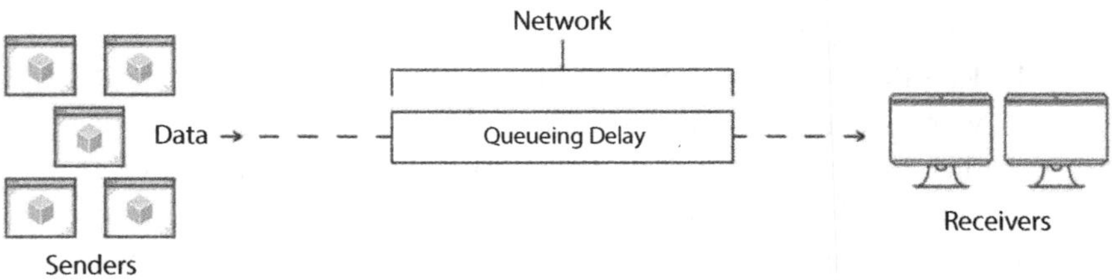


**Figure 6.5** A scenario of network congestion.

equipment with limited bandwidth capacity might struggle to keep up with current data demands, leading to congestion.
- **Bottlenecks**: A bottleneck is a point in the network that restricts data flow, similar to a single-lane bridge on a highway. Bottlenecks can occur due to limitations in specific network devices (such as routers or switches) and can cause congestion even if the overall network capacity is sufficient.

### 6.5.2 Network Congestion Implication

The effects of network congestion depend on how you use your internet connection:

- **Real-time applications**: Activities such as online gaming, video conferencing, and live streaming are highly sensitive to network congestion. They require low latency (fast response time) and consistent data flow for smooth operation. Congestion can cause lag, stuttering, and frequent disconnects, significantly impacting your experience.
- **Web browsing**: Although noticeable, moderate congestion might not significantly hinder Web browsing as much as real-time applications. You might experience slower loading times or occasional page freezes.
- **File downloads**: Downloads might take longer to complete due to congestion, but unless the data loss is critical, the impact might be less severe.

Some common visible signs that a distributed network might be experiencing network congestion is when one faces slower loading times for Web pages and applications and gets frequent buffering during video streaming and when users lag in online games, frequently disconnect from video calls or online applications, and see difficulty in uploading or downloading files.

## 6.6 Communication Load

The computing nodes in a distributed environment exchange intermediate results over the network to calculate the final output that increases communication expenses or overheads [16]. Due to this performance of distributed computing applications, which involves joining, sorting, or even machine learning execution time increases. For example, in Hadoop cluster at Facebook, the observation is that data shuffling contributes to 33% of execution time. This communication creates a bottleneck for convolution neural network implementation in distributed environments such as AlexNet [17]. The communication load is distributed among participating nodes in a manner that improves overall system performance. The division of work among computing nodes should be balanced, but it is an issue because some processors always do more or less work than other nodes. In a worse situation, even some processing nodes do not do any processing and are idle.

The communication load issue is handled using the loading balancing process [18]. The load-balancing process divides work or tasks equally between participating nodes. The aim here is to give equal work to all the computing nodes and not overwhelm a few nodes with work. A good balancing strategy should follow these goals:

- Maximizing overall system performance minimizing delays and use of resources
- A fair job allocation regardless of their origin
- Keeping the system performance handling partial failures

There are two approaches, static and dynamic load balancing, which can be used depending on the situation. In the static approach, the information about system parameters is taken into consideration before distributing the workload and is fixed during the execution. These strategies are deterministic or probabilistic.

### 6.6.1 A Deterministic Strategy

Based on a fixed criterion, various tasks are assigned to processors, whereas probabilistic strategy uses probability ratio to make assignments. For instance, if in any strategy extra task is moved from processor "A" to processor "B," this situation is called deterministic, but if a strategy transfers an extra task from "A" to "B" using a probability value of 0.7 and to processor "C" with a probability value of 0.3, it is called probabilistic strategy [18]. A major disadvantage of any static solution is that it ignores changes in working conditions and overall workload. The plus side of static algorithms is their simplicity and ease of analysis. In the dynamic approach, no assumption related to processing information is made in advance; it does not have any prior information about where the task is going to be executed and in what condition. The dynamic load balancing constantly checks for ongoing changes in the system workload and accordingly redistributes the workload.

### 6.6.2 Bidding Strategy

The strategy is based on the bids by processing nodes wanting to execute tasks available on overloaded processing nodes. The overloaded node chooses the best from all competing nodes wanting to take control over some tasks on the overloaded node. In general, bid information consists of the workload status of a processing node. The overloaded processing node chooses to whom it wants to send some of its tasks after receiving bid information from other competing nodes. The limitation is that one processor can become overloaded after winning many bids. To resolve this, some bidders may have the option to reject the task sent by the straggler. After rejecting, the processing node can send a message to an overloaded node about task rejection. Since processor load depends on the outcome of received messages from bidders, the final results would not be as effective as it seemed in the beginning [19–22].

### 6.6.3 Drafting Strategy

The drafting strategy allows process migration and ends up achieving load balancing. The strategy aims to maximize the processor utilization and minimize the communication load. The issues in the bidding strategy can be reduced by drafting a policy method by making all processing nodes occupied through load balancing, and it does not distribute workload among participating processing nodes. Some tasks may be migrated from an overloaded processing node to another node that has less load.

### 6.6.4 Greedy Strategy

In this strategy, the current state of the processing node is calculated by a function $f(n)$, where $n$ is the number of tasks at hand. The arriving task at $P$ and $n > 0$, then processor $P$ searched for a remote processing node that has $n <= 0$. If the search is successful, then the specific task is transferred there. The efficiency of this policy depends on the function $f(n)$. Here, condition $f(n) < n$ must hold to achieve good performance. Some selected functions in such a situation are $n-1$, $n/2$, $n/3$, $n/5$, etc. Some research states that

$f(n) = n/3$ yields the best results; this greedy strategy outperforms the threshold strategy where $T = 1$ in several scenarios.

### 6.6.5 Threshold Strategy

The strategy works by choosing a value for parameter $T$, which decides whether a task is executed on the local or remote node in a distributed environment. The threshold value is queue length, which is the number of processes in service plus the number of processes waiting in the queue. Threshold value assumes static value in an implementation of Algorithm [4] and [5]. The computing node executes the arriving task on the local node until this processing node threshold is reached. Upon reaching the threshold, the processor randomly chooses another processor and checks that to determine if the task transfer to the probed processor makes the threshold value above its limit. If the limit of the threshold is not reached, the task is transferred, and then the processing node executes the task, else the task is transferred to a third processing node. The selection of the third processing node is performed in the same manner as before. The operations keep taking place until a certain limit is reached, known as the probing limit. When the probing limit is reached, it means no processor is found, and the task is finally executed locally. The exchange of information does not take place among processing nodes to decide on task transfer that reduces communication overhead. An advantage of the strategy is that extra transfer to the processing node is avoided and reaches the threshold limit, saving time.

## 6.7 Conclusion

In today's digital landscape, effectively managing network issues and utilizing advanced communication tools are essential for organizational success. By addressing challenges such as latency, bandwidth limitations, packet loss, and connectivity issues, businesses can ensure smooth operations and improved productivity. Implementing solutions such as network monitoring, prioritizing critical traffic, and upgrading infrastructure helps mitigate congestion. Investing in robust information technology management practices and cutting-edge technologies not only enhances operational efficiency but also positions organizations for sustained growth and competitiveness in the digital era. The chapter provides an overview of various problems and issues in distributed computing, also explaining how these are handled for better performance.

## References


1. Kumar, A. and Mishra, A., Network congestion and mitigation strategies in organizational settings. *J. Netw. Comput. Appl.*, 148, 102448, 2020.
2. Johnson, T. and Lee, S., Enhancing productivity through effective communication tools in modern organizations. *Int. J. Bus. Commun.*, 58, 3, 365–382, 2021.
3. Smith, R. and Patel, K., Understanding packet loss and its impact on real-time applications. *IEEE Commun. Mag.*, 57, 12, 23–29, 2019.
4. Thompson, L. and Kim, J., Strategies for reducing network latency in enterprise environments. *Proceedings of the IEEE International Conference on Network Management*, pp. 124–131, 2022, August.
5. Chowdhury, M., Zaharia, M., Ma, J., Jordan, M.I., Stoica, I., Managing Data Transfers in Computer Clusters with Orchestra, in: *Proceedings of the ACM SIGCOMM 2011 Conference, SIGCOMM âA˘ Z11*, New York, NY, USA, Association for Computing Machinery, pp. 98–109, 2011.
6. Williams, M., Bandwidth limitations and solutions in digital workplaces. *J. Internet Serv. Appl.*, 14, 2, 45–56, 2023.
7. Davis, R. and Nguyen, P., The role of advanced communication tools in enhancing organizational efficiency. *J. Organ. Comput. Electron. Commer.*, 30, 4, 315–329, 2020.
8. Dinari, H., Inter-Process Communication (IPC) in Distributed Environments: An Investigation and Performance Analysis of Some Middleware Technologies. *Int. J. Mod. Educ. Comput. Sci.*, *15*, 2, 36, 2020.
9. Hao, Y., Troemner, M., Li, W., Lale, E., Yang, L., Shen, L., Alnaggar, Md., Di Luzio, G., Cusatis, G., An interprocess communication-based two-way coupling approach for implicit–explicit multiphysics lattice discrete particle model simulations. *Eng. Fract. Mech.*, 310, 110515, 2024.
10. Tonci, N., Torquati, M., Mencagli, G., Danelutto, M., Distributed-memory fastflow building blocks. *Int. J. Parallel Program.*, *51*, 1, 1–21, 2023.
11. Cipar, J., Ho, Q., Kim, J.K., Lee, S., Ganger, G.R., Gibson, G., Xing, E., Solving the straggler problem with bounded staleness, in: *14th Workshop on Hot Topics in Operating Systems (HotOS XIV)*, 2013.
12. Kou, W. and Park, S.Y., A distributed energy management approach for smart campus demand response. *IEEE J. Emerging Sel. Top. Ind. Electron.*, *4*, 1, 339–347, 2022.
13. Nava, J.J., Lee, J.J., Lee, H., HPPython: Extending Python with HPspmd for Data Parallel Programming, in: *Proceedings of the 2023 2nd International*

*Symposium on Computing and Artificial Intelligence*, pp. 91–94, 2023, October.

14. Yazdeen, A.A., Zeebaree, S.R., Sadeeq, M.M., Kak, S.F., Ahmed, O.M., Zebari, R.R., FPGA implementations for data encryption and decryption *via* concurrent and parallel computation: A review. *Qubahan Acad. J.*, *1*, 2, 8–16, 2021.
15. Li, W., Liu, D., Chen, K., Li, K., Qi, H., Hone: Mitigating stragglers in distributed stream processing with tuple scheduling. *IEEE Trans. Parallel Distrib. Syst.*, *32*, 8, 2021–2034, 2021.
16. Ji, B., Wang, Y., Song, K., Li, C., Wen, H., Menon, V.G., Mumtaz, S., A survey of computational intelligence for 6G: Key technologies, applications and trends. *IEEE Trans. Ind. Inf.*, *17*, 10, 7145–7154, 2021.
17. Ng, J.S., Lim, W.Y.B., Luong, N.C., Xiong, Z., Asheralieva, A., Niyato, D., Miao, C., A comprehensive survey on coded distributed computing: Fundamentals, challenges, and networking applications. *IEEE Commun. Surv. Tutorials*, *23*, 3, 1800–1837, 2021.
18. Chen, X., Liu, Z., Kim, I., A parallel computing framework for solving user equilibrium problem on computer clusters. *Transportmetrica A: Transp. Sci.*, *16*, 3, 550–573, 2020.
19. De Giusti, A.E., Structured Parallel Programming: Patterns for Efficient Computation. *J. Comput. Sci. Technol.*, 15, 01, 43–44, 2015.
20. Chowdhury, M., Zaharia, M., Ma, J., Jordan, M.I., Stoica, I., Managing data transfers in computer clusters with orchestra. *ACM SIGCOMM Comput. Commun. Rev.*, *41*, 4, 98–109, 2011.
21. Zhou, Q., Guo, S., Lu, H., Li, L., Guo, M., Sun, Y., Wang, K., Falcon: Addressing stragglers in heterogeneous parameter server *via* multiple parallelism. *IEEE Trans. Comput.*, *70*, 1, 139–155, 2020.
22. Robertazzi, T.G., Shi, L., Robertazzi, T.G., Shi, L., Divisible loads and parallel processing, in: *Networking and Computation: Technology, Modeling and Performance*, pp. 101–137, 2020.

7

# Infinite Horizons: Empowering Business Education Through Metaverse

**Shikha Mishra[1] and Sujit S. Nair[2*]**

[1]*Department of Human Resource, Amity Business School, Amity University, Noida, India*
[2]*MBA (Technology Management), Amity Business School, Amity University, Noida, India*

## Abstract

The study is developed on the metaverse technology of education to disrupt change and enhance creativity, innovation, and engagement *via* students. For this reason, its aim is to provide a narrative review of the academic literature and some illustrative cases that have been using empirical evidence in making tentative claims about benefits, costs, and longer-term educational outcomes. Outcomes imply that metaverse environments can be readily conducive to learners in interaction, critical thinking and processing information, and problem solving. This so-called *metaverse* is the learning fun tagger that stands in an immersive interactive environment, which makes teaching–learning bridge between your reading knowledge (thorough) and its practical implication. That integration will not be without pain and struggle, however; there are challenges from the technological front too, including overcoming hardware limitations and a reliable internet connection; also, open the Pandora box with data privacy and digital justice. It will be a theme in the upcoming paper that makes a case for strategic infrastructure investments and broader educator training to maximize these metaverse elements. Nevertheless, the use of metaverse technology is a must for education and preparing students to live in their screens. The paper did say that introduced carefully and well-studied in subsequent years; it could potentially alter "the future of education" by making students more digitally savvy citizens. The work should be of interest to educators, policymakers, and technologists, hoping to leverage metaverse technology for improved learning environments.

***Keywords:*** Virtual reality, metaverse, practical training, deep learning

**Corresponding author*: sujitsignals@gmail.com

Sandhya Avasthi and Suman Lata Tripathi (eds.) Distributed and Parallel Computing, (135–152)

## 7.1 Introduction

Metaverse technology implication from the dawn of time, the notion that appears moderately new is indeed a ventricle and has its ordinary foundations in science fiction. Neal Stephenson, in his science fiction novel *Snow Crash*, described metaverse as a successor to the internet, first using this idea back in 1992. Improvements in technology over the last couple of decades have brought this concept from science fiction to a potential reality. Metaverse today is described as a collective virtual shared space that resides on the convergence of virtually enhanced physical reality and physically persistent virtual spaces. A metaverse is a virtual universe with an interactive environment where users can meet using avatars in real time, think of it as being built on top of blockchain, virtual reality/augmented reality (VR/AR) tech, and artificial intelligence (AI). Relevance and promise for educators on the learning side of things, in particular with education written large, broadly put it as offering an evolutionary opportunity for improving learner experience. This is due to the fact that traditional modes of education, viz., lectures, text books, and exams, do not attract student attention, whereas a job in hand will always excite them. But metaverse technology, on the other hand, is likely to break loose by providing elementary immersion and interactive into such platform. It gives rise to dynamic learning spaces that foster creativity, innovation, and engagement, way out of the curriculum theory–practice demarcation.

**Problems and limitations**: Metaverse holds great promise; however, an educational future shaped by metaverse is impeded on multiple fronts. For metaverses to materialize, support technical infrastructures from high-speed internet and great hardware are needed. Alongside that, there may also be barriers to metaverse adoption in education due to a lack of the necessary infrastructure. In conclusion, deliveries for future work, he said at the start of his presentation, must face these and other ethical dilemmas (with particular reference to students in this case as data subjects). Heidelberg University, Department of Computer Science, Hasso Plattner Institute (HPI) is also exploring research frontiers in privacy and security questions about data collection methods used in metaverse environments, as well who gets to utilize it. Also, it is vital to ensure that all students are exposed on an even field toward metaverse tech because digital divide will only be advantageous at education level. Brown and White (2023) have a different notation that advocates for educators to get the appropriate training needed to be able to use metaverse tools. So, educator-specific skills and knowledge are needed in order for educators to apply that technology into their pedagogy, as well as having them prepare themselves with the foreseeable challenge.

**(a) Objectives of the study.** The purpose of this study is intended to result in an investigation into metaverse technologies and how they might be valuably applied for the promotion of creativity and innovation engagement linked with 21st century skills when used within a pedagogical paradigm. This article is part of this line, and the researchers will look at a metaverse technology and its ability in educational environments. We review the literature, which includes case studies and empirical data for a comprehensive picture of how metaverse technology transforms education in general.

**(b) What is metaverse technology?** Metaverse technology is a kind of virtual universe, which mingles realities with the physical one and offers real-time coexistence of each user by their digital avatar. It ranges from VR, AR, and blockchain to AI piece parts, which combined gives birth to interactive experiences. Users will have access to different space from this type of spaces in which operations such as meetings, gaming, or even for business and education purposes are carried out. From the time this idea was originated, it has evolved from promising futuristic remedy to now as outright practical solution in use cases including, but not limited to, education.

**(c) A metaverse for education**: Perhaps metaverse will born educational spaces with real experiential and interactive learning environments. According to Johnson *et al.* [25], real-world simulations within metaverse environments increase student engagement and motivation: interactive scenarios. It lets the students discover and in turn learn complex subject matters that they would have learned through memorization otherwise. Meanwhile, Smith Jones, who published academically and reviewed type post in 2023, has found that students learn to be better critical thinkers and problem solvers from metaverse learning because they can experience real-world situations virtually. This type of learning adds a significant tangible flavor to one's theoretical knowledge; hence, future action is built on real experience, not only sedentary as nicely argued here.

## 7.2 Challenges and Concerns

Metaverse technology might one day revolutionize education (and make immersive metaverse itself!). When Disney's metaverse arrives to compete with, it will be facing a big challenge: This kind of technical infrastructure is also what makes the experience in metaverse mostly closer over high-speed internet and powerful computers. Meeting this vision of metaverse technology in education will remain a tall order if the infrastructure to deliver it is not available [4]. There are of ethical considerations as well—for data privacy, digital equity will have to be discussed furthermore. One of the ways in which this will happen is with data coming overwhelmingly from metaverse environments, and just like real life being treated as static advertising wastelands, the privacy and security are a concern, and a big issue could be creating equal access to metaverse tech for all students, because lack of availability keeping some groups out on that can definitely exacerbate certain no-fashionable kinds of education inequities. Also, refer to Brown and White (2023), who discuss the need for training educators in these tools and how metaverse is not without its other limiting factors that come along with its dawn.

**(a) Engagement in student life**

The surveys and case studies suggest that using metaverse environments increases the engagement of students. ***Introduction***: The use of metaverse tools in research has concluded as to the positive influence on the motivation and interest of students almost twofold compared with traditional methods. Because metaverse spaces are immersive, students can become involved in their learning and generally retain a higher level of understanding than with more traditional forms [5].

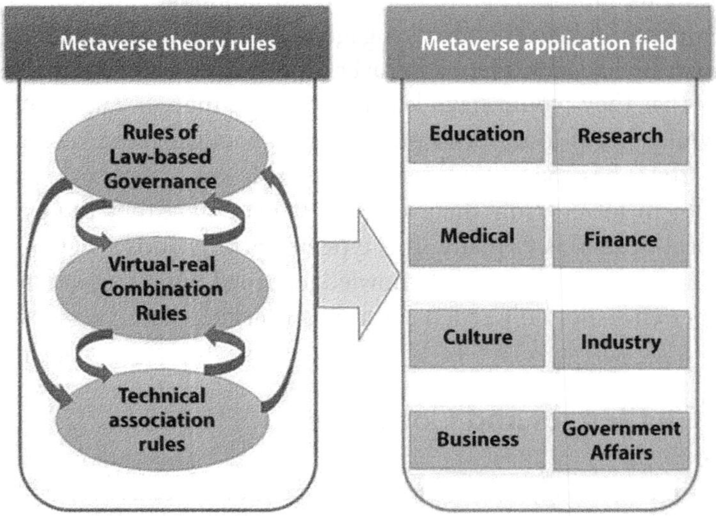


**Figure 7.1** Exploring the key characteristics and theoretical framework for research on the Metaverse (by Chuanxiang Song, Seong-Yoon and Kwang-Seong, 5 Jun 2023).

**(b) High school metaverse case study**: A high school that implemented metaverse technology into their science curriculum found it to be more enjoyable for the students and lifted some student performance grades in assessments as they were working with virtual laboratories and simulations, while others stayed on traditional methods According to CNet, the hands-on experience and immersion of students in their discovery increased; students were apparently more easily able to learn math and subjects that had previously been found difficult [6].

Figure 7.1 illustrates the theoretical foundation and classification of metaverse applications across diverse domains such as education, medical, finance, and governance, highlighting the combination of virtual-real rules and law-based governance frameworks.

## 7.3 Rules of Law–Based Governance

Higher-level critical thinking and problem-solving Educators also report that metaverse learning platforms are effective in encouraging students to be innovative and accurate when it comes to the academic crucible of thought. The theoretical knowledge they gain can be expanded into practical projects using VR simulation, and these orchestration platforms enable a deeper cultivation on the part of students. When students in a strategic management class were analyzed after using the metaverse simulation, they solved problems better than those who took the traditional course. The simulation frees students so that they can make tactical decisions and explore market changes with constraints acting inside the artificial enterprise environment counting as serious learning activities promoting decision-making skills.

**(a) Promoting collaborative and teamwork toggles**
In addition, its virtual space improves or allows the various activities and projects that students do in a digital manner to be carried out together. This model of teaching also aids in preparing students for the realities and expectations of a contemporary workspace. Finally, a third comes from an engineering school with students who underwent virtual project–based learning where they had to remotely design and simulate all aspects of a new product. So, using this hack in a metaverse environment, two cities (Brazil and Paraguay) could add each other (move to the same place) and participate in real time together sharing their notions about it. According to the report, students exhibited better collaboration and communication

skills when working together as a team for projects than in traditional lecture settings.

**(b) Downside: technological/ethical**
While there were returns, different challenges also surfaced. For academic institutions, one of the greatest limitations to incorporating metaverse technologies arose from a considerable outlay in terms of hardware and an installed internet connection. Metaverse-based formats had other problems, as many students and faculty did not have the necessary technology to participate in this learning login. Furthermore, a thought was given to data security that is an ethical issue and questions on digital equity. Privacy concerns are also an issue around data collection and access in metaverse environments. Equally an important question is how to make sure that participation in the world of metaverses offers equal possibilities for all students and not simply reinforce existing educational gaps as growing disparity in access will need to be addressed [7].

## 7.4 Possible Implementations in Educational Framework of Metaverse Technology

The introduction of metaverse technology in educational field must be financially supported as it will involve investing money for building the technological infrastructure and demands time from trainers to learn how exactly they can use and create things on this new vast platform. A transparent framework that ethically describes pedagogy aims at campaign level as well as requires leading and executing all of the pedagogical aspirations. This would mean integrating existing and emerging technologies (with possible partnership with tech developers) to customize metaverse experiences suited for educational purposes [7]. For instance, a way metaverse technology could be introduced is by starting small with pilot projects and scaling as shown. For example, a school might introduce simulation-based teaching in metaverse for one class and study how it affects student engagement as well as academic achievement before scaling to other classes too. In short, it can avoid having an organization go wide and not be worked out by putting some checks to a process. As shown in Figure 7.2, the metaverse ecosystem supports a variety of use cases ranging from virtual learning and workspaces to blockchain-based virtual marketplaces, underlining its multi-sectoral adaptability.

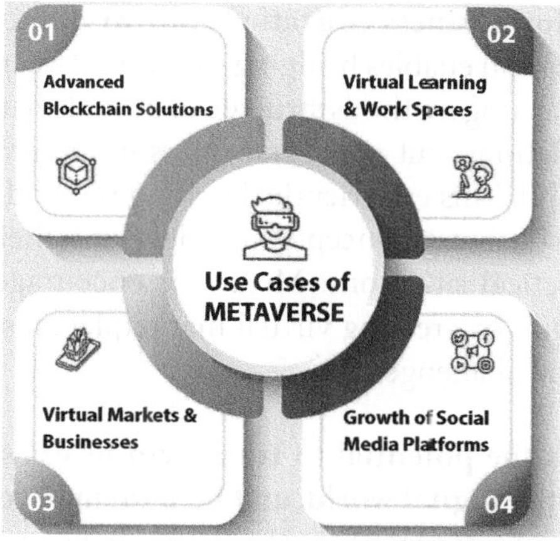


**Figure 7.2** Metaverse use cases and applications. Source:- https://www.mooglelabs.com/blog/metaverse-solutions-the-various-use-cases-and-benefits.

## 7.5 Understanding Metaverse

**Future research directions.** Future study could focus on longitudinal studies examining the long-term benefits of metaverse-based educational interventions. As a result, there is a need for a more thorough investigation of the capabilities and limits of these metaverse tools/platforms at all levels (K to 12 to higher education) and across all disciplines. Additional research must be conducted: ethical and legal dimensions (data privacy, digital equity) to specify how to make best use of a metaverse in education. The depth cards above show a dynamic scan of how the technology could be integrated and also serve to introduce participants further completely into the possibility of negative consequences. Real-world use of metaverse technology in education requires investment to meet capital and infrastructure needs. Although metaverse has adequate capacities in the educational sector, tech inclusion requires a significant capital commitment [8]. **Smooth and continuous smartphone interaction**: For high-speed internet, this is critical because there may be meetings, presentations, and so on that have to be finished on time, and one is unwilling to miss them due to bumpy connections where only a little amount of data can travel through readily. The setup for truly immersive experiences gets considerably more complex when using VR headgear and AR devices.

**(a) Implications for business education industry**: Integrating metaverse into business education enables bridging the gap between theory and practice. Traditional learning methods struggle to provide hands-on experience and realistic simulations, but metaverse offers immersive simulations and virtual endeavors [9]. This experiential learning method deepens students' understanding of business concepts and develops their ability to apply knowledge to practical situations. Metaverse encourages entrepreneurial ideas and innovation by creating virtual marketplaces, startup incubators, and entrepreneurial challenges.

**(b) Metaverse has the potential to transform business education, prepare students for the digital world, and help them become sophisticated and innovative professionals** [3]. However, challenges such as accessibility, inclusiveness, privacy, and ethics must be addressed, as does careful planning, infrastructure, and training [12]. Despite these limitations, metaverse has the potential to alter business education, prepare students for the digital world, and develop sophisticated and innovative professionals. Embracing modern technology has a chance to alter learning and determine the future of business education [10].

## 7.6 Explore the Transformational Potential of Metaverse for Business Education

Figure 7.3 presents a conceptual framework of factors influencing users' intention to adopt metaverse educational platforms, including perceived usefulness, ease of use, social influence, and privacy concerns.

**Virtual business design**. Metaverse's virtual business simulation provides outstanding opportunity for creative and innovative business education. This simulation engages students in a realistic and dynamic virtual environment, allowing them to actively participate in business difficulties [9]. Metaverse allows students to make strategic decisions, assess market trends, and manage finances in a realistic and authentic environment.

**(a) Implications for career education work**: The gap between theory and practice. Traditional learning methods struggle to provide hands-on experience and realistic thinking; however, metaverse provides immersive thinking and realistic endeavors [9]. This experiential learning approach increases students' grasp of business ideas and allows them to apply their knowledge in real-world circumstances. Metaverse fosters entrepreneurial

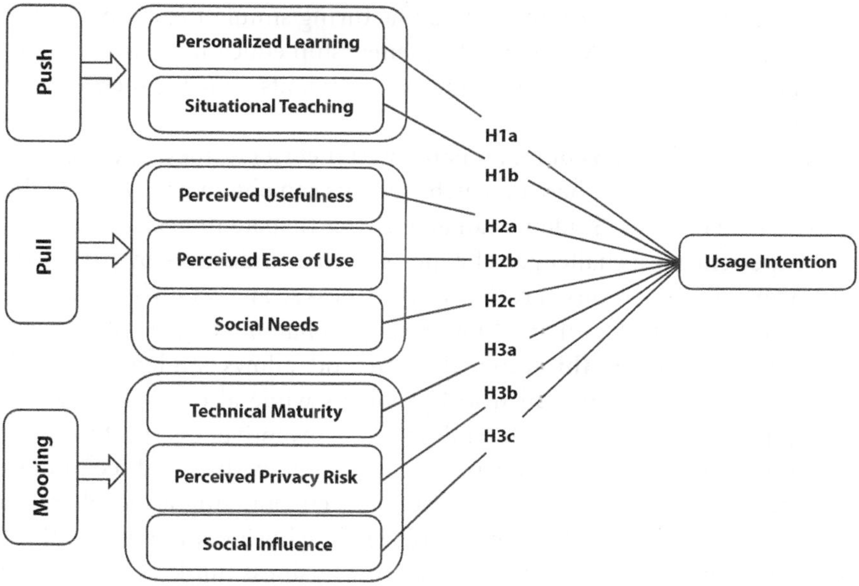


**Figure 7.3** Conceptual framework elucidating the influential factors affecting the intention to utilize metaverse education application platforms.

thinking and innovation by developing virtual marketplaces, business incubators, and entrepreneurial challenges. This enables students to discuss and revise their business ideas in a safe setting [3]. Issues like as accessibility, inclusivity, confidentiality, and ethics must be addressed. Metaverse-based learning necessitates thorough design, planning, and training [12]. Despite these limitations, metaverse offers the potential to alter business education, prepare students for the digital age, and develop talented and inventive professionals. Embracing emerging technology has the potential to change learning and find the future of business education [10].

**(b) Critical thinking and problem-solving skills**: Students who engage in these immersive experiences not only increase their understanding of entrepreneurial thinking, but also build critical thinking and problem-solving abilities as they navigate a simulated tough business world. This transforming approach teaches students to analyze and plan based on trends and market dynamics. It allows you to do things and make judgments, but the complexity and limits in today's corporate environment are huge. Engaging in this type of participatory thinking enables students to think critically, solve problems creatively, and build creative approaches to meet challenges and possibilities that are emerging types. As a result, metaverse serves as a catalyst for students to unleash their creativity, foster an innovative culture, and improve their ability to adapt to a quickly changing business environment, manufacturing simulations in particular. Successful use of metaverse in entrepreneurship education has the ability to generate task-specific theories that help students enhance their creativity and innovation [15].

**(c) Virtual simulations of real business**: At metaverse, these theories provide an exciting atmosphere in which students can obtain practical insights into a range of areas. Students can actively participate in decision-making and experience the challenges of experts in their industries by participating in virtual simulations of real-world business scenarios such as advertising campaigns, product marketing, or supply chain management.

**(d) Develop critical thinking**: This method allows students to apply theoretical principles to real-world problems while also developing critical thinking, problem-solving abilities, and inventiveness. Furthermore, metaverse allows students to experiment with new ideas and techniques, test their potential, and create a secure and encouraging atmosphere for creativity to develop. Metaverse rewards leading business students to think beyond the box, invent solutions, and grow business thinking. It prepares students to drive innovation and define the future of business and use the assignment. Role-playing in metaverse is an effective technique for encouraging creativity and innovation in professional education. By including students in virtual work scenarios, this intervention allows them to take on roles and actively participate in simulated decision-making [15].

**(e) Interactive approach**: This interactive approach allows students to use critical thinking skills in real-world situations, build problem-solving abilities, and discover new strategies. Metaverse activities enable kids to think outside the box, question standard methods, and experiment with innovative solutions [13]. They create a dynamic learning environment in which students can take risks, learn from mistakes, and enhance their decision-making abilities. By incorporating metaphysics into practical operations, business education transcends typical classroom bounds and creates limitless opportunities for creativity and innovation in future company leaders.

**(f) The virtual skills project**: Mentors play a significant part in business education by assisting students in reaching their goals. Since metaverse emerged as a strong instrument to stimulate creativity and innovation in entrepreneurship education, virtual mentorships have been a significant component in harnessing its revolutionary potential [16]. This program provides excellent possibilities for entrepreneurial students to cross geographical boundaries and meet with industry experts and advisors. Mentors at metaverse can help you get useful ideas, exchange real-world experiences, and navigate a dynamic and ever-changing work environment.

(g) **Virtual mentoring**: Students are exposed to a variety of perspectives, fresh ideas, and thought-provoking applications of industry skills in creativity, which evolve to take on complicated shapes [17]. Metaverse also defines a virtual mentoring program that enables students to learn about the newest emerging technology trends while engaging in discussions that foster new ideas and entrepreneurial initiatives [18]. Metaverse's virtual mentoring program not only stimulates creativity and invention, but also equips business students with the skills and connections they need to flourish in a quickly changing business model.

## 7.7 Innovation and Design Ideas Forum

Fostering innovation and creative thinking among business students is critical in today's fast changing business world. The mix of innovation and systems thinking workshops at metaverse represents an intriguing chance to change established approaches to business education. By immersing participants in a genuine atmosphere that invites experimentation, cooperation, and creative problem solving, this session reveals metaverse's true potential as a catalyst for creativity and innovation [20]. In this virtual space, students can engage in active activities that promote ideation, prototype development, and iterative design processes. They may discover new ideas, question assumptions, and use technology to solve complicated business problems in a supportive and comprehensive digital environment [2].

(a) **Embracing innovation and design thinking workshops**: Entrepreneurship education may empower students to think outside the box, produce disruptive ideas, and become ready adaptive and adaptable innovators to handle the difficulties of today's corporate world. A few further possibilities come in form of a virtual business tour. One of the most important and exciting aspects of metamaterials in business education is virtual business trips. Textbooks and case studies have traditionally been used by business students to gain insight into real-world company issues [21]. However, metaverse overcomes these constraints by offering a one-of-a-kind interactive platform on which students can build virtual tours of well-known organizations, industries, and trade exhibits. These virtual business travels offer students a unique opportunity to visit various corporate environments, study business processes, and interact with virtual representatives. This revolutionary approach to entrepreneurship education fosters creativity and innovation, allowing students to grow across industries, spot new trends, and learn from successful firms.

(b) **Ethical decision situations**: In metaverse, where creativity and innovation meet business education, ethical decision-making scenarios are viewed as intriguing opportunities to teach about professional obligations and ideals [12]. Metaverse offers a one-of-a-kind platform for business students to enhance theoretical skills and raises major ethical issues. These situations enable students to examine complex business issues, evaluate ethical considerations, and make educated decisions in accordance with ethical norms. Students develop ethical reasoning, critical thinking, and empathy through engaged participation in this virtual ethical decision-making activity, all of which are required to analyze the intricacies of the corporate world [19]. *Metaverse business course instructor*. Metaverse's ability to produce realistic scenarios allows students to observe firsthand the implications of their decisions, offering a deeper knowledge of the impact of ethical choices on individuals, organizations, and society as a whole of their future work [19].

(c) **Metaverse integration**: It raises numerous ethical difficulties. Organizations, trainers, and manufacturers all work to promote entrepreneurship education. These elements emphasize responsible technology use, privacy, inclusivity, and authenticity. Second, metaverse is used to gather more information about user interactions and behaviors. Ethical considerations involve transparent data collection, informed consent, and making sure robust data safeguards are in place to preserve private data. Users can also assume virtual personas in metaverse. The implications of deception, truth, and trust in educational settings present ethical concerns. Fourth, sustaining educational equity standards necessitates ensuring that all students have equal access to the opportunities and resources that metaverse offers.

(d) **Promoting digital literacy**: Users, including professors and students, must have a comprehensive understanding of metaverse. Promoting digital literacy and obtaining consent are two ethical considerations while doing metaverse-based instruction. *Mapping cross-cultural collaboration*. Cross-cultural business simulations in the meta edition are an effective technique to include creativity and innovation into business education. In today's globalized world, the ability to understand multiple cultures and work well with individuals from diverse origins is crucial for economic success.

(e) **Simulated cross-cultural business**: The meta version's participatory and interactive aspect allows students to engage in simulated cross-cultural business cases that test their awareness of cultural nuances, communication styles, and business practices. These simulations teach students cultural intelligence, empathy, and how to adapt to virtual surroundings modeled after real-world international commercial interactions. Cross-cultural business analogies can help students enhance their problem-solving abilities, communication skills, and decision-making processes, allowing them to thrive in an increasingly linked and multicultural workplace.

(f) **Data analysis and visualization**: Data analysis and visualization are crucial components of business education because they provide students with the knowledge they need to make educated decisions and motivate plans. By adding meta definition into business education, an exciting new dimension arises, offering students more possibilities to deal with data in a dynamic and engaging manner [11]. Metaverse is a platform where students may interact with virtual datasets, use sophisticated visualization tools, and run data-driven simulations to develop a better understanding of challenging business issues. Students who participate in this virtual environment will learn how to research real-world data challenges, apply analytical approaches, and successfully communicate results. Metaverse boosts learning, develops creativity and innovation in data analysis, and promotes critical thinking among students.

## 7.8 Continuing Education and Career Development

In a rapidly evolving business education landscape, metaverse integration provides new opportunity for ongoing learning and professional growth [14]. Metaverse is a dynamic and immersive environment where business students can participate in a range of virtual courses, workshops, and tools, allowing them to gain new talents, improve current skills, and keep on top of industry trends and advances that exist today. This approach to learning continues to promote a culture of lifelong learning, allowing students to adapt to a quickly changing corporate environment while remaining at the forefront of innovation. One of the primary benefits of continuous learning in metaverse is the availability of various learning experiences and materials [1]. Through virtual classrooms, webinars, and interactive modules, students can connect with critical topics and explore emerging trends.

## 7.9 Takeaways

In addition to typical educational programs, Metaverse provides a unique immersive experience that fosters creativity and innovation. Metaverse offers experiential learning opportunities through VR simulations, AR situations, and gamified learning settings [21]. Students can actively participate in simulated business issues, communicate with virtual teams, and test new ideas in a safe setting. This practical learning technique not only enhances problem-solving abilities, but it also promotes creativity and entrepreneurial thinking. With metaverse as an instructional tool, business students can push the boundaries of creativity and innovation while developing the skills required to thrive in a quickly changing business world [11]. Lifelong learning and professional development in metaverse have enormous potential to enable creativity and innovation in business education.

## 7.10 Ethical and Legal Issues

Data privacy and security are likely the most pressing ethical concerns in any metaverse technology. The same is true for how private information about users can be obtained. Institutions should have a personal data protection plan in place because this is the most secret data they should have for the student. This includes safe encrypted data storage and cloud-based access restrictions. According to the paper, we require precise policies and standards for how data should be exchanged in such a metaverse. Students and instructors should have access to this handbook so that they can understand their legal rights and the policy implications.

**(a) Digital equity and broadband access**: The successful implementation of metaverse technology in education outweighs all other outcomes, which can only be realized by prioritizing digital equality. The fact that this resulted in a world of difference demonstrates what happens when we remove all of these obstacles to broader society, regardless of whether they conflict with preexisting systems or can simply carry it on their own. That is why everyone, whether online or at a university, should have equal access to experimenting with metaverse technologies. This may necessitate funding for those who do not have access to home equipment, as well as training support that allows all to be fully engaged in online learning. Metaverse platforms should provide accessibility capabilities to accommodate students with disabilities.
**(b) Ethical use of virtual worlds**: However, virtual worlds do not teach the only method to use this in education, which is a problem because data privacy and accuracy are only two parts of a broader puzzle when it comes to ensuring the ethical application of laws. However, neither considers the production of metaverse content and activity. As a result, educators must include the requirements of disabled children into authentic learning opportunities. Metaverse offers a code of conduct for students to safeguard

their safety. Safe learning in digital twin environments requires teachers to be aware of cyberizing or inappropriate content and respond accordingly.

## 7.11 Future Prospects and Innovations

Every other way, Cotise X Reality technology is improving virtual learning. VR headsets will be improved with higher-quality displays and more accurate motion tracking to provide a more realistic simulation-like experience. Similar improvements in AR could allow the virtual component to blend so seamlessly into our surrounding scene that it will have a major influence on learning.

**(a) Blending fibers with emerging technologies**: Federal Realty Investment Trust can broaden its educational efforts by mixing metaverse tech fibers with new emerging technologies such as AI and blockchain. This technology also provides individualized learning by leveraging AI to provide personalized feedback and input depending on students' preferences and dislikes. This demonstrates how an AI-powered virtual teacher can adapt to demanding assignments while benefiting students the most. Blockchain technology improves data security and transparency by enabling independent verification of student progress/degree [22]. This may make certification easier, increasing the legitimacy of academic degrees.
**(b) Expand functionality**: Metaverse technology has no practical applications. These virtual worlds can be used to encourage learning and interest in subjects such as STEM (Science, Technology, Engineering, and Mathematics), Humanities, and Arts [23]. One hypothetical example is VR simulations for surgery, which allow future doctors to practice and refine their abilities without risk. Art students can also explore with AR and begin with 3D models, both of which foster creativity while incorporating technology. Because of its adaptable technology, metaverse is ideal for improving education in a variety of fields.

## 7.12 Conclusion

Metaverse offers significant potential to enhance education by providing immersive and engaging experiences, stimulating creativity, and boosting student productivity. Although it may seem complex, incorporating metaverse into education represents a key step in embracing educational reform and preparing students for a digitally driven future [24]. One of the primary considerations is how educators and policymakers can harness this virtual technology to create innovative learning environments, while emphasizing ethical considerations in various crisis scenarios. To fully realize the potential of metaverse in education, further research and development are necessary. Continued collaboration between industry and educational institutions will help refine and optimize the use of virtual worlds in classrooms. Technological advancements present an exciting opportunity to build a dynamic, interactive learning environment that can inspire and engage students in entirely new ways.

## References

1. De Felice, *et al.*, Examining the Influence of Metaverse Education Application Platforms on Creativity: A Systematic Literature Review. *Appl. Sci.*, 13, 5682, 2023.
2. Mitra, Metaverse: An Ecosystem for Innovative Blended Education and Training. *J. Metaverse*, 3, 66–72, 2023.
3. Setiawan, and Anthony, Metaverse for Business: A Comprehensive Review Based on 7 Layers of Metaverse, in: *Proceedings of the 2022 International Conference on Information Management and Technology (ICIM Tech)*, Semarang, Indonesia, 11–12 August 2022, pp. 687–692, 2022.
4. Lin, *et al.*, Metaverse in Education: A Visionary Approach, Opportunities, and Challenges, 18–23, 2022, arXiv 2022, arXiv:2211.14951.
5. Soriani, and Bonafede, Metaverse and Education: Exploring Pedagogical Perspectives for Future Learning. *J. Incl. Methodol. Technol. Learn. Teach.*, 3, 4–8, 2023, Available online: https://www.inclusiveteaching.it/index.php/inclusiveteaching/article/view/54 (accessed on 5 June 2023).
6. Mistretta, The Metaverse—A Transformative Space for Educational Alternatives. *AI Comput. Sci. Robot. Technol.*, 2022.
7. Mystakidis, Metaverse: Unveiling Potential. *Encyclopedia*, 2, 486–497, 2022.
8. Hwang, and Chien, Clarifying Definitions, Roles, and Research Avenues of the Metaverse in Education: An Artificial Intelligence Perspective. *Comput. Educ. Artif. Intell.*, 3, 100082, 2022.
9. Rospigliosi, Metaverse or Simulacra? Roblox, Minecraft, Meta and the Shift to Virtual Reality for Education, Socialization, and Work. *Interact. Learn. Environ.*; Taylor Francis Abingdon UK, 30, 1–3, 2022.
10. Rahman, *et al.*, Leveraging Metaverse Technology in Education Domain. *J. Metaverse*, 3, 79–86, 2023.
11. Mustafa, Evaluating Education through Metaverse Technology. *Tech. Soc. Sci. J.*, 32, 278, 2022.

12. Kaddoura, and Al Husseiny, The Growing Presence of Metaverse in Education: Navigating Challenges, Exploring Opportunities, and Addressing Ethical Considerations. *PeerJ Comput. Sci.*, 9, e1252, 2023.
13. Kshetri, *et al.*, Metaverse and Its Impact on Higher Education Institutions. *IT Prof.*, 24, 69–73, 2022.
14. Wang, *et al.*, Unraveling the Development, Evolution, and Research Prospects of Educational Metaverse. *Educ. J.*, 11, 254–260, 2022.
15. Singh, *et al.*, Metaverse in Education: A Comprehensive Overview, in: *Applying Metalytics to Measure Customer Experience in the Metaverse*, pp. 135–142, 2022.
16. Yue, Breaking Barriers between Teachers and Students through Metaverse Technology in Education: Insights from Shenzhen City, China, in: *Proceedings of the 2022 13th International Conference on E-Education, E-Business, E-Management, and E-Learning (IC4E)*, Tokyo, Japan, 14–17 January 2022, pp. 40–44.
17. Wang, *et al.*, Exploring Potential Applications of the Metaverse in Higher English Education. *Open J. Soc. Sci.*, 11, 450–459, 2023.
18. Kumar, Gupta, Bapat, Empowering Retail Managers: Utilizing the Power of ChatGPT. *J. Bus. Strategy*, 2023.
19. Knox, The Metaverse: Navigating Tech Frontiers with Serious Business. *Postdigital Sci. Educ.*, 4, 207–215, 2022.
20. Shaikh, A., Kumar, Jani, Mitra, García-Tadeo, Devarajan, The Role of Machine Learning and Artificial Intelligence in Crafting a Digital Classroom and its Sustainable Impact on Education during COVID-19. *Mater. Today Proc.*, 56, 3211–3215, 2021.
21. Gim, Bae, Kang, Metaverse Learning: Exploring the Interplay between VR-Based Education Quality, Self-Determination, and Learner Satisfaction, in: *Proceedings of the 2022 IEEE/ACIS 7th International Conference on Big Data, Cloud Computing, and Data Science (BCD)*, Danang, Vietnam, 4–6 August 2022, pp. 279–284.
22. Govindarajan, Business School in the Metaverse Part 1: Insights from a Pilot Course, Harvard Business Publishing Education, 2022, Available online: https://www.hbsp.harvard.edu/inspiring-minds/business-school-in-the-metaverse (accessed on 23 June 2023).
23. Bapat, and Chitnis, Assessing the Effectiveness of University Website for University Admissions during COVID-19 Crisis. *Shodh Sarita*, 7, 114–121, 2020.
24. Pioneering India's First MBA in Metaverse, Education India Today, 2023, Available online: https://www.indiatoday.in/education-today/news/story/this-university-launched-indias-first-mba-in-metaverse-2341 809-2023-03-02 (accessed on 5 June 2023).
25. Johnson, A., Smith, B., Clark, C., The Impact of Metaverse Simulations on Student Engagement and Motivation. *J. Virtual Learn.*, 2022.

# 8

# Paradigm Shifts and Future Directions in Distributed Data Management for Decentralized Networks

**Bishnu Kant Shukla[1*], Bhupender Parashar[2], Vikas Kumar Singla[3] and Shivam Verma[4]**

*[1]Department of Civil Engineering, JSS Academy of Technical Education, Noida, India*
*[2]Department of Mathematics, JSS Academy of Technical Education, Noida, India*
*[3]Department of Mechanical Engineering, JSS Academy of Technical Education, Noida, India*
*[4]Department of Mechanical and Industrial Engineering, New Jersey Institute of Technology, Newark (New Jersey), USA*

***Abstract***

New data and knowledge management methods are being developed for decentralized systems and the future Internet. The evolution of distributed data management and how it is necessary for decentralized architectures to be more efficient, reliable, and scalable will be examined in this chapter. Novel frameworks and architectures are examined to handle decentralized networks' massive and varied datasets. Current academic research shows the complexity of configurable data analytics engines and domain-specific languages, which address heterogeneous data sources and high ingestion rates. Advanced data analytics frameworks are needed as the Internet of Things (IoT) becomes more ingrained in decentralized ecosystems. Edge computing designs that reduce network congestion and latency are covered in this chapter. In IoT environments, scalability and real-time processing are crucial. As big data in distributed systems become more important, strong data management solutions are needed. Comparing technologies and methods for big dataset scalability and dependability is the focus of this chapter. Case studies and practical deployments show how distributed data management systems may increase operational efficiency and decision-making across different sectors. Current trends and prospective study areas in distributed data management are discussed in this

**Corresponding author*: bishnukantshukla@gmail.com

Sandhya Avasthi and Suman Lata Tripathi (eds.) Distributed and Parallel Computing, (153–182)

chapter. Blockchain technology for data security, quantum computing, and artificial intelligence/machine learning in data analytics are examples. Chapter summarizes distributed data management in decentralized systems' present and future. These systems are crucial to maximizing the next-generation Internet's potential and require continual development and study in this ever-changing field.

***Keywords*:** Distributed data management, decentralized systems, Internet of Things (IoT), big data analytics, edge computing, future internet technologies

## 8.1 Introduction

The world of data management is going through a change now because more and more people are using decentralized systems, and the Internet architecture is evolving too. While traditional centralized ways of handling data have been effective, in their right they are facing challenges when it comes to keeping up with today's scattered environments. These settings revolve around the prevalence of Internet of Things (IoT) devices such as gadgets' the ability to process data at the networks edge and dealing with amounts of data, all of which call for a fresh look, at current norms. The growing volume of data generated from a range of sources requires the implementation of methods to ensure effectiveness and reliability, in managing data processes with scalability [1, 2].

Distributed data management is crucial, in handling data as networks grow more complex and extensive. These systems separate data across nodes of using a centralized system like before. This approach enhances accessibility and reliability by preventing issues that can arise with a point of control and storage. Increasing interest in distributed systems is fueled by the need to support applications that require availability, resilience to failures, and seamless integration of data, from origins [1, 3]. In the field of IoT, the integration of multiple devices, which continuously collect data, complicates data management mainly due to the sheer volume and variety of data generated [4]. Managing IoT data is further complicated due to the diversity of data types and the need for immediate analysis.

Modern information systems prioritize distributed data management, particularly in distributed networks where data are generated, processed, and stored across multiple nodes. Distributing data across multiple nodes can improve fault tolerance and load balancing, ensuring uninterrupted operation even in the face of node failures [5, 6]. Large data environments demand the integration of distributed data management solutions. These systems can accommodate various data storage formats, including NoSQL databases. IoT applications are favored for their ability to handle large amounts of data, which are typically utilized in industrial applications [7].

Data processing techniques and storage options are made more complex by distributed data management systems. A few of these techniques, such as parallel and distributed processing frameworks, simplify the process of managing large datasets by distributing jobs across multiple processing nodes. The system's horizontal scaling is heightened by this approach, which involves adding more nodes to optimize data processing speed and increase network scale. It is focused in exploring new architectures and framework to support the large, diverse datasets typical of distributed networks [8]. A thorough examination is necessary to comprehend data analysis engines that are flexible and programming languages designed to handle specific problems in such situations. It not only addresses the challenges of integrating IoT into distributed environments but also explores how IoT impacts distributed data management [9, 10]. The paper analyzes various techniques for big data analytics and presents a comparison of technologies and methods for managing massive amounts of data in distributed systems. Additionally, the methods are evaluated for their ability to be scaled up, as well as when they perform well and are ultimately useful. The utilization of predictive analytics models, data mining techniques, and machine learning (ML) algorithms is a key aspect of big data analytics.

## 8.2 Paradigm Shifts in Distributed Data Management

### 8.2.1 Evolution of Data Management Paradigms

As technology advances, so do the changing needs of modern information systems, which are reflected in new paradigms being developed for data management. Initially, data management was mainly centralized, with all processing and storage activities handled by a single server or swapping and merging multiple servers. Although centralized solutions are straightforward to design and operate, they present substantial limitations in terms of performance, stability, or fault tolerance [11]. Large-scale applications are no longer able to handle the growing demands for real-time processing and increasing data volumes, which can be accommodated by centralized systems.

### 8.2.2 Impact of Decentralized Architectures

Decentralized architectures enhance the concept of distributed data management by eliminating centralized points of control. Decentralized systems are characterized by the autonomous nature of each node, but also by its ability to collaborate with other nodes in pursuit of a common aim. By eliminating any single point of failure or vulnerability, this architectural design enhances both fault tolerance and security [12]. Decentralized architectures are well-suited for situations where data are produced and utilized at the margins, like IoT ecosystems.

### 8.2.3 Key Technological Drivers

Various technological advancements are driving the shift toward distributed and decentralized approaches to data management. This trend is largely due to the rapid growth of IoT devices. The vast amounts of information generated by these devices necessitate immediate analysis and handling. Incorporating a wide range of data sources and formats necessitates the use of IoT data management solutions that are scalable. This is particularly true for digital signage applications [13]. One of the primary technological drivers is edge computing. Through edge computing, latency is reduced, bandwidth is conserved, and real-time analytics is facilitated through data handling at the network's boundary. It is especially critical in applications where quick decisions are required, such as driverless cars and industrial automation systems [14]. The advancements in artificial intelligence (AI) and machine learning (ML) are the primary drivers of distributed data management. By analyzing vast amounts of data, AI and ML algorithms can uncover intricate patterns and valuable insights that aid in making informed decisions. The development of distributed data management systems requires the integration of these technologies [15–17].

## 8.3 Emergent Architectures and Frameworks

### 8.3.1 Overview of Emergent Architectures

Emergent architectures for distributed data management are designed to meet the complex needs of modern data-intensive applications. By utilizing these designs, it becomes feasible to manage diverse and extensive datasets effectively, guaranteeing the capacity to handle increasing workloads, recover from failures during testing, and analyze data in real time. The shift from monolithic to microservices architectures is a significant and relevant development. Microservices architectures make it easier to partition application components, which improves the system's flexibility and durability [18]. Developers can concentrate on code and functionality in serverless architectures because cloud providers handle underlying

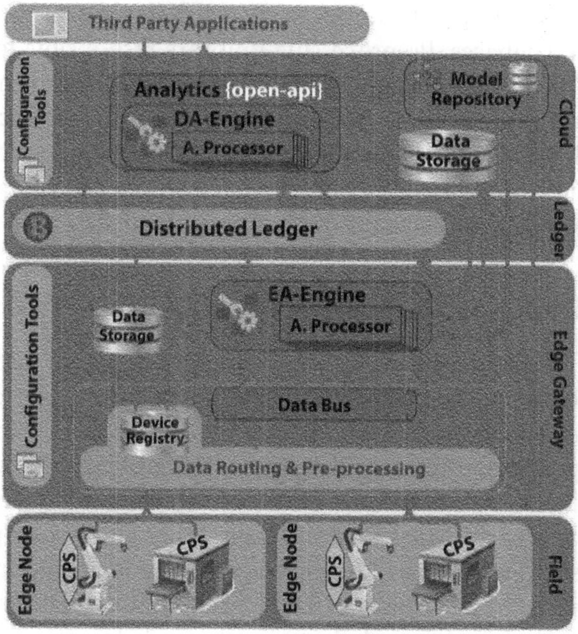


**Figure 8.1** The architecture of the distributed data analytics engine [22].

infrastructure scalability and operation automatically [19]. Additionally, hybrid architectures that integrate elements of cloud and edge computing are emerging.

These architectures leverage centralized cloud storage to process and store large amounts of data, as well an edge device for rapid and real-time processing [20]. The use of Docker and Kubernetes as containerization tools and orchestration is also a crucial aspect of emergent architectures [21]. These technologies facilitate the implementation, expansion, and administration of applications in distributed environments while maintaining uniformity and dependability. Figure 8.1 demonstrates the distribution and interaction of the Distributed Data Analytics Engine, which is comprised of all the essential components of a distributed data management system. Specifically, its aim is to efficiently handle the vast amount, varied varieties, and rapid pace of data generated in present-day decentralized networks [22].

The diagram in Figure 8.1 illustrates the configuration of a distributed data analytics system. Several components are included in the system, including data ingestion modules, preprocessing units, core analytics engines, and storage systems. These data ingestion modules aggregate information from different sources, such as IoT devices, social media, and transactional databases. Preprocessing units are responsible for the initial processing, transformation, and enrichment of data, which is necessary for its preparation for later analysis. By utilizing ML and statistical methods, the core analytics engines generate various analytical models to extract relevant insights from data. The storage systems offer efficient storage and easy access to processed data for querying and reporting [23].

### 8.3.2 Domain-Specific Languages in Data Analytics

Domain-specific languages (DSLs) have emerged as potent instruments for managing distributed data, providing tailored solutions that cater to specific domains. However, they differ from other approaches. In contrast to general-purpose programming languages, DSLs offer high-level abstractions and constructs that directly correspond to domain concepts and processes. This approach makes intricate tasks easier and boosts productivity [24]. Encapsulating domain knowledge within a language framework is one of the primary advantages of DSLs in distributed data management. This is particularly important. Nonprogrammer domain specialists can now contribute more easily to system creation and optimization. In big data analytics, DSLs can offer resources for analyzing, processing, and consuming data [25].

In distributed data management, DSLs offer several benefits, such as facilitating simplified operations, increased efficiency, improved performance, and easy integration with existing frameworks. The focus on specific fields in their architecture allows specialists to efficiently utilize their specialized knowledge, leading to more efficient and scalable data management solutions. In Figure 8.2, adaptable data preprocessing at the edge is emphasized to process data in close proximity to its source, rather than relying on centralized data centers.

Figure 8.2 illustrates an architecture where edge devices preprocess data—filtering, aggregating, and transforming—before sending it to central systems for further analysis [26, 27]. This setup reduces transmission delays, minimizes network congestion, and enables real-time data processing. Key components include:

- **Data ingestion modules**: Collect raw data from various edge devices, supporting multiple formats and protocols.
- **Preparation units**: Perform data cleaning, normalization, and aggregation to improve quality and reduce volume.

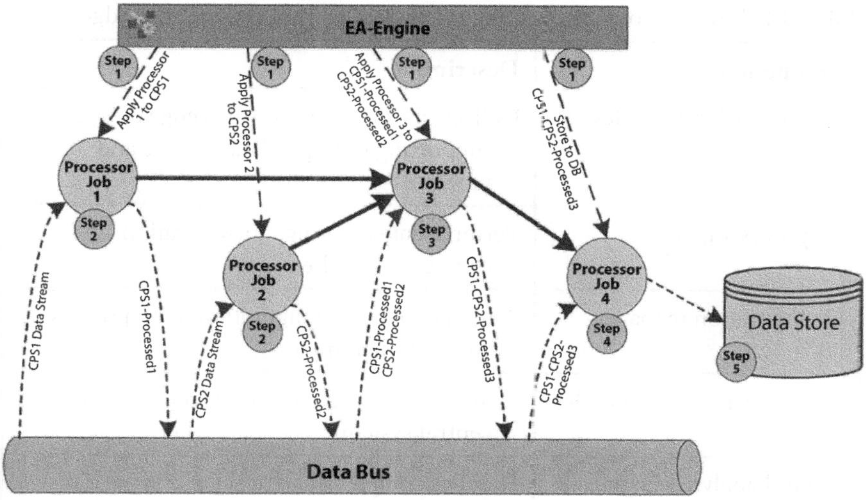


**Figure 8.2** Customizable edge data preprocessing [22].

- **Configuration manager**: Allows dynamic adjustment of preprocessing rules and parameters.
- **Data transmission modules**: Securely and efficiently transfer preprocessed data to central systems using low-latency protocols.
- **Central analytics engine**: Conducts advanced analytics while edge devices handle initial preprocessing, optimizing performance.

Developers can use an XML-based DSL to customize the EA-Engine's operations, defining streaming analytics functions through combinations of processors [28]. The EA-Engine supports three types:

- **Preprocessors**: Filter and prepare data streams for further analysis.
- **Storage processors**: Store data streams in repositories, ensuring data persistence.
- **Analytics processors**: Perform analytics on data streams, from statistical tasks to ML.

These processors form analytics pipelines described in Analytics Manifests, which define the processing functions executable by the EA-Engine based on available devices and data sources. The EA-Engine

**Table 8.1** Key components of configurable data preprocessing at the edge.

| Component | Description |
|---|---|
| Data ingestion modules | Collect raw data from various edge devices, supporting multiple data formats and protocols |
| Preprocessing units | Perform data cleaning, normalization, and aggregation at the edge |
| Configuration manager | Allows dynamic configuration of preprocessing rules and parameters |
| Data transmission modules | Ensure secure and efficient data transfer to central systems |
| Central analytics engine | Handles complex analytical tasks using data processed at the edge |

executes these edge analytics pipelines, whereas the Distributed Analytics Engine in the cloud handles factory-wide analytics, ensuring scalable, real-time analytics across distributed environments.

Implementing adjustable data preparation at the edge has substantial implications for the efficiency and scalability of distributed data management systems. By delegating preprocessing duties to the edge (as described in Table 8.1), the system may effectively manage increasing quantities of data, enhance efficiency, minimize latency, and enhance the responsiveness of real-time applications.

By including these elements, the structure enables effective and expandable data administration, tackling the difficulties presented by the immense volumes of data produced in decentralized networks.

## 8.4 Integration of IoT

### 8.4.1 IoT Ecosystem and Data Management Challenges

The IoT system is characterized by a vast network of connected devices, sensors, and systems that generate and exchange data on premise. From smart homes and smartphones to industrial mechanization and urban areas, this ecosystem encompasses a wide range of applications. The large volume, wide range, and rapid pace of data creation have made the integration of IoT with distributed data management systems a challenging

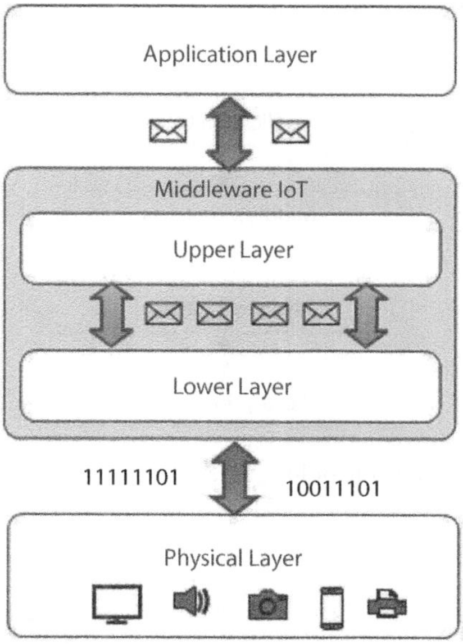


**Figure 8.3** IoT framework [31].

endeavor. Proper data management requires the use of robust frameworks that can analyze data in real time, provide secure data transmission, and offer efficient storage solutions [29]. Maintaining the quality and consistency of data from various sources is a significant challenge in managing IoT data. Another significant issue to consider is the security and privacy of IoT data, given the potential sensitivity that may be present [30].

A diagrammatic representation of an IoT middleware architecture can be seen in Figure 8.3. Management of request messages and response transmission for middleware services is carried out by the top layer, which also interacts with applications. The physical layer communicates with the lower layer, which facilitates the exchange of binary data and control instructions between devices. This hierarchical design guarantees optimal communication and data processing from edge devices to cloud-based analytics.

Figure 8.4 presents a comprehensive analysis of the several layers of an IoT system, namely, perception, network, middleware, application, and business [32]. Every layer in the IoT system has distinct duties and responsibilities that collectively enhance the performance and dependability of the system.

Figure 8.5 depicts the connection between the data distribution service (DDS) and an IoT middleware using a communication interface

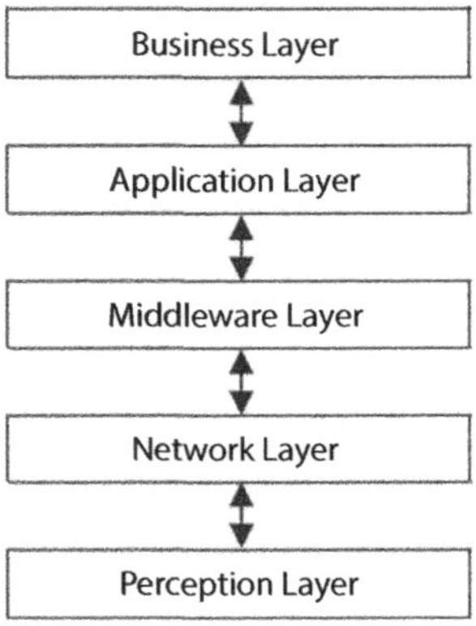


**Figure 8.4** Five-layer architecture of IoT [32].

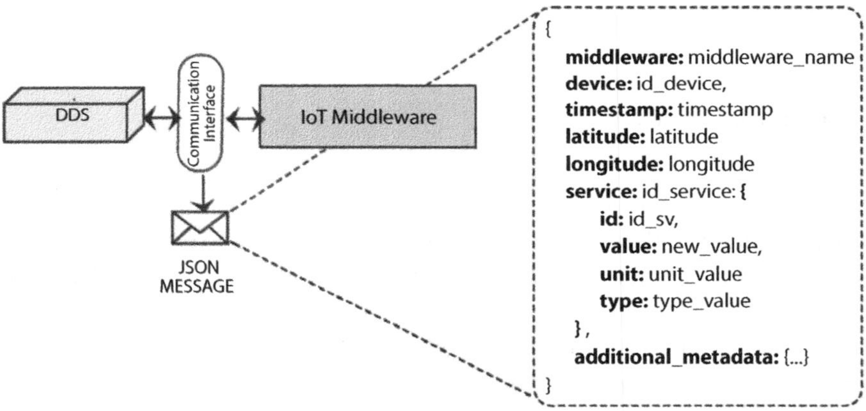


**Figure 8.5** The distributed data service–internet of things middleware communication interface [31].

module. The registered middleware is required to transmit duplicates of all messages that are exchanged, and these messages are captured by the DDS through this port. JSON enables compatibility with different middleware systems by differentiating data sources. The JSON structure contains attributes such as middleware name, device identifier, service identification, and metadata like geo-location and data type. These attributes help in transmitting, processing, and storing data efficiently [31, 33, 34]. This bridges the gap between the generation of raw data and its utilization in analytics and decision-making [35].

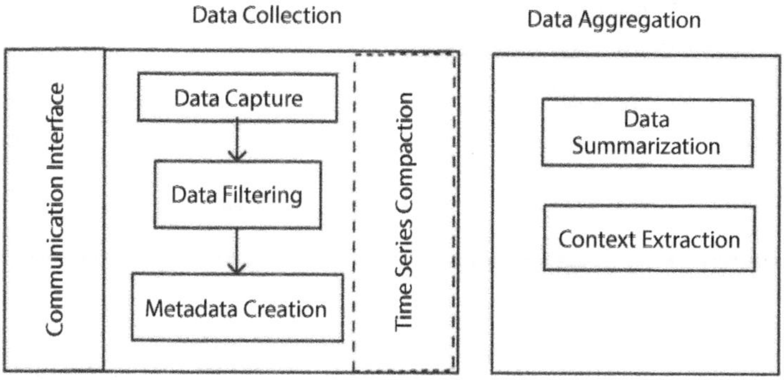


**Figure 8.6** Components of DDS [31].

## 8.5 Edge Computing and Big Data Analytics

### 8.5.1 Benefits of Edge Computing

Rather than depending on centralized data centers, edge computing is a new way of handling distributed data by processing it near its source. There are several benefits to this method, including reduced delay, decreased use of network resources, and better data analysis in real time. The use of edge computing greatly reduces the processing and response time for data by conducting computations at the network's edge [36–39]. Edge devices can perform on-premises data processing to aggregate and sort before being transferred to the cloud. By using this method, the network's volume of data transmission can be reduced [40].

The organization and management of data from multiple devices are facilitated by the DDS used in IoT middleware, as demonstrated in Figure 8.6. In the DDS design, there are two main components: gathering data and aggregating it. Data collection in this aspect involves gathering data from various IoT middleware systems and storing it in a database for future use. The DDS can be consolidated with information from various sources using this feature for future processing [31].

### 8.5.2 Big Data Management in Distributed Systems

Managing big datasets in distributed systems involves managing their storage, processing, and analysis across multiple nodes. The decentralized architecture of these systems enables the simultaneous processing of data, leading to a substantial enhancement in performance and scalability. Big data management relies on key technologies such as distributed file

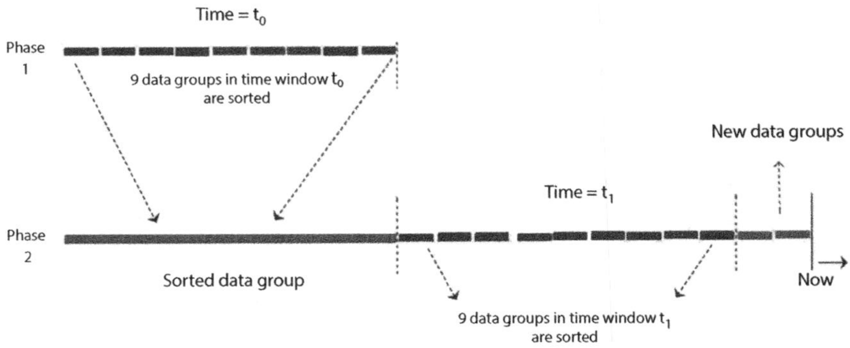


**Figure 8.7** Example of organization in time series [31].

systems, including the Hadoop distributed file system (HDFS), and distributed processing frameworks such as Apache Spark [41–43]. HDFS offers a scalable and resilient storage solution by spreading data across numerous nodes, allowing for efficient data retrieval and redundancy. Apache Spark enhances HDFS by providing a high-performance computing framework that speeds up data processing operations using in-memory processing. Collectively, these technologies serve as the foundation of most big data analytics systems, empowering organizations to efficiently and expeditiously analyze extensive volumes of data [44].

Figure 8.7 illustrates the structure and manipulation of time-series data in a distributed data management system, with a specific emphasis on data compression and reconfiguration. Time-series compaction module arranges and categorizes data into specific time intervals, which can be modified in accordance with the computational environment to optimize efficiency. The purpose of this process is to manage large amounts of sensor data and conserve storage space. Despite the network activity level, the data compression shown in this image results in unvarying and persistent groups of data.

## 8.6 Data Aggregation and Summarization Techniques

### 8.6.1 Importance of Data Aggregation

IoT and big data environments require the use of distributed data management systems, which involve data aggregation. Data integration involves combining data from various sources to produce a condensed and efficient dataset that is easier on the eyes [45]. By optimizing data processing and

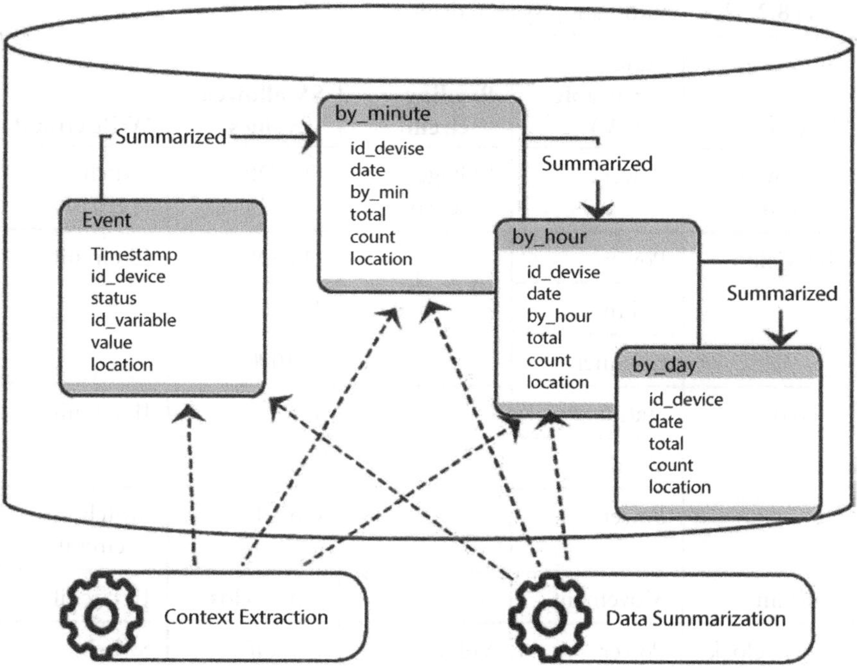


**Figure 8.8** Component of data aggregation [31].

storage, data aggregation provides an important advantage. Consolidating information at transitional points, such as edge devices or gateways, can reduce the amount of data that must be transmitted to central data centers, which will preserve bandwidth and minimize latency [46].

Figure 8.8 illustrates the structure of a data aggregation system in an IoT framework, emphasizing the concurrent operations of collecting and aggregating data. The data collection component acquires unprocessed data from different IoT middleware, while the aggregation component preprocesses and condenses these data at regular intervals (such as minutes, hours, or days) to improve real-time processing [31, 47].

## 8.6.2 Case Studies and Practical Implementations

Data aggregation and summarizing approaches are widely used in many case studies and practical applications across diverse fields. Various examples demonstrate the adaptability and efficiency of various strategies in enhancing data management and analytics [48]. Table 8.2 presents a range of devices utilized in home automation, emphasizing their roles, state

**Table 8.2** Home automation system devices.

| Device | State variable (SV) | Reading circuit | SV allowed values | Write circuit |
|---|---|---|---|---|
| Microwave oven | Power | Voltage sensor | On, Off | Switch circuit |
| Television | Power | — | On, Off | IR circuit |
| | Volume | | 1–100 | |
| | Channel | | 1–1000 | |
| Stereo | Station | — | 1–6 | IR circuit |
| | Volume | | 1–100 | |
| | Power | | On, off | Switch circuit |
| Curtain | Movement | — | Open, close | IR circuit |
| Alarm clock | Power | Voltage sensor | On, off | Switch circuit |
| Coffee pot | Power | Voltage sensor | On, off | Switch circuit |
| Gate | Distance | Distance detector | 2–700 | — |
| | Movement | — | Open, close, stop | IR circuit |

variables, and permissible values, together with their reading and writing circuits. These devices produce significant volumes of data that must be collected and summarized for efficient monitoring and control [49].

Table 8.3 illustrates the quantity of devices in a UIoT-DDS (User Interface of Things – Data Distribution Service) configuration, highlighting the necessity for strong data management solutions to effectively handle data from various sensors, actuators, gateways, control units, and user interfaces [50].

In order to assess the effectiveness of the intended DDS, this part provides data from two tests involving the modeling of a home automation

**Table 8.3** Quantity of UIoT-DDS devices.

| No. of producers | No. of homes | Year | Month | Day |
|---|---|---|---|---|
| 4 | 142,857 | 458.91 TB | 37.72 TB | 1.26 TB |
| 3 | 95,238 | 305.92 TB | 25.15 TB | 0.84 TB |
| 2 | 63,492 | 203.96 TB | 16.76 TB | 0.56 TB |
| 1 | 33,600 | 107.92 TB | 8.87 TB | 0.9 TB |

IoT scenario. The initial simulation involves the analysis of data produced by numerous households equipped with home appliances and devices that are controlled by the UIoT middleware [39]. The purpose of this experiment is to assess the two components of DDS (data collecting and data aggregation), which will be referred to as the UIoT-DDS study. The second simulation involves a comparison between the DDS data collector and a comparable collector in the Kaa middleware [10], within a home automation IoT setup that is similar to the previous scenario. The purpose of this second study, known as the Kaa collector study, is to showcase the efficiency of the DDS data collector in managing a substantial amount of data in comparison to the Kaa collector.

Both experiments utilize an emulated smart home system that consists of seven devices as outlined in Table 8.2. The computing environment used for the case study evaluates data collection and aggregation consists of a cluster of four machines. Each machine is equipped with an Intel Xeon 2.5-GHz processor with eight cores, 8 GB of RAM, 500 GB of HD, and 1 Gb Ethernet. Each node was configured with the Ubuntu Linux 14.04 operating system, together with Apache Kafka 0.8.2, Apache Storm 0.9.5, Apache Cassandra 2.2.6, and Streamparse 2.0.0.

In order to simulate message exchange between the User Interface of Things (UIoT) and the DDS, Kafka producers are configured to generate a total of eight million messages concurrently. Each message consists of 160 bytes. Table 8.3 displays the quantity of residences and the quantity of devices depicted in the simulation, along with the amount of data transmitted at various time intervals. The calculation relies on a procedure that retrieves data from devices at regular intervals of 10 seconds and transmits messages of 160 bytes accordingly.

## 8.7 Advanced Applications and Case Studies

### 8.7.1 Domestic and Industrial Applications

The incorporation of distributed data management systems has had a substantial influence on both household and industrial applications, resulting in better operational efficiency, instantaneous decision-making, and expanded data analytics capabilities. Smart home systems can optimize energy use, boost security, and improve inhabitants' quality of life by collecting and analyzing data from many sensors [48].

The implementation of distributed data management systems in industrial settings has significantly transformed operations in various sectors such as manufacturing, logistics, and energy. IoT systems gather extensive data from sensors integrated into machinery and equipment, enabling predictive maintenance, process optimization, and real-time monitoring.

Figure 8.9 depicts a centralized dashboard utilized to monitor and oversee the implementation of the EA-Engine. The EA-Engine, also known as the edge analytics engine, does data processing at the edge, delivering immediate analytics and valuable insights. The dashboard presents essential performance indicators (KPIs), measurements on system health, and analytics outcomes, empowering operators to promptly make well-informed decisions. The visual interface consolidates data from multiple sources, providing a full overview of the system's performance and operational state [22, 50]. The dashboard's capacity to deliver instantaneous feedback and analytics is essential for both household and industrial applications. Within a smart home environment, the dashboard has the capability to exhibit energy consumption patterns, notify homeowners about security breaches, and modify settings according to occupancy and personal

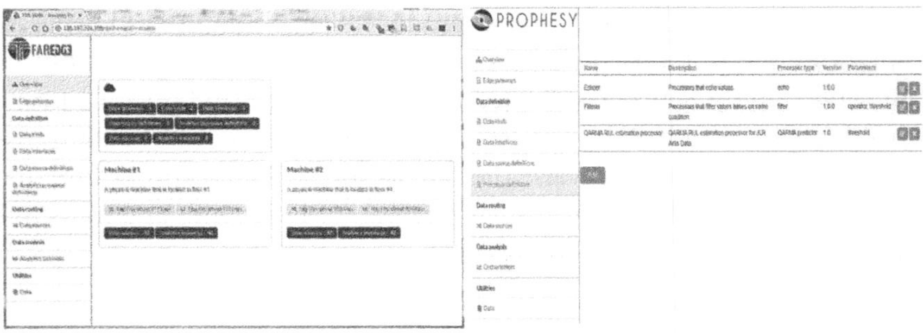


**Figure 8.9** Management dashboard for the EA-engine implementation [22].

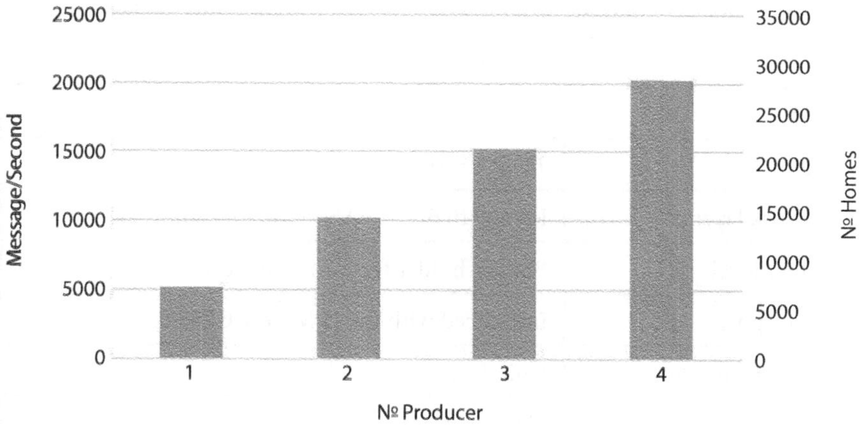


**Figure 8.10** Result from the kaa collector [31].

preferences. Within industrial settings, the dashboard serves as a tool for operators to oversee production lines, identify irregularities, and enhance procedures, thus guaranteeing optimal and efficient system performance.

Figure 8.10 displays the results obtained by the Kaa IoT platform, which gathers and analyzes data from different IoT devices. The Kaa platform offers a versatile and expandable solution for overseeing IoT data, facilitating the immediate gathering, processing, and presentation of data [31]. The diagram illustrates the combined data from several sensors, emphasizing patterns, deviations, and valuable information that may be utilized to enhance operations and facilitate data-based decision-making [51]. The Kaa collector results are especially advantageous for industrial applications that require real-time analysis of massive volumes of sensor data. In a logistics setting, the Kaa platform may monitor the whereabouts and state of items, granting insight into the supply chain and facilitating proactive handling of possible problems. Through the analysis of gathered data, firms can better their inventory management, minimize delays, and optimize customer happiness. Table 8.4 presents comprehensive specifications of the Gloriot sensor nodes employed in the Cooja simulation environment. Power consumption, communication range, data rate (including any optional default value), and various other sensor categories are included in the specifications. By examining the sensor nodes' capabilities and constraints, the table provides insights that aid in the design and implementation of effective IoT solutions [52].

**Table 8.4** Specifications of the gloriot sensor nodes in the cooja environment.

| Part | Description |
|---|---|
| Flash | Up to 1 Mbyte |
| Radio | TI CC2520 |
| Network layer | IPv6 with 6LoWPAN standards 802.15.4 |
| Battery level | Battery holder for 2 AAA batteries |
| Sensor port | Interfaced with the IRMote-CC2520 |
| Propagate model | Unit disk graph model |
| Node position | Fixed without mobility |
| Warming | 120 s |
| Micro | STM32f405-ARM32-bit-Cortex-M4-CPU |
| LP operation | Sleep, stop, and standby modes VBAT supply for RTC, 2032-bit backup-registers + optional 4 KB backup SRAM |
| Simulation time | 2 h |
| Routing level | RPL based on border router |
| Application layer | Gloriot interface + COAP |
| Radio rate | 30 m–1 dBm in simulation and 2 m in experimental |
| Number of nodes | 50 randomly-deployed nodes |
| Sensors | Sensors: temperature/humidity(SHT15) |
| Data generating | Every 20 s and 30 s UDP packet |
| Sink/root node position | X/2, Y0 |

Table 8.5 displays a comparative examination of the suggested data aggregation technique in contrast to other conventional methods in both indoor and outdoor environments [53].

Table 8.6 offers a comprehensive analysis of different sensor nodes utilized in diverse settings. It emphasizes variations in specifications such as power consumption, communication range, data rate, sensor types, and battery life.

**Table 8.5** Outcomes from in-depth experiments comparing the suggested method to alternative strategies in outdoor and indoor environment.

| Protocol | Aggregated (%) | Packet delivery ratio (%) | Receive | Sent | Drop |
|---|---|---|---|---|---|
| LA-RPL (indoor) | 34.11 | 98.7 | 82,665 | 83,718 | 1053 |
| RPL (outdoor) | 0 | 95.7 | 77,987 | 81,430 | 3443 |
| A-RPL (indoor) | 11.03 | 96.4 | 78,132 | 80,993 | 2861 |
| BD-RPL (outdoor) | 0 | 96.9 | 79,004 | 81,450 | 2446 |
| M-RPL (indoor) | 6.78 | 93.1 | 73,369 | 78,830 | 5461 |
| M-RPL (outdoor) | 9.83 | 95.2 | 73,650 | 77,329 | 3679 |
| RPL (indoor) | 0 | 91.9 | 75,313 | 81,874 | 6561 |
| A-RPL (outdoor) | 13.26 | 96.7 | 79,931 | 82,584 | 2653 |
| BD-RPL (indoor) | 0 | 96.4 | 80,334 | 83,326 | 2992 |
| LA-RPL (outdoor) | 37.7 | 99.1 | 82,151 | 82,880 | 729 |

This comprehensive comparison table provides specifications of different sensor nodes, emphasizing disparities in power consumption, communication range, data rate, sensor types, battery life, and cost. These complex applications and case studies highlight the sizable effect of distributed data management systems in residential as well as industrial settings. These systems utilize advanced technologies such as IoT, edge computing, and real-time data analytics to achieve higher operational efficiency, better decision-making, and improved resource management [62–67].

**Table 8.6** Detailed comparison of various sensor nodes and their specifications.

| Specification | Node A | Node B | Node C | Node D | Ref. |
|---|---|---|---|---|---|
| Power consumption | 0.5 W | 0.3 W | 0.4 W | 0.6 W | [54] |
| Communication range | 100 m | 150 m | 120 m | 130 m | [55] |
| Data rate | 250 kbps | 500 kbps | 300 kbps | 400 kbps | [56] |
| Sensor types | Temp, humidity | Temp, pressure | Humidity, pressure | Temp, humidity | [57] |
| Battery life | 2 years | 1.5 years | 1 year | 2.5 years | [58] |
| Cost | $50 | $60 | $55 | $70 | [59] |
| Operating temperature | −20°C to 70°C | −10°C to 60°C | −30°C to 80°C | −15°C to 75°C | [60–62] |
| Data storage capacity | 1 GB | 2 GB | 1.5 GB | 2.5 GB | [63] |
| Network protocol | ZigBee | Wi-Fi | LoRa | Bluetooth | [64–66] |
| Deployment environment | Indoor | Outdoor | Indoor/outdoor | Outdoor | [67] |

## 8.8 Future Directions in Distributed Data Management

### 8.8.1 Blockchain for Enhanced Data Security

The use of blockchain ensures the security and legitimacy of data exchanges by providing a centralized ledger that cannot be altered. A cryptographic hash for each block in the blockchain is accompanied by a timestamp and transaction data [68]. The blocks themselves are called "blocks." This setup provides a strong defense against manipulation and dishonesty. Decentralized data management using blockchain can help ensure the integrity and confidentiality of data transfers between IoT devices. The preservation of data integrity and provenance is particularly significant in industries such as supply chain management, healthcare, and financial services [69]. Smart contracts are written-in contracts that can be executed by themselves.

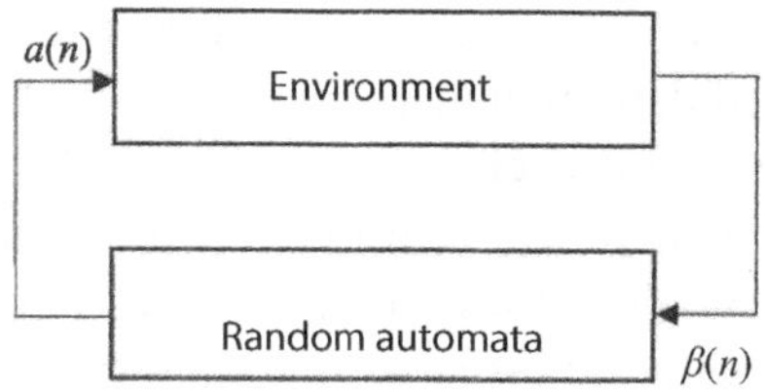


**Figure 8.11** Stochastic learning mechanisms [32].

### 8.8.2 AI and ML in Data Analytics

Distributed data management is poised to be revolutionized by the integration of AI and ML, which offer powerful instruments for analyzing and comprehending massive amounts of data. AI and ML algorithms can identify patterns, create precise forecasts, and offer valuable insights that aid in making informed decisions [70]. Machine learning models, particularly those utilizing deep learning techniques, can analyze vast amounts of data to identify intricate patterns and connections [71]. AI and ML play a crucial role in improving data security. The use of AI-driven approaches, such as anomaly detection, behavioral analysis, and automated threat response, facilitates the rapid identification and mitigation of security threats as they arise [72].

Stochastic learning automata, which are units of adaptive decision-making in ML, are illustrated in Figure 8.11. The use of stochastic learning automata in distributed data management is demonstrated in a diagram to optimize system performance and decision-making processes [32, 73]. For dynamic and uncertainty-independent scenarios, stochastic learning automata are particularly useful.

### 8.8.3 Prospective Research Avenues

The future of distributed data management is filled with abundant potential for study and innovation. Several crucial domains are positioned to propel progress in this field:

- **Integration of blockchain and AI**: The integration of blockchain technology and AI can bolster data security and improve analytical capabilities. Research in this field can investigate the utilization of AI algorithms to identify irregularities and authenticate transactions on the blockchain.

This would guarantee the trustworthiness and dependability of distributed data management systems [74].

- **Quantum-resistant cryptography**: With the increasing prevalence of quantum computers, it is crucial to design cryptography algorithms that are resistant to quantum attacks. Conducting research on quantum-resistant encryption will guarantee the security of distributed data management systems against potential quantum threats [75].
- **Federated learning**: This method entails training ML models on distributed devices without transmitting raw data to a central server. Federated learning improves privacy and minimizes bandwidth consumption, making it well-suited for remote settings. Research should prioritize enhancing federated learning methods and tackling obstacles associated with model correctness and convergence [76].
- **Edge AI**: By incorporating AI capabilities to the edge of the network, it becomes possible to obtain immediate insights and make decisions in close proximity to the data source. Research in edge AI can investigate the optimization of algorithms for energy-efficient devices and the smooth integration with central data management systems [77].
- **Adaptive security mechanisms**: It is essential for the future of distributed data management to create adaptable security systems that utilize AI and ML to promptly address changing threats. The research could prioritize the development of resilient and self-repairing security frameworks capable of autonomously detecting and mitigating threats [78].

The future directions in distributed data management involve a variety of cutting-edge technology and approaches. Blockchain, quantum computing, AI, and ML are poised to revolutionize the field by providing improved security, efficiency, and analytical capabilities [79, 80]. By investigating these potential research paths, the field can persistently progress, confronting increasing obstacles and revealing novel prospects for expansion and advancement.

## 8.9 Conclusion

- The study highlights the significant progress in distributed data management, moving away from large centralized systems and toward more efficient, scalable, resilient distribution architectures. The progress of this development has been significantly boosted by the use of key technologies like IoT, edge computing, and big data analytics. IoT integration in distributed systems has introduced new challenges and opportunities, as the devices produce vast amounts of data that must be processed and managed immediately. This helps to reduce latency and bandwidth problems that interfere with effective data processing at the edge, which is also essential. For large datasets in distributed environments, efficient methods of collection and condensation are needed to reduce data size while improving data accuracy and allowing for prompt decision-making.

- Practical and real-world examples demonstrate the effectiveness and adaptability of distributed data management systems in smart devices, industrial IoT, and logistics.
- These systems demonstrate significant improvements in operational efficiency, safety, and decision-making capabilities. Additionally, the report discusses areas that could be studied and improved upon in the future, including the use of blockchain for enhanced data protection, research outcomes from quantum computing, or the integration of AI and ML into data analysis. These technologies are projected to maintain the dispersed nature of data management.
- Continuous innovation is crucial to keeping up with the rapid advancements in technology. The integration of blockchain, quantum computing, and AI will require modifications in distributed data management solutions. These improvements may lead to improved security, effectiveness, and analytical capabilities, adapting to the evolving needs of modern applications. New challenges will arise in managing and analyzing the ever-larger and more complex data. Continuous innovation ensures that systems remain capable of effectively managing these issues, thereby fostering industry acceptance and enabling organizations to access cutting-edge data management solutions.
- Distributed data management is anticipated to play a significant role in the development of data-driven applications.
- Various industries are increasingly relying on the ability to handle and scrutinize large amounts of data in real time. The integration of modern technology will significantly enhance

the capabilities of these systems, making them essential tools for enterprises and organizations. This will be interdisciplinary cooperation among researchers, engineers, and the industry to work together on how to handle complex problems of dispersed data management. With so much new information, it becomes imperative to devise sustainable and scalable solutions that maximize resource usage, minimize environmental harm, and ensure smooth scalability.

- Despite the technical advancements, distributed data management is experiencing significant growth and demand for effective data processing and analysis. The future of distributed data management has great potential to revolutionize data management and utilization across different applications and industries by actively embracing continuous innovation and promoting collaboration.

## References

1. Yi, Z., Hongkai, Z., Yongyu, W., Yulian, X., Xiaoyan, Z., Improved DataX Data Synchronization Technique for Distribution Grid Data Middleware Implementation, in: *2024 IEEE 3rd International Conference on Electrical Engineering, Big Data and Algorithms (EEBDA)*, 2024, February, IEEE, pp. 1260–1266.
2. Rawat, S., Shukla, B.K., Sihag, P., Srivastav, Y., Singh, H.K., Environmental effects and sustainable hydropower development: A review of deployment research, environmental valuation and iot sensors integration. *AIP Conf. Proc.*, 3050, 1, 040008, 2024, February, AIP Publishing.
3. Gubbi, J., Buyya, R., Marusic, S., Palaniswami, M., Internet of Things (IoT): A vision, architectural elements, and future directions. *Future Gener. Comput. Syst.*, 29, 7, 1645–1660, 2013.
4. Sheng, Z., Yang, S., Yu, Y., Vasilakos, A.V., McCann, J.A., Leung, K.K., A survey on the IETF protocol suite for the Internet of Things: Standards, challenges, and opportunities. *IEEE Wireless Commun.*, 20, 6, 91–98, 2013.
5. Atzori, L., Iera, A., Morabito, G., The Internet of Things: A survey. *Comput. Netw.*, 54, 15, 2787–2805, 2010.
6. Sun, Y., Song, H., Jara, A.J., Bie, R., Internet of Things and Big Data Analytics for Smart and Connected Communities. *IEEE Access*, 4, 766–773, 2016.
7. Kune, R., Konugurthi, P.K., Agarwal, A., Chillarige, R.R., Buyya, R., The anatomy of big data computing. *Softw.: Pract. Exper.*, 46, 1, 79–105, 2016.

8. Guo, C. and Chen, J., Big data analytics in healthcare, in: *Knowledge technology and systems: Toward establishing knowledge systems science*, pp. 27–70, Springer Nature Singapore, Singapore, 2023.
9. Cui, Y., Ma, Z., Wang, L., Yang, A., Liu, Q., Kong, S., Wang, H., A survey on big data-enabled innovative online education systems during the COVID-19 pandemic. *J. Innov. Knowl.*, 8, 1, 100295, 2023.
10. Hu, H., Wen, Y., Chua, T.S., Li, X., Toward scalable systems for big data analytics: A technology tutorial. *IEEE Access*, 2, 652–687, 2014.
11. Shoetan, P.O., Oyewole, A.T., Okoye, C.C., Ofodile, O.C., Reviewing the role of big data analytics in financial fraud detection. *Fin. Acc. Res. J.*, 6, 3, 384–394, 2024.
12. Stonebraker, M. and Çetintemel, U., "One size fits all" an idea whose time has come and gone, in: *Making Databases Work: The Pragmatic Wisdom of Michael Stonebraker*, pp. 441–462, 2018.
13. Mansour, M., Gamal, A., Ahmed, A.I., Said, L.A., Elbaz, A., Herencsar, N., Soltan, A., Internet of things: a comprehensive overview on protocols, architectures, technologies, simulation tools, and future directions. *Energies*, 16, 8, 3465, 2023.
14. Satyanarayanan, M., The Emergence of Edge Computing. *Computer*, 50, 1, 30–39, 2017.
15. White, T., *Hadoop: The Definitive Guide*, O'Reilly Media, Sebastopol, California, USA, 2012.
16. Crosby, M., Pattanayak, P., Verma, S., Kalyanaraman, V., Blockchain Technology: Beyond Bitcoin. *Appl. Innov. Rev.*, 2, 6–19, 2016.
17. Jordan, M.I., and Mitchell, T.M., Machine Learning: Trends, Perspectives, and Prospects. *Science*, 349, 6245, 255–260, 2015.
18. Qiu, H., Banerjee, S.S., Jha, S., Kalbarczyk, Z.T., Iyer, R.K., {FIRM}: An intelligent fine-grained resource management framework for {SLO-Oriented} microservices, in: *14th USENIX Symposium on Operating Systems Design and Implementation (OSDI 20)*, pp. 805–825, 2020.
19. Roberts, M., *Serverless Architectures on AWS: With Examples Using AWS Lambda*, Manning Publications, Shelter Island, New York, USA, 2018.
20. Ahmadi, S., Security Implications of Edge Computing in Cloud Networks. *J. Comput. Commun.*, 12, 02, 26–46, 2024.
21. Burns, B., Grant, B., Oppenheimer, D., Brewer, E., Wilkes, J., Borg, Omega, and Kubernetes. *Commun. ACM*, 59, 5, 50–57, 2016.
22. Kefalakis, N., Roukounaki, A., Soldatos, J., Configurable distributed data management for the Internet of the Things. *Information*, 10, 12, 360, 2019.
23. Sadique, K.M., Rahmani, R., Johannesson, P., DIdM-EIoTD: Distributed identity management for edge Internet of Things (IoT) devices. *Sensors*, 23, 8, 4046, 2023.
24. Fowler, M., *Domain-Specific Languages*, Addison-Wesley Professional, Boston, Massachusetts, USA, 2010.

25. Hudak, P., Building domain-specific embedded languages. *ACM Comput. Surv. (CSUR)*, 28, 4es, 196, 1996.
26. Voellmy, A. and Hudak, P., Nettle: Taking the Sting out of Programming Network Routers. *Proceedings of the 16th ACM SIGPLAN International Conference on Functional Programming*, pp. 235–246, 2013.
27. Ngo, T.T.T., Pinet, F., Sarramia, D., Kang, M.A., A mediation system for continuous spatial queries on a unified schema using Apache Spark. *Big Earth Data*, 8, 1, 115–141, 2024.
28. Farooq, O., Singh, P., Hedabou, M., Boulila, W., Benjdira, B., Machine learning analytic-based two-staged data management framework for internet of things. *Sensors*, 23, 5, 2427, 2023.
29. Hellerstein, J.M., Stonebraker, M., Hamilton, J., Architecture of a Database System. *Found. Trends Databases*, 1, 2, 141–259, 2007.
30. Hasan, M.K., Weichen, Z., Safie, N., Ahmed, F.R.A., Ghazal, T.M., A Survey on Key Agreement and Authentication Protocol for Internet of Things Application. *IEEE Access*, 12, 61642–61666, 2024.
31. Cruz Huacarpuma, R., de Sousa Junior, R.T., De Holanda, M.T., de Oliveira Albuquerque, R., García Villalba, L.J., Kim, T.H., Distributed data service for data management in internet of things middleware. *Sensors*, 17, 5, 977, 2017.
32. Homaei, M.H., Salwana, E., Shamshirband, S., An enhanced distributed data aggregation method in the Internet of Things. *Sensors*, 19, 14, 3173, 2019.
33. Rath, K.C., Khang, A., Roy, D., The Role of Internet of Things (IoT) Technology in Industry 4.0 Economy, in: *Advanced IoT Technologies and Applications in the Industry 4.0 Digital Economy*, pp. 1–28, CRC Press, Boca Raton, Florida, USA, 2024.
34. Hussain, A. and Qureshi, K.N., Standards and Policies Adoption for AIoT Networks, in: *Artificial Intelligence of Things (AIoT)*, pp. 49–76, CRC Press, Boca Raton, Florida, USA, 2024.
35. Kolekar, V.K., Oswal, M., Wankhade, Y., Shirke, G., Sondur, A., Wable, P., Smart City IoT Data Management with Proactive Middleware. *IJRITCC*, 11, 5, 319–329, 2023.
36. Sadatdiynov, K., Cui, L., Zhang, L., Huang, J.Z., Salloum, S., Mahmud, M.S., A review of optimization methods for computation offloading in edge computing networks. *Digital Commun. Netw.*, 9, 2, 450–461, 2023.
37. Gill, S.S., Quantum and blockchain based Serverless edge computing: A vision, model, new trends and future directions. *Internet Technol. Lett.*, 7, 1, e275, 2024.
38. Carvalho, G., Cabral, B., Pereira, V., Bernardino, J., Edge computing: current trends, research challenges and future directions. *Computing*, 103, 5, 993–1023, 2021.
39. Alwakeel, A.M., An overview of fog computing and edge computing security and privacy issues. *Sensors*, 21, 24, 8226, 2021.
40. Martinez-Rendon, C., González-Compeán, J.L., Sánchez-Gallegos, D.D., Carretero, J., CD/CV: Blockchain-based schemes for continuous verifiability

and traceability of IoT data for edge–fog–cloud. *Inf. Process. Manage.*, 60, 1, 103155, 2023.
41. Al-Masri, E., Souri, A., Mohamed, H., Yang, W., Olmsted, J., Kotevska, O., Energy-efficient cooperative resource allocation and task scheduling for Internet of Things environments. *Internet Things*, 23, 100832, 2023.
42. Singh, R.K., Developing a big data analytics platform using Apache Hadoop Ecosystem for delivering big data services in libraries. *Digit. Libr. Perspect.*, 40, 2, 160–186, 2024.
43. Dwivedi, R., Tiwari, A., Bharill, N., Ratnaparkhe, M., Mogre, P., Gadge, P., Jagadeesh, K., A novel apache spark-based 14-dimensional scalable feature extraction approach for the clustering of genomics data. *J. Supercomput.*, 80, 3, 3554–3588, 2024.
44. Al-Jumaili, A.H.A., Muniyandi, R.C., Hasan, M.K., Paw, J.K.S., Singh, M.J., Big data analytics using cloud computing based frameworks for power management systems: Status, constraints, and future recommendations. *Sensors*, 23, 6, 2952, 2023.
45. Dikaiakos, M.D., Pallis, G., Katsaros, D., Mehra, P., Vakali, A., Cloud Computing: Distributed Internet Computing for IT and Scientific Research. *IEEE Internet Comput.*, 13, 5, 10–13, 2009.
46. Oliveira, F., Costa, D.G., Assis, F., Silva, I., Internet of Intelligent Things: A convergence of embedded systems, edge computing and machine learning *Internet Things*, 26, 101153, 2024.
47. Errami, S.A., Hajji, H., El Kadi, K.A., Badir, H., Spatial big data architecture: from data warehouses and data lakes to the Lakehouse. *J. Parallel Distrib. Comput.*, 176, 70–79, 2023.
48. Miorandi, D., Sicari, S., De Pellegrini, F., Chlamtac, I., Internet of Things: Vision, applications and research challenges. *Ad Hoc Networks*, 10, 7, 1497–1516, 2012.
49. Lee, J., Bagheri, B., Kao, H.A., A Cyber-Physical Systems architecture for Industry 4.0-based manufacturing systems. *Manuf. Lett.*, 3, 18–23, 2015.
50. Nie, Q., Tang, D., Liu, C., Wang, L., Song, J., A multi-agent and cloud-edge orchestration framework of digital twin for distributed production control. *Rob. Comput. Integr. Manuf.*, 82, 102543, 2023.
51. Askar, S.K., Deep forest based internet of medical things system for diagnosis of heart disease. *ARO-the Sci. J. koya Univ.*, 11, 1, 88–98, 2023.
52. De Benedictis, A., Flammini, F., Mazzocca, N., Somma, A., Vitale, F., Digital twins for anomaly detection in the industrial internet of things: Conceptual architecture and proof-of-concept. *IEEE Trans. Ind. Inf.*, 19, 12, 11553–11563, 2023.
53. Chithaluru, P., Al-Turjman, F., Kumar, M., Stephan, T., Computational-intelligence-inspired adaptive opportunistic clustering approach for industrial IoT networks. *IEEE Internet Things J.*, 10, 9, 7884–7892, 2023.

54. Gupta, N. and Kumar, A., Study on the wireless sensor networks routing for Low-Power FPGA hardware in field applications. *Comput. Electron. Agric.*, 212, 108145, 2023.
55. Akyildiz, I.F., Su, W., Sankarasubramaniam, Y., Cayirci, E., A survey on sensor networks. *IEEE Commun. Mag.*, 40, 8, 102–114, 2002.
56. Gungor, V.C. and Hancke, G.P., Industrial wireless sensor networks: Challenges, design principles, and technical approaches. *IEEE Trans. Ind. Electron.*, 56, 10, 4258–4265, 2009.
57. Hac, A., *Wireless sensor network designs*, John Wiley & Sons, Hoboken, New Jersey, USA, 2003.
58. Heinzelman, W.B., Chandrakasan, A.P., Balakrishnan, H., An application-specific protocol architecture for wireless microsensor networks. *IEEE Trans. Wireless Commun.*, 1, 4, 660–670, 2002.
59. Bhatia, S., Jaffery, Z.A., Mehfuz, S., A Comparative Study of Wireless Communication Protocols for use in Smart Farming Framework Development, in: *2023 3rd International Conference on Intelligent Communication and Computational Techniques (ICCT)*, 2023, January, IEEE, pp. 1–7.
60. Stankovic, J.A., Research directions for the Internet of Things. *IEEE Internet Things J.*, 1, 1, 3–9, 2008.
61. Akyildiz, I.F. and Vuran, M.C., *Wireless sensor networks*, John Wiley & Sons, Hoboken, New Jersey, USA, 2010.
62. Yick, J., Mukherjee, B., Ghosal, D., Wireless sensor network survey. *Comput. Networks*, 52, 12, 2292–2330, 2008.
63. Anastasi, G., Conti, M., Di Francesco, M., Passarella, A., Energy conservation in wireless sensor networks: A survey. *Ad Hoc Networks*, 7, 3, 537–568, 2009.
64. Li, L., Podder, P., Hoque, E., A formal security analysis of ZigBee (1.0 and 3.0), in: *Proceedings of the 7th Symposium on Hot Topics in the Science of Security*, 2020, September, pp. 1–11.
65. Paul, B., Assi, C., Kaddoum, G., LoRaWAN network planning. *IEEE Trans. Green Commun. Networking*, 8, 4, 1413–1426, 2024.
66. Ali, J., Zafar, M.H., Hewage, C., Hassan, S.R., Asif, R., The advents of ubiquitous computing in the development of smart cities—A review on the internet of things (IoT). *Electronics*, 12, 4, 1032, 2023.
67. Vasseur, J.-P. and Dunkels, A., *Interconnecting Smart Objects with IP: The Next Internet*, Morgan Kaufmann, Waltham, Massachusetts, USA, 2010.
68. Nakamoto, S. and Bitcoin, A., A peer-to-peer electronic cash system. *Bitcoin*, 4, 2, 15, 2008, URL: https://bitcoin. org/bitcoin. pdf.
69. Yli-Huumo, J., Ko, D., Choi, S., Park, S., Smolander, K., Where is current research on Blockchain technology?—A systematic review. *PLoS One*, 11, 10, e0163477, 2016.
70. Pugliese, R., Regondi, S., Marini, R., Machine learning-based approach: Global trends, research directions, and regulatory standpoints. *Data Sci. Manage.*, 4, 19–29, 2021.

71. Karthikeyan, S. and Nagamani, G.M., An Architecture of Cyber-Physical System for Industry 4.0, in: *Digital Transformation: Industry 4.0 to Society 5.0*, pp. 259–283, Springer Nature Singapore, Singapore, 2024.
72. Chio, C. and Freeman, D., *Machine Learning and Security: Protecting Systems with Data and Algorithms*, O'Reilly Media, Sebastopol, California, USA, 2018.
73. Abofathi, Y., Anari, B., Masdari, M., A learning automata based approach for module placement in fog computing environment. *Expert Syst. Appl.*, 237, 121607, 2024.
74. Dinh, T.T.A., Liu, R., Zhang, M., Chen, G., Ooi, B.C., Wang, J., Untangling Blockchain: A Data Processing View of Blockchain Systems. *IEEE Trans. Knowl. Data Eng.*, 30, 7, 1366–1385, 2018.
75. Bernstein, D.J. and Lange, T., Post-quantum cryptography. *Nature*, 549, 7671, 188–194, 2017.
76. Ji, S., Tan, Y., Saravirta, T., Yang, Z., Liu, Y., Vasankari, L., Pan, S., Long, G., Walid, A., Emerging trends in federated learning: From model fusion to federated x learning. *Int. J. Mach. Learn. Cybern.*, 15, 1–22, 2024.
77. McEnroe, P., Wang, S., Liyanage, M., A survey on the convergence of edge computing and AI for UAVs: Opportunities and challenges. *IEEE Internet Things J.*, 9, 17, 15435–15459, 2022.
78. Buczak, A.L. and Guven, E., A Survey of Data Mining and Machine Learning Methods for Cyber Security Intrusion Detection. *IEEE Commun. Surv. Tutor.*, 18, 2, 1153–1176, 2016.
79. Tripathi, S.L. and Mahmud, M., *Explainable Machine Learning Models and Architecture*, Wiley & Scrivener Publishing LLC, USA, 2023, https://doi.org/10.1002/9781394186570.
80. Ghai, D., Tripathi, S.L., Saxena, S., Chanda, M., Alazab, M., *Machine Learning Algorithms for Signal and Image Processing*, Wiley IEEE Press, USA, 2022, DOI:10.1002/9781119861850.

9

# Autonomy and Adaptive Architectures in Distributed Systems

**Bishnu Kant Shukla[1]*, Bhupender Parashar[2], Vikas Kumar Singla[3] and Shivam Verma[4]**

*[1]Department of Civil Engineering, JSS Academy of Technical Education, Noida, India*
*[2]Department of Mathematics, JSS Academy of Technical Education, Noida, India*
*[3]Department of Mechanical Engineering, JSS Academy of Technical Education, Noida, India*
*[4]Department of Mechanical and Industrial Engineering, New Jersey Institute of Technology, Newark (New Jersey), USA*

## *Abstract*

The convergence of autonomy and adaptive architectures in distributed systems heralds a transformative era for the next-generation Internet, marking a significant leap from traditional centralized frameworks. This chapter delves into the intricate symbiosis between autonomous agents and multiagent systems (MASs) within the decentralized paradigm, underscoring their pivotal role in enhancing system adaptability, resilience, and scalability. Through a meticulous examination of the conceptual underpinnings and evolutionary trajectory of MAS, the discourse extends to the nuanced definition and operationalization of autonomy within these distributed networks. Architectural models and adaptive strategies are scrutinized, revealing their instrumental function in fostering robust, scalable, and efficient decentralized systems. A series of case studies spanning smart grids, water distribution, and transportation systems serve as empirical testaments to the pragmatic application and potential of MAS in real-world scenarios. The chapter presents a forward-looking discussion on the challenges and future directions, highlighting the imperative for scalability, security, and privacy considerations in the relentless pursuit of autonomous and adaptive distributed systems. The present chapter not only enriches the academic discourse but also provides valuable insights for practitioners navigating the complexities of decentralized systems and the next-generation Internet.

**Corresponding author*: bishnukantshukla@gmail.com

Sandhya Avasthi and Suman Lata Tripathi (eds.) Distributed and Parallel Computing, (183–218)

***Keywords:*** Autonomy, distributed systems, multiagent systems, adaptive architectures, decentralized paradigm, next-generation internet

## 9.1 Introduction

Added to technology and the need for reliable, adaptable, and effective solutions, distributed systems have been transformed. Although some centralized frameworks are effective in certain contexts, they frequently lack the necessary adaptation and handling of complex, expansive, and ever-evolving environments. This has resulted in the study and acceptance of decentralized paradigms using autonomy and adaptive systems. Networked systems require multiagent systems (MASs). MAS is a system of self-governing agents who interact with each other and their environment to achieve personal and shared goals. These systems are ideal for complex, fluctuating, and volatile environments where centralized control is not feasible. The intelligence, self-organization, and collaborative problem-solving of MASs make them ideal for applications such as smart grids, water distribution, transportation systems [1, 2], and autonomous navigation. Decree and scalability are the primary objectives of decentralization. Decentralized systems reduce the number of single points of failure by sharing decision-making and computational weight among multiple nodes, resulting in more resource-efficient utilization. Managing the growing complexity and scale of distributed systems requires decentralization. Real-time processing and dynamic environment adaptation are made possible by decentralization [3]. The Internet is being shaped by the presence of autonomous and adaptable organizations. Self-regulating, self-curing, and evolving systems can be managed by autonomous agents and adaptive mechanisms in distributed systems. Changes in user requirements, network conditions, and environmental factors demand flexibility. Hence, adaptability is crucial. Accordingly, self-governing and flexible distributed systems are becoming more popular among academic and business research communities [4, 5].

It explores the potential of distributed systems' autonomy and adaptive architectures, which holds great promise for the future Internet. This course covers topics such as autonomy, adaptive architectures, and MASs. The work delineates these notions, examines their evolution, and highlights centralized viewpoints. Specifically, the investigation examines distributed system architectural models and agent-based modeling. It delves into the design and implementation of MASs, highlighting their strengths and weaknesses. Furthermore, it explores the adaptive strategies for robustness and elasticity of distributed systems. It explores how systems organize themselves, bounce back from failure, or change with conditions. Smart grids, water distribution, and transportation networks are utilized to illustrate the practical implementation of multiagent networks (MAS) in the chapter. In addition, the paper briefly discusses MAS applications in various fields, with a particular emphasis on autonomous navigation systems (ANSs). The latest projects and instances of MAS utilization in unmanned surface vehicles (USVs) and autonomous vessels are discussed [6, 7]. It investigates collision avoidance techniques for autonomous navigation and MAS. It involves testing various algorithms to ensure safe and efficient navigation [8]. In addition, the study explores how network architecture, including theoretical graph structures, impacts the reliability and performance of distributed systems [9].

The primary obstacles and opportunities for self-governing and flexible distributed systems are outlined in this paper. This involves dealing with issues of scalability, security, and privacy as well as new technology. This initiative aims "to improve scholarship on distributed systems" and will offer useful insights to professionals and scholars working in decentralized architectures and the future Internet. By utilizing charts and tables from current research, the analysis and discussion will be enhanced by providing a visual and empirically based perspective.

## 9.2 Conceptual Framework

Understanding autonomy, adaptive architectures, and MASs is essential for the creation of autonomous and adaptable distributed systems. However, other areas may differ from this. The functionality and efficiency of modern distributed systems are based on these concepts.

### 9.2.1 Definition of Key Concepts

#### *9.2.1.1 Autonomy*

Different components or agents can make independent decisions and act independently, allowing for distributional autonomy without human intervention. Perceive, analyze, and act to achieve objectives are capabilities of autonomous agents. The development of robust and effective systems that can withstand changes in conditions is dependent on the proficiency acquired. The ability of automated systems to learn and improve over time is crucial for managing practical applications [10].

#### *9.2.1.2 Adaptive Architectures*

Adaptive designs are designed to cope with environmental or internal changes. Rearranging components, setting up adjustments for optimal performance, and optimizing resource usage are carried out dynamically. The system's effectiveness and dependability are dependent on the system being able to handle changes in network conditions, workload, and external factors. The scale and complexity of dispersed systems often make fixed designs unsuitable, necessitating flexibility [11].

#### *9.2.1.3 Multiagent Systems*

In MASs, individuals and groups work together as agents to achieve specific objectives. The system benefits from the cooperation of agents, even though each functions independently. In dynamic, multidimensional environments, MAS effectively distributes computational workload and decision-making tasks. This decentralized approach improves flexibility, scale, and reliability. MAS is well-suited for applications in robotics, telecommunications, and transportation technologies, as well as smart grids [12].

#### *9.2.1.4 The Evolutionary Trajectory of MAS*

MAS has been elevated in the domains of artificial intelligence, machine learning (ML), and distributed computing. In its early stages, MAS concentrated on fundamental interactions. Technological progress has led to a significant improvement in agent capabilities and interaction complexity. Complex tasks in challenging environments can be accomplished by modern MASs, which employ advanced algorithms to learn, adapt, and coordinate. Learning algorithms that leverage past experiences to enhance performance is a significant advancement. Optimal behavior is achieved by agents through trial and error, which is known as reinforcement learning [13]. Synchronization and information exchange are enhanced through the implementation of better communication protocols and network topologies. The integration of MASs with Internet of Things (IoT) and edge computing has significantly augmented their applications and potential. Larger MASs can be made possible through processing capacity and connectivity, thanks to these technologies. Complex distributed systems emphasize the importance of MAS in this evolution [14].

### 9.2.2 Importance of Decentralized Paradigms

Decentralized ideas must be able to be durable and adaptable in distributed systems. The advantage of decentralized systems is that they enable the sharing of control and decision-making among multiple nodes or agents, which allows for greater fault tolerance, scalability, and resource use.

Node failures do not impact the resilience of decentralized systems, making them resilient [15]. Furthermore, scaling is a benefit of using decentralized paradigms, which is particularly true for distributed systems. Increasing the number of nodes or agents leads to an even distribution of computational workload and communication, which reduces congestion and improves performance. Large quantities of data or users are effectively managed by these systems [16, 17]. Composed distributed systems can be enhanced through the use of MASs, autonomy, and adaptive architectures. MAS and decentralized models are now more widely accepted due to their ability to handle complex, ever-changing environments.

## 9.3 Architectural Models

### 9.3.1 Overview of Emergent Architectures

In distributed systems, components can collaborate to achieve goals. The designs differ, but they are compatible with client–server, peer-to-peer (P2P), and hybrid models. Nevertheless, the client–server architecture is prevalent, where a central server provides services to client nodes [18]. P2P environments enable resource provision and solicitation to be distributed among all nodes simultaneously. All the nodes act as both clients and servers, transferring resources. Scalability and fault tolerance are key factors in the development of P2P networks for file sharing, blockchain, and collaborative applications [19]. Hybrid models involve both client–server and P2P relationships. Although peers share information directly, a central server can also synchronize data and balance efficiency with scalability [20]. The management of data processing, latency, and resource usage are crucial for modern IoT-edge computing systems. This is advantageous for real-time applications such as driverless cars and industrial IoT systems [21].

### 9.3.2 Agent-Based Models

The goal of agent-based models (ABMs) involves the use of independent agents to interact with each other and their environment in order to achieve specific objectives. Every agent operates independently, depending on its local knowledge and functions [22].

#### *9.3.2.1 Agent Architecture and Control Flow*

Perception, decision-making, action, and communication are the components of an agent's architecture in a MAS. The flow of information and cooperation in Figure 9.1 is reflected in the hierarchical structure [23].

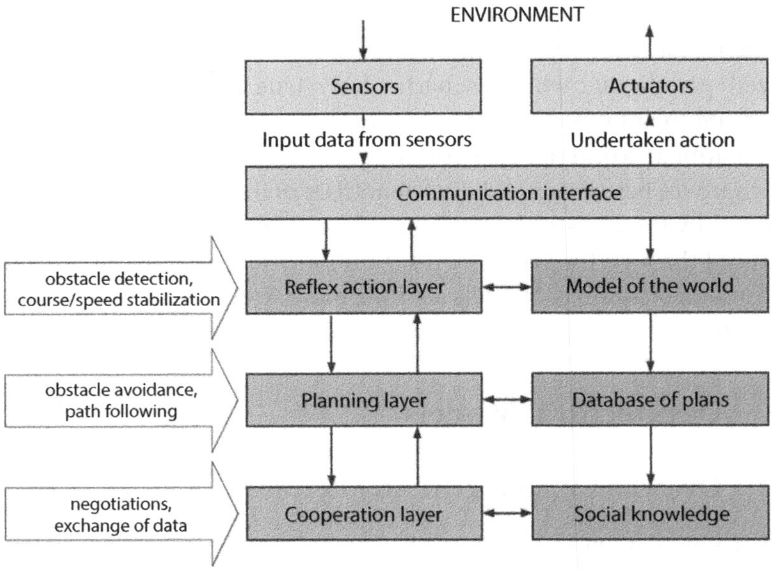


**Figure 9.1** Framework for agent architecture and control dynamics [2].

The ABM incorporates attributes such as autonomy, social competence, responsiveness, and initiative. Table 9.1 provides a concise overview of the crucial characteristics necessary for efficient agent performance in a MAS [24].

## 9.4 Adaptive Strategies in Distributed Systems

Adaptive methods are necessary for distributed systems to operate and grow efficiently in response to environmental changes, while maintaining optimal performance. This is particularly true of adaptive approaches. These remedies involve the use of flexibility principles and procedures that optimize the system's ability to withstand and expand. Learning algorithms strive to optimize their responses for similar scenarios. The use of historical data enables reinforcement learning to aid in the development of methods for optimizing rewards. Adapting to changing circumstances and user demands requires continuous improvement [32].

**Table 9.1** Overview of key agent characteristics.

| Category | Description | Attribute | Importance | Ref. |
|---|---|---|---|---|
| Abilities | The ability to perceive the surroundings using senses, analyzing immediate inputs and sequences of perceptions to develop a comprehensive historical comprehension | Perception | Essential | [25] |
| Abilities | Multiple viewpoints: the ability to manipulate capabilities without limitations and the ability to act independently from other things or functions, including working without human interaction | Autonomy | Essential | [26–28] |
| Abilities | Agents adjust their behavior and interactions with their surroundings by drawing on their previous experiences | Adaptation | Optional | [29] |
| Abilities | Agents communicate with other agents, even people | Communication | Essential | [29] |
| Location | Agents possess the ability to engage in communication and share data with other agents, including individuals | Situatedness | Essential | [29] |

*(Continued)*

**Table 9.1** Overview of key agent characteristics. (*Continued*)

| Category | Description | Attribute | Importance | Ref. |
|---|---|---|---|---|
| Location | Network interoperability refers to the capacity to seamlessly navigate between different networks and function on diverse equipment | Mobility | Optional | [26, 29] |
| Behavior | Agents are programmed to make decisions that maximize their performance results | Rationality | Optional | [25] |
| Behavior | Agents possess objectives that extend beyond instantaneous reactions to stimuli; they proactively engage in actions to accomplish these objectives, which entail cognitive processes such as logical thinking, strategizing, bargaining, and collaborating with others | Proactiveness | Optional | [26, 29, 30] |
| Behavior | Agents rapidly adapt their behavior in reaction to changes in the environment | Reactivity | Essential | [29, 30] |
| Behavior | Agents participate in interactive and dynamic relationships with other agents, exerting influence on one another's behaviors | Social | Essential | [31] |

### 9.4.1 Mechanisms for System Resilience and Scalability

Distributed systems employ techniques to address faults, spread workloads, and oversee resources, guaranteeing both resilience and scalability. Fault tolerance ensures the continued operation of a system even in the event of component failures by the implementation of redundancy, replication, and checkpointing. Redundancy ensures the presence of backup components, replication creates copies of data, and checkpointing preserves system states for the sake of recovery [33].

Load balancing is a technique that uniformly distributes workloads, hence preventing bottlenecks and improving performance. The techniques employed consist of round-robin scheduling, least connections, and dynamic algorithms [34]. Scalable designs facilitate the expansion of systems and the effective management of demand by employing horizontal scaling (adding nodes) and vertical scaling (improving existing nodes). Microservices designs divide applications into smaller, autonomous services to enhance scalability [35]. Elasticity enables systems to dynamically allocate resources according to demand, hence ensuring optimal utilization and cost-effectiveness. Cloud systems employ autoscaling to manage resources dynamically, which is essential for handling varying workloads [36]. Self-healing solutions facilitate the automatic identification and correction of errors, thus guaranteeing uninterrupted operation. Automated failover and self-repairing software are essential elements [37].

Adaptability, resilience, and scalability are essential attributes for distributed systems. These systems utilize ML, fault tolerance, load balancing, scalable architectures, elasticity, and self-healing mechanisms to effectively handle changing situations, maintain availability, and efficiently meet increasing needs.

## 9.5 Case Studies

### 9.5.1 Smart Grids

Smart grids improve the dependability, effectiveness, and ecofriendliness of electrical supplies through the integration of digital communication and automation. Smart grids, in contrast to traditional one-way grids, employ bidirectional communication and sophisticated management to accommodate fluctuations in consumption and output, integrate renewable energy sources, and enhance dependability. One important aspect is the integration of infrastructure components such as the national power grid and gas transmission system, which improves efficiency and minimizes environmental harm [38].

### 9.5.2 Geographical and Functional Infrastructure Interdependence

Figure 9.2 depicts the physical and operational interconnection between the national electrical grid and gas transmission infrastructure of Great Britain. It emphasizes their functions within the larger energy environment.

The integration of electricity and gas networks in smart grids guarantees a dependable energy provision. The electricity system is dependent on natural gas, particularly for gas-fired power plants, whereas the gas network utilizes electrical infrastructure for the purpose of controls and monitoring. This interaction improves the resilience of the system by adjusting to fluctuations in demand, integrating renewable energy sources, and effectively responding to emergencies [39].

Smart technologies offer the capacity to monitor and control in real time, enhancing performance and stability. Advanced metering infrastructure collects data on energy usage, detects malfunctions, and improves the efficiency of energy distribution. Distributed energy resources such as

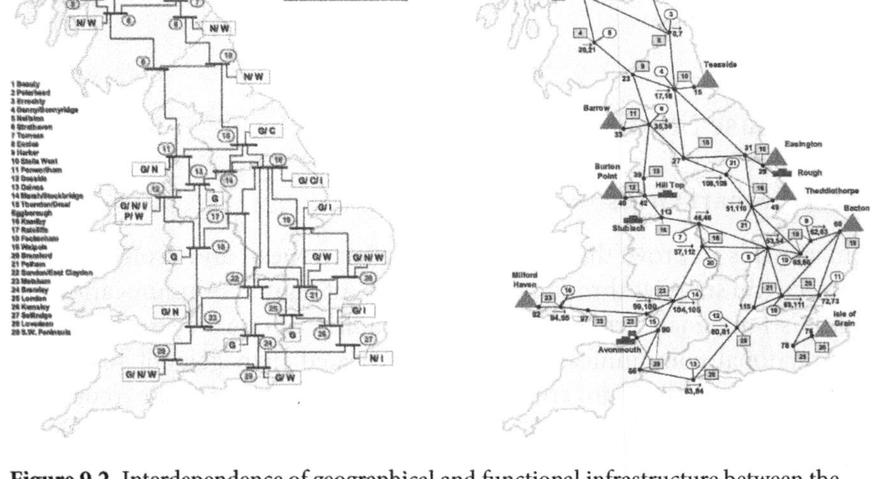


**Figure 9.2** Interdependence of geographical and functional infrastructure between the national electricity grid (left) and the gas transmission system (right) in Great Britain [39].

solar panels, wind turbines, and battery storage systems decentralize the production of energy, hence enhancing the flexibility and resilience of the power grid [40].

### 9.5.3 Water Distribution Systems

Water distribution systems convey potable water from treatment facilities to residential, commercial, and industrial establishments. The integration of autonomous and adaptive designs enhances efficiency, reliability, and sustainability [41].

#### *9.5.3.1 Adaptive Water Management*

Adaptive water management involves real-time monitoring and automated control, as well as predictive analytics to optimize operations and maintenance. Meters and sophisticated sensors are utilized to monitor water quality, pressure, and flow rates without interruption. By detecting any anomalies, such as leaks, these devices can quickly identify and correct the problem [41]. Are geographic information systems (GISs) and supervisory control and data acquisition (SCADA) systems crucial? Whereas GISs display the actual structure of water network, SCADA enables real-time control and monitoring [42].

#### *9.5.3.2 Leak Detection and Management*

Water leakage in distribution systems leads to increased costs and water loss. Sound sensors, pressure recorders, and smart meters are among the advanced technologies used for leak detection. ML algorithms can analyze the data to predict leaks and prioritize maintenance tasks. The control of network pressure can be achieved through adaptive methods as well [43]. The goal of pressure management is to decrease the strain on pipes and the likelihood of leaking. Pressure reduction valves and variable speed pumps are utilized to adjust flow rates based on the demand [44].

#### *9.5.3.3 Water Quality Monitoring*

Maintaining the cleanliness of water is essential. The pH, turbidity, chlorine levels, and microbiological contaminants are monitored by autonomous systems. Both alerts and automatic actions are used to reduce health hazards by dealing with deviation from established norm. These technologies promptly identify the sources of contamination and provide prompt action [45].

### 9.5.4 Transportation Systems

Integrating self-governing and flexible designs into transportation systems enhances effectiveness, security, and environmental friendliness, rendering it indispensable for infrastructure. Contemporary networks necessitate the synchronization of road, rail, aviation, and maritime modes. Intelligent technology facilitates efficient traffic management, mitigates congestion, and improves mobility [46].

#### *9.5.4.1 Intelligent Transportation Systems*

Integrating self-governing and flexible designs into transportation systems enhances effectiveness, security, and environmental friendliness, rendering it indispensable for infrastructure. Contemporary networks necessitate the synchronization of road, rail, aviation, and maritime modes. Intelligent technology facilitates efficient traffic management, mitigates congestion, and improves mobility [46].

#### *9.5.4.2 Traffic Management*

Adaptive traffic management systems utilize up-to-the-minute data to optimize the flow of vehicles and minimize traffic congestion. Traffic lights equipped with sensors adapt their timing according to present conditions, thereby decreasing waiting periods and enhancing traffic flow. Traffic management centers gather data from multiple sources to observe patterns and deal with issues or congestion [47].

#### *9.5.4.3 Public Transportation*

Autonomous and adaptive technology improves the dependability and effectiveness of public transport. Implementing real-time tracking technology for buses, trains, and other transportation modes allows for accurate arrival predictions and improved service management. Autonomous vehicles and trains function with enhanced precision, hence decreasing delays and enhancing safety. Furthermore, these systems offer significant data that can be used for the purpose of strategizing and enhancing routes and timetables [48].

## 9.6 Application of MASs

MASs are utilized in marine and unmanned vehicle operations to achieve autonomous navigation, coordination, and control. MASs utilize a vast amount of agents to enhance efficiency, safety, and resilience. This section focuses on the use of MASs in ships and unmanned vehicles, which are designed to handle complex and dynamic situations that require high levels of coordination and flexibility. MAS is responsible for autonomous navigation, collision prevention, and successful mission execution [49].

### 9.6.1 Autonomous Surface Ships

By utilizing MASs, these ships can perform complex tasks without human supervision, leading to increased safety and operational efficiency [49]. Figure 9.3 illustrates the structure and flow of control in agent systems, emphasizing the interaction between different modules to provide seamless and secure navigation.

### 9.6.2 Unmanned Surface Vehicles

USVs employ sophisticated marine autonomous systems to autonomously navigate and function in unrestricted waters. These systems integrate sensors, communication devices, and algorithms to identify barriers, devise paths, and adapt in real time to prevent collisions [50]. Figure 9.3 depicts the arrangement and sequence of operations in agent systems, emphasizing the interactions between modules for the purpose of ensuring secure navigation.

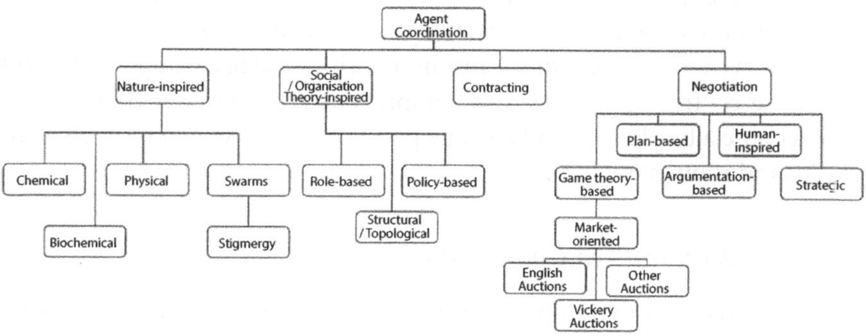


**Figure 9.3** Typical coordination models documented in research [39].

### 9.6.3 Swarm Robotics

Swarm robotics uses multiple autonomous robots working together more efficiently than individually. In marine and unmanned vehicle scenarios, swarms perform synchronized searches, survey underwater environments, or execute coordinated maneuvers. MAS-based control systems provide high fault tolerance and scalability, ideal for complex, large-scale missions [51].

### 9.6.4 Autonomous Underwater Vehicles

Autonomous underwater vehicles (AUVs) conduct underwater exploration and data collection independently. They map ocean floors, monitor marine life, and inspect infrastructure. MASs enable precise depth control, navigation, and sensor integration. AUVs reduce the need for human divers, enhancing safety and efficiency [52].

### 9.6.5 Hybrid MASs

Hybrid MASs integrate USVs, AUVs, and aerial drones to carry out intricate activities across several domains. A master of advanced studies in marine and unmanned operations provides the advantages of self-governance, flexibility, and efficiency. They do intricate tasks, adjust to dynamic settings, and function with minimal human intervention [53]. Table 9.2 illustrates the various uses and advantages of MASs in enhancing the functionalities of ships and unmanned vehicles.

### 9.6.6 Common Coordination Models in MAS

#### *9.6.6.1 Centralized Coordination*

Centralized coordination refers to the management of a system by a central actor or a small group. They engage in decision-making, assign tasks, and supervise the allocation of resources. This strategy is highly efficient when the central agent possesses comprehensive knowledge. However, it can become a bottleneck and a single point of failure, which restricts scalability and robustness [62].

#### *9.6.6.2 Decentralized Coordination*

Decentralized coordination involves the distribution of decision-making authority among all agents. Every individual utilizes local data and interacts

**Table 9.2** Collaborative systems for maritime and autonomous vehicles.

| Objective | Optimization goals | Approach | Task type | Controlled system | Remarks | Year | Authors |
|---|---|---|---|---|---|---|---|
| Autonegotiation, collision avoidance | Details not specified | Geometrical methods | Cooperation | Ship | Two ships encounter, might not be COLREGs compliant | 2008 | [54] |
| Formation control | APF path planning with sliding mode control | Leader-following consensus | Cooperation | USVs + UAV | Different task | 2021 | [55] |
| Collision avoidance in UAV swarms | Safety, energy consumption, response time | Multiagent reinforcement learning | Cooperation | UAV | Different control object | 2022 | [56] |
| Formation control | Sampled-data consensus protocol | Leader-following consensus | cooperation | USV | Different task | 2019 | [57] |
| Training a team of USVs | Optimizing agents' coordination decisions | Genetic-based fuzzy rule training algorithm | Cooperation | USV | Different task | 2019 | [58] |

*(Continued)*

**Table 9.2** Collaborative systems for maritime and autonomous vehicles. (*Continued*)

| Objective | Optimization goals | Approach | Task type | Controlled system | Remarks | Year | Authors |
|---|---|---|---|---|---|---|---|
| Maneuver negotiation | No optimization | Algorithms for automated lane change and distance keeping | Cooperation | Car | Concept stage | 2016 | [59] |
| Searching water region by a team of UUVs | Minimize the total time | UUV operation algorithm | Cooperation | UUV | different task | 2019 | [59] |
| Autonegotiation, collision avoidance | Best set of reciprocal trajectories | Evolutionary sets of safe trajectories | Cooperation | Ship | Concept stage | 2013 | [60] |
| Maneuver autonegotiation, collision avoidance | Best set of reciprocal trajectories | Evolutionary sets of safe trajectories | Cooperation | Ship | Data acquisition | 2015 | [61] |

with colleagues. This solution is capable of managing higher workloads and minimizing the chance of failure. However, it can be intricate and may require the use of advanced algorithms to ensure efficient synchronization [63].

#### *9.6.6.3 Hierarchical Coordination*

Hierarchical coordination combines elements of centralization and decentralization. Superior agents supervise subordinate ones, making judgments at different hierarchical levels. This method improves efficiency, scalability, and coordination across the entire system [64].

#### *9.6.6.4 Market-Based Coordination*

Market-based coordination uses economic concepts to distribute resources and assign responsibilities. Agents compete by submitting bids that are determined by their skills and schedule, and the bid with the highest value is selected as the winner. This promotes efficiency and is effective when resources are scarce. Nevertheless, it necessitates a well-defined assessment method and can be computationally intensive [65].

#### *9.6.6.5 Contract Net Protocol*

The contract net protocol is a coordinating mechanism utilized in MASs. Managers communicate assignments, subcontractors submit bids, and managers allocate contracts to the most suitable candidate [66]. The system is adaptable and allocates jobs in real time, but it necessitates effective communication and negotiation.

## 9.7 Autonomous Navigation Systems

Through the use of artificial intelligence (AI), ML, sensor fusion, and real-time data processing, ANSs enable vessels to navigate without human intervention. The following section provides a brief overview of the ANS, with an emphasis on USVs as the main focus [67, 68].

### 9.7.1 Examples of Recently Developed USVs

Various applications require USVs that are made possible by advancements in ANS. Such systems are widely used. Table 9.3 summarizes their

**Table 9.3** Recent developments in unmanned surface vehicles (USVs).

| Country | Application | Max speed | Length [m] | Mission endurance | Payload | USV | Ref. |
|---|---|---|---|---|---|---|---|
| Israel | Naval and security missions | 40 kn | 11 or 9 | >48 h | — | Protector | [69] |
| Israel | Military/defense | 60 kn | 11.9 | 350 nm | 2200 kg | Katana | [70] |
| USA | Ocean surveying | 6 kn | 7.5 | 25 days at 2 kn | 500 kg | C-Worker 7 | [71] |
| USA | Military/defense | 35 kn | 6.5 | — | — | C-Target 6 | [72] |
| USA | Military/defense | 50 kn | 9.6 | — | — | C-Target 9 | [73] |
| USA | Ocean surveying | 6.5 kn | 5.8 | 30 days | — | C-Worker 6 | [74] |
| Norway | Hydroacoustic applications | 12 kn | 8 | 20 days at 4 kn | — | Sounder | [75] |
| Poland | Military/defense | 30 kn | 5.7 | 8–130 h | 1000 kg | Edredon | [76, 77] |

essential features and capabilities, demonstrating the various applications and advantages of USVs with ANS.

ANSs are technological innovations that transform marine operations by enabling ships to navigate and execute tasks without human intervention. Table 9.4 provides a comprehensive overview of the various applications and advantages of these sophisticated systems.

Figure 9.4 depicts an ANS designed specifically for USVs. The system consists of:

- **Advanced sensor module** combines information from nautical charts, radars, AIS, stereo vision, lidars, and GPS.
- **Data fusion module** integrates sensor data to create an accurate representation of the environment.
- **Collision avoidance module** utilizes sophisticated algorithms to detect and carry out secure maneuvers in collaboration with the obstacle detection and avoidance system [86].
- **Route planning module** is responsible for determining a path based on both mission requirements and weather conditions.

**Table 9.4** Studies on autonomous maritime vessels.

| Years | Aim | Type of analysis/ experiments | Vessel category | Project | Ref. |
|---|---|---|---|---|---|
| 2017–2022 | Coastal navigation | Planned model testing and vessel operation | 79.5 m, fully electric container ship, 120 TEU | Yara Birkeland | [78] |
| 2016–2022 | Marine research and exploration | Scheduled Atlantic crossing for 2022 | 5-meter trimaran Mayflower 400 | MAS | [79] |
| 2016–2019 | Urban aquatic transportation | Comprehensive prototype development | 5 m, electric passenger ferry milliAmpère | Autoferry | [80] |
| 2015–2019 | Techniques for navigation and guidance | Large-scale experimental trials | Autonomous passenger ferries | Autosea | [81] |
| 2018 | Coastal navigation | Demonstration of a fully autonomous ferry | 53.8 m, ferry Finferries Falco | SVAN | [82] |
| 2015–2018 | Remote-controlled vessel | Concept validation through theoretical analysis | Not specified | AAWA | [83] |
| 2013 | Coastal navigation | Conceptual ship design | 60 m, 1300 DWT, battery-operated | ReVolt | [84] |
| 2012–2015 | Long-distance navigation, self-guided navigation | Feasibility study and theoretical evaluation | Dry bulk carrier, 75,000 DWT, speed: 16 knots | MUNIN | [85] |

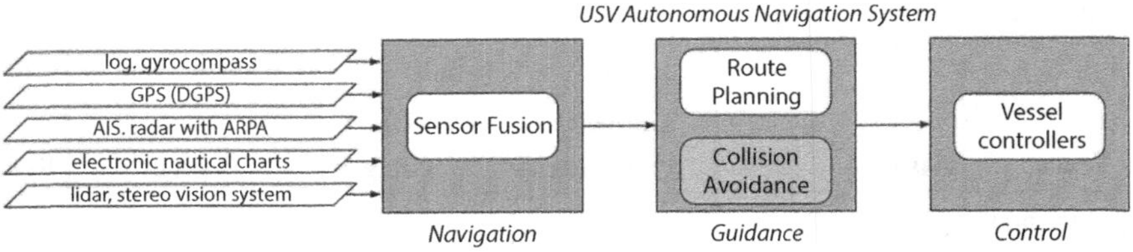


**Figure 9.4** Autonomous navigation system for unmanned surface vehicles (USVs) [2].

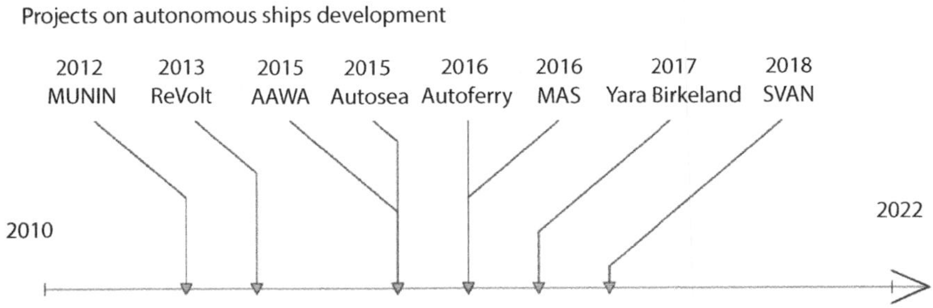


**Figure 9.5** Timeline of recent autonomous ship projects [2].

- **Motion control system** computes control forces to accurately track the intended trajectory or perform collision avoidance maneuvers.
- **Communication systems** facilitate instantaneous data exchange with other vessels and marine traffic control [87].

Figure 9.5 displays a chronological representation of recent endeavors in autonomous ship technology, such as MUNIN, FLAGSHIP, Kongsberg Maritime's project, and Rolls Royce's effort. It showcases the progress and significant achievements in this field [88].

## 9.8 Collision Avoidance Algorithms

Collision avoidance is essential for autonomous navigation, since it guarantees the safe functioning of USVs by preventing any instances of collisions. Multiple collision avoidance methods are available, each with unique benefits and constraints. This section analyzes these methodologies, contrasts various algorithms, and investigates the execution of the trajectory base algorithm (TBA) [89].

### 9.8.1 Comparison of Collision Avoidance Algorithms

Table 9.5 assesses different collision avoidance algorithms, with a specific emphasis on their application in maneuver autonegotiation systems. The methods are compared by evaluating their computational complexity, accuracy, and adaptability [90].

Table 9.6 extends this comparison, offering further perspectives on the efficacy and appropriateness of each method for various situations.

Table 9.6 demonstrates that certain algorithms outperform others in particular areas, such as having a low computational complexity or high accuracy. Meanwhile, some algorithms provide a well-rounded blend of qualities. The selection is contingent upon the particular requirements and limitations of the application [94].

**Table 9.5** Evaluation of collision avoidance algorithms for maneuver autonegotiation systems—part 1.

| COLREGs | Year | Type | Method | Dynamic obstacles | Static obstacles | Ref. |
|---|---|---|---|---|---|---|
| Priority determined according to COLREGs | 2013 | Deterministic | Cooperative Path Planning (CPP) | Basic and advanced encounters | Fixed point-based obstacles (buoys) | [91] |
| Penalties for COLREGs violations | 2012 | Stochastic | Evolutionary Sets of Safe Ship Trajectories (ESoSST) | Basic and advanced encounters | Coastal lines and shallow areas | [92] |
| Area influenced by COLREGs (CA) | 2010 | Stochastic | Evolutionary algorithm, Collision-Avoidance Negotiation FramewOrk (CANFO) | Basic and advanced encounters | Stationary vessel | [93] |
| Potentially noncompliant with COLREGs | 2008 | Deterministic | Collision-Avoidance Negotiation FramewOrk (CANFO) | Dual ship interactions | Not accounted for | [54] |
| COLREGs compliance enforced based on ship domain shape and size | 2022 | Deterministic | Trajectory Base Algorithm (TBA) | Basic and advanced encounters | Coastal lines, shallow areas, point-based obstacles | [2] |

**Table 9.6** Evaluation of collision avoidance algorithms for maneuver autonegotiation systems—part 2.

| Perspective | Year | Consistency | Execution time | Optimization parameters | Ref. |
|---|---|---|---|---|---|
| Views of both vessels | 2008 | Confirmed | Not specified | Information not provided | [54] |
| Consistency across all vessels' views | 2010 | Not confirmed | 200–800 seconds | Path length, average speed, travel time, engine adjustments | [93] |
| Perspective of the leading vessel | 2012 | Not confirmed—minor variations possible | Up to 1 minute | Minimum trajectory deviations in a set | [92] |
| Consistency across all vessels' views | 2013 | Confirmed | 7 seconds for complex scenarios | Course alteration of 30 degrees | [91] |
| Perspective of the leading vessel/all vessels | 2022 | Confirmed | Less than 1 second | Shortest possible path | [2] |

### 9.8.2 Implementation of TBA

The TBA is a predictive technique used to avoid collisions by anticipating the future courses of both the autonomous vessel and adjacent obstacles. TBA examines these paths to forecast collisions and modify the vessel's route.

Figure 9.6 depicts the TBA flowchart, which begins with input data regarding the courses, speeds, bearings, and distances of all vessels. A preliminary candidate trajectory is subsequently analyzed.

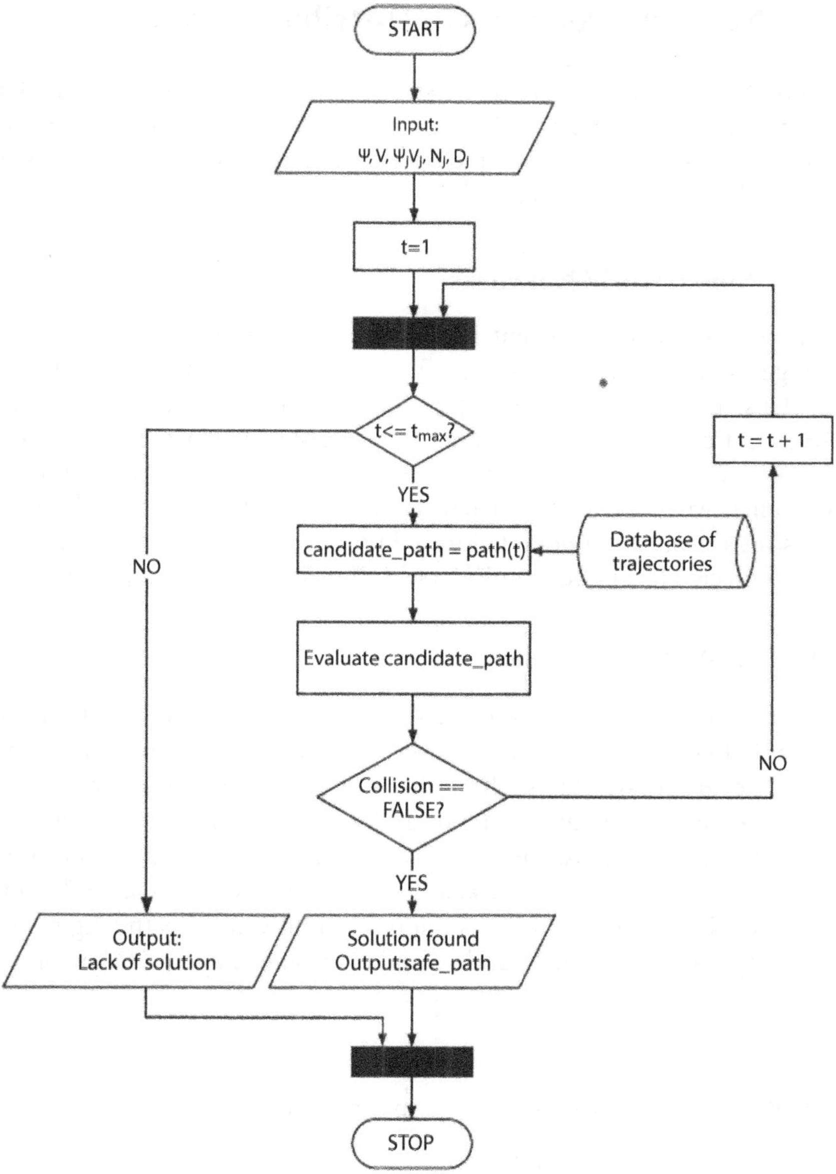


**Figure 9.6** Flowchart of the trajectory-based algorithm [2].

## 9.9 Network Properties in Distributed Systems

Comprehending the performance, stability, and scalability of distributed systems is dependent on their network characteristics. The concept of graph theory presents a structured approach to analyze these attributes, as outlined by Albert and Barabási [95] in Table 9.7.

### 9.9.1 Small-World Networks

Small-world networks exhibit high levels of local clustering and short average path lengths, facilitating efficient access to most nodes within a few steps. This architectural design, which is frequently used in social networks and certain distributed systems, achieves a balance between local interactions and long-range connections in order to improve communication. Small-world networks efficiently disseminate information and exhibit robustness against random failures through a combination of densely interconnected local nodes and sparsely connected global nodes [96].

### 9.9.2 Scale-Free Networks

Scale-free networks follow a power-law degree distribution, with a few nodes (hubs) having many connections and the majority having few. This trend appears in systems such as the Internet and biological networks. Scale-free networks may withstand random failures but are vulnerable to targeted attacks on hubs. Hubs are essential for communication and resilience, yet they offer a risk if hacked [97]. Table 9.7 examines several graph patterns, offering metrics such as unpredictability, mean path length, and clustering coefficient to help understand distributed systems' behavior.

**Table 9.7** Key characteristics of principal theoretical graph structures.

| Graph structure | Average path length | Randomness | Clustering coefficient |
|---|---|---|---|
| Scale free | Short | Moderately high | Medium |
| Small world | Medium | Moderate | High |
| Regular graph | Long | Structured | High |
| Random graph | Short | Unstructured | Low |

### 9.9.3 Robustness and Fault Tolerance

Scale-free networks are resistant to random failures due to their hub-centric topology, which ensures fault tolerance. Even after many failures, highly connected nodes maintain network functionality. However, they are subject to targeted hub attacks. Small-world networks with a high clustering coefficient are resistant to localized disturbances, resulting in improved local robustness [98].

### 9.9.4 Scalability

Both small-world and scale-free networks are very scalable. Small-world networks may accommodate new nodes without affecting their structure. Scale-free networks, with their power-law distribution, automatically handle growth by connecting new nodes to existing hubs while retaining network efficiency. Scalability is critical when extending dispersed systems, such as big IoT deployments [99].

### 9.9.5 Application-Specific Design

The network architecture chosen should be appropriate for the needs of the application. For example, a distributed system for analyzing massive datasets could benefit from a small-world network to improve data aggregation and processing. In contrast, a distributed sensor network for environmental monitoring might employ a scale-free architecture to improve robustness and data collecting [100]. Graph structures analyze network properties to provide insights into the design and optimization of distributed systems.

## 9.10 Challenges and Future Directions

Autonomous and adaptive distributed systems provide major development and deployment issues. Addressing these concerns is critical to guaranteeing scalability, security, privacy, and compatibility with emerging technology.

(1) **Scalability**: Scalability is a major difficulty in distributed systems, as it involves managing rising workloads by adding resources such as nodes or processing power. Systems must

retain performance and dependability without increasing complexity or cost.

(2) **Horizontal versus vertical scaling**: Horizontal scaling adds new nodes, but vertical scaling improves the resources of current nodes. Horizontal scaling is preferable due to its flexibility and fault tolerance, but it poses issues in network administration, data consistency, and load distribution [101].

(3) **Load balancing**: Distributing workloads across many nodes eliminates bottlenecks. It entails equally distributing duties and dynamically changing resource distribution in response to demand. Advanced methods, including ML, can forecast demand and optimize resource distribution [102].

(4) **Data consistency**: Maintaining consistent data across a big, dispersed network is difficult. Balancing eventual consistency, which allows for transient variations, and strong consistency, which ensures immediate uniformity but may compromise performance, is critical [103].

(5) **Scalability metrics and evaluation**: Throughput, latency, and fault tolerance are key scalability metrics and evaluation parameters. P2P systems have fast data transmission rates and error resilience, although they may have higher latency than client–server models. Edge computing combines high throughput with low latency, making it ideal for real-time applications.

### 9.10.1 Security and Privacy Considerations

Security and privacy are key considerations in distributed systems, especially as they grow increasingly networked. Ensuring security and preserving user data are critical to successful adoption.

(1) **Data encryption**: Encrypting data at rest and in transit is critical for preventing unauthorized access. End-to-end encryption and secure protocols (TLS/SSL) are widely utilized [104].

(2) **Access control**: Strong access control guarantees that only authorized users have access to resources. Role-based access control and attribute-based access control are popular methods for managing permissions [105].

(3) **Anomaly detection**: It is critical to detect and respond quickly to security risks. ML algorithms examine network traffic and system behavior to detect abnormalities that may suggest breaches, resulting in alerts and automated responses [106].

(4) **Privacy-preserving computation**: Protecting user privacy during data processing is difficult. Techniques such as differential privacy, homomorphic encryption, and secure multiparty computation enable data analysis while protecting individual privacy [107].

## 9.10.2 Integration with Emerging Technologies

Integrating dispersed systems with emerging technologies such as blockchain, AI, and the IoT creates new opportunities and difficulties.

### *9.10.2.1 Blockchain*

Blockchain offers a decentralized, secure method for managing transactions and data, improving transparency, security, and trust in distributed systems. However, solving the high computing requirements and scalability concerns is critical [108].

### *9.10.2.2 Artificial Intelligence*

AI improves distributed systems by enabling intelligent decision-making, predictive analytics, and automation. AI integration necessitates sophisticated data management and processing to accommodate high data volumes from distributed nodes [109].

### *9.10.2.3 Internet of Things*

The IoT is a network of interconnected devices that generate massive amounts of data that must be handled and analyzed quickly. Distributed systems offer the foundation for IoT applications, but they must be designed to withstand the tremendous size and complexity of IoT ecosystems [110].

Scalability, security, privacy, and interaction with emerging technologies are critical to the advancement of distributed systems. Advanced techniques and resilient frameworks can improve efficiency, dependability, and security, resulting in new breakthroughs and applications.

## 9.11 Conclusion

According to this study, the Internet could be transformed by utilizing autonomy and adaptive architectures in distributed systems. This demonstrated how decentralized MASs can increase flexibility, strength, and expansion. The use of solid frameworks in efficient operation was demonstrated by various architectural models, such as agent-based and hierarchical systems. Practical uses and advantages of MAS were showcased in smart grid, water distribution systems, and transportation case studies. In addition, the analysis of network properties in distributed systems demonstrated how graph designs affect performance and dependability. Collision avoidance algorithms, scalability, security, privacy, and integration with new technologies were identified as potential issues.

Implementation and management of distributed systems have been addressed in this article with helpful tips. MAS has been demonstrated to enhance system efficiency and reliability across various industries through detailed case studies. Understanding network characteristics is essential in the design of scalable, high-performance architectures. Safer autonomous systems require algorithms that avoid collisions and safeguard security and privacy. The research on MAS and adaptive architecture is established by this article. Comparing architectural models and graph structures contributes to more efficient and stable distributed systems. The focus of innovative research and development can be on scalability, security, and integration with emerging technology. By addressing these problems, distributed systems and applications can be greatly improved. Data indicate potential research areas. The growing size and complexity of distributed systems necessitate the implementation of advanced load balancing and data consistency measures. The use of hybrid methods can involve the integration of various scaling tactics. The connection between distributed systems demands security and privacy. Future research will need to focus on anomaly detection and better encryption and access control. Safeguarded data can be obtained through new privacy-preserving computation methods that enable appropriate analytics.

The integration of blockchain, AI, and IoT can enhance the performance of distributed systems. The improvement of dispersed systems can be achieved through the implementation of seamless integration by researchers. Whereas blockchain ensures transactions are secure and open, AI also offers intelligent decision-making and predictive analytics. Distributed systems become more flexible and efficient with the use of adaptive algorithms based on ML. Researchers should focus on developing algorithms that can learn from environmental data and modify system behavior in real time to enhance performance and resilience. With the growing prevalence of dispersed systems, energy and environmental effect must also be considered. Future research should concentrate on energy-efficient designs and sustainable behaviors to mitigate the impact of distributed system environmental effect. The benefits and drawbacks of autonomy and adaptive architectures are present in distributed systems. New research and practical implementations could help practitioners and researchers solve these problems and create more efficient, secure, and scalable distributed systems that will revolutionize multiple sectors.

## References


1. Julian, V. and Botti, V., Multi-Agent Systems. *Appl. Sci.*, 9, 7, 1402, 2019.
2. Lazarowska, A. and Żak, A., A Concept of Autonomous Multi-Agent Navigation System for Unmanned Surface Vessels. *Electronics*, 11, 18, 2853, 2022.
3. Arzovs, A., Judvaitis, J., Nesenbergs, K., Selavo, L., Distributed Learning in the IoT–Edge–Cloud Continuum. *Mach. Learn. Knowl. Extr.*, 6, 1, 283–315, 2024.
4. Marik, V., Gorodetsky, V., Skobelev, P., Multi-agent technology for industrial applications: Barriers and trends, in: *2020 ieee international conference on systems, man, and cybernetics (smc)*, 2020, October, IEEE, pp. 1980–1987.
5. Beckman, P., Dongarra, J., Ferrier, N., Fox, G., Moore, T., Reed, D., Beck, M., Harnessing the computing continuum for programming our world, in: *Fog Computing*, pp. 215–230, John Wiley & Sons, Ltd., Chichester, United Kingdom, 2020.
6. Jelen, G., Babic, J., Podobnik, V., A multi-agent system for context-aware electric vehicle fleet routing: A step towards more sustainable urban operations. *J. Clean. Prod.*, 374, 134047, 2022.
7. Nantogma, S., Zhang, S., Yu, X., An, X., Xu, Y., Multi-USV Dynamic Navigation and Target Capture: A Guided Multi-Agent Reinforcement Learning Approach. *Electronics*, 12, 7, 1523, 2023.
8. McKinnon, R.C., *The Cause, Effect, and Control of Accidental Loss*, CRC Press, Boca Raton, Florida, USA, 2023.
9. Forti, S., Bisicchia, G., Brogi, A., Declarative continuous reasoning in the cloud-IoT continuum. *J. Log. Comput.*, 32, 2, 206–232, 2022.
10. Srirama, S.N., A decade of research in fog computing: Relevance, challenges, and future directions. *Softw.: Pract. Exper.*, 54, 1, 3–23, 2024.
11. Donta, P.K., Murturi, I., Casamayor Pujol, V., Sedlak, B., Dustdar, S., Exploring the potential of distributed computing continuum systems. *Computers*, 12, 10, 198, 2023.

12. Koru, A.T., Ramírez, A., Sarsılmaz, S.B., Sipahi, R., Yucelen, T., Dogan, K.M., Containment Control of Multi-Human Multi-Agent Systems Under Time Delays. *IEEE Trans. Syst. Man Cybern.: Syst.*, 54, 3344–3356, 2024.
13. Bai, W., Zhang, W., Cao, L., Liu, Q., Adaptive control for multi-agent systems with actuator fault *via* reinforcement learning and its application on multi-unmanned surface vehicle. *Ocean Eng.*, 280, 114545, 2023.
14. Bisicchia, G., Forti, S., Pimentel, E., Brogi, A., Continuous QoS-compliant orchestration in the Cloud-Edge continuum. *Softw.: Pract. Exper.*, 54, 2191–2213, 2023.
15. Pearl, J. and Mackenzie, D., *The Book of Why: The New Science of Cause and Effect*, Basic Books, Inc., New York, New York, USA, 2018.
16. Villari, M., Fazio, M., Dustdar, S., Rana, O., Ranjan, R., Osmotic computing: A new paradigm for edge/cloud integration. *IEEE Cloud Comput.*, 3, 6, 76–83, 2016.
17. Kirchhoff, M., Parr, T., Palacios, E., Friston, K., Kiverstein, J., The Markov blankets of life: autonomy, active inference and the free energy principle. *J. R. Soc. Interface*, 15, 138, 20170792, 2018.
18. Gill, S.S., Wu, H., Patros, P., Ottaviani, C., Arora, P., Pujol, V.C., Haunschild, D., Parlikad, A.K., Cetinkaya, O., Lutfiyya, H., Stankovski, V., Modern computing: Vision and challenges. *Telemat. Inform. Rep.*, 13, 100116, 2024.
19. Danelutto, M., Dazzi, P., Torquati, M., Structuring the Continuum, in: *International Conference on Advanced Information Networking and Applications*, 2024, April, Springer Nature Switzerland, Cham, pp. 212–223.
20. Uslu, B.C. and Agent, M.A., The role of MAS interoperability for IoT applications: A survey on recent advances in manufacturing systems. *J. Fac. Eng. Archit. Gazi Univ.*, 38, 2, 1279–1297, 2023.
21. Xia, J., Luo, Y., Liu, Z., Zhang, Y., Shi, H., Liu, Z., Cooperative multi-target hunting by unmanned surface vehicles based on multi-agent reinforcement learning. *Def. Technol.*, 29, 80–94, 2023.
22. Herrera, J.L., Berrocal, J., Forti, S., Brogi, A., Murillo, J.M., Continuous QoS-aware adaptation of Cloud-IoT application placements. *Computing*, 105, 9, 2037–2059, 2023.
23. Niu, Y., Zhu, F., Wei, M., Du, Y., Zhai, P., A Multi-Ship Collision Avoidance Algorithm Using Data-Driven Multi-Agent Deep Reinforcement Learning. *J. Mar. Sci. Eng.*, 11, 11, 2101, 2023.
24. Keogh, K. and Sonenberg, L., Designing multi-agent system organisations for flexible runtime behaviour. *Appl. Sci.*, 10, 15, 5335, 2020.
25. Brewka, G., Artificial Intelligence—A Modern Approach by Stuart Russell and Peter Norvig, in: *Series in Artificial Intelligence*, vol. 11, pp. 78–79, Prentice Hall, Englewood Cliffs, NJ, USA, 1996.
26. Nwana, H.S., Software agents: An overview. *Knowl. Eng. Rev.*, 11, 3, 205–244, 1996.
27. Hexmoor, H., A model of absolute autonomy and power: Toward group effects. *Connect. Sci.*, 14, 4, 323–333, 2002.

28. Castelfranchi, C. and Falcone, R., From automaticity to autonomy: the frontier of artificial agents, in: *Agent autonomy*, pp. 103–136, 2003.
29. Franklin, S. and Graesser, A., Is it an Agent, or just a Program?: A Taxonomy for Autonomous Agents, in: *International workshop on agent theories, architectures, and languages*, 1996, August, Springer Berlin Heidelberg, Berlin, Heidelberg, pp. 21–35.
30. Wooldridge, M., Intelligent agents: The key concepts, in: *ECCAI Advanced Course on Artificial Intelligence*, pp. 3–43, Springer Berlin Heidelberg, Berlin, Heidelberg, 2001.
31. Macal, C.M. and North, M.J., Tutorial on agent-based modeling and simulation, in: *Proceedings of the Winter Simulation Conference*, 2005, December, IEEE, p. 14, 2005.
32. Hou, C., Data-Submission Control of Web Service-Based Multi-Agent System. *IEEE Trans. Serv. Comput.*, 17, 2165–2179, 2024.
33. Li, Y., Li, X., Wei, X., Wang, H., Sim-real joint experimental verification for an unmanned surface vehicle formation strategy based on multi-agent deterministic policy gradient and line of sight guidance. *Ocean Eng.*, 270, 113661, 2023.
34. Hudson, N., Khamfroush, H., Baughman, M., Lucani, D.E., Chard, K., Foster, I., QoS-aware edge AI placement and scheduling with multiple implementations in FaaS-based edge computing. *Future Gener. Comput. Syst.*, 157, 250–263, 2024.
35. Neha, B., Panda, S.K., Sahu, P.K., Sahoo, K.S., Gandomi, A.H., A systematic review on osmotic computing. *ACM Trans. Internet Things*, 3, 2, 1–30, 2022.
36. Pezzulo, G., D'Amato, L., Mannella, F., Priorelli, M., Van de Maele, T., Stoianov, I.P., Friston, K., Neural representation in active inference: Using generative models to interact with—and understand—the lived world. *Ann. N. Y. Acad. Sci.*, 1534, 1, 45–68, 2024.
37. Terra, M.B. and Gondim, J.J., NERD: a network exfiltration rootkit detector based on a multi-agent artificial immune system, in: *2021 Workshop on Communication Networks and Power Systems (WCNPS)*, 2021, November, IEEE, pp. 1–7.
38. Massa, J., Forti, S., Paganelli, F., Dazzi, P., Brogi, A., A declarative reasoning approach to conflict management in Intent-Based Networking, in: *2024 27th Conference on Innovation in Clouds, Internet and Networks (ICIN)*, 2024, March, IEEE, pp. 228–233.
39. Herrera, M., Pérez-Hernández, M., Kumar Parlikad, A., Izquierdo, J., Multi-agent systems and complex networks: Review and applications in systems engineering. *Processes*, 8, 3, 312, 2020.
40. Kimovski, D., Saurabh, N., Jansen, M., Aral, A., Al-Dulaimy, A., Bondi, A.B., Galletta, A., Papadopoulos, A.V., Iosup, A., Prodan, R., Beyond von neumann in the computing continuum: Architectures, applications, and future directions. *IEEE Internet Comput.*, 28, 6–16, 2023.

41. Russo, G.R., Ferrarelli, D., Pasquali, D., Cardellini, V., Presti, F.L., QoS-aware offloading policies for serverless functions in the Cloud-to-Edge continuum. *Future Gener. Comput. Syst.*, 156, 1–15, 2024.
42. Hou, C., Zhou, C., Wu, C.G., Cong, R., Li, K., Optimization of Cloud-Based Multi-Agent System for Trade-Off Between Trustworthiness of Data and Cost of Data Usage. *IEEE Trans. Autom. Sci. Eng.*, 21, 106–122, 2022.
43. Hu, G.J. and Vardanega, T., An architectural view on the compute continuum: Challenges and technologies, 2023, Available at SSRN 4328069.
44. Casamayor Pujol, V., Morichetta, A., Murturi, I., Kumar Donta, P., Dustdar, S., Fundamental research challenges for distributed computing continuum systems. *Information*, 14, 3, 198, 2023.
45. Park, J., Kang, M., Lee, Y., Jung, J., Choi, H.T., Choi, J., Multiple Autonomous Surface Vehicles for Autonomous Cooperative Navigation Tasks in a Marine Environment: Development and Preliminary Field Tests. *IEEE Access*, 11, 36203–36217, 2023.
46. Pujol, V.C., Donta, P.K., Morichetta, A., Murturi, I., Dustdar, S., Edge intelligence—research opportunities for distributed computing continuum systems. *IEEE Internet Comput.*, 27, 4, 53–74, 2023.
47. Kaur, A., Kumar, R., Saxena, S., Osmotic computing and related challenges: A survey, in: *2020 Sixth International Conference on Parallel, Distributed and Grid Computing (PDGC)*, 2020, November, IEEE, pp. 378–383.
48. Wright, J. and Bourke, P., Markov Blankets and Mirror Symmetries—Free Energy Minimization and Mesocortical Anatomy. *Entropy*, 26, 4, 287, 2024.
49. Sharma, V., Jayakody, D.N.K., Qaraqe, M., Osmotic computing-based service migration and resource scheduling in Mobile Augmented Reality Networks (MARN). *Future Gener. Comput. Syst.*, 102, 723–737, 2020.
50. Oliveira, S., Badarnah, L., Barakat, M., Chatzimichali, A., Atkins, E., Beyond energy services: A multidimensional and cross-disciplinary agenda for home energy management research. *Energy Res. Social Sci.*, 85, 102347, 2022.
51. Bueno, A., Rubio, B., Martín, C., Díaz, M., Functions as a service for distributed deep neural network inference over the cloud-to-things continuum. *Softw.: Pract. Exper.*, 54, 1297–1311, 2024.
52. Bocci, A., Forti, S., Brogi, A., Sustainable Cloud-Edge Infrastructure as a Service, in: *2023 12th Mediterranean Conference on Embedded Computing (MECO)*, 2023, June, IEEE, pp. 1–4.
53. Liu, Y., Liu, J., He, Z., Li, Z., Zhang, Q., Ding, Z., A survey of multi-agent systems on distributed formation control. *Unmanned Syst.*, 12, 1–14, 2023.
54. López Escobar, J.J., Díaz-Redondo, R.P., Gil-Castiñeira, F., Unleashing the power of decentralized serverless IoT dataflow architecture for the Cloud-to-Edge Continuum: a performance comparison. *Ann. Telecommun.*, 79, 1–14, 2024.
55. Hu, Q., Yang, C., Cheng, H., Xiao, B., Planned Route Based Negotiation for Collision Avoidance Between Vessels. *TransNav: Int. J. Mar. Navig. Saf. Sea Transp.*, 2, 4, 363–368, 2008.

56. Xue, K. and Wu, T., Distributed consensus of USVs under heterogeneous UAV-USV multi-agent systems cooperative control scheme. *J. Mar. Sci. Eng.*, 9, 11, 1314, 2021.
57. Huang, S., Zhang, H., Huang, Z., Multi-UAV Collision Avoidance using Multi-Agent Reinforcement Learning with Counterfactual Credit Assignment, 2022, arXiv preprint arXiv:2204.08594.
58. Wang, L., Yue, W., Zhang, R., Consensus for multiple unmanned surface vehicle (MUSV) systems with Markov switching topologies. *Pol. Marit. Res.*, 26, 1, 145–152, 2019.
59. Han, W., Zhang, B., Wang, Q., Luo, J., Ran, W., Xu, Y., A multi-agent based intelligent training system for unmanned surface vehicles. *Appl. Sci.*, 9, 6, 1089, 2019.
60. Zak, A., Control of unmanned underwater vehicle as a member of vehicles team performing a given task. *Trans. Marit. Sci.*, 8, 01, 18–25, 2019.
61. Hornauer, S. and Hahn, A., Towards marine collision avoidance based on automatic route exchange. *IFAC Proc. Vol.*, 46, 33, 103–107, 2013.
62. Szlapczynska, J., Data acquisition in a manoeuver auto-negotiation system. *TransNav: Int. J. Mar. Navig. Saf. Sea Transp.*, 9, 3, 343–348, 2015.
63. Sadeeq, M.A. and Zeebaree, S., Energy management for internet of things *via* distributed systems. *J. Appl. Sci. Technol. Trends*, 2, 02, 80–92, 2021.
64. Donta, P.K., Sedlak, B., Casamayor Pujol, V., Dustdar, S., Governance and sustainability of distributed continuum systems: A big data approach. *J. Big Data*, 10, 1, 53, 2023.
65. Michalitsi-Psarrou, A., Papageorgiou, I.L., Ntanos, C., Psarras, J., Agent-Based Simulation to Measure the Effectiveness of Citizen Sensing Applications—The Case of Missing Children. *Appl. Sci.*, 11, 14, 6530, 2021.
66. Qiao, Y., Yin, J., Wang, W., Duarte, F., Yang, J., Ratti, C., Survey of deep learning for autonomous surface vehicles in marine environments. *IEEE Trans. Intell. Transp. Syst.*, 24, 4, 3678–3701, 2023.
67. Massa, J., Forti, S., Paganelli, F., Dazzi, P., Brogi, A., Declarative Provisioning of Virtual Network Function Chains in Intent-based Networks, in: *2023 IEEE 9th International Conference on Network Softwarization (NetSoft)*, 2023, June, IEEE, pp. 522–527.
68. Sharma, M., Tomar, A., Hazra, A., Edge computing for industry 5.0: fundamental, applications and research challenges. *IEEE Internet Things J.*, 11, 19070–19093, 2024.
69. Mahapatra, A., Mishra, K., Pradhan, R., Majhi, S.K., Next generation task offloading techniques in evolving computing paradigms: Comparative analysis, current challenges, and future research perspectives. *Arch. Comput. Methods Eng.*, 31, 3, 1405–1474, 2024.
70. Wu, H. and Wang, J., Distributed information fusion based trajectory tracking for USV and UAV clusters *via* multi-agent deep learning approach. *Aerosp. Syst.*, 7, 1–15, 2024.

71. Lazarowska, A. and Żak, A., Real-time path planning for Autonomous Navigation Systems of Unmanned Surface Vehicles, in: *2022 26th International Conference on Methods and Models in Automation and Robotics (MMAR)*, 2022, August, IEEE, pp. 408–413.
72. Available online: https://www.l3harris.com/all-capabilities/c-target-7-asv (accessed on 28 May 2024).
73. Available online: https://www.l3harris.com/all-capabilities/c-target-6-asv (accessed on 28 May 2024).
74. Available online: https://www.l3harris.com/all-capabilities/c-target-9-asv (accessed on 28 May 2024).
75. Available online: https://www.unmannedsystemstechnology.com/company/autonomous-surface-vehicles-ltd/ (accessed on 28 May 2024).
76. Kongsberg Maritime Ltd., Sounder USV, Available online: https://www.kongsberg.com/maritime/products/marine-robotics/uncrewed-surface-vehicle-sounder/ (accessed on 28 May 2024).
77. Kalinowski, A. and Małecki, J., Polish USV 'EDREDON'and non-European USV: a comparative sketch. *J. Mar. Eng. Technol.*, 16, 4, 416–419, 2017.
78. Kang, Z., Gao, M., Liao, Z., Zhang, A., Collaborative communication-based ocean observation research with heterogeneous unmanned surface vessels. *Front. Mar. Sci.*, 11, 1388617, 2024.
79. Kliushnikov, I., МЕТОД ВИЗНАЧЕННЯ СТРУКТУРИ ТА СКЛАДУ МУЛЬТИАГЕНТНОЇ СИСТЕМИ МОНІТОРИНГУ МАЛИХ МОДУЛЬНИХ РЕАКТОРІВ ПОБУДОВАНОЇ НА ОСНОВІ БЕЗПІЛОТНИХ ЛІТАЛЬНИХ АПАРАТІВ. ***Системи управління навігації та зв'язку. Збірник наукових праць***, 4, 74, 22–29, 2023.
80. Kongsberg, YARA Birkeland—Autonomous Ship Project, Available online: https://www.kongsberg.com/maritime/support/themes/autonomous-ship-project-key-facts-about-yara-birkeland/ (accessed on 28 May 2024).
81. Promare, Mayflower Autonomous Ship (MAS), Available online: https://mas400.com (accessed on 28 May 2024).
82. NTNU, Autoferry—Autonomous All-Electric Passenger Ferries for Urban Water Transport, Available online: https://www.ntnu.edu/autoferry (accessed on 28 May 2024).
83. NTNU, Autosea—Sensor Fusion and Collision Avoidance for Autonomous Surface Vehicles, Available online: https://www.ntnu.edu/autosea/ (accessed on 28 May 2024).
84. Rolls-Royce, SVAN—Safer Vessel with Autonomous Navigation, 2018, Available online: https://breakingwaves.fi/wp-content/uploads/2019/06/SVAN-presentation.pdf (accessed on 28 May 2024).
85. Rolls-Royce, Remote and Autonomous Ship—The Next Step, Available online: https://www.rolls-royce.com/~/media/Files/R/Rolls-Royce/documents/customers/marine/ship-intel/aawa-whitepaper-210616.pdf (accessed on 28 May 2024).

86. DNV GL, The ReVolt. A New Inspirational Ship Concept, Available online: https://www.dnvgl.com/technology-innovation/revolt/index.html (accessed on 28 May 2024).
87. MUNIN, Maritime Unmanned Navigation through Intelligence in Networks, Available online: http://www.unmanned-ship.org/munin/about/ (accessed on 28 May 2024).
88. Balouek-Thomert, D., Perez, I., Faulstich, S.D., Holmes, H.A., Altintas, I., Parashar, M., Keynote Talk: Leveraging the Edge-Cloud Continuum to Manage the Impact of Wildfires on Air Quality, in: *2023 IEEE International Conference on Pervasive Computing and Communications Workshops and other Affiliated Events (PerCom Workshops)*, 2023, March, IEEE, pp. 27–31.
89. Brogi, A., Microservices Beyond COVID-19, in: *Joint Post-proceedings of the Third and Fourth International Conference on Microservices (Microservices 2020/2022)*, Schloss-Dagstuhl-Leibniz Zentrum für Informatik, 2023.
90. Rebol, M. and Pietroszek, K., Artificial Reality Continuum, in: *Encyclopedia of Computer Graphics and Games*, pp. 126–132, Springer International Publishing, Cham, 2024.
91. Podile, V., Kulshrestha, N., Goswami, S., Durga, L., Rachanasree, B., Reddy, T.P., Sarojini, P.S., The Future of Business Management with the Power of Distributed Systems and Computing, in: *Meta-Heuristic Algorithms for Advanced Distributed Systems*, vol. 1, p. 1, 2024.
92. Chaysri, P., Spatharis, C., Blekas, K., Vlachos, K., Unmanned surface vehicle navigation through generative adversarial imitation learning. *Ocean Eng.*, 282, 114989, 2023.
93. Tam, C. and Bucknall, R., Cooperative path planning algorithm for marine surface vessels. *Ocean Eng.*, 57, 25–33, 2013.
94. Szlapczynski, R. and Szlapczynska, J., On evolutionary computing in multi-ship trajectory planning. *Appl. Intell.*, 37, 155–174, 2012.
95. Albert, R. and Barabási, A.L., Statistical mechanics of complex networks. *Rev. Mod. Phys.*, 74, 1, 47, 2002.
96. Parashar, M., Cloud2Things 2023: 3rd Workshop on From Cloud to Things: harnessing pervasive data in the Computing Continuum-Program.
97. Repetto, M., Interface To Security Functions: An Overview And Comparison Of I2nsf And Openc2. *IEEE Commun. Stand. Mag.*, 7, 4, 60–67, 2023.
98. Tam, C. and Bucknall, R., Path-planning algorithm for ships in close-range encounters. *J. Mar. Sci. Technol.*, 15, 395–407, 2010.
99. Boccaletti, S., Latora, V., Moreno, Y., Chavez, M., Hwang, D.U., Complex networks: Structure and dynamics. *Phys. Rep.*, 424, 4–5, 175–308, 2006.
100. Newman, M.E., The structure of scientific collaboration networks. *Proc. Natl. Acad. Sci.*, 98, 2, 404–409, 2001.
101. Terra, M.B.D.S., NERD (Network Exfiltration Rootkit Detector): um sistema imune artificial multi-agente para detecção de rootkits por exfiltração em rede, 2021.

102. Sowiński, P., Lacalle, I., Vaño, R., Palau, C.E., Autonomous Choreography of WebAssembly Workloads in the Federated Cloud-Edge-IoT Continuum, in: *2023 IEEE 12th International Conference on Cloud Networking (CloudNet)*, 2023, November, IEEE, pp. 454–459.
103. Monti, F., Rinderle-Ma, S., Cortés, A.R., Zheng, Z., Mecella, M. (Eds.), *Service-Oriented Computing: 21st International Conference, ICSOC 2023, Rome, Italy, November 28–December 1, 2023, Proceedings, Part I*, vol. 14419, Springer Nature, 2023.
104. Raghav, Y.Y. and Kait, R., Edge Computing Empowering Distributed Computing at the Edge, in: *Emerging Trends in Cloud Computing Analytics, Scalability, and Service Models*, pp. 67–83, IGI Global, Hershey, Pennsylvania, USA, 2024.
105. Martins, A.B., Recomendação de Pontos de Interesse para Grupos-Uma Abordagem baseada em Sistemas Multi-Agente e no Feedback dos Turistas (Doctoral dissertation), 2023.
106. Finocchio, F., Tonci, N., Torquati, M., MTCL: a multi-transport communication library, in: *European Conference on Parallel Processing*, 2023, August, Springer Nature Switzerland, Cham, pp. 55–67.
107. Freed, M., Bielinska, S., Buckley, C., Coptu, A., Yilmaz, M., Messnarz, R., Clarke, P.M., An Investigation of Green Software Engineering, in: *European Conference on Software Process Improvement*, 2023, August, Springer Nature Switzerland, Cham, pp. 124–137.
108. Selmi, I., Kabachi, N., Ben Abdallah, S., Ghedira Guegan, C., Baazaoui, H., Adaptive Multi-agent-based Alert System for Diseases' Detection, in: *Advanced Information Networking and Applications: Proceedings of the 34th International Conference on Advanced Information Networking and Applications (AINA-2020)*, Springer International Publishing, pp. 734–745, 2020.
109. Abdelmoniem, A.M., Leveraging The Edge-to-Cloud Continuum for Scalable Machine Learning on Decentralized Data, 2023, arXiv preprint arXiv:2306.10848.
110. Segumpan, R.G. and Zahari, J.S.A. (Eds.), *Mixed Methods Perspectives on Communication and Social Media Research*, Routledge, London, United Kingdom, 2023.

# 10

# Distributed Consensus Frequency Control in Networked Microgrid

**Jeevitha Kandasamy[1]*, J. Jenitha[2], M.R. Mohanraj[3], Jenifer Amla. L.[4], G. Mahalakshmi[1] and Ponrekha M.[5]**

[1]*Department of Electrical and Electronics Engineering, Sri Krishna College of Engineering and Technology, Kovaipudur, Coimbatore, India*
[2]*Department of Electrical and Electronics Engineering, Adhiyamaan College of Engineering, Hosur, Tamil Nadu, India*
[3]*JKKN College of Engineering and Technology, Komarapalayam, Tamil Nadu, India*
[4]*Department of Electrical and Electronics Engineering, Karpagam College of Engineering, Myleripalayam, Coimbatore, Tamil Nadu, India*
[5]*Department of Electrical and Electronics Engineering, Karpagam Academy of Higher Education, Coimbatore, Tamil Nadu, India*

## *Abstract*
Microgrids (MGs) have been more well-known recently as practical answers to a variety of energy-related problems, helping to move away from conventional centralized energy distribution systems. Utilizing waste heat optimally, integrating renewable energy (RE) sources with zero emissions, managing power supply and demand effectively, and enhancing grid resilience in unfavorable environmental circumstances are just a few of the benefits of MGs. Although they have advantages, variations in energy supply and load demand might cause stability problems for individual MGs. In order to overcome this, nearby MGs can be linked together to create a networked MG, which will increase the system's overall flexibility and dependability. This research work employs time-domain simulation to analyze the stability of networked microgrid (NMG) systems, with a focus on frequency of operation. The primary loop of load frequency control (LFC), which regulates frequency variations in the event of minor disturbances, is essential for preserving frequency stability. In the event of network islanding, the LFC secondary loop brings the system frequency back to normal. In the past, researchers have regulated the frequency of NMGs both centrally and decentralically using conventional

**Corresponding author*: jeevivijaya19@gmail.com

Sandhya Avasthi and Suman Lata Tripathi (eds.) Distributed and Parallel Computing, (219–234)

controllers. However, recent focus has switched toward artificial neural network distributed consensus frequency control because of limited adaptability of artificial intelligence (AI). With the help of distributed consensus control, this research work proposes FOPID (fractional-order proportional integral derivative) adaptive distributed controller as a distributed manner for cooperative MG operation in NMGs, which require distributed computing to function and be controlled effectively. Distributed computing allows for improved control mechanisms, real-time data processing, scalability, and enhanced dependability through the use of adaptive distributed controllers and AI. The suggested controller performs better when managing disruptions such as changes in RE sources and load perturbation.

***Keywords***: Artificial neural network, fractional-order proportional integral derivative adaptive controller, distributed control, networked microgrid

## 10.1 Introduction

A microgrid (MG) is a defined, small-scale electrical network that operates as a cohesive, controllable system. It can operate alone in island mode or grid connected. An isolated MG is one that runs completely off the grid and is unable to connect to a larger electrical grid. Nanogrids are the lowest versions of MGs. Networked MG is the interconnection of MG cluster as shown in Figure 10.1. Grid-connected MGs usually run in parallel with the conventional wider-area synchronous grid, but they can also separate and function independently in island mode when necessary due to technical. With this capability, the MG area's supply security is improved, allowing it to function as an emergency power source and smoothly switch between connected and islanded modes [1].

An MG that is self-sufficient generates electricity on its own and is supported by an energy storage system. It is used in areas where it is costly and impractical to transmit power from a centralized source. Small islands and isolated rural regions would benefit greatly from this technique for accessing electricity [2]. Additionally, a self-sufficient MG skillfully integrates various dispersed generation sources, particularly renewable energy sources. MGs face difficulties in managing control and protection since they are required to produce all ancillary services in-house for system stability [3–5]. Furthermore, with low short-circuit levels, selectively functioning protection systems can be challenging. Meeting demands for energy that go beyond electricity, including heating and cooling, is another crucial component. This adaptability promotes cross-sectoral energy consumption by allowing the

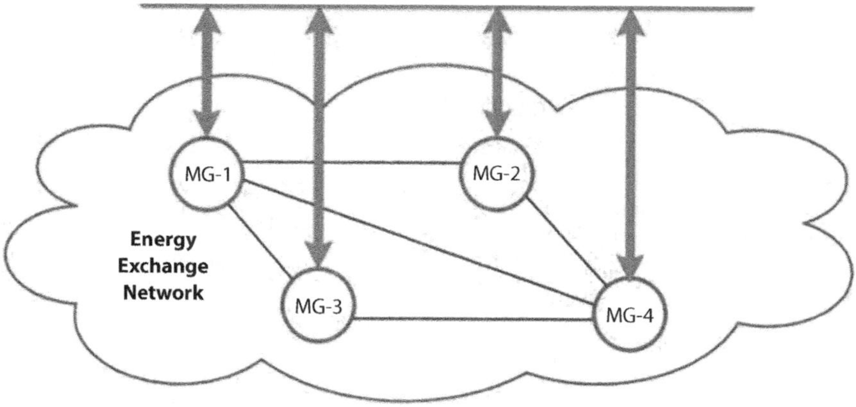


**Figure 10.1** Interconnected microgrid.

replacement of energy carriers and improving efficiency through the use of waste heat for home hot water, heating, and cooling.

MGs can be categorized into three primary topologies based on the different architectures that are necessary to manage the energy flow from various sources into the electrical grid.

**AC MG**: Using AC/AC converters to link sources of power with AC output to the AC terminal, power sources can modify the frequency and voltage as required. DC/AC converters are needed for connecting sources of power having DC output to the AC bus.
**DC MG**: DC/DC converters are used to connect DC output power sources either directly with the DC bus or through them. Through AC/DC converters, AC output sources are integrated with the DC bus. The schematic diagram of AC and DC bus system is shown in Figure 10.2.
**Hybrid MG**: This MG has a bidirectional converter that makes it easier for the AC and DC buses to exchange electricity [6–8].

In order to efficiently manage power sharing inside MG, a number of research employed distributed control to maintain the frequency of the MG. Recent advances in control systems have greatly benefited from the capabilities of neural network (NN). There are significant obstacles, even though a few research have used NN for constructing fractional-order proportional integral derivative (FOPID) and PID controllers utilizing traditional gradient algorithms for load frequency control (LFC) applications.

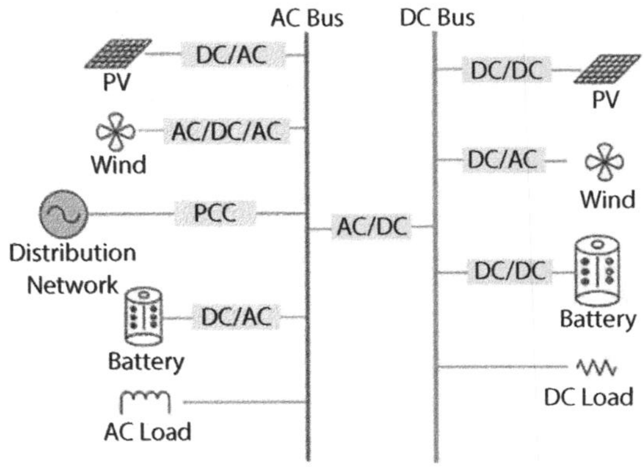


**Figure 10.2** Schematic diagram of AC and DC bus system.

The gradient approach frequently requires unreasonably long training times, and there are no organized methods for gain initialization. Furthermore, there are problems with traditional gradient-based tuning methods, which can lead to the system being unstable. The conventional tuning methods such as particle swarm optimization (PSO) [9–12], gravity search algorithm (GSA) [13–15], and moth flame optimization (MFO) [16–18] are used to obtain the gain parameters of various controller. Artificial neural network (ANN) optimization of controller gains may be able to resolve these problems. PID controller tuning is commonly done using PSO technique. This approach optimizes the controller settings to meet desired system performance, drawing inspiration from the social behavior of fish schools and flocks of birds. In PSO-oriented PID tuning, probable solutions are represented in the realm of parameters by a group of particles. The locations of distinct particles, which are modified based on their own and nearby experiences, serve as a representation of the control parameters. Reducing a cost function typically associated with performance standards or system flaws is the ultimate objective. Iterative updates bring particles closer to the optimal PID settings, increasing the precision, security, and speed of response of the system. Driven by the gravitational pull among celestial bodies, GSA provides a different approach to optimizing PID controllers. To maximize PID settings, this method models the interaction of gravity between collections of solutions, like in celestial bodies in a gravitational field. In GSA-based PID tuning, each solution represents a potential set of PID parameters, and their performance is evaluated using a specified objective variable related to system performance.

Solutions gravitate toward one another, just like heavenly planets do; stronger remedies, or others with better outcomes, have a larger effect.

Like bodies gravitationally attracted to one another, solutions are repeatedly modified toward regions of greatest efficiency. PID controllers are optimized using a metaheuristic approach. MFO improves PID settings by replicating the relationships between magnetic dipoles and taking cues from the way magnetic forces behave in the natural world. In MFO-based PID tuning, each solution's performance is evaluated in relation to a set of PID parameters using a predefined fitness equation according to system performance criteria. Solutions interact with each other by repelled and appealing interactions that depend on their distances and fitness levels, just like magnetic dipoles do. Through iterative updates, solutions migrate toward regions of superior fitness, much like dipoles of magnets align in a field of magnetic attraction.

For a variety of applications, ANNs offer a number of advantages. They excel in being adaptable, accurately simulating complex nonlinear relationships, and handling data in parallel to expedite calculations. ANNs replace human feature engineers because they are resistant against noise and can generalize learned patterns to new data. They can scale to handle large datasets and are versatile, appropriate for a variety of applications from control to classification. Because of these qualities, ANNs are great tools for precisely and quickly resolving a variety of real-world problems. This research provides an adaptive ANN technique to build a distributed FOPID controller for managing the frequency of the NMG system.

By employing ANNs to generate the initial gain values, the NN-based FOPID controller's robustness is increased. The energy distribution of the ANN is reduced by using a neural technique, which improves the NMG system's capacity to control frequency. Distributed computing can improve the efficiency and dependability of NMGs. Distributed computing is an interdisciplinary approach to computational tasks to allow for the combination and control of multiple MGs within a larger network. This approach is critical for addressing several energy-related concerns, such as optimizing the use of waste heat, integrating carbon-free sources of clean energy, and ensuring effective control of supply as well as demand for electricity.

One of the primary functions of machines in NMGs is their ability to handle real-time data processing and analysis. This capacity is necessary to maintain grid stability and dependability, especially in the face of changing energy supplies and varying load requirements. Distributed computing enables the continuous monitoring and prompt response necessary for the successful oversight of these dynamic settings. Distributed computing also increases the durability of NMGs by distributing control tasks among multiple nodes. This decentralization increases the system's overall resiliency and ensures that it can continue to operate even in the case of a node failure. Advanced control systems such as FOPID configuration adaptive distributed controlling systems and ANN distributed group decision control require distributed computing's flexibility and processing capacity. Within the context of LFC, distributed computing enables the effective operation of the network's two main loops of control. The fast resolution of variations in frequency and the prompt return of the network's frequency to its initial values following disruptions are ensured by the deployment of a distributed method. The stability and dependability of NMGs are largely dependent on distributed computing, which supports these complex control mechanisms. The following sums up this paper's main contributions:

- The design of a distributed FOPID controller that is adaptive and uses ANNs to control the frequency of NMG systems
- Assessing the suggested controller performance in various circumstances and looking into how well it can adjust to changes in load demand
- Evaluation of the suggested ANN-based FOPID control method for NMG systems in comparison to conventional techniques for fine-tuning FOPID and PID controllers

This chapter is ordered as follows:

Section 10.2 describes the transfer function of the NMG model. Section 10.3 describes the design of proposed controller. Section 10.4 focuses on results and discussion and the last section concludes the work and suggests directions for future research.

## 10.2 System Model

An NMG, which consists of three identical MGs; is the system that is being studied in this chapter. Every MG incorporates distributed generators (DGs) with capacities of 250, 250, and 400 kW for wind, sun, and biodiesel sources, respectively. Each MG has a total installed capacity of 1 MW as a result. To improve grid stability and energy management, each MG includes an energy storage device in the form of a 100-kW battery. Every MG's DGs and energy etorage system (ESSs) are linearized under particular operating circumstances to make frequency analysis and system modeling easier. A more straightforward depiction of the components' dynamic behavior is made possible by this linearization technique, which facilitates a thorough examination of the frequency response and system performance. Through the integration of these linearized models, scholars may get a deeper understanding of the behavior of the NMG in diverse circumstances, hence aiding in the creation of efficient control tactics and operational protocols for forthcoming MG deployments. Below are the small-signal models that were produced following linearization for each MG:

Solar power generation (SPG):

$$G_{\mathrm{SPG}}(s) = \frac{K_{\mathrm{SPG}}}{1 + sT_{\mathrm{SPG}}} \tag{10.1}$$

Wind power generation (WPG):

$$G_{\mathrm{WPG}}(s) = \frac{K_{\mathrm{WPG}}}{1 + sT_{\mathrm{WPG}}} \tag{10.2}$$

Biodiesel power generation (BDPG):

$$G_{\mathrm{BDPG}}(s) = \frac{K_{\mathrm{VA}}}{(1 + sT_{\mathrm{VA}})} \frac{K_{\mathrm{BD}} K_{\mathrm{BE}}}{(1 + sT_{\mathrm{BE}})} \tag{10.3}$$

The Appendix contains information on the system parameters in detail.

## 10.3 Distributed Control Technique

This section outlines the distributed control developed for the NMG system. It provides a detailed description of the ANN-designed FOPID controller for all MGs.

The following dynamics are used to establish consent between MGs about the upkeep of system frequency through the use of a basic consensus technique and its derivative $\dot{x}_i = u_i$, as follows:

$$\dot{x}_i = a_{ij}(f_i - f_j) \tag{10.4}$$

The frequency at $i^{\mathrm{th}}$ MG and $j^{\mathrm{th}}$ MG is represented by $f_i$ and $f_j$.

The inertia response of MG greatly affects its frequency stability. In the event of load imbalances or variations, the system's intrinsic inertia plays a critical role in maintaining the frequency of the MG. In order to reduce frequency fluctuations inside the MG, the inertia control stage acts as the main defensive mechanism against load changes. The kinetic energy contained in the spinning generator components determines the inertia constant of a conventional system.

### 10.3.1 ANN Tuned FOPID Distributed Controller

The energy function for distributed control of NMG is formulated using a Lyapunov-based approach, which characterizes the behavior of NN as follows:

$$E = \frac{1}{2} e(t)_i^2 \tag{10.5}$$

In distributed manner, the controller controls the MG's frequency ($f_i$) in order to achieve a stable system.

The output of distributed FOPID controller is:

$$u_i(t) = K_{pi}(f_i - f_j) + K_{ii}\, D^{-\lambda}(f_i - f_j) + K_{di} D^{\mu}(f_i - f_j) \tag{10.6}$$

where $K_{pi}$, $K_{ii}$, and $K_{di}$ are the FOPID controller of $i^{th}$ NMG. $\lambda$ and $\mu$ are the fractional orders.

A better edition of the traditional PID controller that provides more resilience and flexibility for managing dynamic systems is FOPID controller. With the FOPID controller, fractional calculus concepts are applied, permitting noninteger values in its parameters, in contrast to the integer-order PID controller, which uses integer values for its derivative, integral, and proportional gains. FOPID controllers provide for more accurate modifications to the dynamics of the system due to the fractional orders in the proportional, integral, and derivative terms [21–23]. This is especially useful in situations where standard PID controllers can find it difficult to achieve satisfactory results. Fractional orders allow the FOPID controller to capture noninteger dynamics and extended memory systems, among other complicated system phenomena. Iterative optimization approaches or specific tuning methods are frequently used to determine the ideal fractional orders and gains for FOPID controllers in order to achieve the desired system performance. Applications for FOPID controllers may be found in many domains, such as biomedical engineering, robotics, aerospace, and process control, where accurate and reliable management of dynamic systems is crucial.

The three primary layer types that make up an ANN architecture [19, 20] are the input layer, hidden layer or layers, and output layer as shown in Figure 10.3. Without any feedback loops, data move from the input layer to the output layer *via* one or more hidden layers in a feedforward ANN. Below is a brief explanation of every layer:

**Input layer**: Data characteristics or input variables are represented by neurons in the input layer. Each input layer neuron is associated with a single input data characteristic. In the input layer, the dimensionality of the input data dictates how many neurons are present.
**Hidden layer**: It processes the incoming data by sitting between the input and output layers. All of the neurons in the preceding layer, either the input layer or another hidden layer, send inputs to each neuron in a hidden layer, which then computes the weighted total of these inputs. Before being sent to the following layer, each neuron's output is subsequently processed by an activation function. The intricacy of the issue and the intended model performance might affect how many hidden layers and neurons there are in each hidden layer.
**Output layer**: Using the calculations carried out in the hidden layers, the output layer generates the predictions or outputs of the network. The type of prediction job determines how many neurons are in the output layer. In a regression work, for example, there would be one neuron for each continuous output variable, but in a classification task with two classes, there would normally be one neuron in the output layer representing each class.

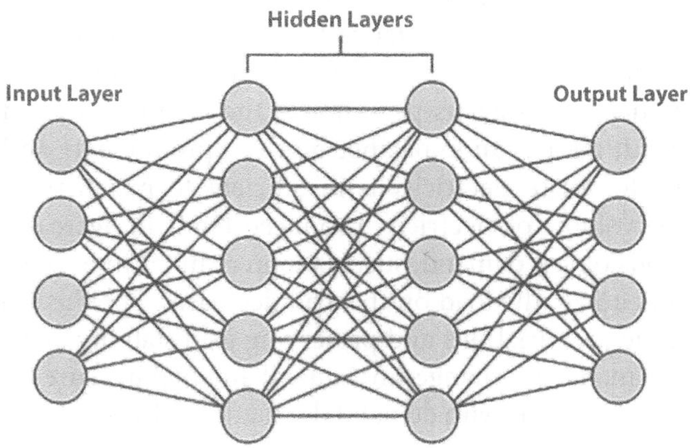


**Figure 10.3** The architecture of ANN.

## 10.4 Results and Discussion

The proposed ANN-based FOPID controller for an interconnected NMG system is put into effect in this section and compared with other standard FOPID. Power networks experience frequency variation due to a variety of reasons, all of which have an impact on the dynamic behavior of the grid. Unexpected variations in demand lead to load inequities, which are one of the primary issues. This inequality could be the result of sudden changes in production loads or quick adjustments in client demand. Frequency variations can also result from unintended discontinuation from the grid or from equipment breakdowns that reduce generating capacity. The increase in unpredictability to the producing mix caused by the inclusion of energy from renewable sources such solar and wind exacerbates frequency fluctuations. The reliability of the grid is also significantly impacted by communication delays, administration system motion, and the generators' response time to variations in demand.

Frequency is further exaggerated by grid disruptions, such as faults and line tripping incidents, which upset the delicate equilibrium between generation and demand. Furthermore, frequency variations can be impaired by fault clearance delays and network resonance phenomena, particularly during system-wide interruptions. The decreasing inertia in present-day power systems with significant renewable energy penetration exacerbates frequency aberrations, requiring strong management methods to guarantee grid stability. It is essential to comprehend these complex reasons in order to put mitigation plans into action and guarantee the dependability of power systems.

In actuality, changes in the demand conditions within a power system can cause frequency variations. Unexpected variations in the demand for energy disrupt the complex balance between generation and consumption, hence affecting the frequency of the grid. For example, during periods of high demand, such as peak hours, the load on the grid increases considerably. If there is an imbalance between productivity and load, and the capacity to create electricity is insufficient to match this increasing demand, the volume of electricity produced tends to decrease. However, during periods of low demand, such as soon at nighttime when industrial activity slows down, the load on the grid decreases. For this reason, minimizing frequency variations and preserving grid stability depend heavily on efficiently managing changes in demand and making sure that generating capacity stays in line with demand fluctuations. The performance of the proposed controller is investigated for load demand variation scenarios:

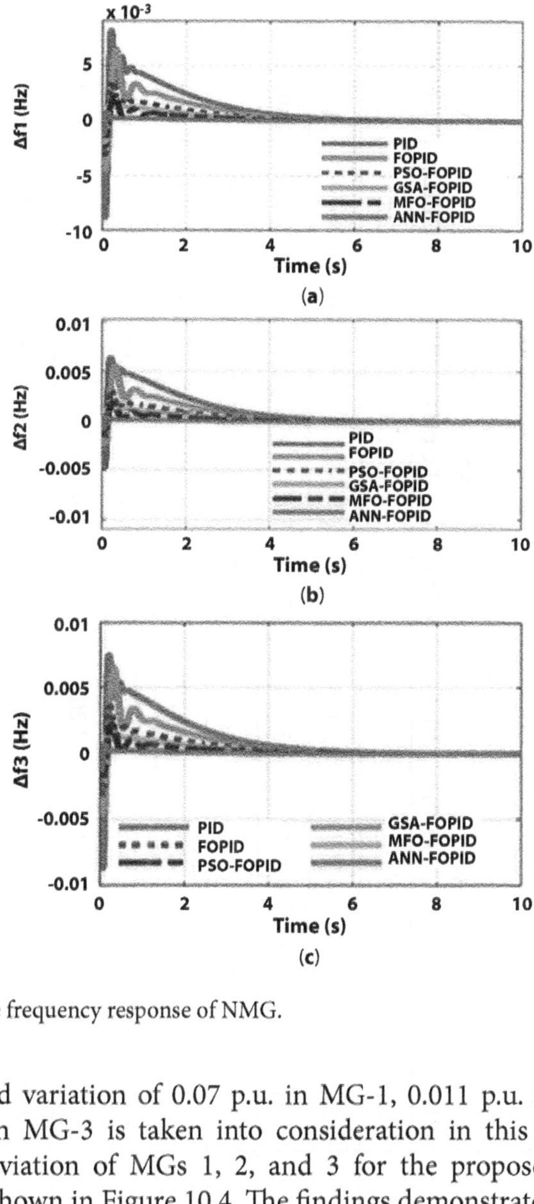


**Figure 10.4** The frequency response of NMG.

A step load variation of 0.07 p.u. in MG-1, 0.011 p.u. in MG-2, and 0.0017 p.u. in MG-3 is taken into consideration in this scenario. The frequency deviation of MGs 1, 2, and 3 for the proposed distributed controller is shown in Figure 10.4. The findings demonstrate that, in comparison to conventional tuned PID and FOPID controllers, the proposed ANN-FOPID controller effectively mitigates frequency oscillations with improved transient performance metrics are shown in Table 10.1.

**Table 10.1** Performance measures.

| | $\Delta f_1$ | | | $\Delta f_2$ | | | $\Delta f_3$ | | |
|---|---|---|---|---|---|---|---|---|---|
| | PID | FOPID | ANN-FOPID | PID | FOPID | ANN-FOPID | PID | FOPID | ANN-FOPID |
| IAE $\times 10^{-03}$ | 10.1200 | 7.1254 | 5.0125 | 10.256 | 6.3486 | 4.5555 | 10.603 | 7.700 | 4.5182 |
| ITAE $\times 10^{-05}$ | 3.1254 | 1.2541 | 0.5681 | 3.1555 | 1.6114 | 0.5822 | 3.0380 | 1.4570 | 0.5497 |
| ISE $\times 10^{-05}$ | 3.5464 | 1.5846 | 0.5845 | 3.1440 | 1.6580 | 6.1155 | 2.6130 | 1.7210 | 0.0462 |
| ITSE $\times 10^{-03}$ | 14.145 | 12.125 | 10.185 | 15.320 | 12.2700 | 7.5270 | 15.560 | 12.2500 | 6.6370 |
| Settling time (s) | 5.12503 | 5.4857 | 4.2565 | 6.0293 | 5.9187 | 4.5533 | 5.9870 | 4.9272 | 4.2625 |
| Rise time (s) $\times 10^{-05}$ | 9.4255 | 8.0255 | 7.0266 | 7.8975 | 6.9009 | 2.2154 | 5.6989 | 5.5381 | 5.2425 |
| Peak time (s) | 0.17552 | 0.1369 | 0.1025 | 0.2035 | 0.2025 | 0.2011 | 0.3325 | 0.2524 | 0.2181 |
| Peak magnitude | 0.0055 | 0.0050 | 0.0025 | 0.0045 | 0.0033 | 0.0031 | 0.0087 | 0.00877 | 0.0031 |
| Absolute error $\times 10^{-05}$ | 6.3261 | 5.699 | 4.145 | 9.1255 | 8.4221 | 7.3054 | 2.6585 | 1.8795 | 1.5945 |

The following are the definitions for different transient and steady-state measures:

- Steady-state error: A range of numbers representing the difference, over an infinite period of time, between the system output and the reference input
- Peak overshoot: The greatest deviation from the final value that the system reaction is capable of achieving
- Total absolute error (TAE): The total of all absolute errors during a period of time
- The total absolute error compounded by time over time is known as the integral time absolute error, or ITAE.
- The total square of the mistake over time is known as the integral square error, or ISE.
- The total time square error (ITSE) is calculated by multiplying the error's square by the passage of time.
- Setting time (ST): The time required for the output to reach the steady state

## 10.5 Conclusion

The research work describes an ANN-based distributed adaptive FOPID controller designed for frequency deviation in NMG systems. ANN is used to identify the initial controller settings, and network dynamics are used to handle uncertainty. The neural network uses a gradient descent method for weight updates, which guarantees effective adaptation. Superior performance in both steady-state and transient behavior is demonstrated by evaluation against various optimization-based FOPID controllers (PSO, GSA, and MFO) and traditional PID control. In particular, there are significant benefits with the suggested ANN controller, especially when load varies. The goal of future research is to further improve operational efficiency and durability in NMG systems by investigating cooperative control in conjunction with distributed control rules.

## References

1. Alsafran, A.S., A feasibility study of implementing ieee 1547 and ieee 2030 standards for microgrid in the kingdom of saudi arabia. *Energies*, 16, 4, 1777, 2023.

2. Fu, Q., Montoya, L.F., Solanki, A., Nasiri, A., Bhavaraju, V., Abdallah, T., Yu David, C., Microgrid generation capacity design with renewables and energy storage addressing power quality and surety. *IEEE Trans. Smart Grid*, 3, 4, 2019–2027, 2012.
3. Abdelghany, M.B., Al-Durra, A., Gao, F., A coordinated optimal operation of a grid-connected wind-solar microgrid incorporating hybrid energy storage management systems. *IEEE Trans. Sustain. Energy*, 15, 1, 39–51, 2023.
4. Polevaya, N.A., Optimal Microgrid Formation to Improve Power Supply Reliability, in: *2024 Conference of Young Researchers in Electrical and Electronic Engineering (ElCon)*, IEEE, pp. 838–842, 2024.
5. Alhasnawi, B.N., Jasim, B.H., Rahman, Z.A.SA., Guerrero, J.M., Dolores Esteban, M., A novel internet of energy based optimal multi-agent control scheme for microgrid including renewable energy resources. *Int. J. Environ. Res. Public Health*, 18, 15, 8146, 2021.
6. Anjaiah, K., Dash, P.K., Bisoi, R., Dhar, S., Mishra, S.P., A new approach for active and reactive power management in renewable based hybrid microgrid considering storage devices. *Appl. Energy*, 367, 1234295, 2024.
7. Dey, B., Márquez, F.P.G., Basak, S.K., Smart energy management of residential microgrid system by a novel hybrid mgwoscacsa algorithm. *Energies*, 13, 13, 3500, 2020.
8. Favuzza, S., Mitolo, M., Moradi, S., Musca, R., Zizzo, G., A General Methodology for Short-circuit Calculations in Hybrid AC/DC Microgrids. *IEEE Trans. Ind. Appl.*, 3, 2742–2749, 2023.
9. Almadhor, A., Rauf, H.T., Khan, M.A., Seifedine Kadry, and Yunyoung Nam. "A hybrid algorithm (BAPSO) for capacity configuration optimization in a distributed solar PV based microgrid. *Energy Rep.*, 7, 7906–7912, 2021.
10. Hussain, A., Shah, S.D.A., Arif, S.M., Heuristic optimisation-based sizing and siting of DGs for enhancing resiliency of autonomous microgrid networks. *IET Smart Grid*, 2, 2, 269–282, 2019.
11. Bagheri Tolabi, H., Ara, A.L., Hosseini, R., An enhanced particle swarm optimization algorithm to solve probabilistic load flow problem in a micro-grid. *Appl. Intell.*, 51, 3, 1645–1668, 2021.
12. Karthikumar, K. and Senthil Kumar, V., A new opposition crow search optimizer-based two-step approach for controlled intentional islanding in microgrids. *Soft Comput.*, 25, 2575–25885, 2021.
13. Li, N., Su, Z., Jerbi, H., Abbassi, R., Latifi, M., Furukawa, N., Energy management and optimized operation of renewable sources and electric vehicles based on microgrid using hybrid gravitational search and pattern search algorithm. *Sustain. Cities Soc.*, 75, 103279, 2021.
14. Kumar, N. and Jain, D.K., Optimal coordination of overcurrent relays for microgrid operation using JAYA algorithm. *e-Prime Adv. Electr. Eng. Electron. Energy*, 7, 100467, 2024.

15. Kumar, N. and Jain, D.K., Development of an Adaptive Protection Scheme for Microgrid Operation Suitable for Grid-Connected and Islanded Mode. *J. Oper. Autom. Power Eng.*, 7, 100467, 2024.
16. Elkholy, M.H., Senjyu, T., Metwally, H., Farahat, M.A., Irshad, A.S., Hemeida, A.M., Lotfy, M.E., A resilient and intelligent multi-objective energy management for a hydrogen-battery hybrid energy storage system based on MFO technique. *Renew. Energy*, 222, 119768, 2024.
17. Karnavas, Y.L. and Nivolianiti, E., Optimal load frequency control of a hybrid electric shipboard microgrid using jellyfish search optimization algorithm. *Appl. Sci.*, 13, 10, 6128, 2023.
18. Noman, A.M., Aly, M., Alqahtani, M.H., Almutairi, S.Z., Aljumah, A.S., Ebeed, M., Mohamed, E.A., Optimum Fractional Tilt Based Cascaded Frequency Stabilization with MLC Algorithm for Multi-Microgrid Assimilating Electric Vehicles. *Fractal Fract.*, 8, 3, 132, 2024.
19. Jain, S., Ahuja, R.K., Gupta, A., Arya, Y., Hybrid intelligent h-AFSA-ANN controller for the SPV-BESS-DG-based DC microgrid integrated system. *Electr. Eng.*, 1–26, 2024.
20. Mariyaraj, A. and Thankappan, S.P., IoT-integrated smart energy management system with enhanced ANN controller for small-scale microgrid. *Electr. Eng.*, 1–35, 2024.
21. Wang, H., Zeng, G., Dai, Y., Bi, D., Sun, J., Xie, X., Design of a fractional order frequency PID controller for an islanded microgrid: A multi-objective extremal optimization method. *Energies*, 10, 10, 1502, 2017.
22. Jena, N.K., Sahoo, S., Naik, A.K., Sahu, B.K., Mohanty, K.B., Frequency control of an AC microgrid with fractional controller, in: *Green Technology for Smart City and Society: Proceedings of GTSCS 2020*, Springer Singapore, pp. 277–288, 2021.
23. Jena, N.K., Sahoo, S., Nanda, A.B., Sahu, B.K., Mohanty, K.B., Frequency regulation in an islanded microgrid with optimal fractional order PID controller, in: *Advances in Intelligent Computing and Communication: Proceedings of ICAC 2019*, Springer Singapore, pp. 447–457, 2020.

# Appendix

$G_{BDPG}(s)$ - transfer function of simplified BDPG, $K_{BD}$ -participation factor of BDPG unit and its value is 0.25, $K_{VA}, T_{VA}$ – gain and time constant of value actuator and its value is 1 and 0.05 s, $K_{BE}, T_{BE}$ - gain and time constant of engine and its value are 1 and 0.5 s. $G_{SPG}$ - transfer function of SPG, $K_{SPG}, T_{SPG}$ – gain and time constant of SPG, and it value is 1 and 0.15 s. $G_{WPG}$ - transfer function of WPG, $K_{WPG}, T_{WPG}$ – gain and time constant of WPGS, and it value are 1 and 0.15 s.

## Appendix

# 11

# Navigating Trust in Distributed Systems

**Pooja Dehankar[1] and Susanta Das[2*]**

*[1]Ajeenkya DY Patil School of Engineering, Pune, Maharashtra, India*
*Affiliated to Savitribai Phule Pune University, Pune, Maharashtra, India*
*[2]School of Engineering, Ajeenkya DY Patil University, Pune, Maharashtra, India*

***Abstract***

The need for network and system security has increased due to the growth of services and applications in *ad hoc* and Internet-based contexts, as well as the complexity and quick development of computer systems and communication networks. As a result of the growing number of cyber-attacks on networks and systems, people's trust in the application of distributed networks and networks has suffered. In order to ensure the resources' availability, integrity, and privacy in networked distributed systems, there is a growing need for the development of innovative trust and security approaches. The foundation for distributed systems is trust. The inherent difficulties in building trust in distributed systems result from things such as dispersed ownership and control, inconsistent security and reliability levels, and the lack of centralized authority. Despite their decentralized character, these difficulties highlight the necessity of strong processes to promote confidence among system participants and components. This chapter delves into the complex aspects of trust in distributed systems, looking at the difficulties that arise, the methods used to build and preserve it, and the wider ramifications for system architecture and functionality. The techniques used to foster trust in distributed systems are examined in this chapter. This covers reputation systems, distributed governance models, consensus algorithms such as proof of work and proof of stake, and cryptographic approaches such as digital signatures and safe multiparty computation. By guaranteeing data integrity, confirming identities, rewarding integrity, and facilitating decentralized decision-making, each of these tactics seeks to increase trust. The wider effects of trust in distributed systems are discussed in this chapter, with special attention to system privacy, scalability, security, and resilience. Trust shapes the architecture, protocols, and functioning

**Corresponding author*: susanta2024das@yahoo.com; susanta2024das@gmail.com

Sandhya Avasthi and Suman Lata Tripathi (eds.) Distributed and Parallel Computing, (235–256)

of distributed systems by influencing the trade-offs and design decisions made during development.

***Keywords*:** Distributed systems, cyber-attacks, data integrity, privacy, security, trust models

## 11.1 Introduction

Trust in distributed systems (DSs) goes beyond simple reliability. It includes the confidence in the security, privacy, and integrity of data and services exchanged among nodes. Trust is dynamic and context-dependent, inclined by factors such as network conditions, node behaviors, and system configurations. In DSs, where computing resources are spread across multiple nodes and geographical locations, the concept of trust plays essential role. Trust forms the foundation upon which continuous communication, collaboration, and functionality are built. This chapter explores the complex nature of trust in DSs, delving into its significance, challenges, and the various mechanisms employed to establish and maintain trust in these complex environments. In DSs, trust is an important idea that is essential to guaranteeing and improving system security [1].

The authorization systems in place are unable to offer strong and capable instruments to effectively oversee security on the scale needed for the current Internet. The creation and implementation of systems that make the Internet more programmable are placing growing pressure on these processes. Furthermore, it appears that the trend toward "increased flexibility through programmability" is quickening with the introduction of ideas such as mobile agents and active networking. The shortcomings of conventional authorization procedures led to the development of DS security strategy based on trust management. When making an authorization decision, engines for managing trust eliminate requirement to determine "identities." Rather, they use a programming language to communicate rights and limitations. This enables modern, scalable security measures to be standardized and to be more flexible and expressive. Additionally, trust-management technique offers advantages such as system designs that motivate administrators and developers to carefully analyze and explicitly declare an application's (app's) security policy, as well as evidence that the required transactions adhere to regional norms. In this work, we analyze the shortcomings of current authorization procedures [2].

### 11.1.1 Trust in Distributed Computing Ecosystem

Trust is an enabling technology, which makes it important to include in DSs. With it, safe, seamless agent-based apps and online commerce will be possible. Many scholars utilize and presume a highly precise meaning of trust in relation to problems such as authentication or the ability to pay for goods, despite the necessity to standardize trust and its related notions [3]. Large distributed computing systems that link entire nations or even corporations are becoming more and more common. Without a shared trusted agent, these organizations' relationships are characterized by a need for cooperation and rivalry. In DSs, trust and security are closely intertwined. A theory of trust can be used for many different things, such as designing mechanisms that are resilient to trust failures and building authentication servers based on relationships of trust [4].

Distributed computing and security services, among other emerging digital environments and infrastructures, have created new avenues for resource usage, communication, and information sharing in recent years. But when distributed services are deployed, it becomes unclear how much we can rely on service providers—individually or collectively—not to breach security regulations. Determining the answer to this issue is essential for choosing reliable service providers and developing trustworthy DSs [5].

### 11.1.2 Trust in the Internet of Things

When working with the Internet of Things (IoT) and DSs, trust is essential. Thus, trust must be taken into account at every level of system development in order to create, improve, and adapt such systems. However, a framework would be necessary for trust-based design and development in order to direct system developers in extracting a comprehensive set of needs while also averting any disputes. Due to the variety of people, devices, and systems, as well as the intricate relationships among system components, a framework that can adapt to changing circumstances is necessary to handle trust and development concerns [6]. Entities in DSs are dispersed across many security domains and lack prior knowledge of each other. DSs and the security elements that make them up, such as entities, credentials, certificates, trust ideals, and rules are fluid and always evolving in this context. In order to support the dispersed and dynamic nature of these systems and their constituent parts, models of access control and trust-building strategies are required [7].

Novel DSs include mobile *ad hoc* networks and peer-to-peer (P2P) networks that are emerging as a result of the quick growth of network and communication technology. A crucial consideration in these DSs is trust. The various entities in a DS can have up-to-date, consistent trustworthiness information maintained by a versatile, general-purpose trust-management system. As a result, trust management research is still ongoing. There are still many intriguing research questions to be answered, such as the storage of trust and reputation values [8].

We have observed the evolutionary emergence of a novel breed of DSs in recent years. These systems have a lot in common: they are autonomous within their administrative areas, highly decentralized, and scalable to the Internet. The ability to work together in both known and unknown realms is most crucial. Peer-to-peer apps and open Web services are two prime examples. In DSs, permission is typically identity-based and uses access control lists (ACL), for example. However, because of the requirement to deal with unknown users, or strangers, and the necessity of managing a potentially huge number of users and/or resources, techniques based on preset identities are inappropriate for the new breed of DSs [9].

For all parties involved, particularly the manufacturers and consumers of the program, software dependability in DSs has always been a top priority. Large-scale distributed apps, such as e-government, e-commerce, multimedia services, and end-to-end automotive solutions, have several models developed to evaluate or forecast their dependability; yet, these systems continue to have reliability problems. To guarantee the dependability of a DS, it is necessary to evaluate the dependability of every single part or element in enterprise distributed apps prior to projecting or evaluating the dependability of the entire system. Additionally, transparent fault detection and recovery protocols must be implemented to ensure smooth user interaction [10].

The dependability of processing components, communication channels, software redundancy, and data files are all aspects of a distributed processing system's reliability, which is a crucial design criterion. Apps and files in a DS have redundancy, which is not captured by the conventional terminal-pair reliability. We present two reliability metrics: distributed program reliability, which expresses the likelihood that a program requiring multiple computers to operate successfully will be executed, and DS reliability, which measures the likelihood that every one of the system's designated distributed programs will function [11].

Object orientation, a focus on distribution, and the use of parallelism to boost speed are just a few of the traits that the new breed of database systems and general-purpose operating systems share. The challenge of keeping multicomponent distributed apps consistent in the face of concurrency and failures arises for both kinds of systems as a result. It is also reasonable to anticipate that large programs will incorporate both general purpose and database components [12]. For DSs to keep current copies of shared data on several computers connected to a network, data replication is utilized. But even after decades of study, little is known about the methods used to provide consistency in duplicated systems. In fact, it has been discovered that a large number of published algorithms were false at some point, including those that included purportedly automated proofs of correctness [13].

A widespread move toward software distribution as the primary computer paradigm has been sparked by recent rapid technology advancements. Security flaws have become more dangerous in tandem with this, which frequently prevents people from implementing and adopting security features. Although security is widely accepted to be important, particularly in open and collaborative environments, there is a significant lack of systematic approaches (methodologies) for designing secure DSs in survey literature [14].

The open-source DSs have gained popularity due to the information age's explosive growth. In a distributed setting, there has never been a bigger need for security and protection. Enforcing a policy across the system has been the traditional approach to security, but this methodology is ineffective for large DSs where completely new security threats and vulnerabilities are appearing. Our contention is that an alternative framework is required, one that prioritizes user-definable regulations over the "system as enforcer." The choice of security level should be available to users, who should only have to pay for what is actually needed. Furthermore, people have to take ultimate responsibility for their own safety [15].

Networks for data communication are becoming a necessary component of contemporary life. Sheer systems and networks may now be connected, thanks to the standardization of communication protocols. Open systems are globally connected, enabling services such as electronic financial transfers, resource sharing, and remote computing. All of these apps must be evaluated for potential security breaches in order to deliver secure delivery of the services they are designed to provide. Furthermore, it is important to assess how apps must be designed to safeguard information transfer against various potential dangers [16].

## 11.2 Transparency Basics

An essential paradigm for building DSs is the process of composing systems recursively to create transparently dispersed systems that are functionally identical. The degree of recursive transparency that can be attained is largely dependent on the capability and semantics provided by the underlying systems. Because of this, it is critical that systems be built with functionality that scales smoothly in a distributed setting. Being able to intercept a system's fundamental processes and extrapolate their significance in a dispersed setting is essential for creating a clear addition to that framework. In order to intercept and extend operations that traverse certain interfaces, with clearly specified interfaces and the necessary reflective capabilities, the underlying system must have a clear structure. Thus, while designing extensible DSs, reflection and transparency are both crucial. Although transparent expansions to microkernel architectures as the foundation for object-oriented systems are feasible, this can become unduly cumbersome due to the current generation of object-oriented programming languages' lack of reflective capabilities. To create languages whose implementation and computational model are more compatible with the underlying platforms that support them, more study is needed [17].

Among the things that show access transparency are Web browsing, SQL queries, and the file system in the Network File System (NFS). Location transparency is exemplified by the NFS file system and Web pages. A couple prominent instances of concurrency transparency include the NFS file system and the network of ATMs. Two instances of replication transparency are Web page mirroring and distributed database management systems. Database management systems are among failure transparency. Web pages and NFS are the systems that make migration transparency possible. Transparency in performance enables the system to be adjusted to perform better when the load changes. The World Wide Web is the best-DS example of implementing scaling transparency [18].

## 11.3 Heterogeneous and Homogeneous DSs

DSs come in two flavors: heterogeneous (like grid, cloud, and P2P) and homogeneous (like cluster). These kinds of systems are susceptible to a number of issues, including load balancing, fault tolerance, resource selection, and quality of service. One important topic in DS design is fault tolerance. In this context, we refer to the failure that results from a software or hardware malfunction in system as fault. Furthermore, they need to develop failure-tolerant approaches that aim to identify and fix these problems so that the system can continue to function even in the face of these defects [19].

### 11.3.1 Trust Concepts

Trust cannot be adequately defined for each individual. It is too nebulous. It could come in as many varieties as the number of participants or items. Additionally, it could change depending on the circumstance. At different times and by different people, it is interpreted and understood in different ways. Social trust and human trust are influenced by a number of variables. The clear indicators of whether or not to trust a certain individual to complete a work are their past experiences, level of skill, suggestions, etc. Nevertheless, there are additional implicit cognitive components of trust, such as selfishness, reciprocativeness, and philanthropy [20]. Most of the time, they are concealed, and only human conduct can account for them. Because of this, it is exceedingly challenging to describe and explain trust in a unique way. It is feasible to simulate agent confidence in MAS by taking into account each of these factors. A list of ideal trust components from numerous significant papers [21, 22] that are particularly relevant to Internet of People (IoP) is reputation, recommendation basic trust, general trust, situational trust, transitivity utility risk, and reciprocation. Comprehending human behavior in the context of IoT can pose challenges to the calculation of trust.

### 11.3.2 Inadequacies with Security Mechanisms

The ACL is one of the operating system's security features. The access privileges that a principal possesses on an object (resource) are listed in this ACL. For example, the "permissions" mechanism in the UNIX file system is basically an ACL. Nevertheless, these ACLs are regrettably insufficient for DSs. The principal's identity is known in operating system (OS) but unknown in DS. In network computing contexts, these straightforward password-based protocols are insufficient because authentication is achieved through username/password mechanisms [23]. Delegation makes it possible for administrative duties to be distributed. It is essential for DS's scalability. The entity enforcing policy, or the last link in the delegation chain in DS, specifies policy (or authorization) in the form of an ACL. As a result, locally defined subpolicies become inconsistent [24]. Since a DS primarily works with data—whether it is in motion or not—across the domains of data sourcing, distribution, storage, and utilization in services, every component and interface in this data chain is directly subject to the traditional CIA (confidentiality, integrity, and availability) properties. Information leakage risks such as side-channel attacks and covert-channel attacks are among the dangers to secrecy. An interruption or denial of data access poses a risk to availability. Any compromise of data accuracy, such as a breach of data consistency as noticed by the distributed participants, is referred to as an integrity aspect. This covers the various forms of consistency that are available for storage and transactional services, such as strong, weak, relaxed, eventual, etc. As a result, in order to secure the data elements of a DS, it is necessary to take into account not only the data threats posed by viruses, malicious apps, and code, but also the threats that are related to resources, access control, data transportation, and coordination services [25]. Each administrative entity in a DS is assigned a unique local trust model, which can be utilized by many users and other entities due to the vast number of these entities. The authentication methods listed above are all unsecure, insufficient, and not scalable. The reason for all of these counterintuitive and troublesome mechanisms is that there are no any suitable replacements for DS [26].

## 11.4 Trust Management

The authorization decision, certificate storage and retrieval, and trust negotiation are the three main components of trust management systems (TMSs), which in reality consist of a multitude of subsystems and operations. Access control decisions have implications for the elements and semantics of authorization decisions. The low-level representation of access control elements including credentials and rules, certificate storage, and retrieval pertains to the actual location of certificates [27, 28].

With the use of trust management, risk may be reduced, and benign businesses' network activity can be guaranteed. One of the jobs is gathering the data required to create a trustworthy relationship; another is actively preserving and modifying the one that currently exists. The trust-management technique was established as a response to inadequacies of outdated authorization procedures for DS security. The requirement to ascertain "identities" in order to grant authorization is eliminated by trust-management engines. Rather, they use a programming language to communicate rights and limitations. This makes it possible to standardize and enhance the flexibility and expressiveness of contemporary, scalable security solutions.

The plan comprises system architectures that motivate developers and administrators to carefully evaluate and articulate an app's security policy, as well as verification that requested transactions adhere to local norms [29].

Based on how they are architecturally designed, trust-management techniques fall into one of three categories: completely distributed, semidistributed, or central. Distributed trust management functions without the need for a central server, in contrast to its centralized counterpart. Behavior-based dynamic trust management and credential-based (or policy-based) static trust management are the two primary categories into which trust management is usually divided. The unified technique enables direct authorization of critical security actions through the formulation and interpretation of security policies, credentials, and relationships. The limitations of earlier permission processes led to the development of these trust-management techniques.

The process of defining security credentials and the notion of establishing security policies are combined in TMSs. Specific trust assignments between public keys that connect keys to identities and carry out specific functions are specified by credentials. These technological advancements facilitate the specification, enhancement, and assignment of policies among the various tiers of a policy hierarchy. Consequently, the technique resolves the scalability and consistency issues with ACL. Credentials define precise trust relationships between public keys that connect keys to identities and carry out defined functions. These technologies make it easier to specify, improve, and delegate policies among the different levels of a policy hierarchy. Consequently, the method fixes the problems with ACL consistency and scalability [30].

## 11.5 Components' Roles

A crucial part of the trust management architecture that offers trust management functions is Trust Manager. The logic behind the Trust Inference Engine is rudimentary and arbitrary. Established trust ties make up the Trust Policy Base. The trust relationships inside the trust base are dynamically updated by the Trust Update. Trust decision: Provide interested parties that rely on an owner host's judgment by generating a traveling calculation. When making decisions about trust, a variety of elements are taken into account, including recommendations for trust from other individuals, long-term observations of behaviors associated to trust, and an initial set of relationships related to trust [31].

## 11.6 User Authentication and Access Control

Historically, the primary sources of security for solitary computers and small networks have been user authentication and access control. Through the app of system-based controls to verify the identity of an individual or process, these physical procedures explicitly permit or prohibit the usage, modification, or viewing of a computer resource. These systems, however, fall short of meeting the increased flexibility required by distributed networks, such as the Internet, and ubiquitous/pervasive computer environments since these networks lack central control and its users are not preset. Users expect locally hosted information and services to be available to them at all times and places in ubiquitous systems, which raises serious security risks and complicates access management. A distributed TMS consists of the following: creating a security policy, giving organizations credentials, confirming the credentials' compliance with the policy, entrusting others with your confidence, rescinding rights, and assessing users' access privileges. Distributed trust management, when combined with Public Key Infrastructure and Role-Based Access Control, is an infrastructure that offers an extremely adaptable way to enforce security in pervasive computing environments [32].

## 11.7 Trust Framework Pillars

The term "environment" refers to the technological aspects of the existing infrastructure as well as the supply chain, society, culture, institutions, ethics, race, religion, and so forth. Customers include attributes unique to people, such as gender, age, occupation, psychological state, habits, abilities, and physical and cognitive capacity, in addition to the intelligence level in the event that system users are not human. The commercial factors that impact confidence are addressed by commercial requirements. In order to evaluate the interplay between the factors in each pillar, technology is crucial. It is quite challenging to watch and evaluate a relationship like this. The trust evaluation module should be integrated with the app to provide a realistic evaluation, as services are often unreliable and a standalone trust assessment module could be quite costly for an enterprise setting [6].

## 11.8 Trust Metrics

The first type of trust is based on a host's capacity to complete a task to the initiator host's criteria. Each time a conversation takes place, the initiator host assesses the outcome and records the target host's degree of expertise. This maintained value provides the host with firsthand knowledge in determining their own level of trust, as well as a standing value that extra hosts can draw upon when making decisions of their own. The belief that a host is dependable and consistent in offering perceptive analysis and direction constitutes the second type of trust. This kind is based on a variety of traits: The total number of interactions a host has with other hosts determines its activity level. This feature indicates a host's level of activity as well as how trustworthy and current their information is. The degree to which two hosts are comparable is determined by the similarity of their regard for reputation. The two hosts who are more alike evaluation processes and values are, the more credible one's advice will be to the other. A host's popularity is determined by how many encounters they have had with a particular host. The degree of acceptance and likability among other hosts is determined by a host's popularity. How cooperative a host is can be determined by looking at the ratio of interactions to total service requests. This characteristic will determine a host's inclination to engage with and assist others [33].

## 11.9 Trust Models and Mechanisms

Due to their ability to offer users a variety of easily accessible sharing environments, P2P networks have garnered a lot of attention lately. The flexibility of P2P networks leads to security holes. Due to their frequent interactions with strangers or other peers, peers are vulnerable to a variety of hazards. A strong trust management architecture is necessary in open environments to keep untrustworthy peers out of the system. GenTrust is a revolutionary trust paradigm for P2P networks created *via* genetic programming. A peer assesses the reliability of a fellow peer based on traits and suggestions. Because the method does not rely on a central authority, it is compatible with P2P network's decentralized design. The idea is quite effective against all kinds of attacks [34].

Large-scale systems that use P2P system design benefit greatly from its low cost of ownership, robustness, scalability, and site autonomy. But there are also a lot of disadvantages to this strategy, such as problems with trust and a lack of peer supervision and cooperation. For a P2P organized large-scale network computing system, we offer a fully described trust model and an explanation of the tactics employed in it. The concept of keeping up a recommender network that may be used to locate references to a target domain forms the basis of the methodology. The simulation's findings show that the trust model may be used to pinpoint trouble spots and support the development and preservation of confidence [35].

Online e-commerce companies use trust models that are based on recommendations. In an online environment, communication between users and services and anonymous parties is required. For risk management in online environments, trust models are becoming a vital tool. While doing transactions, it is a good idea to assess each other's performance. When determining whether or not to do business with a specific entity in the future, an entity can find trust from the collective ratings on that particular entity. Its main flaw is that it cannot ensure the caliber of suggestions. Subjective assessment criteria can differ, and unscrupulous parties could make biased suggestions. The decision-making authority of the inquiring bodies is retained while assessing the caliber of ideas and the reliability of recommenders [36].

To address the issue of disparate estimate processes for the same online service, a naive Bayesian network is employed in Song *et al.* [37] to the recommendations trust model. The foundation of the Eigen trust model is the idea of transitive trust [38]. Finding pretrusted peers that ensure algorithm convergence and steer clear of hostile collectives is a significant issue when employing this technique.

In order for the weighted majority technique [39] to function, recommenders that are unable to identify deceptions are given smaller weights. A trust opinion cannot be produced using the requester's own trust standard.

In role-based trust management, users' trustworthiness is assessed by a trust domain, which assigns roles to them based on the certificates they have provided. The users were assigned the identical task, but their enforcement of different behaviors ought to have altered their trustworthiness. To the role, variables representing cumulative behaviors are introduced. Behavior-aware credentials are introduced to characterize the imposed behavior-based trust movement policy. The current trust status is represented by behavior variables, which are also utilized to construct role reputation and domain reputation. Credentials that consider reputation provide context for the trust movement policy that is based on reputational shifts. Trust domains provide access control and trust constraints that are specific to local roles in the role-based TMS. Whether or not access users are assigned any local tasks will depend on their certificates. Nonetheless, the certificates are released by a separate domain or a local domain. How to accept certificates from other domains will be outlined in policies related to trust delegation. The credentials provide a real time (RT)-friendly explanation of policy of trust and trust delegation. These prerequisites create a network of confidence between names. Lastly, trust domain will be able to validate the users' requests based on the local roles that have been assigned to the access users [40].

The main issue to be resolved is trust evaluation for the trust model, and a substantial field of information security study is trusted computing. During the app model design phase, thorough analysis, verification, and theoretical trust analysis are necessary to ensure the security of the trust model for trusted computing. This method of assessing trust accepts direct, recommended, and indirect forms of trust as legitimate. The main measure of direct trust is subject satisfaction, which is mostly based on how well two subjects communicate with one another. When a subject accepts or believes in the experience-based information that another subject provides, this is known as recommendation trust. The trust chain that makes up indirect trust is composed of a series of recommendations [41].

Although these organizations and their processes are called zero-trust, trust-free, or trustless, it would be false to think that one can function fully in a decentralized autonomous organization without trust. These groups engage in cooperation and business dealings. To characterize the DAO 707 as less trust-intensive would seem more appropriate, given that it demands less trust from its members on a number of levels [42].

The predicted value of the beta distribution is used by the beta reputation system (BRS) to express trust. Real numbers between 0 and 1 represent its trust degrees. BRS calculates trust based on the agent's personal experiences as well as outsiders' viewpoints. The quantity of positive and negative feedback is represented by 2-tuples (r, s) in these data. BRS handles erroneous opinions with a straightforward discounting process. The amount of discounting is determined by how much faith the BRS has in the agents who offer their opinions. BRS gives an agent's opinions a high discount if it believes that they are an extremely unreliable source of services. According to the theory of trust transitivity, an agent can be relied upon to give excellent (honest) opinions if they can be trusted to perform a certain service [43].

## 11.10 Trust in Sensor Networks

A method for choosing reliable cluster heads in a cluster-based wireless sensor network (WSN), as well as a distributed trust-based architecture. The model makes use of both direct and indirect data from reliable nodes. Packet loss rate, data packets, and control packets are the three characteristics that are traditionally weighted in order to model trust. Every node keeps a trust table for all neighboring nodes, and only upon request does the cluster head receive these values. This method lessens the impact of negative publicity because it is not predicated on hearsay [44].

To determine whether sensor nodes are reliable and to filter (delete) data that have been received from malicious nodes. In their model, the authors posit that all sensor nodes are highly populated, time is synchronized, and each sensor node is cognizant of its own location. There is no trust update, and the traditional technique of calculating trust entailed weighting the trust criteria according to the app [45].

A watchdog mechanism to keep an eye on other nodes, gauge reputation, and ultimately gauge trust. A binary event, such a successful or unsuccessful transaction, can have uncertainty included in its description using the Bayes theorem. The initial values of the variables are (1) and (0), respectively, representing the degree of uncertainty and stranger trust [46].

A safe cluster formation algorithm to stop hostile or hacked nodes from becoming cluster chiefs and to make it easier to create trusted clusters using predistributed keys. They used the beta distribution to simulate trust based on positive and negative interactions. By merging them with those from time $t$, the successful/unsuccessful interactions at time $t + 1$ are updated. Their trust architecture is developed within the context of a cluster-based network topology with nodes having unique local IDs [47].

## 11.11 Apps of TMSs

Resource sharing and management in collaborative virtual project teams (VPTs) environments will get harder as the demand for transparent information increases. Assessing the trust between coworkers using the recommended VPT model and the analytical findings for the needs of resource sharing in a VPT will help determine how to optimize resource allocation and collaboration, ultimately improving the team's overall performance. In real-world VPT situations, the trust evaluation method improves secure resource sharing by taking worker previous access records into account. Although negative trust values are used to foster mistrust between coworkers, direct and indirect trust values are used to foster more trust. The technique for assessing coworker trust has some disadvantages, but it also provides a secure means of satisfying VPT requirements for resource security and adaptability between VPTs [48].

Users of any DS must work in a secure environment. Security becomes much more important when people share sensitive information and goods over a network. One example of a DS where security is essential is an e-commerce site. It is crucial that transactions cannot be undone, messages stay secret and unchangeable, and resources can be accessed only by those who have been properly authorized and authenticated. These features require a suitable security layer in order to enable access and exchange between E-commerce platforms and the customers they serve. They are offered by a distributed security management system (DSMS). Resource sharing, secure communication, and access among the various distributed apps, items, databases, and organizations that comprise the system are managed by the DSMS, a security middleware for e-commerce servers. In order to allow authorized consumers to securely retrieve and transmit data to the system, it is meant to serve as a secure interface between customers and merchant databases. The server needs to be of the best quality and have a high error tolerance because it needs to remain online at all times. It must also have an intuitive feature set and interface [49].

Globally, people now primarily communicate and interact through online social networks, or online social networks (OSNs). The foundations of privacy have been under threat in recent years as technology has developed and offered active members of online communities' additional benefits and social significance. While sharing private content with friends and colleagues is common on OSNs, users might not always be fully aware of the risk that they are inadvertently giving away personal information to adversaries, data harvesters, social bots, spammers, or other parties. Stopping this information leakage is one of the main objectives of the relationship-based, trust-based, information flow control, and access control security paradigms created for OSNs. The model uses publicly available data points to characterize the quality of the network interactions, including the total number of friends, the age of the user account, and the length of the friendship. It also evaluates the degree of trust between users and ascertains the information flow between them to ascertain if users in their network are friends or enemies. Lastly, it enhances social network privacy management and provides more precise and useful options for information sharing [50].

## 11.12 DSs Advantages and Challenges

Remote service access is one advantage of distributed computing.

Distributed Computing: Distribute tasks among multiple computers to boost throughput.

Specialized Equipment: Perform different tasks on equipment configured for that specific use.

Load Balancing: Utilize redundancy in service processing to divide labor efficiently.

Distributed Data Storage: Implement redundancy in data storage systems to improve I/O speed and shorten download times (e.g., mirroring at multiple sites), providing fault tolerance in case one component malfunctions.
Scalability: Performance can be enhanced by acquiring more equipment.
Complexity: Distributed computing can be complex to implement, especially for legacy applications.
Compatibility Issues: Legacy apps may not be designed for distributed environments.
Improved Performance: Distributed computing can significantly improve performance and throughput.
Fault Tolerance: Distributed systems can provide fault tolerance and redundancy, ensuring system availability.
Scalability: Distributed systems can be scaled horizontally by adding more equipment.

Research on distribution transparency is still ongoing. A variety of issues, including as security, authentication, fault tolerance, process scheduling, and dependability, are still problematic. Performance demands a large overhead in communications, and load balancing is often difficult [51].

More and more standalone, independently produced components are being integrated into software systems. This combination is only practical when the parts are interoperable or able to work together to complete a task or tasks for the user. Disparities in middleware technology, communication protocols, and data formats utilized by the various components frequently cause compatibility issues. The inclusion of mediators, who carry out the required data translations and suitably coordinate the actions of the components, allows components to cooperate despite these discrepancies. However, in the present and the future, interoperability will remain a significant problem for DSs that are highly dynamic and heterogeneous [52].

## 11.13 Artificial Intelligence for Trust Management

Determining node trust can be made more accurate and successful in distributed networks by implementing artificial intelligence (AI) approaches. A kind of AI known as "machine learning" uses historical data to predict or react to future data. It involves simulating human observational learning with computers so that more effective systems can be created by using historical data and knowledge. The powerful powers can also be applied to trust evaluation. Past interaction data play a major role in determining trust, and machine learning is essentially the art of creating predictions based on past data. Systems and target entities can have their trust levels dynamically updated by evaluating trust using machine learning approaches. The trust evaluation model becomes more accurate and dynamic with the addition of machine learning [53]. The methodology gains flexibility by utilizing machine learning techniques to ascertain the trust level. Consequently, the model exhibits increased dynamic adaptability and is more receptive to novel interactions. Furthermore, the implementation of a penalty mechanism lessens the effect of erroneous feedback, especially when it comes from dishonest nodes, such as collusive deceit nodes [54].

## 11.14 Conclusion

Modern computing relies heavily on trust, which is a constantly developing and essential component. Building robust and safe DSs that support our networked digital world will require tackling the issues and adopting cutting-edge trust mechanisms as technology develops. The concept of trust in DSs is complex and essential to maintaining the efficiency, security, and dependability of contemporary technology infrastructures. We have looked at a number of aspects of trust in this chapter, including trust models. One such model is P2P trust, which is crucial for building and preserving relationships of trust between entities in DSs. The difficulties with trust in DSs have also been covered. DSs rely on trust to facilitate data sharing, collaboration, and communication across heterogeneous networks. We can continue to build confidence in DSs and advance the creation of dependable and secure decentralized ecosystems by utilizing trust models, strong trust metrics, efficient trust-management techniques, and cutting-edge technology. The complexity of trust in DSs, where variables such as system architecture, communication protocols, and network topology all affect trust dynamics, is one of the main lessons to be learned. Furthermore, the chapter has provided insight into cutting-edge technologies that are transforming trust mechanisms, such as AI. Even with these developments, developing and preserving trust in DSs are still hampered by issues with scalability, interoperability, and privacy. It will take interdisciplinary teams with knowledge in computer science, cryptography, economics, and law to solve these problems. With continuous research and development aimed at improving security, transparency, and user empowerment, the future of trust in DSs seems promising.

## References

1. Xiu, D. and Liu, Z., A formal definition for trust in distributed systems, in: *Information Security: 8th International Conference, ISC 2005, Singapore,*

*September 20-23, 2005. Proceedings 8*, Springer, Berlin Heidelberg, pp. 482–489, 2005.

2. Jøsang, A., The right type of trust for distributed systems, in: *Proceedings of the 1996 workshop on New security paradigms*, pp. 119–131, 1996.
3. Grandison, T. and Sloman, M., A survey of trust in internet applications. *IEEE Commun. Surv. Tutor.*, 3, 4, 2–16, 2000.
4. Rangan, P.V., An axiomatic basis of trust in distributed systems, in: *Proceedings. 1988 IEEE Symposium on Security and Privacy*, IEEE Computer Society, pp. 204–204, 1988.
5. Schryen, G., Volkamer, M., Ries, S., Habib, S.M., A formal approach towards measuring trust in distributed systems, in: *Proceedings of the 2011 ACM symposium on applied computing*, pp. 1739–1745, 2011.
6. Dorodchi, M., Abedi, M., Cukic, B., Trust-based development framework for distributed systems and IoT, in: *2016 IEEE 40th Annual Computer Software and Applications Conference (COMPSAC)*, vol. 2, IEEE, pp. 437–442, 2016.
7. Ahadipour, A. and Schanzenbach, M., A survey on authorization in distributed systems: Information storage, data retrieval and trust evaluation, in: *2017 IEEE Trustcom/BigDataSE/ICESS*, pp. 1016–1023, IEEE, 2017.
8. Li, H. and Singhal, M., Trust management in distributed systems. *Computer*, 40, 2, 45–53, 2007.
9. Yao, W., *Trust management for widely distributed systems*, No. UCAM-CL-TR-608, University of Cambridge, Computer Laboratory, 2004.
10. Ahmed, W. and Wu, Y.W., A survey on reliability in distributed systems. *J. Comput. Syst. Sci.*, 79, 8, 1243–1255, 2013.
11. Raghavendra, C.S., Prasanna Kumar, V.K., Hariri, S., Reliability analysis in distributed systems. *IEEE Trans. Comput.*, 37, 3, 352–358, 1988.
12. Birman, K.P., Maintaining consistency in distributed systems, in: *Proceedings of the 5th workshop on ACM SIGOPS European workshop: Models and paradigms for distributed systems structuring*, pp. 1–6, 1992.
13. Gomes, V.BF., Kleppmann, M., Mulligan, D.P., Beresford, A.R., Verifying strong eventual consistency in distributed systems. *Proc. ACM Program. Lang.*, 1, OOPSLA, 1–28, 2017.
14. Uzunov, A., Fernandez, E., Falkner, K., Engineering security into distributed systems: A survey of methodologies. *J. Univers. Comput. Sci.*, 18, 20, 2920–3006, 2012.
15. Wulf, W.A., Wang, C., Kienzle, D., A new model of security for distributed systems, in: *Proceedings of the 1996 workshop on New security paradigms*, pp. 34–43, 1996.
16. Prabhu, M.M. and Raghavan, S.V., Security in computer networks and distributed systems. *Comput. Commun.*, 19, 5, 379–388, 1996.
17. Stroud, R., Transparency and reflection in distributed systems, in: *Proceedings of the 5th workshop on ACM SIGOPS European workshop: Models and paradigms for distributed systems structuring*, pp. 1–5, 1992.
18. Mantena, S.R., Transparency in distributed systems, The University of Texas at Arlington, 2019.

19. Ledmi, A., Bendjenna, H., Hemam, S.M., Fault tolerance in distributed systems: A survey, in: *2018 3rd International Conference on Pattern Analysis and Intelligent Systems (PAIS)*, IEEE, pp. 1–5, 2018.
20. Falcone, R. and Castelfranchi, C., Social trust: A cognitive approach, in: *Trust and deception in virtual societies*, pp. 55–90, 2001.
21. Marsh, S.P., *Formalising trust as a computational concept*, 1994.
22. Abdul-Rahman, A. and Hailes, S., A distributed trust model, in: *Proceedings of the 1997 workshop on New security paradigms*, pp. 48–60, 1998.
23. Lampson, B., Abadi, M., Burrows, M., Wobber, E., Authentication in distributed systems: Theory and practice. *ACM Trans. Comput. Syst. (TOCS)*, 10, 4, 265–310, 1992.
24. Yahalom, R., Klein, B., Beth, T., Trust relationships in secure systems-a distributed authentication perspective, in: *Proceedings 1993 IEEE computer society symposium on research in security and privacy*, IEEE, pp. 150–164, 1993.
25. Suri, N., Distributed systems security knowledge area issue, The Cyber Security Body Of Knowledge, 2019.
26. Nagaraj, S.V., Access control in distributed object systems: problems with access control lists, in: *Proceedings Tenth IEEE International Workshop on Enabling Technologies: Infrastructure for Collaborative Enterprises. WET ICE 2001*, IEEE, pp. 163–164, 2001.
27. Chapin, P.C., Skalka, C., Sean Wang, X., Authorization in trust management: Features and foundations. *ACM Comput. Surv. (CSUR)*, 40, 3, 1–48, 2008.
28. Dadhich, P., Dutta, K., Govil, M.C., Trust enhanced authorization for distributed systems. *Int. J. Sci. Eng. Res.*, 40, 2011.
29. Blaze, M., Feigenbaum, J., Ioannidis, J., Keromytis, A.D., The role of trust management in distributed systems security, in: *Secure Internet programming: security issues for mobile and distributed objects*, pp. 185–210, 1999.
30. Sharma, A., Pilli, E.S., Mazumdar, A.P., Gera, P., Towards trustworthy Internet of Things: A survey on Trust Management applications and schemes. *Comput. Commun.*, 160, 475–493, 2020.
31. Li, N., Mitchell, J.C., Winsborough, W.H., Design of a role-based trust-management framework, in: *Proceedings 2002 IEEE Symposium on Security and Privacy*, IEEE, pp. 114–130, 2002.
32. Boukerche, A. and Ren, Y., A trust-based security system for ubiquitous and pervasive computing environments. *Comput. Commun.*, 31, 18, 4343–4351, 2008.
33. Tajeddine, A., Kayssi, A., Chehab, A., Artail, H., A comprehensive reputation-based trust model for distributed systems, in: *Workshop of the 1st International Conference on Security and Privacy for Emerging Areas in Communication Networks*, IEEE, pp. 116–125, 20052005.
34. Tahta, U.E., Sen, S., Can, A.B., GenTrust: A genetic trust management model for peer-to-peer systems. *Appl. Soft Comput.*, 34, 693–704, 2015.
35. Azzedin, F. and Maheswaran, M., Trust modeling for peer-to-peer based computing systems, in: *Proceedings International Parallel and Distributed Processing Symposium*, IEEE, p. 10, 2003.

36. Li, L., Trust derivation and recommendation management in a trust model, in: *2008 International Conference on Intelligent Information Hiding and Multimedia Signal Processing*, IEEE, pp. 219–222, 2008.
37. Song, W., Phoha, V.V., Xu, X., An adaptive recommendation trust model in multiagent system, in: *Proceedings. IEEE/WIC/ACM International Conference on Intelligent Agent Technology, (IAT)*, IEEE, pp. 462–465, 2004.
38. Kamvar, S.D., Schlosser, M.T., Garcia-Molina, H., The eigentrust algorithm for reputation management in p2p networks, in: *Proceedings of the 12th international conference on World Wide Web*, pp. 640–651, 2003.
39. Wang, Y. and Vassileva, J., Bayesian network-based trust model, in: *Proceedings IEEE/WIC International Conference on Web Intelligence (WI 2003)*, IEEE, pp. 372–378, 2003.
40. Li, L., Zhang, S., Fan, L., Behavior-aware role based trust management, in: *2008 The 9th International Conference for Young Computer Scientists*, IEEE, pp. 1919–1924, 2008.
41. Ou, W., Wang, X., Han, W., Wang, Y., Research on trust evaluation model based on TPM, in: *2009 Fourth International Conference on Frontier of Computer Science and Technology*, IEEE, pp. 593–597, 2009.
42. Pazaitis, A., De Filippi, P., Kostakis, V., Blockchain and value systems in the sharing economy: The illustrative case of Backfeed. *Technol. Forecast. Soc. Change*, 125, 105–115, 2017.
43. Jelenc, D., Hermoso, R., Sabater-Mir, J., Trček, D., Decision making matters: A better way to evaluate trust models. *Knowledge-Based Syst.*, 52, 147–164, 2013.
44. Crosby, G.V., Pissinou, N., Gadze, J., A framework for trust-based cluster head election in wireless sensor networks, in: *Second IEEE Workshop on Dependability and Security in Sensor Networks and Systems*, IEEE, p. 10, 2006.
45. Hur, J., Lee, Y., Yoon, H., Choi, D., Jin, S., Trust evaluation model for wireless sensor networks, in: *The 7th International Conference on Advanced Communication Technology, 2005, ICACT 2005*, vol. 1, IEEE, pp. 491–496, 2005.
46. Ganeriwal, S., Balzano, L.K., Srivastava, M.B., Reputation-based framework for high integrity sensor networks. *ACM Trans. Sens. Netw. (TOSN)*, 4, 3, 1–37, 2008.
47. Pissinou, N. and Crosby, G.V., Cluster-based reputation and trust for wireless sensor networks, in: *2007 4th IEEE consumer communications and networking conference*, IEEE, pp. 604–608, 2007.
48. Chen, T.-Y., Chen, Y.-M., Chu, H.-C., Developing a trust evaluation method between co-workers in virtual project team for enabling resource sharing and collaboration. *Comput. Ind.*, 59, 6, 565–579, 2008.
49. Ehikioya, S.A. and Olukunle, A.A., A formal model of distributed security for electronic commerce transactions systems. *Int. J. Networked Distrib. Comput.*, 7, 2, 68–84, 2019.

50. Voloch, N., Gal-Oz, N., Gudes, E., A trust based privacy providing model for online social networks. *Online Soc. Netw. Media*, 24, 100138, 2021.
51. Malhotra, D., A framework for trust and reputation in distributed environments. *Int. J. Res. Rev. Comput. Sci.*, 2, 2, 617, 2011.
52. Issarny, V. and Bennaceur, A., Composing distributed systems: Overcoming the interoperability challenge, in: *Formal Methods for Components and Objects: 11th International Symposium, FMCO 2012, Bertinoro, Italy, September 24-28, 2012, Revised Lectures 11*, Springer Berlin Heidelberg, pp. 168–196, 2013.
53. Tripathi, S.L. and Mahmud, M., *Explainable Machine Learning Models and Architecture*, Wiley & Scrivener Publishing LLC, USA, 2023, https://doi.org/10.1002/9781394186570.
54. Li, Z., Fang, W., Zhu, C., Gao, Z., Zhang, W., Ai-enabled trust in distributed networks. *IEEE Access*, 2023.

# 12

# Trust in Distributed Systems, Distributed Ledger, Blockchain, and Related Technologies

**Shikha Verma[1]*, Priya Mishra[1] and Sandhya Avasthi[2]**

[1]*Department of Computer Applications, ABES Engineering College, Ghaziabad, India*
[2]*Department of CSE, ABES Engineering College, Ghaziabad, India*

***Abstract***
Distributed trust, reliant on a group of people rather than a single entity, epitomizes a decentralized trust paradigm. Enabled by blockchain technology, it ensures security, immutability, and transparency. Through consensus processes and cryptographic procedures, participants' confidence is fostered and sustained, facilitating secure and open communication. As distributed trust gains wider acceptance, it holds the potential to revolutionize industries, streamline processes, and foster international collaboration. A recording system that is distributed ledger technology (DLT), recording digital asset transactions, allows for simultaneous recording across multiple locations. DLT differs from traditional databases by lacking an administrative database and central features. DLT includes the technology architecture and rules facilitating simultaneous record update, validation, and access across distributed ledgers.

***Keywords***: Cryptocurrency, distributed ledger, serverless computing, blockchain, distributed ledger technology (DLT), IoT

## 12.1 Introduction

Trust encompasses various dimensions beyond mere security, including aptitude, benevolence, accessibility, strength, and dependability, together

**Corresponding author*: shikhasaxena83@gmail.com

Sandhya Avasthi and Suman Lata Tripathi (eds.) Distributed and Parallel Computing, (257–280)

with features unique to each user. The subjective likelihood that one person expects another to carry out an action that is essential to their well-being is known as reliability trust. But trust goes beyond this [1–3], because decision trust is the readiness of one side to feel secure enough to rely on someone or something in a particular scenario, even when there may be unfavorable consequences. Behavior trust and reputation are pivotal concepts in trust assessment. Behavior trust [4, 5], defined as the confidence in a device's competence to perform as expected within a specific context and timeframe, is integral to every online transaction. Conversely, reputation serves as an indirect trust mechanism [6–8], where trustworthiness is evaluated based on past behavior observations within a specific context and timeframe. In addition, trust is referred to as model that is decentralized and depends on participating nodes in the system.

The complication of trust in the Internet of Things (IoT) setting [9, 11–14] is combined by the varied units organized within it, including physical devices, requests, facilities, and persons. Each unit may remark and measure belief in a different way, making it impossible to find a remarkable standpoint. Trust affairs spread crossways numerous stages and gatherings, from human users believing service workers to devices winning in machine-to-machine connections. Moreover, the energetic and clear nature of IoT connections often includes imperfect information exchange among devices, requiring the outline of standing mechanisms.

To address these challenges, trust mechanisms in IoT must be capable of transmission trust values to devices with nominal management overhead and without relying on centralized entities. Moreover, as IoT services frequently trust on organized chains of facilities, guaranteeing belief across the entire deal chain becomes imperative. Defining and establishing trust in the IoT realm are a multifaceted endeavor, deeply intertwined with the intricacy of the IoT network [10] and the diverse interactions within it. Therefore, trust mechanisms must be adaptive, decentralized, and capable of addressing the exclusive tasks posed by the IoT landscape.

## 12.2 Trust in Distributed Ledger

The previous few ages have seen rise in tendency among corporations to approve professional models positioned on making value proposals that blend products and services. However, trust-related challenges have hindered the full implementation of these innovative business models. This chapter explores as well as evaluates how decentralized individuals' trust and cooperation might be improved by distributed ledgers such as blockchains [15] in a chain network. Through the development of a demonstrator, we illustrate the feasibility of decentralizing value chains within specific parameters.

These days, a ledger usually acts as the primary record, whether in book or digital form, for managing economic transactions measured in monetary units of a/c across various a/c types, commonly utilized in bookkeeping [16]. Although the concept of ledgers has deep roots in human civilization, serving as a means to arrange and monitor assets and resources since ancient times. Dating back 5000 years to Babylonia, the earliest forms of written language essentially functioned as ledgers for managing grains and other resources [17]. The ability to manage resources efficiently and reliably enabled the development and management of big cities, facilitated collaboration on a broader scale. Up to the creation of the double-entry bookkeeping system in northern Italy in the 14th century, ledger remained a crucial component of society [18, 19].

Advent of the double-entry approach marked a significant shift in society, offering advantages over the old traditional systems. Notably, the double-entry system was more transparent and easier to comprehend, laying the groundwork for our modern economy. This system, coupled with the introduction of fiat money, where the currency's worth is guaranteed by nations rather than tied to precious metals, facilitated global collaboration and eased cross-border trade. The blockchain is a novel kind of ledger that has surfaced in recent years [20].

### 12.2.1 Double-Spending Problem

In 2008, the idea of blockchain surfaced as a way to address the peer-to-peer network double-spending issue [21]. The potential that digital assets and currencies can be spent more than once by making duplicates of themselves gives rise to this issue. The first blockchain system, Bitcoin, was introduced by Nakamoto [21], laying the groundwork for a technology that is currently extensively used. As a result, many of the flaws and restrictions of the first system have been addressed in the creation of second-generation distributed ledgers [21].

However, critics continue to raise concerns, particularly regarding the technology's energy consumption, with estimations suggesting significant energy expenditure, especially during peak periods [22]. Second-generation blockchains have sought more efficient implementations, yet challenges persist, hindering the technology's competitiveness against centralized solutions [23]. Distributed ledger solutions require collective resources to maintain trust and security, making them comparatively costlier and harder to manage from a single-agent perspective. While offering traceability and transparency, the distributed nature of data in blockchain networks compromises scalability and raises privacy concerns [23].

In today's cryptocurrency networks, privacy issues are often addressed by allowing users to remain anonymous. However, future applications, such as logistics tracking, may face integrity challenges if using distributed ledgers for purposes beyond currency exchange. Critics also argue that blockchain solutions do not inherently guarantee indisputability, as they do not address the procedure of registration of info into the ledger, including the conversion of physical world data into digitized form.

## 12.3 Trust Management in Edge-Based IoT Systems

Management of trust in edge-based IoT systems is a crucial area of focus on ensuring the reliability of interactions between edge network and IoT nodes together. Following an extensive study of the literature obtained in our survey, we have identified several key features and requirements that a trust management framework should possess. We will delve into the proposals found in our literature review, examining how each addresses these

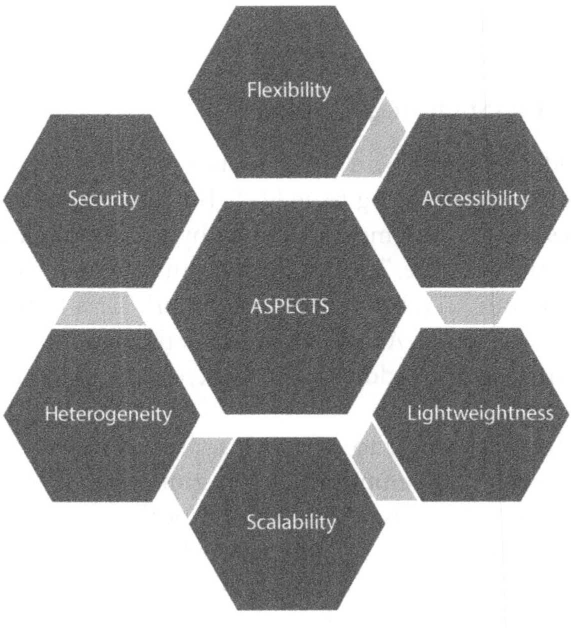


**Figure 12.1** Requirements for management of trust in edge-based IoT systems.

features and requirements. This analysis will be presented in Figure 12.1, providing a clear overview of the coverage of each proposal in fulfilling the identified features and requirements.

## 12.4 A Taxonomy of Trust Computation Frameworks for Edge-Based IoT Systems

The purpose of this section is to list the knowledge gaps in the area of trust in edge-based IoT systems. Six parameters—trust composition, trust propagation, trust aggregation, trust update, trust generation, and trust with blockchain—are used to classify the various trust computation models now in use. Notably, these characteristics are orthogonal, and our classification is not mutually exclusive. Blockchain-based models could benefit from a similar strategy that takes composition, aggregation, and other viewpoints into account. The six parameters are described as follows:

i. **Trust composition**: Social trust (ST) and quality of service (QoS) are the two elements that make up trust composition. The ability of an IoT device to deliver high-quality service is represented by QoS, whereas the social connections among IoT device owners are reflected in ST. QoS and ST consider trust, privacy, centrality, connectedness, honesty, and confidence among other criteria. ST is further divided into two categories: direct and indirect trust. Whereas indirect trust represents the confidence the community, or a portion of it, has in a device, direct trust examines interactions between two devices.

ii. **Trust propagation**: This parameter looks at the nodes' mutual trust propagation. Generally, two types of schemes exist: decentralized and centralized. When IoT devices spread trust to others without depending on a centralized organization (like a MANET or WSN), this is known as distributed propagation. An edge server or other centralized entity is necessary for centralized propagation.

iii. **Trust aggregation**: The process of combining trust values derived from node input or self-observation is known as trust aggregation.

iv. **Trust update**: Trust principles are classically modernized through event-driven or dynamic-driven organizations.

In event-driven updates, a node's belief data are rested subsequent to an incidence. Dynamic-driven informs occasionally involve assembly indication and informing trust through combination mechanisms.

v. **Trust formation**: This restriction defines in what way trust is recognized based on certain belongings. Trust creation can be single-trust, where only one belonging is measured, or multitrust, applying multidimensional trust by leveraging numerous belongings.

vi. **Trust with blockchain**: Any blockchain technology–based financial application is designed in a way that it builds trust in all digital transactions. In the context of digital currency, blockchain has become trust-building technology.

## 12.5 Trust in Distributed Databases

Trust plays a vital role in actual distributed database systems, where high accessibility and responsibility tolerance are paramount. Duplication is a common method used to attain these objectives. This chapter equivalences numerous existing duplication techniques in terms of application and boundaries, while also presenting a novel duplication technique called TIRS (trust-based intelligent replication system).

TIRS controls trust mechanisms through data read and write processes, enhancing its flexibility against faulty or malicious nodes. Through the incorporation of belief into the replication protocol, TIRS demonstrates [24] strong fault acceptance and high-speed data reading capabilities. Trust in distributed databases is paramount for guaranteeing the integrity, security, and data availability across multiple nodes in a networked environment. It includes several critical dimensions, including reliability, safety, constancy, performance, and fault tolerance. Reliability is essential for keeping the accuracy and stability of data, even in the face of disappointments or disruptions. Security measures, such as encoding and access controls, are energetic for shielding data from illegal access and malicious attacks. Consistency ensures that all nodes in the distributed system have access to the most up-to-date and synchronized data, preventing conflicts or inconsistencies. Performance considerations, such as scalability and latency, are crucial for meeting user wants and ensuring efficient data processing. Fault tolerance mechanisms, including repetition and redundancy, help mitigate the impact of node failures and ensure continuous data availability. Trust in distributed databases is built on a strong basis of reliability, safety, constancy, performance, and fault tolerance, which collectively instill confidence in the integrity and reliability of the distributed database system.

## 12.6 Trust in Blockchain

To make cryptocurrency transactions easier, Nakamoto fashioned blockchain technology back in 2008 [25]. The application of blockchain knowledge to distributed ledger schemes and other economic activities has been the subject of more fresh research [26]. In a matter of minutes, many entities may share data and transactions, thanks to blockchain technology, all without the need for third-party intervention or verification. This can be achieved with a shared data framework that generates real-time self-updates using computer algorithms [27].

In current years, there has been significant attention in blockchain technology as a decentralized solution. Blockchain offers various advantages, including decentralization, encryption algorithms, immutable data storage, consensus mechanisms, etc. [28, 29]. Once information is verified and stored on the blockchain by consensus nodes, it remains permanently recorded unless a majority (more than 51%) of the network nodes are simultaneously controlled. This characteristic presents an opportunity to address security issues arising from centralized data storage.

Traditional consensus methods include DPoS (delegated proof of stake) [30], PoW (proof of work) [30], and PoS (proof of stake) [30]. But some academics are experimenting with novel ways by fusing several consensuses, such as PoA (proof of authority), Bitchain-NG, and proof of elapsed time [31].

These blockchain consensus mechanisms effectively enhance trust among network nodes in distributed systems, thereby overcoming security vulnerabilities associated with single points of failure and potential data breaches from attacks on central nodes.

Also, blockchain functions as a distributed ledger kept by multiple nodes, eliminating the necessity for mediators and dipping cost, although many current agreement mechanisms rely heavily on on-chain calculation, leading to matters such as separations and cooperation delays. Splits present doubt and uncertainty into the blockchain, while consensus postponements pose tests for broader IoT applications. Therefore, finding an equilibrium among competence and safety remains an important task in blockchain research and development.

Through this multipurpose nature of blockchain, belief is a vital element in the operation and extensive acceptance of blockchain technology. At its heart, belief is vital for validating communications within a blockchain network. Applicants must feel assured that transaction is exactly noted and stated by the network's harmony. Additionally, belief plays an important role in preserving the integrity of data stored on the blockchain. The immutability of the ledger relies severely on belief to ensure that data run unalterable and loyal over time. Smart contracts, which are integral to blockchain, rely on trust for their fruitful implementation. Operators must have assurance that the code will execute as intended without requiring intermediaries. Decentralization, another critical aspect of blockchain, depends on trust to ensure that selections are complete in the network's best benefits. Finally, trust is serious for the safety of blockchain networks and the safeguarding of user assets, providing users with sureness that their transactions and data are shielded from illegal access. Figure 12.2 shows the trust model of blockchain.

Trust in blockchain stems from its primary principles of transparency, decentralization, and immutability. The goal is given below:

**Transparency**: Blockchain transactions are crystal clear to all network members, in difference to traditional systems where transactions are authenticated and recorded by a central authority such as a bank or

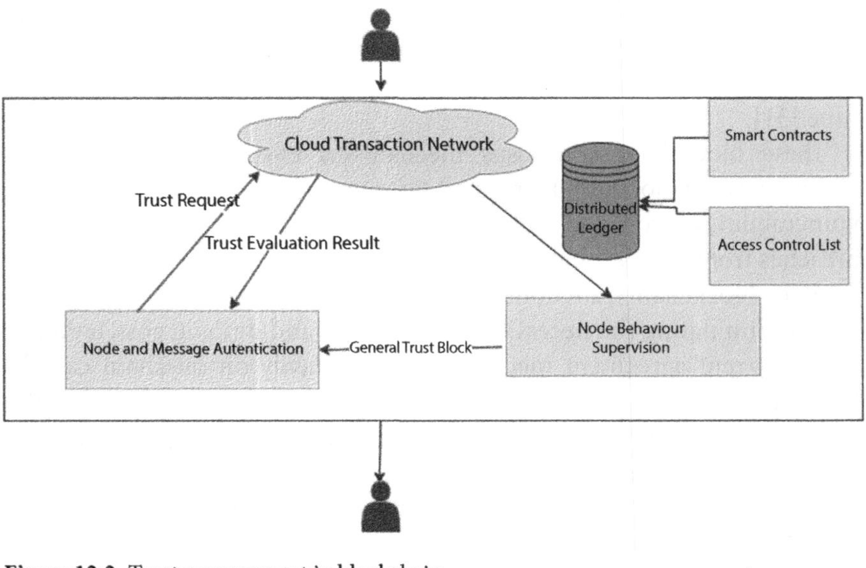


**Figure 12.2** Trust management in blockchain.

government.Anyone can see the whole transaction history because of this visibility, which ensures transparency and fosters user trust. Also, blockchain's decentralized structure does away with the need for a single leading party. Somewhat blockchain functions through a network of nodes, each of which keeps a duplicate copy of the ledger. Because transactions are accepted and recorded by network participants through consensus, this decentralization decreases the prospect of fraud or manipulation. We can understand it through an actual state. For example, in instruction to pay currency to party B using a cryptocurrency based on blockchain, party A must broadcast the transaction to the network, and each node must autonomously confirm its legality. The transaction is close to the blockchain and added to a block after a consensus is gained. By confirming that transaction records cannot be changed without the consent of the majority of participants, this procedure helps the dependability and trustworthiness of blockchain technology.

**Immutability**: The blockchain's immutability transaction serves as a support of the technology's consistency and trustworthiness. It indicates that when a transaction is firmly noted on the blockchain, it becomes unchallengeable, impermeable to changes or removals. This immutableness does not happen suddenly, but rather a meticulously engineered attribute is achieved through a combination of cryptographic mechanism, especially symmetric key and consensus mechanisms, rendering the blockchain tamper-proof.

Cryptographic hashing, an important aspect of blockchain technology, entails the alteration of transactional data into a distinct, fixed-length character string called a hash.

This process is executed through sophisticated cryptographic algorithms, ensuring that each transaction is mapped to a distinct hash. Even a small change to the transactional data would produce a totally distinct hash, thereby helping as a digital fingerprint that facilitates the detection of any tampering attempts.

Also, the immutableness of blockchain transactions is upheld through consensus mechanisms, which arrange the validation and acceptance of transactions by network participants. Protocols such as PoW or PoS mandate that all nodes in the network reach consensus on the validity of transactions before they are appended to the blockchain. This decentralized validation process ensures that no single entity can individually adjust transactional data. Any attempt to change a transaction would necessitate the collusion of a majority of network participants, a formidable challenge in a decentralized ecosystem.

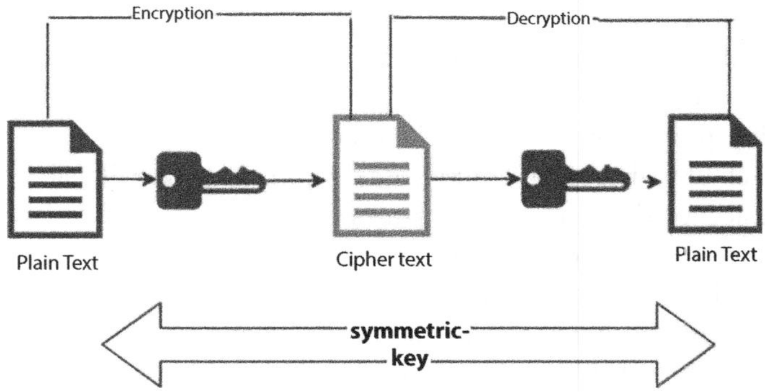


**Figure 12.3** Encryption and decryption.

Consider a scenario where somebody initiates a transaction to transfer digital assets to a blockchain of network. Upon broadcasting the transaction to the system, it undergoes difficult validation by network nodes, as shown in Figure 12.3, with each node independently verifying its authenticity. Once authenticated, the transaction is bundled into a block, where it is hashed and added to the blockchain. This process ensures that the deal becomes an unchallengeable record, firmly embedded in the blockchain's ledger for eternity.

In essence, the immutability of blockchain transactions serves as a bedrock of trust and integrity within the ecology. It promises users that their data are safeguarded against tampering and manipulation, fostering confidence in the reliability of blockchain technology for a myriad of applications across diverse industries.

**Smart agreements**: An innovative feature of smart agreements of blockchain technology is allowing for the automation and execution of contractual agreements without the need for intermediaries. These self-executing contracts can repeatedly enforce agreements whenever encoded circumstances are met since the terms and conditions of these contracts are directly embedded into the blockchain's code. This feature not only streamlines the contract execution process but also enhances trust among parties involved, as it ensures that agreements are executed precisely as intended, without the potential for human error or manipulation.

As an illustration, look at a condition where two parties enter into smart contract facilitated by the Ethereum's blockchain. They decide that upon the distribution of a specific amount of merchandise, a predetermined payment will be automatically released between the parties. The terms of this agreement are encoded into a smart contract deployed on the Ethereum blockchain. Once the goods are distributed, the smart contract separately verifies this event by accessing external data sources or relying on predefined conditions within the blockchain itself. Upon confirming the fulfillment of the terms, the smart contract automatically triggers the transaction of money from sender to receiver account, all without the need for intermediaries or manual intervention.

This automated execution of contractual agreements not only eliminates the need for trust in intermediaries but also enhances trust between the contracting parties. Since the terms of the agreement are enforced by code and recorded on an unchallengeable blockchain ledger, sender and receiver can have confidence that the agreement will execute exactly as specified, without the risk of disputes or inconsistencies. Furthermore, smart contracts extend beyond simple payment agreements and can be utilized in many sectors, including supply chain management, real estate, insurance, and more.

**Security**: Blockchain employs sophisticated cryptographic techniques to ensure the security of transactions and data, instilling trust among users by safeguarding in contradiction of unauthorized access and interfering. Two primary cryptographic methods, public-key cryptography and cryptographic hashing, play essential roles in this security framework.

Public-key cryptography, also known as asymmetric cryptography, is used to secure transactions on the blockchain. In this technique, each participant in the network possesses a pair of cryptographic keys: a public key and a private key. The public key is nearby to all members and is used to encrypt data, whereas the private key is known only to its owner and is used to decrypt the encrypted data. When a transaction is started on the blockchain, it is encrypted using the recipient's public key. Only the receiver, who holds the conforming private key, can decrypt and access the transaction details. This ensures the privacy and integrity of transactions, as only authorized party can access and confirm the transaction data. Cryptographic hashing, on the other hand, is employed to protect the integrity of data stored on the blockchain. Hash purposes generate fixed-size, unique fingerprints of input data, known as hashes. These hashes are computed based on the satisfaction of the data, making it practically impossible to reverse-engineer the unique input from the hash. In the context of blockchain, cryptographic hashing is used to create a safe and tamper-proof record of transactions and blocks. Each block in the blockchain covers a hash of the previous block, forming a chain that links all transactions together. Any change to the data within a block would result in a change in its hash, thus canceling subsequent blocks. This inherent link between blocks ensures the immutability and integrity of the blockchain, as any altering attempts would be easily detected and disallowed by the network.

For example, let us consider a scenario where A wants to send funds to B using a blockchain-based cryptocurrency. When A starts the transaction, it is encrypted using B's public key, ensuring that only B can access and decrypt the transaction details using his private key. Additionally, the transaction details are hashed to make a unique fingerprint, which is recorded in a block along with other transactions. The hash of this block comprised the subsequent block, forming a chain of blocks that are cryptographically linked. Any attempt to change the transaction data or the content of a block would result in a change in its hash, alerting the network to the tampering attempt and preserving the integrity of the blockchain.

**Consensus mechanisms**: Blockchain networks apply consensus mechanisms such as PoW or PoS to authorize transactions and uphold the integrity of the ledger, thereby fostering trust among participants. These mechanisms ensure that all network nodes settle on the soundness of transactions before they are added to the blockchain, enhancing confidence in the correctness and reliability of the system. For instance, in a PoW system like that used by Bitcoin, network nodes compete to solve complex mathematical puzzles in order to validate transactions and create new blocks. This process requires significant computational power, and the first node to solve the puzzle earns the right to add the new block to the blockchain. The remaining of the network then verifies the validity of the block, ensuring consensus is reached before it is believed as part of the ledger. Similarly, validators are selected to produce new blocks in a PoS system, such as Ethereum 2.0, based on the quantity of cryptocurrency they own and are ready to "stake" as collateral. Because trying to validate fraudulent transactions can result in the forfeiture of their staked funds, validators are motivated to operate honorably.

## 12.7 Serverless Computing

Serverless computing has transformed cloud computing, altering how developers create and deploy applications. They have gained importance in recent times due to its benefits such as reduced costs, decreased latency, eliminating the need for management, and its scalability. Unlike old-style server-based models that need developers to manage server infrastructure, serverless computation precises away servers, letting developers to focus solely on coding and deploying functions. At its core, serverless computing functions on a "pay as you proceed" principle, where billing for users is incomplete to the resources used during function implementation, rather than for lazy server time.

## 12.7.1 Functions of Serverless Computing

A key feature of serverless computing is its automatic scaling, dynamically adjusting resource allocation based on call. This ensures best performance, even during sudden traffic spikes. Moreover, serverless architectures [5] promote high accessibility and fault tolerance, with cloud providers handling infrastructure maintenance and repetition automatically, minimizing downtime. Few functions of serverless computing are shown in Figure 12.4. Serverless computing includes Backend as a Service (BaaS) and Function as a Service (FaaS). Baas handles user management, messaging, and storage services [32].

Besides these rewards, security and trust are the subjects faced by these systems. The necessity for trust in serverless computing stems from numerous factors. Users necessitate trust that serverless platforms will implement their functions reliably, devoid of downtime or service interruptions. Given that developers rely on these stages to operate critical business functions and applications, any downtime or service disturbance could result in significant consequences, including revenue loss and deterioration of customer trust. Let us consider a real-world example of how security and

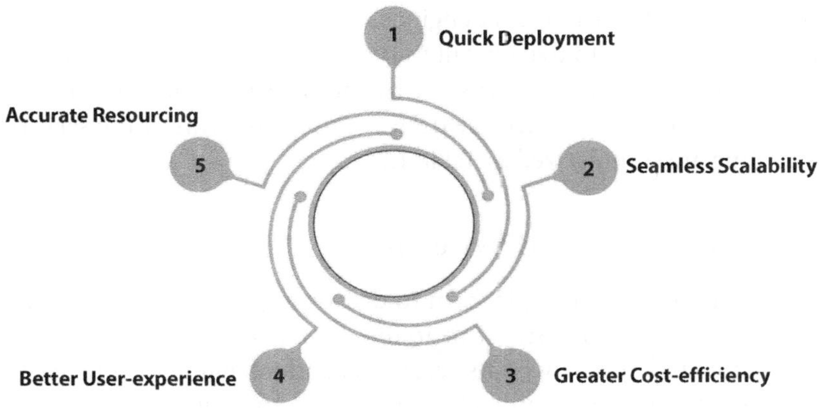


**Figure 12.4** Functions of serverless computing.

trust in serverless computing are vital for a healthcare application. Imagine a healthcare organization emerging a serverless application for storing and processing patient health records in the cloud. This application allows medicinal professionals to access patient data securely and professionally, enabling them to make well-versed decisions and provide timely care. In this scenario, safety is paramount to protect the subtle health information stored in the application. Patients trust the healthcare organization to precaution their data and ensure its confidentiality, integrity, and availability [33].

### 12.7.2 Serverless Computing Performance and Benefits

Users anticipate serverless stages to furnish high-performance computing resources to efficiently execute functions with receptiveness. Trust in serverless computing involves confidence that the platform can expertly handle varying workloads and dynamically scale to meet demand, all while upholding low latency and negligible overhead. Let us delve into a real-world example to illustrate the meaning of performance and trust in serverless computing.

Consider a popular e-commerce platform [34] that utilizes serverless computing to handle its product recommendation engine. This recommendation engine is crucial for providing personalized product proposals to users based on their browsing history, purchase behavior, and other relevant data. As the e-commerce platform acknowledges fluctuating traffic throughout the day, particularly during peak shopping seasons or publicity events, the performance of the recommendation engine becomes essential to ensure a seamless user experience. In this scenario, users trust the serverless platform to deliver high-performance computing resources to efficiently execute the reference engine's functions with receptiveness. They expect the platform to dynamically scale resources in real time to handle sudden spikes in traffic and ensure that product references are delivered promptly without any noticeable delays. Various benefits of the serverless computing are summarized in Table 12.1.

### 12.7.3 Trust in Serverless Computing

By trusting the serverless platform to deliver high-performance computing resources and seamlessly scale to meet demand, the e-commerce platform can confidently rely on its recommendation engine to enhance user engagement, drive sales, and deliver a superior shopping experience. This fosters trust and loyalty among users, who expect consistent performance

**Table 12.1** Summary of benefits of serverless computing.

| SN | Benefits | Description |
|---|---|---|
| 1 | Cost-effective | There is an abstraction from server infrastructure that provides less expenditure on hardware. The user is charged according to usage. |
| 2 | Scalability | Serverless computing solves resource allocation problem, so developers do not have to worry about application scalability matters/issues. As user request increases, application automatically scales up. |
| 3 | Server-side management | Cloud provider manages and maintains software and hardware. It manages all deployment software. They also deal with administration operations. |
| 4 | Easy deployment | Deployment is easy in serverless computing. Developer needs to uploaded necessary functions and then can release software. |
| 5 | Reduced latency | The applications are not hosted on server; hence, code can be executed anywhere on network. Cloud vendors run the application on servers near the end user machine. |

and responsiveness from the platform, especially during critical moments such as peak shopping periods or promotional campaigns. Ultimately, act and trust in serverless computing play a vital role in ensuring the success and competitiveness of online businesses in today's digital scene.

Trust in serverless computing is seriously unfair by the reputation and track record of the cloud service provider bringing the platform. Users must have faith that the provider boasts a proven history of dependability, security, and performance to inspire confidence in the platform's capabilities. Let us consider a scenario in India where a popular food delivery startup, "QuickBite," chooses to transition to serverless computing for its order processing and delivery management system. QuickBite has been experiencing rapid growth in its user base and order volumes across numerous cities in India. With this development, the company faces tests in managing its existing infrastructure, which struggles to handle peak order loads during busy hours, leading to occasional idle time and delays in order processing. To address these challenges, QuickBite decides to travel its order processing and delivery management system to a serverless computing platform on the condition that they are done by a reputable cloud service provider with a strong presence in India. The cloud service provider has built a hard standing in the Indian market for its dependability, security, and presentation [35]. It has a track record of serving many Indian businesses across diverse industries, including e-commerce, financial technology, and healthcare, and has gathered trust among customers for its robust infrastructure and support services. By partnering with this trusted cloud service provider, QuickBite gains confidence in the serverless platform's capabilities to competently handle its order processing needs. The provider's platform proposes autoscaling features that dynamically allocate resources based on demand, safeguarding that QuickBite can flawlessly handle spikes in order volumes throughout peak hours without experiencing stoppage or performance issues.

Additionally, the cloud service provider's safety measures, including encryption, access controls, and submission with Indian data protection regulations, reassure QuickBite that its customers' info and payment details are safeguarded against illegal access or breaches. The company can migrate its order processing and delivery management system to the serverless platform, and its knowledge improves reliability, scalability, and security. The platform professionally processes orders, optimizes delivery routes, and provides real-time updates to customers, attracting the overall user experience. By leveraging serverless computing from a trusted cloud service provider, vendors strengthen their position in the competitive market. The company can focus on expanding its business and serving more clients while relying on the provider's reliable and secure substructure to support its operations. This belief in the serverless platform's capabilities authorizes vendors to innovate and scale their business deprived of worrying about the underlying technology infrastructure.

### 12.7.4 Compliance

Trust spreads to adherence to controlling requirements and industry standards. Users seek assurance that serverless platforms fulfill pertinent regulations and standards, such as GDPR, Health Insurance Portability and Accountability Act (HIPAA), or SOC2, to ensure data protection and arrangement with legal obligations. For example, businesses such as MediTech, a healthcare technology firm, exemplify the importance of trust finished adherence to regulatory requirements and industry standards. MediTech offers a cloud-based electronic medical records system to hospitals and clinics, requiring strict obedience to regulations such as the Personal Data Protection Bill and standards set by the Ministry of Health and Family Welfare. This safeguards the protection of patients' sensitive medical data and arrangements with legal obligations. Clients rely on MediTech's promise of data security and compliance to safeguard their patients' information, thereby reinforcing belief in the company's services.

### 12.7.5 Monitoring and Support

Users rely on serverless platforms to propose comprehensive monitoring, logging, and support services to address any issues, optimize performance, and ensure seamless operation of their functions and applications. Trust in serverless computing hinges on confidence that the platform delivers robust monitoring and support capabilities to tackle any challenges that may arise. In the Indian context, consider a startup like "TechServe" that specializes in developing digital answers for local businesses. Utilizing a serverless platform, TechServe has goals to deploy and achieve its applications efficiently. Their reliance on this platform extends to expecting it to provide essential nursing, logging, and support services crucial for ensuring unified operations. Through comprehensive nursing tools, TechServe can track vital performance metrics such as response times and user interactions, allowing them to promptly address any issues that may influence their applications' functionality. Additionally, robust logging competencies enable TechServe to examine user behavior and ensure compliance with local data confidentiality regulations. As an inauguration, TechServe heavily leans on the support services provided by the platform, seeking timely assistance from technical experts to resolve any technical challenges they face. Eventually, trust in serverless computing for TechServe breaks on the platform's aptitude to deliver tailored monitoring and support services, ensuring the smooth operation and optimization of their digital solutions within the Indian market landscape.

## 12.8 Trust in Cloud Computing

Delivering computer services over the Internet (sometimes known as "the cloud") on a pay-per-use basis includes servers, storage, databases, networking, software, and more. Cloud service providers offer resources and services that operators can access in place of owning physical infrastructure or data centers. These facilities are scalable and flexible and can be rapidly provisioned, enabling organizations to innovate, deploy requests, and manage data more efficiently. Trust is crucial in cloud computing due to several reasons described in this section.

### 12.8.1 Data Security and Privacy

Organizations entrust cloud workers with sensitive data, such as exclusive information, customer records, and monetary data. They need a declaration that this information is protected from unwanted access, breaches, or data loss. Trust is important in cloud computing, permeating every aspect of its adoption and use. For instance, a healthcare organization such as "MediCare Clinic" trusts cloud services to firmly store the electronic health records of patients [37]. They trust their cloud worker to implement stringent safety measures, such as encoding and access controls, to protect sensitive medicinal information and comply with regulations such as HIPAA. Likewise, an e-commerce platform [36], like "ShopNow," depends on cloud infrastructure for its site hosting. Trust in the cloud provider's dependability ensures continuous service, critical for meeting customer stresses, especially during peak shopping periods. Whether it is regulatory compliance, presentation optimization, or disaster recovery, trust forms the bedrock of fruitful cloud adoption, enabling organizations to innovate and thrive in today's digital landscape.

### 12.8.2 Service Reliability and Availability

Businesses trust cloud services to be obtainable and accessible whenever needed [38]. Trust in the cloud provider's substructure and network reliability ensures minimal stoppage and uninterrupted operations. Businesses rely heavily on cloud services to ensure their processes are available and accessible whenever needed. For example, consider a global e-commerce retailer, "GlobalMart," which utilizes cloud services to host its online store. GlobalMart trusts its cloud provider to continue robust infrastructure and network reliability, ensuring nominal downtime and uninterrupted access to its website for customers worldwide. This trust in the cloud provider's dependability allows GlobalMart to offer seamless shopping knowledge, even during high-traffic events such as periodic sales or product launches. Without this belief, GlobalMart would risk losing income and customer trust due to service disturbances or outages. Therefore, trust in the cloud provider's substructure and network reliability is essential for businesses to preserve continuous processes and meet customer prospects.

### 12.8.3 Compliance and Regulatory Requirements

Regulations controlling data handling, storage, and transfer apply to a wide range of subdivisions. Cloud providers must demonstrate compliance with these rules to instill trust in their clientele and ensure legal adherence. Regarding the field of cloud computing, compliance with regulatory standards is paramount, particularly for industries subject to stringent data handling and storage regulations. For example, consider a financial institution, "SecureBank," which relies on cloud-based storage solutions for sensitive customer financial data. SecureBank trusts its cloud workers to comply with manufacturing guidelines such as the Payment Card Industry, Data Security Standard, or the Sarbanes Oxley Act, [39], which govern the safe handling and storing of financial information. This trust ensures that SecureBank's data leftovers are secure, auditable, and compliant with regulatory standards, mitigating the risk of financial penalties or reputational damage due to noncompliance [40–42]. Likewise, a healthcare organization such as "MediCare Clinic" entrusts its patient health accounts to cloud services, relying on the cloud provider's obedience to regulations such as HIPAA to safeguard patient secrecy and confidentiality. Without trust in the cloud provider's adherence to regulatory necessities, organizations would face lawful and working challenges, underscoring the critical rank of compliance in cloud computing.

### 12.8.4 Performance and Scalability

Cloud services should be able to scale dynamically to meet changing demand and performance requirements. Trust in the cloud provider's infrastructure and scalability capabilities ensures that applications can handle fluctuations in workload effectively. Cloud providers frequently offer disaster regaining and backup answers to help organizations improve from unforeseen outages, data loss, or ruins. Trust in the cloud provider's tragedy recovery processes ensures business steadiness and data resilience.

## 12.9 Conclusion

Trust has many dimensions when it comes to distributed technologies such as cloud computing, serverless computing, grid computing, distributed databases, and blockchain. The primary notion in trust involves many actors such as trustors and trustees. In distributed databases, trust safeguards high availability and fault tolerance, vital for real-time operations.

Various repetition techniques, including the innovative TIRS, improve resilience by incorporating trust mechanisms during data operations, protecting against faults and malicious nodes. First developed for crypto-currency transactions, blockchain has changed to serve distributed ledger systems and more. It eases rapid data and transaction conversation without third-party confirmation, leveraging shared data outlines and algorithms for instant information. In this chapter, serverless computing and cloud computing are discussed, giving details about how to build trust in this type of distributed technology.

## References

1. Buccafurri, F., Fotia, L., Lax, G., Privacy-preserving resource evaluation in social networks, in: *Proceedings of the 10th Annual International Conference on Privacy, Security and Trust*, IEEE, 2012.
2. Buccafurri, F., Fotia, L., Lax, G., Allowing non-identifying information disclosure in citizen opinion evaluation, in: *Proceedings of the International Conference on Electronic Government and the Information Systems Perspective*, Springer, 2013a.
3. Buccafurri, F., Fotia, L., Lax, G., Allowing privacy-preserving analysis of social network likes, in: *Proceedings of the 11th Annual Conference on Privacy, Security and Trust*, IEEE, 2013b.
4. Buccafurri, F., Fotia, L., Lax, G., A privacy-preserving e-participation framework allowing citizen opinion analysis. *Electron. Gov. Int. J.*, 11, 3, 185–206, 2015.
5. Azzedin, F., Taxonomy of reputation assessment in peer-to-peer systems and analysis of their data retrieval. *Knowl. Eng. Rev.*, 29, 4, 463, 2014.
6. Comi, A., Fotia, L., Messina, F., Pappalardo, G., Rosaci, D., Sarné, G.M.L., Using semantic negotiation for ontology enrichment in e-learning multi-agent systems, in: *Proceedings of the 9th International Conference on Complex, Intelligent, and Software Intensive Systems*, IEEE, 2015.
7. Comi, A., Fotia, L., Messina, F., Rosaci, D., Sarnè, G.M.L., A qos-aware, trust-based aggregation model for grid federations, in: *OTM Confederated International Conferences "On the Move to Meaningful Internet Systems"*, Springer, 2014.
8. Comi, A., Fotia, L., Messina, F., Rosaci, D., Sarné, G.M.L., Grouptrust: Finding trust-based group structures in social communities, in: *International Symposium on Intelligent and Distributed Computing*, Springer, 2016.
9. Fortino, G., Fotia, L., Messina, F., Rosaci, D., Sarné, G.M.L., A meritocratic trust-based group formation in an IoT environment for smart cities. *Future Gener. Comput. Syst.*, 108, 34–45, 2020.

10. Meo, P.D., Fotia, L., Messina, F., Rosaci, D., Sarné, G.M.L., Providing recommendations in social networks by integrating local and global reputation. *Inf. Syst.*, 78, 58–67, 2018.
11. Fortino, G., Fotia, L., Messina, F., Rosaci, D., Sarné, G.M.L., A blockchain-based group formation strategy for optimizing the social reputation capital of an IoT scenario. *Simul. Modell. Pract. Theory*, 108, 102261, 2021.
12. Messina, F., Pappalardo, G., Comi, A., Fotia, L., Rosaci, D., Sarné, G.M.L., Combining reputation and QoS measures to improve cloud service composition. *Int. J. Grid Util. Comput.*, 8, 2, 142–151, 2017.
13. Wang, K., Chen, C.-M., Liang, Z., Hassan, M.M., Sarne, G.M.L., Fotia, L., Fortino, G., A trusted consensus fusion scheme for decentralized collaborated learning in massive iot domain. *Inf. Fusion*, 72, 100–109, 2021.
14. McKnight, D.H. and Chervany, N.L., The Meanings of Trust. Technical Report MISRC Working Paper Series 96-04, University of Minnesota, Management Information Systems Research Center, 1996.
15. Wenngren, J., Lundgren, M., Ericson, A., Lugnet, J., Distributed ledger technologies building trust in value chains? *2020 3rd International Symposium on Small-scale Intelligent Manufacturing Systems (SIMS)*, Gjovik, Norway, pp. 1–6, 2020, doi: 10.1109/SIMS49386.2020.9121489.
16. Lusiani, M., Pancot, C., Sangster, A., Vedovato, M., Bookkeeping, but not for profit: A special form of double entry in a 16th century Venetian charity. *The British Accounting Review*, 55, 5, 101175, 2023. https://doi.org/10.1016/j.bar.2023.101175.
17. Cripps, E.L., The Structure of Prices in the neo-Sumerian Economy (I). *SAT*. 2, 669, 2014.
18. Yamey, B.S., Notes on the origin of double-entry bookkeeping. *Account. Rev.*, 22, 3, 263–272, 1947.
19. Carruthers, B.G. and Espeland, W.N., Accounting for rationality: Double-entry bookkeeping and the rhetoric of economic rationality. *Am. J. Sociol.*, 97, 1, 31–69, 1991.
20. Zheng, Z., Xie, S., Dai, H.N., Chen, X., Wang, H., Blockchain challenges and opportunities: A survey. *Int. J. Web Grid Serv.*, 14, 4, 352–375, 2018.
21. Nakamoto, S., *Bitcoin: A peer-to-peer electronic cash system*, Manubot, 2019.
22. Nowiński, W. and Kozma, M., How can blockchain technology disrupt the existing business models? *Entrep. Bus. Econ. Rev.*, 5, 3, 173–188, 2017.
23. Avasthi, S., Jain, K., Prakash, A., Sanwal, T., A Blockchain Architecture for Secure Decentralized System and Computing, in: *2024 3rd International conference on Power Electronics and IoT Applications in Renewable Energy and its Control (PARC)*, 2024, February, IEEE, pp. 415–420.
24. Khayat, G. and Maalouf, H., Trust in real-time distributed database systems. *2017 8th International Conference on Information Technology (ICIT)*, Amman, Jordan, pp. 572–579, 2017, doi: 10.1109/ICITECH.2017.8080061.
25. Kumar, R., Badwal, L., Avasthi, S., Prakash, A., A Secure Decentralized E-Voting with Blockchain & Smart Contracts, in: *2023 13th International*

*Conference on Cloud Computing, Data Science & Engineering (Confluence)*, 2023, January, IEEE, pp. 419–424.

26. Li, X., Jiang, P., Chen, T., Luo, X., Wen, Q., A survey on the security of blockchain systems. *Future Gener. Comput. Syst.*, 107, 841–853, 2020, [Google Scholar] [CrossRef] [Green Version].
27. Dorri, A., Kanhere, S.S., Jurdak, R., Gauravaram, P., Blockchain for IoT security and privacy: The case study of a smart home, in: *Proceedings of the 2017 IEEE International Conference on Pervasive Computing and Communications Workshops (PerCom Workshops)*, Kona, HI, USA, 13–17 March 2017, pp. 618–623, [Google Scholar].
28. Novo, O., Blockchain Meets IoT: An Architecture for Scalable Access Management in IoT. *IEEE Internet Things J.*, 5, 1184–1195, 2018, [Google Scholar] [CrossRef].
29. Sun, Y., *et al.*, Dt-dpos: A delegated proof of stake consensus algorithm with dynamic trust. *Procedia Comput. Sci.*, 187, 371–376, 2021.
30. Yang, Z., Yang, K., Lei, L., Zheng, K., Leung, V.C.M., Blockchain-Based Decentralized Trust Management in Vehicular Networks. *IEEE Internet Things J.*, 6, 1495–1505, 2019, [Google Scholar] [CrossRef].
31. Seh, A.H., Zarour, M., Alenezi, M., Sarkar, A.K., Agrawal, A., Kumar, R., Ahmad Khan, R., Healthcare Data Breaches: Insights and Implications. *Healthcare*, 8, 133, 2020.
32. Hassan, H.B., Barakat, S.A., Sarhan, Q.I., Survey on serverless computing. *J. Cloud Comput.*, 10, 1–29, 2021.
33. Vijayasekaran, G. and Duraipandian, M., An Efficient Clustering and Deep Learning Based Resource Scheduling for Edge Computing to Integrate Cloud-IoT. *Wirel. Pers. Commun.*, 124, 3, 1–16, 2022, [Google Scholar] [CrossRef].
34. Kumari, A. and Sahoo, B., Serverless architecture for healthcare management systems, in: *Handbook of research on mathematical modeling for smart healthcare systems*, pp. 203–227, IGI Global, 2022.
35. Datta, P., *et al.*, Valve: Securing function workflows on serverless computing platforms. *Proceedings of The Web Conference 2020*, 2020.
36. Shafiei, H., Khonsari, A., Mousavi, P., Serverless computing: a survey of opportunities, challenges, and applications. *ACM Comput. Surv.*, 54, 11s, 1–32, 2022.
37. Enes, J., Expósito, R.R., Touriño, J., Real-time resource scaling platform for big data workloads on serverless environments. *Future Gener. Comput. Syst.*, 105, 361–379, 2020.
38. Hien, P.T., Adaptive Fault Tolerance Mechanisms for Enhancing Service Reliability in Cloud Computing Environments. *Eigenpub Rev. Sci. Technol.*, 7, 1, 252–265, 2023.
39. Birje, M.N., *et al.*, Cloud computing review: concepts, technology, challenges and security. *Int. J. Cloud Comput.*, 6, 1, 32–57, 2017.

40. Avasthi, S., Chauhan, R., Acharjya, D.P., Significance of preprocessing techniques on text classification over hindi and english short texts, in: *Applications of Artificial Intelligence and Machine Learning: Select Proceedings of ICAAAIML 2021*, Springer Nature Singapore, Singapore, pp. 743–751, 2022.
41. Kumar, R., Avasthi, S., Tripathi, S.L., Architecture of Blockchain-Enabled Decentralized Systems, in: *Decentralized Systems and Distributed Computing*, pp. 53–74, 2024.
42. Tripathi, S.L. and Mahmud, M., *Explainable Machine Learning Models and Architecture*, Wiley & Scrivener Publishing LLC, USA, 2023, https://doi.org/10.1002/9781394186570.

# 13

# Strategy to Improve Psychological Elements and Customer Service in Intelligent Health Systems

**Mani Dublish[1*], Anita Pati Mishra[2] and Shikha Mittal[3]**

[1]*Department of Computer Applications, Ajay Kumar Garg Engineering College, Ghaziabad, U.P., India*
[2]*School of Information and Technology, IMS Noida, Uttar Pradesh, India*
[3]*Department of Management, Raj Kumar Goel Institute of Technology, Ghaziabad, Uttar Pradesh, India*

## *Abstract*

In order to make sure that the creation fulfills the needs and proficiencies of the handler, especially in standings of protection and manager understanding, design processes such as human-centered proposal, which involve the end user through the product growth and testing procedure, can be extremely important. Human-centered design's systematic and iterative approach can frequently provide difficulties when the competitive, linked health industry places demand on design teams for quick and efficient product development life cycles. Our goal was to develop an organized approach based on the ideas of human-centered design that would enable developers and designers to guarantee that user needs are considered at every stage of the design process, all the while keeping development moving quickly. In order to evaluate and improve the usability, humanoid aspects, and worker involvement of a linked healthiness structure called the WIISEL (Wireless Insole for Independent and Safe Elderly Living) system—a structure intended to endlessly evaluate descent menace by measure gait and stability constraints allied through fall risk—we first present the methodology and its justification in this chapter.

***Keywords***: Human elements, integrated health, human-centered design, evaluation of usability, graphical interface design, health

**Corresponding author*: manidublish2@gmail.com

Sandhya Avasthi and Suman Lata Tripathi (eds.) Distributed and Parallel Computing, (281–298)

## 13.1 Introduction

A phrase used to describe the use of health technology to provide remote patient care is "connected health," which also includes concepts related to eHealth, telehealth, telemedicine, and mHealth [1]. Fitness, nutrition, and activity trackers are becoming more and more common connected health goods, along with blood pressure and heart rate monitors, thermometers, weighing scales, and diabetes management tools. The quantified-self movement, a contemporary phenomenon in which people try to monitor their own behavioral, physiological, and environmental data, is typified by all of these [2]. With the right clinical-based information technology (IT) infrastructure in place, these tools, systems, and services may empower people to take charge of their own health and well-being in the comfort of their own homes—all while staying in touch with medical professionals. In addition to promoting healthy behaviors to prevent or lessen health issues, this model can also help with chronic disease self-management, lower the number of medical visits, support continuous health monitoring for both individuals and entire groups, and offer tailored, localized, and on-demand interventions [3].

The market for linked healthcare is expanding as a result of a growing emphasis on lowering healthcare expenses for individuals of all ages. According to a Geisinger Health Plan study, heart patients who used connected health monitoring after discharge experienced a 44% reduction in hospital readmissions [4]. Agboola *et al.* found a similar decrease in heart failure–related readmissions, with a 48% decrease observed in the first 30 days following discharge [5].

Numerous interconnected health gadgets have similar characteristics; they are usually small, electronic modules that perform one or more particular medical tasks. These gadgets typically include wearable clips or belts, touch or nontouch screens, speakers, buttons, switches, and other components. They are also typically made to measure some component of an individual's health state [6]. As shown in Figure 13.1 mobile phones and connected health devices, such as blood pressure or heart rate monitors, can be synchronized, with the phone serving as a platform for communication, storage, and exchange of data.

Several features set connected health devices apart from other medical or health equipment that could be used in a surgical, clinical, or hospital setting [7]. Healthcare professionals may not always be the users of connected health devices, which are intended to be used in the home by unsupervised users. User interfaces (UIs) on connected health devices are

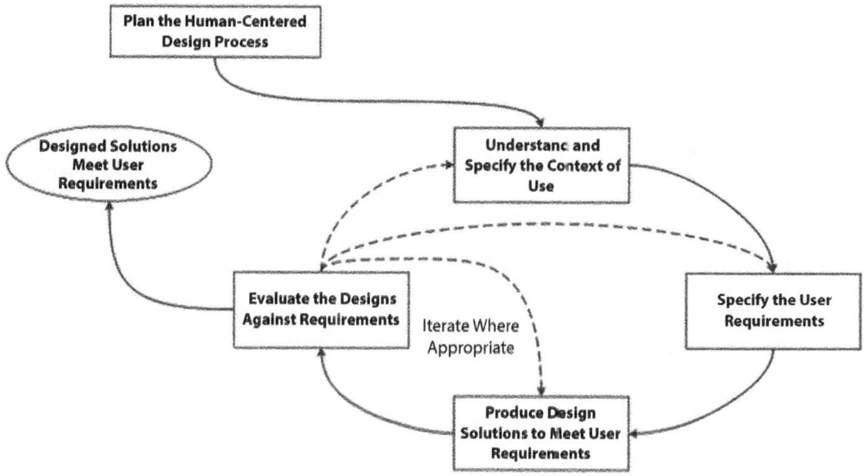


**Figure 13.1** Four essential stages comprise human-centered design: (1) identify the client and the scenario in which they will be using the design; (2) define the consumers necessities; (3) create layout alternatives; and (4) assess creates in light of demands.

made up of both hardware and software components and necessitate a certain amount of human–computer interaction. Connected health devices require UIs with strong usability features because it is likely that old, disabled, or infirm users would use these devices.

Users may be asked to do tasks that are above their capacity by the UI aspects of linked health devices [8]. As shown in Figure 13.2 poor interface design has been noted to be the reason for the failure of many otherwise good items in the marketplace, whereas mediocre products have grown as a result of appealing and user-friendly interface design [9]. Consequently, the usability and human factor aspects of the device interfaces, and consequently the user experience they offer, are crucial variables to take into account when designing connected health technologies.

Usability is "the extent to which a user can use a product to achieve specific goals with effectiveness, efficiency, and satisfaction in a specified context," according to the International Organization for Standardization (ISO) [10]. Human factors refer to the application of human capabilities (physical, sensory, emotional, and intellectual) and limitations to the design and development of tools, devices, systems, environments, and organizations [11]. This definition is provided by the American National Standards Institute and the Association for the Advancement of Medical Instrumentation. The definition of user experience is the opinions and reactions of users arising from their use of a good or service [12].

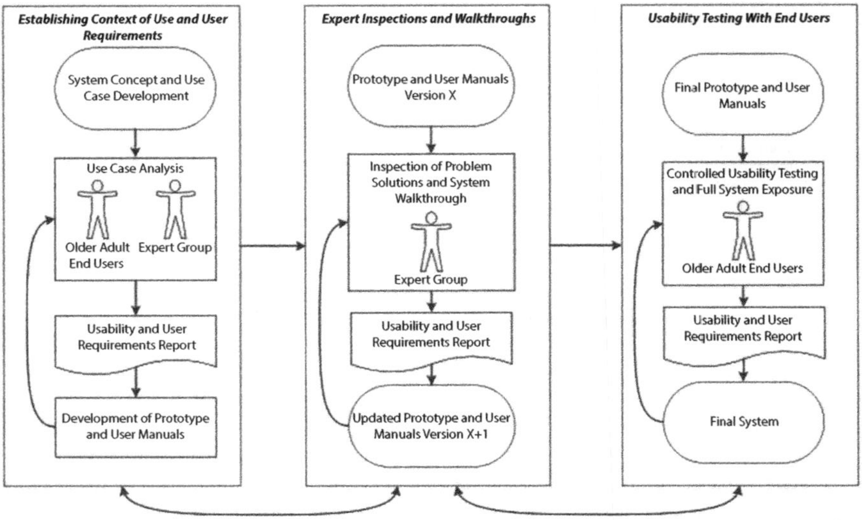


**Figure 13.2** The human-centered design process we used to create our linked health app.

In order to review market resubmissions, the Food and Drug Administration (FDA) requires proof of end user involvement during the design phase [13]. The Agency for Healthcare Research and Quality has also called for usability and human factors evaluation of medical devices and systems during the design process [14, 15].

## 13.2 Design with User in Mind

The goal of the design concept known as "user-centered design" (UCD) is to center the design process around the end user. Norman [16], who proposed rules that designers could adhere to so that their interfaces would produce acceptable usability results, is credited with coining the phrase in the 1980s. The "person who will ultimately be using the product" is the end user, and since then, a large number of designers, researchers, and policymakers have advocated a variety of strategies and techniques that aim to incorporate the end user in the design process.

The ISO expanded the concept of UCD to "address impacts on a number of stakeholders, not just those typically considered as users" in their 2010 standard ISO 9241-210, designating the process as human-centered design (HCD) [16, 17]. Therefore, from now on in this work, we will refer to UCD as HCD. According to the ISO 9241-210 standard, HCD is "an approach to systems design and development that aims to make interactive systems more usable by applying human factors/ergonomics and usability knowledge and techniques and focusing on the use of the system." The guideline also explains how adopting a design strategy that enhances human aspects and usability may be advantageous [8, 18, 19].

## 13.3 Designing Networked Medication Equipment with a Human Center

We have already talked about how connected health devices are becoming more and more significant in the global healthcare system [20]. It has been demonstrated that several linked health devices contain interface features that may present challenges for older adult or disabled users [21]. In terms of use context and UI needs, we have also demonstrated that linked health devices and systems are distinct from other medical equipment [13]. We have now covered the essential elements and technical specifications of HCD. The question "Why is all of this important for connected health system design?" then arises.

In light of the previous discussion, we believe that the design of connected health devices requires a customized HCD methodology. We will now go into further detail about our reasoning for this belief by focusing on three particular needs. It is essential to have a detailed prototype or specification of the interface prior to assessing the interface's navigation using a cognitive walkthrough methodology. The application of HCD to health devices and systems varies greatly, as demonstrated by these and numerous more instances [10, 22]. It also demonstrates the variety of usability and human factors testing methods that designers and engineers can use to get user input.

Numerous testing and assessment methods that are widely used now were created by the late 1980s; therefore, many of these activities are not new [23, 24]. However, we believe that many of the related health publications lack comprehensive information about the activities conducted during the design process, especially with respect to ISO 9241-210, as well as a thorough assessment of the activities' success or failure [25].

## 13.4 Testing Usability with End Users

In summative user testing, end users are shown the upgraded prototypes (Requirement 2). Although field testing with end users in places such as their homes is more beneficial, the test can also be conducted in controlled environments such as a laboratory. The development team must prioritize and address issues found by the tests one after the other, repeating testing as needed (Requirement 4). It is recommended to maintain brief test cycles with a limited number of participants in each cycle.

### 13.4.1 Suggested Activities

It is recommended that user testing be done; it is well-described in the literature [26] and entails observing people as they interact with the system interface. Although there is a loss of realism in the actual world, laboratory sessions offer greater control over the experiment and more reliable data when it comes to this kind of monitoring. Although the data may be more difficult to accurately quantify, it can yield richer observations of users in more natural use environments. The administrator will frequently ask the subject to think aloud during the initial stages of user testing so that the observer may get a sense of the mental process the user is using to confront and try to solve usability and human factors issues [27] (Requirements 1 and 5).

The user behavior is recorded *via* cameras, voice recorders, and note-taking. User satisfaction (Requirement 3) is measured and recorded using scales such as the Quebec User Evaluation of Satisfaction With Assistive Technology, the System Usability Scale, the After-Scenario Questionnaire, the NASA Task Load Index, the visual analog scale, and 5-point Likert scale questionnaires [20, 28]. An instance of a Likert questionnaire item could be, "I have no trouble reading the text on the screen." The user is then asked to indicate on a scale of 1 to 5 how much they agree or disagree with the item. By keeping track of task completion times, error rates, and completion rates, efficiency and effectiveness can be quantified [29].

### 13.4.2 Outcomes

If necessary, an extremely sophisticated prototype that has undergone additional user testing or professional scrutiny can be completed. Requirements 7 to 9 and 1 to 5 are satisfied by this phase. It is acceptable and required to repeat activities inside each phase (Requirement 4). After every stage, all issues are noted and documented in organized reports on human factors and usability, or in some other format, so that all parties involved are aware of the issues and that all modifications and issues are recorded (Requirement 9).

## 13.5 Framework Required in Healthcare Fiction for Human-Based Design

It is important to note that there have been published descriptions of several HCD approaches to healthcare technology design in the literature. Vermeulen *et al.* [23], for instance, provided a multiphasic methodology for the design of an activity monitor for older adults. The phases comprised the following: context and user analysis, user requirement identification, interface development, and laboratory interface evaluation. Using an HCD methodology, Schaeffer collected user requirements through focus groups and surveys in order to develop interface prototypes for insulin pumps. In their initial design step, Chouvarda *et al.* [22] presented icon and interface concepts to end users as part of an HCD process for a telepsychology app.

Thus, in addition to making sure that our methodology complies with ISO 9241-210's six HCD guiding principles, we will also be adding three extra requirements that our methodology needs to fulfill. These three additional requirements are outlined below and will be referred to as Requirements 1 to 3:

- **Requirement 1**: Our approach will, to the greatest extent feasible, adhere to the procedures delineated in ISO 9241-210 and provide a thorough account of the tasks executed and results attained in every stage.
- **Requirement 2**: We will use an approach that makes use of quick prototyping, testing, and development.
- **Requirement 3**: The planning of tasks ahead of time and the creation of the necessary documentation will be the main focuses of our methodology.

## 13.6 A Necessary Step to Enable Quick Learning Processes

Furthermore, the connected health space is perceived as a rapidly evolving, fiercely competitive market [30], emphasizing the necessity for devices that can have quick development cycles in addition to meeting acceptable user standards. The link between mobile phones and connected health technology is a punctuation point for this demand. The phones themselves serve as platforms for the gathering, sending, and storing of health data, and mobile applications give users access to their data or to an external device.

The Google Play Store and the Apple App Store offered more than 100,000 mobile health apps for download in 2015 [31]. More than 500 million people are anticipated to use mobile health apps in some capacity by 2016 [32]. Because mobile health devices and apps are becoming more and more popular, they run the risk of being comparatively outdated very quickly [33]. As a result, shorter product lifecycles are required, much as was the case in the software industry in the past. It is possible that this will prevent organizations from integrating a complete HCD technique into their product development cycle. The authors believe that, in light of this finding, it is necessary to provide a thorough explanation of an HCD approach that complies with 9241-210 and is enhanced for usage with linked health devices by simplifying the distinct phases within the HCD procedure.

## 13.7 Requirement for a Planned Approach Setup

It has been noted in the past that developers of linked health solutions frequently focus more on the technological novelty of these systems than on how easy they are to use [34]. It was discovered more recently [35] that criteria are required for the design and development process for linked health devices with regard to usability. The proper documentation of the design process is crucial in the creation of medical devices, especially if the device has to meet a standard like IEC62366-1 from the International Electrotechnical Commission). For market resubmissions to be reviewed by the FDA, proof of end user input throughout the design phase is required [36].

### 13.7.1 Techniques

There are currently nine requirements for the approach that must be met; these will be discussed in this section. These are mentioned below, along with relevant details:

- **Requirement 1**: First and foremost, the design is predicated on a clear comprehension of users, tasks, and settings. We will define the context of usage, user requirements, and user profiles in the first part of our technique.
- **Requirement 2**: All phases of design and development require user input. In every stage, we will try to include both end users and knowledgeable users.

- **Requirement 3**: User-cantered assessment informs and improves the design. At every stage, we will employ assessment methods to attain quantifiable outcomes.
- **Requirement 4**: It is an iterative process. There will be several stages in which we can make modifications to the design after each one; if needed, we can go back to a previous stage of the procedure.
- **Requirement 5**: The complete user experience is addressed in the design. The first phase's use cases will cover every facet of use and serve as a point of reference both before and after each subsequent phase.
- **Requirement 6**: Multidisciplinary viewpoints and talents are included in the design team. We want to integrate many viewpoints from experts, stakeholders, and members of the design team from different disciplines. Any individual participating in the project who is impacted by the actions or results linked to the product under consideration is considered a stakeholder in this context a record. The documentation of all actions, designs, and developments will be included into our process [37]. We will now outline a three-phase process that will satisfy these needs based on these specifications. These three stages have the following labels:
  - **Phase 1**: Setting the user requirements and context of use
  - **Phase 2**: Professional walkthroughs and inspections
  - **Phase 3**: Testing usability with final users Figure 13.2 shows the entire technique.

### 13.7.2 Methodology Application in a Networked Health System

A methodology's application is essential to guaranteeing a linked health system's efficacy, efficiency, and alignment with organizational objectives as shown in Figure 13.3. This is an organized method that you can use in planning and evaluation.

- **Planning and evaluation**: Conduct a SWOT (strengths, weaknesses, opportunities, and threats) analysis of the current systems and procedures to determine their advantages, disadvantages, opportunities, and threats. Give the linked health system specific goals and objectives that take into account things such as better patient outcomes, lower costs, and operational efficiency. Provide a thorough project plan that includes schedules, the distribution of resources, and key performance indicators for success assessment.

- **Engagement of stakeholders**: Determine who the important parties are and involve them, such as administrators, patients, IT personnel, healthcare providers, and government agencies. Make sure that the expectations of the stakeholders are in line with the project's objectives, and ask for their feedback at every stage to encourage support and buy-in.
- **Infrastructure of technology**: Evaluating hardware, software, networking, and security needs is important for the linked health system. Ensure data security, scalability, interoperability, and easy integration by selecting the right technology.
- **Integrating and managing data**: To guarantee the safe gathering, storing, processing, and exchange of healthcare data, implement a strong data management plan. To enable smooth integration with current health information systems, electronic health records, and other pertinent platforms, implement interoperability standards and protocols.
- **Workflow reorganizations**: Find inefficiencies and bottlenecks in the current administrative and clinical operations by analyzing them. Rework processes to maximize resource use, simplify procedures, and take advantage of the connected health system's capabilities.
- **Instruction and training**: To familiarize administrators, other stakeholders, and healthcare professionals with the usage of the linked health system, offer extensive training programmers. Provide continuing instruction and assistance to guarantee that new technologies and workflows are adopted and maintained proficiently.
- **Testing and approval**: Before the connected health system is fully implemented, put it through extensive testing and validation. Conduct pilot studies or simulations to evaluate the system's functionality, usability, and real-world performance.
- **Deployment and implementation**: Start with a pilot deployment in a few departments or facilities and gradually expand the connected health system. Track the implementation process attentively, deal with problems or obstacles right away, and make any adjustments to the plan.

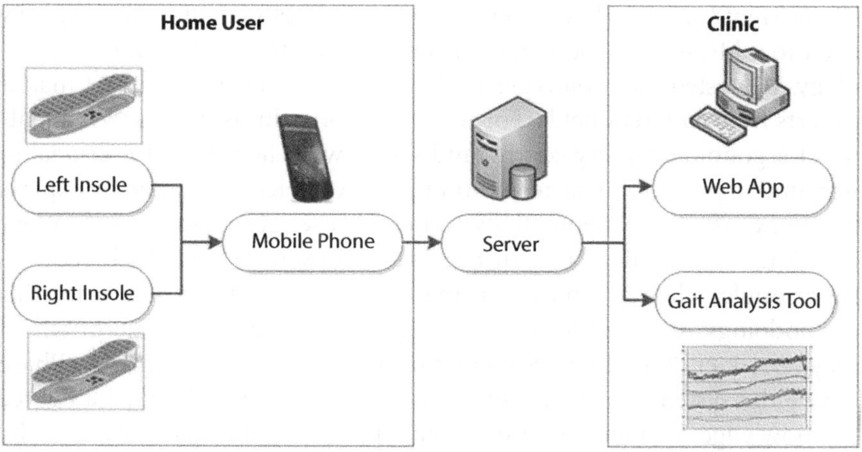


**Figure 13.3** Safe elderly living system that depends on wireless devices.

- **Assessment and ongoing improvement**: Assess the effect of the interconnected health system on important indicators such as cost-effectiveness, patient outcomes, and satisfaction. To promote ongoing system optimization and improvement, get input from stakeholders and take lessons gained into account.
- **Regulation and compliance**: Ensure that all pertinent healthcare laws, rules, and guidelines—such as the Health Insurance Portability and Accountability Act—are followed in terms of data security and privacy. Keep up with regulatory changes and make necessary adjustments to the linked health system to ensure compliance. You may better develop, execute, and optimize a connected health system to improve patient care delivery, boost operational effectiveness, and produce better results throughout the healthcare continuum by using this methodology.

## 13.8 Limitations

Preliminarily, we can state that this system has effectively reached all of the goals we set forth for it. We believe that our suggested methodology, together with the examples of its application in this paper, will offer aspiring designers a methodical guide to follow an HCD process that maintains a consistent framework while enabling quick development cycles. We now need to address some potential constraints we identified in our methodology. We tested the prototypes in Phase 2 exclusively with subject matter experts from different fields. For several reasons, this is the case. As a matter of ergonomic quality control and safety, we believe that it is crucial to wait until a prototype has been thoroughly evaluated and tested by experts before exposing it to a potentially vulnerable user group, in this case, older individuals. It might not seem necessary to exercise this much caution, for example, when it comes to a smartphone app, but our goal is for this methodology to be relevant to all linked health devices, some of which may be riskier than others. Second, the expert feedback provided in Phase 2 gave the system a new viewpoint from an outsider and added a degree of knowledge in interface design, human aspects, and usability that the target end user would not have had [38]. Ultimately, recruiting end users can be costly, so Phase 2 serves as a means of eliminating a large number of usability issues, regardless of how straightforward or intricate they may be, prior to the prototype being made available to end users. However, usability inspection groups within a research group or organization might be formed from stakeholders, designers, and developers who may already be involved in a project or related initiatives. Experts can also be expensive to pay or attract. Heuristics can be used to train those who are not familiar with usability to analyze prototypes [39, 40].

The methodology's introduction of paper prototyping activities in Phase 1 and so-called cheap usability engineering tools in Phase 2 allows it to meet one of its requirements: emphasizing quick prototyping and evaluation. The value of quality could decline as a result of this emphasis on speed. Our methodology, however, places a strong emphasis on the necessity of documentation and phase-by-phase assessment. This will guarantee that recommended improvements are prioritized, distributed, and put into action prior to the start of the following phase. The effectiveness and caliber of user feedback and the necessary modifications will ultimately depend on the caliber and layout of testing and assessments; for this reason, it is critical for design teams to have a specialist usability engineer.

## 13.9 Conclusion

The proposed approach will work well for current design and usability engineering teams in fast-paced, highly competitive industries, as it provides a straightforward yet reliable structure for HCD and development. The tasks that can be completed throughout each step have been thoroughly covered by us. We have additionally provided our rationale for this methodology, highlighting its adaptability and value, especially in terms of enhancing the usability, human aspects, and customer experience of medical device and system designs. The physical environment of healthcare facilities plays a significant role in patient satisfaction. A clean, comfortable, and safe environment can help patients feel more at ease. Regular maintenance and upgrades of facilities and equipment are essential to provide a conducive atmosphere for healing and recovery. Gathering and analyzing patient feedback are critical for continuous improvement. Healthcare providers should have mechanisms in place to collect feedback, whether through surveys, suggestion boxes, or digital platforms. Analyzing this feedback helps identify areas for improvement and implement changes that enhance the patient experience. Engaging with the community builds trust and enhances the reputation of healthcare providers. Educational programs, health workshops, and community health initiatives help build strong relationships with the community, promoting better health outcomes and increasing patient satisfaction.

## References


1. Kvedar, J., Coye, M.J., Everett, W., Connected health: A review of technologies and strategies to improve patient care with telemedicine and telehealth. *Health Aff. (Millwood)*, 33, 2, 194–199, 2014 Feb, [FREE Full text] [doi: 10.1377/hlthaff.2013.0992] [Medline: 24493760].
2. Swan, M., The quantified self: Fundamental disruption in big data science and biological discovery. *Big Data*, 1, 2, 85–99, 2013 Jun, [doi: 10.1089/big.2012.0002] [Medline: 27442063].
3. Kumar, S., Nilsen, W.J., Abernethy, A., Atienza, A., Patrick, K., Pavel, M., *et al.*, Mobile health technology evaluation: The mHealth evidence workshop. *Am. J. Prev. Med.*, 45, 2, 228–236, 2013 Aug, [FREE Full text] [doi: 10.1016/j.amepre.2013.03.017] [Medline: 23867031].
4. Geisenger, Geisenger Health Plan, URL: https://www.geisinger.org/health-plan [accessed 2017-03-04] [WebCite Cache ID 6oi2LhCUF.
5. Agboola, S., Jethwani, K., Khateeb, K., Moore, S., Kvedar, J., Heart failure remote monitoring: Evidence from the retrospective evaluation of a real-world remote monitoring program. *J. Med. Internet Res.*, 17, 4, e101, 2015 Apr 22, [FREE Full text] [doi: 10.2196/jmir.4417] [Medline: 25903278].
6. Harte, R.P., Glynn, L.G., Broderick, B.J., Rodriguez-Molinero, A., Baker, P.M., McGuiness, B., *et al.*, Human centred design considerations for connected health devices for the older adult. *J. Pers. Med.*, 4, 2, 245–281, 2014 Jun 04, [FREE Full text] [doi: 10.3390/jpm4020245] [Medline: 25563225].

7. Preece, A., Reuschel, W., AccessWorld Magazine, Mobile connected health devices: The future of health technology?, 2014 Nov, URL: https://www.afb.org/afbpress/pub.asp?DocID=aw151107 [accessed 2017-03-04] [WebCite Cache ID 6oi6GFAHS].
8. Armijo, D., McDonnell, C., Werner, K., Electronic Health Record Usability: Interface Design Considerations, Agency for Healthcare Research and Quality, Rockville, MD, 2009 Oct, URL: https://healthit.ahrq.gov/sites/default/files/docs/citation/ 09-10-0091-2-EF.pdf [accessed 2017-03-04] [WebCite Cache ID 6oi6wEIZb].
9. Zimmermann, D. and Grötzbach, L., A requirement engineering approach to user centered design, in: *Human-Computer Interaction. Interaction Design and Usability.* HCI 2007. Lecture Notes in Computer Science, vol. 4550, J.A. Jacko (Ed.), pp. 360–369, Springer, Berlin, Germany, 2007.
10. Kushniruk, A.W. and Patel, V.L., Cognitive and usability engineering methods for the evaluation of clinical information systems. *J. Biomed. Inform.*, 37, 1, 56–76, 2004 Feb, [FREE Full text] [doi: 10.1016/j.jbi.2004.01.003] [Medline: 15016386].
11. Katsulis, Z., Ergai, A., Leung, W.Y., Schenkel, L., Rai, A., Adelman, J., *et al.*, Iterative user centered design for development of a patient-centered fall prevention toolkit. *Appl. Ergon.*, 56, 117–126, 2016, [doi: 10.1016/j.apergo.2016.03.011].
12. Association for the Advancement of Medical Instrumentation. ANSI/AAMI HE75-2009: Human Factors Engineering—Design of Medical Devices, Association for the Advancement of Medical Instrumentation, Arlington, VA, 2009.
13. Astbrink, G. and Beekhuyzen, J., The Synergies Between Universal Design and User-Centred Design, Griffith University School of Computing and Information Technology, Brisbane, Australia, 2003 Jan, URL: https://pdfs.semanticscholar.org/9be4/49a9b7f75e271799ebdf0da0bcd47b3c43ba.pdf?_ga=1.160889150.2018493194.1489338408 [accessed 2017-03-12] [WebCite Cache ID 6oudZutG7].
14. Salah, D., Paige, R.F., Cairns, P., A systematic literature review for agile development processes and user centred design integration, in: *Proceedings of the 18th International Conference on Evaluation Assessment in Software Engineering*, London, UK, May 13-14, 2014, [doi: 10.1145/2601248.2601276].
15. Thompson, H., Medical Device Diagnostic Industry, 2012 Sep 07, User-centered design for medical devices: If it isn't documented it doesn't exist URL: http://www.mddionline.com/article/user-centered-design-medical-devices-if-it-isn%E2%80%99t-documented-it-doesn%E2%80%99t-exist [accessed 2017-03-04] [WebCite Cache ID 6oi7BbobZ].
16. Norman, D.A. and Draper, S.W. (Eds.), *User Centered System Design: New Perspectives on Human-Computer Interaction*, Lawrence Erlbaum Associates, Hillsdale, NJ, 1986.

17. Thompson, H., Medical Device Diagnostic Industry, User-centered design for medical devices: If it isn't documented it doesn't exist, 2012 Sep 07, URL: http://www.mddionline.com/article/user-centered-design-medical-devices-iiisn%E2%80%99t-documented-it-doesn%E2%80%99t-exist [accessed 2017-03-04] [WebCite Cache ID 6oi7BbobZ].
18. Applying Human Factors and Usability Engineering to Medical Devices: Guidance for Industry and Food and Drug Administration Staff, US Department of Health and Human Services, Washington, DC, 2016 Feb 03, URL: https://www. fda.gov/downloads/MedicalDevices/../UCM259760.pdf [accessed 2017-03-12] [WebCite Cache ID 6oucXhk6c] Woolgar S. Configuring the user: The case of usability trials. Sociol Rev 1990 May;38(S1):58-99. [doi: 10.1111/j.1467-954X.1990.tb03349.x].
19. Applied Research for Connected Health, US Connected Health Market Analysis Report, Technology Centre, Enterprise Ireland, Dublin, Ireland, 2014 Jun, URL: http://www.arch.ie/wp-content/uploads/2016/06/.
20. Taylor, K., Connected Health: How Digital Technology is Transforming Health and Social Care, Deloitte Centre for Health Solutions, London, UK, 2015, URL: https://www2.deloitte.com/content/dam/Deloitte/uk/Documents/life-sciences-health-care/deloitte-uk-connected-health.pdf [accessed 2017-03-12] [WebCite Cache ID 6oupVUdzr].
21. Norman, D., *The Design of Everyday Things: Revised and Expanded Edition*, Basic Books, New York, NY, 2013.
22. Chouvarda, I.G., Goulis, D.G., Lambrinoudaki, I., Maglaveras, N., Connected health and integrated care: Toward new models for chronic disease management. *Maturitas*, 82, 1, 22–27, 2015 Sep, [doi: 10.1016/j.maturitas.2015.03.015] [Medline:25891502].
23. Vermeulen, J., Neyens, J.C., Spreeuwenberg, M.D., van, R.E., Sipers, W., Habets, H., *et al.*, User-centered development and testing of a monitoring system that provides feedback regarding physical functioning to elderly people. *Patient Prefer. Adherence*, 7, 843–854, 2013, [doi: 10.2147/PPA.S45897] [Medline: 24039407].
24. Schaeffer, N., The role of human factors in the design and development of an insulin pump. *J. Diabetes Sci. Technol.*, 6, 2, 260–264, 2012 Mar 01, [FREE Full text] [doi: 10.1177/193229681200600208] [Medline: 22538134].
25. Zickler, C., Halder, S., Kleih, S.C., Herbert, C., Kübler, A., Brain painting: Usability testing according to the user-centered design in end users with severe motor paralysis. *Artif. Intell. Med.*, 59, 2, 99–110, 2013 Oct, [doi: 10.1016/j.artmed.2013.08.003] [Medline: 24080077].
26. Gould, J.D. and Lewis, C., Designing for usability: Key principles and what designers think. *Commun. ACM*, 28, 3, 300–311, 1985, [doi: 10.1145/3166.3170].
27. Applied Research for Connected Health, US Connected Health Market Analysis Report, Technology Centre, Enterprise Ireland, Dublin, Ireland, 2014 Jun, URL: http://www.arch.ie/wp-content/uploads/2016/06/US-Connected-

Health-Market-Analysis-Report.pdf [accessed 2017-03-12] [WebCite Cache ID 6oupHAAZY].

28. Pogue, D., Scientific American, When will my gadget become obsolete?, 2013 Sep 01, URL: https://www.scientificamerican.com/article/pogue-when-will-my-gadget-become-obsolete[accessed 2017-03-12] [WebCite Cache ID 6ouplCYbk].
29. Vélez, O., Okyere, P.B., Kanter, A.S., Bakken, S., A usability study of a mobile health application for rural Ghanaian midwives. *J. Midwifery Womens Health*, 59, 2, 184–191, 2014, [FREE Full text] [doi: 10.1111/jmwh.12071] [Medline: 24400748].
30. Afacan, Y. and Erbug, C., An interdisciplinary heuristic evaluation method for universal building design. *Appl. Ergon.*, 40, 4, 731–744, 2009 Jul, [doi: 10.1016/j.apergo.2008.07.002] [Medline: 18775531].
31. Sesto, M.E., Irwin, C.B., Chen, K.B., Chourasia, A.O., Wiegmann, D.A., Effect of touch screen button size and spacing on touch characteristics of users with and without disabilities. *Hum. Factors*, 54, 3, 425–436, 2012 Jun, [doi: 10.1177/0018720811433831] [Medline: 22768644].
32. Harte, R., Quinlan, L.R., Glynn, L., Rodriguez-Molinero, A., Scharf, T., Carenas, C., *et al.*, A multi-stage human factors and comfort assessment of instrumented insoles designed for use in a connected health infrastructure. *J. Pers. Med.*, 5, 4, 487–508, 2015 Dec 16, [FREE Full text] [doi: 10.3390/jpm5040487] [Medline: 26694468].
33. Nielsen, J., Nielsen Norman Group, Guerrilla HCI: Using discount usability engineering to penetrate the intimidation barrier, 1994 Jan 01, URL: https://www.nngroup.com/articles/guerrilla-hci/ [accessed 2017-03-05] [WebCite Cache ID 6ojl1s4D2].
34. Chiu, C.C., Vicente, K.J., Buffo-Sequeira, I., Hamilton, R.M., McCrindle, B.W., Usability assessment of pacemaker programmers. *Pacing Clin. Electrophysiol.*, 27, 10, 1388–1398, 2004 Oct, [doi: 10.1111/j.1540-8159.2004.00643.x] [Medline: 15511248].
35. Salah, D., Paige, R.F., Cairns, P., A systematic literature review for agile development processes and user centered design integration, in: *Proceedings of the 18th International Conference on Evaluation Assessment in Software Engineering*, London, May 13-14, 2014, [doi:10.1145/2601248.2601276].
36. Lee, J.C., Judge, T.K., McCrickard, D.S., Evaluating eXtreme scenario-based design in a distributed agile team, in: *Proceedings of the ACM CHI Conference on Human Factors in Computing Systems*, Vancouver, BC, May 7-12, 2011, pp. 863–877, [doi: 10.1145/1979742.1979681].
37. Khajouei, R., Peute, L.W., Hasman, A., Jaspers, M.W., Classification and prioritization of usability problems using an augmented classification scheme. *J. Biomed. Inform.*, 44, 6, 948–957, 2011 Dec, [Doi: 10.1016/j.jbi.2011.07.002].
38. Martínez-Pérez, B., de la Torre-Díez, I., Candelas-Plasencia, S., López-Coronado, M., Development and evaluation of tools for measuring the

quality of experience (QoE) in mHealth applications. *J. Med. Syst.*, 37, 5, 9976, 2013 Oct, [doi:10.1007/s10916-013-9976-x] [Medline: 24014255].
39. Svanaes, D., Alsos, O.A., Dahl, Y., Usability testing of mobile ICT for clinical settings: Methodological and practical challenges. *J. Med. Inform.*, 79, 4, e24–e34, 2010 Apr, [doi: 10.1016/j.ijmedinf.2008.06.014].
40. Tripathi, S.L. and Mahmud, M., *Explainable Machine Learning Models and Architecture*, Wiley & Scrivener Publishing LLC, USA, 2023, https://doi.org/10.1002/9781394186570.

## Abbreviations

| | |
|---|---|
| **CACP** | Center for Advanced Communications Policy |
| **CÚRAM** | Centre for Research in Medical Devices |
| **FDA** | Food and Drug Administration |
| **FP7** | Seventh Framework Programme for Research |
| **GP** | general practitioner |
| **HCD** | human-centered design |
| **ISO** | International Organization for Standardization |
| **UCD** | user-centered design |
| **UI** | user interface |
| **WIISEL** | Wireless Insole for Independent and Safe Elderly Living |

# 14

# New Age Tech's Backbone: Role of Distributed Systems in Paving Path for a Durable Future

**Kadambri Agarwal*** **and Saijal Dahiya**

*Dept. of CSE, ABES Engineering College, Ghaziabad, India*

## *Abstract*

With decentralized systems at its core, the next generation of the Internet is set to completely transform the digital environment. Decentralized systems mean that there is no single authority to control the operations of the internet; it is a mutually connected system of multiple devices, and now with its help, we are aiming to create a revolution in the age of the Internet. Needless to say, our aim is not to remove the existing infra but to improve upon the existing to better the data storage, utilize peer-to-peer networking, and enhance the data transmission and access through the underlying network architecture. This abstract aims to discuss the effects of introducing a decentralized system on infrastructure, communication, and the societal impact. The decentralized system architecture was readily adopted by the world because of the major change of stance it brought about data ownership, security, and overall privacy in the digital world. There is no single head point, which can decide which can stop or give Internet access to the world. There is reduction in single points of failure in architecture because all the necessary operations are usually performed by dispersing data and resources to geographically different locations. This in turn guarantees that the data cannot be easily compromised because there is no single vulnerability that one can attack to enter and malign the network. With the increased digitization and users and communities having a never-seen-before level of authority over the digital assets, this is both the reason for it to be able to happen and the reason we can be safe on it. Although problems arise with the usage of decentralized systems such as difficulty in fault identification, lack of standardization of protocols, less transaction processing speed, and no regulatory oversight present, it has still paved the

**Corresponding author*: kadambriagarwal@gmail.com

Sandhya Avasthi and Suman Lata Tripathi (eds.) Distributed and Parallel Computing, (299–322)

way for better concepts to be actualized, with the major two being Web 3.0 and decentralized artificial intelligence (AI). Broadly speaking, AI refers to mimicking human-like thinking skills to the highest extent possible and involves constant learning and applying. Currently, we are seeing the rise of decentralized AI as a branch of AI that adds the benefits of decentralized architecture to the already useful machine learning and deep learning tool, adding to the scalability factor and enhancing the trust and security in the AI systems. Web 3.0 is believed to be as big of a paradigm shift as the previous two versions were during their time. It believes that there is going to be absolute freedom to the users to use the Internet as per their will and will be based on open-source software and applications will run on decentralized peer-to-peer-networking. The Internet will be more connected and omnipresent and permissionless in nature, focusing more on user interactions and having a bottom-up design. To summarize it all, decentralized systems are going to be one of the pillars of the Internet's evolution providing an opportunity to create a more user-oriented, indiscriminate, and transparent digital experience.

***Keywords*:** IoT, distributed, machine learning, metaverse, blockchain, augmented reality

## 14.1 Introduction

Distributed systems have become the need of the hour. Initially, when humanity took off with its technological developments, it had assumed that if a machine is able to ease the work of man, it would be sufficient. But as we kept on tapping into the various domains, we realized that technology not only can reduce our work but also can create logics and software we rarely imagined of. This breakthrough in perception alongside the continuous efforts in development led to the existence of innovative machine learning, virtual reality (VR) and augmented reality (AR) devices, Internet of Things (IoT), and much more [1–5]. This positive growth in their demand and advancements have proven singular machine systems to be incompetent with the scalability and performance requirements and call for an updated computation mechanism where one can be guaranteed of increased fault tolerance, fast communication, and durability. Fortunately for us, distributed systems were also being developed when the tech boom happened. Distributed systems hit the nerve when they worked on removing dependence on a single machine, in the process removing the existence of single point of failure. Being a loosely coupled system, it has created an environment where various devices can interact, synchronize, and share resources, which in turn created a transparent, more powerful, and resilient computational system where devices can be physically separated with different memory resources even but in parallel can process data to achieve a common outcome [6–9]. A decentralized concurrent network that can share resources, combine individual outputs, and take off the load from one node of the system and divide into many is what we need to continue to expand to new horizons of development. Some of the current technologies that can benefit from the application of distributed systems are as follows:

1. **Smart grids:** Due to the ever-growing need and consumption of electrical energy, the traditional power grids responsible for generation and distribution of electricity have proven themselves to be inefficient in terms of real-time control, transmission loss management, and lower-quality production. Along with this, the environment's deteriorating condition calls for a more sustainable management. This brought the smart grid technology to prominence. It calls for a more equitable distribution among urban and rural areas, forecasts the demand and can be great for controlling assets and secure power system, and takes up less space during installation.
2. **Internet of Things:** No one in today's day and time can claim to not understand the ideas of smart homes, having energy-saving and interconnected devices. But how is this possible? The best way to implement it is to implement the full potential of IoT. Multiple devices that are connected to sensors that can detect and act according to real-time environments and having constant Internet connection are one of the most basic requirements here, but once executed, it can lead to a house that can unlock from your phone, and devices can be put on and off power saving more from afar. It can lead to a more alert alarm system in offices and an easy-to-manage but enhanced lifestyle of the sick and elderly, among its various applications.
3. **Blockchain:** Ideally constructed for finance industry, blockchain technology has found itself useful in many areas such as health and life sciences, thanks to its architecture that involves distributed ledger as well [10, 11]. These ledgers allow decentralized transactions to occur and are the foundation of cryptocurrencies such as Bitcoins. For security, it uses cryptography, preferably asymmetric key, and has been

known for its potential in building the Internet systems soon, owing to its scalability.

4. **Machine learning:** AI is the way to go when one desires to mimic the human way of thinking in machines. To expand on this technology, we now have several subdomains to go forward with, one of them being machine learning, where instead of configuring the method to compute on the device, we feed it with datasets or simply put it in an unfamiliar environment where it can learn and develop the program logic on its own, without human help. It has found its application extensively in natural language processing, self-driving cars, recommendation systems, classification and prediction, etc.
5. **Augmented reality:** It is a combination of the virtual world we create and the real world we live in. It is achieved by augmenting the images generated by a device on the real world providing a simulation that is closest to reality. One of its popular applications involves how well it has actually enhanced learning experience by creating an engaging approach to an already known subject. A large portion of development of AR wishes to make it a universal experience, so much so that each individual can carry the devices with them anywhere.
6. **Distributed databases:** Data are being constantly created everywhere around us. This includes trends, information, conclusions, and predictions made with statistics and tech and also the general database that any organization (big or small) might generate. This can include customer records, sensitive files, reports, employee information, and many other forms of heterogeneous data, which will be easy to handle when you put in one place but at the same time difficult to put in memory of one machine and also increasing security risk and failure chances in the process. Distributed databases are solution to this problem, and database management system (DBMS) provides the mechanism to work on it with ease.
7. **Metaverse:** Just as we have our universe made with stars, galaxies, solar systems, and asteroids, our digital world also has such variety of components such as social media, VR, video conferencing, chatbots, etc., which also form an unconnected yet dependent realm, which is heading toward an advanced and widespread ecosystem at an exponential

pace because of AI, 5G, blockchain, cloud computing, and much more. In the upcoming days, our focus will be on seeing how self-sustaining realm maintains security and trust of users while generating a new economy for them.

## 14.2 Distributed Systems in Smart Grids

Smart grids represent an integration of traditional power grids with advanced digital communication and control technologies, enabling more efficient and reliable electricity delivery. Distributed systems play a crucial role in the implementation and operation of smart grids, offering several advantages, along with some challenges.

### 14.2.1 Advantages of Distributed Systems in Collaboration with Smart Grids

Smart grids implemented with distributed systems tend to better balance the supply and demand of electricity on a real-time basis. This tends to happen when we utilize different digital technologies such as sensors and software that help us to improve overall system efficiency and also help us minimize transmission losses, which leads to optimal energy distribution. The merger of renewable energy resources, which are solar power and wind power, into the grid becomes very easy when we use smart grids. This allows distributed generators to effectively communicate with the central grid in a manner that is seamless and promotes efficient use of clean energy. Distributed system gives us the power of real-time monitoring and control features; this leads to smart grids to automatically identify problems or disturbances without any delay. It helps us to reduce downtime during outages and provide a more dependable supply of electricity; hence, they automatically redistribute power. Real-time data on energy consumed are made visible to the end customer with the help of advanced smart meters and various other technologies. This helps the end customer to accurately calculate their energy consumption bill, and this transparent mechanism also leads to their active participation in grid optimization leading to energy saving and making educated decisions. Distributed systems make it possible to dynamically change electricity flows and control voltage levels, which leads to improvement in smart grid stability, and hence, grid has a stronger resistance to cyberattacks and adverse weather. There is a reduction in cost when smart grids are implemented with distributed systems, which helps to save money for the end customer and utilizes the same by maximizing energy distribution leading to cutting losses and limiting downtime.

### 14.2.2 Disadvantages of Distributed Systems in Collaboration with Smart Grids

The rules surrounding smart grids are yet to mature. Standards, data privacy, and interoperability need to be dealt with to ensure that there is efficient working of the energy sector and fair competition. Also, smart grids generate huge data. Although these data prove to be very useful in the optimization of grid operations, at the same time, it portrays security risks. Constant issues are ensuring data privacy and keeping the data far from cyber threats. Implementing smart grid technology requires advanced hardware, software, and communication infrastructure. Smart grids integrated with distribution systems are often exposed to cybersecurity, including malicious attacks, leading to compromised data and illegal access. The grid data are very critical and hence need overall robust protection and security measures with continuous monitoring for cyberattacks. The process of updating the systems currently in place to meet these technological requirements might be really slow and expensive. Another challenge is the advanced control algorithms and communication protocols, which are the backbone of a distributed system smart grid as they are required for the accurate distribution of energy resources and assets of the grid with end result of maximizing grid operations while maintaining stability and reliability.

### 14.2.3 Working of Distributed Systems in Collaboration with Smart Grids

Distributed systems decentralize intelligence and decision-making powers in smart grids. To monitor the conditions of the grid, detect defects, and make locally wise decisions, the local controllers, sensors, and actuators work independently and in coordination with each other. Then, a reliable and robust infrastructure is required to authorize data exchange and coordination across all distributed grid components, which are smart meters, sensors, and grid devices. This helps all the components to communicate with central control systems using wired or wireless communication technologies, for example, ethernet, Wi-Fi, and cellular networks.

In a distributed generation integrated grid, real-time data from different grid devices and components collected by the smart grids are then processed to gain insights of the grid performance and identify inefficiencies in operations so that it can be clearly optimized. Smart grid distributed control algorithms help in optimization using various techniques, which are used to coordinate assets of the grid, control energy flows, and maintain grid stability and reliability. These advanced algorithms use real-time data AI predictive models to optimize energy dispersion and manage grid congestion. Distributed systems have created a way to incorporate distributed energy resources (DERs) into the grid. These resources (like solar PVs, wind turbines, and battery storage systems that serve as DERs) can be controlled/coordinated to assist in grid stability, ancillary services, and energy optimization.

## 14.3 Distributed Systems in IoT

The IoT represents a network of interconnected devices embedded with sensors, software, and other technologies, enabling them to collect and exchange data (Figure 14.1). Distributed systems are essential for the functioning of IoT ecosystems, offering several advantages along with some challenges.

**Figure 14.1** Showcases the intricate presence of IoT devices around us. Internet of Things access technologies [Infographic]. Adapted from "Internet of Things Access Technologies," by M. Conran, October 24, 2017, Network Insight (network-insight.net). © 2017 Matt Conran.

### 14.3.1 Advantages of Distributed Systems in Collaboration with IoT

Because a distributed system can scale horizontally by adding more devices and nodes to the network, IoT deployments are able to take up the load of increasing numbers of devices and their consequent levels of data being generated. Spreading data processing and storage across many nodes makes a system more reliable and fault-tolerant. If one node crashed or became overloaded, other nodes would be able to continue in operation and deliver the service without any break. Low latency is achieved by distributing the processing work closer to the source, thereby improving the response time and thus can be used in IoT applications for industrial automation, smart city, and healthcare, where real-time data processing and decision-making are involved. The distributed systems have to make sure that computing and storage burdens are spread evenly among all the resources available so that bottlenecks are reduced, and efficiency in the usage of hardware resources is attained in IoT deployments. It supports the dynamic reconfigurability and adaptation of distributed systems to changing network conditions, device configurations, and workload demand. This allows IoT systems to be flexible in adapting to changing requirements and scaling resources on demand.

### 14.3.2 Disadvantages of Distributed Systems in Collaboration with IoT

One can suffer from cyber threats in the IoT distributed systems, such as unauthorized access, breaches of data, and malware attacks. Securing these devices in the IoT, communication channels, and the place where data are stored against cyberattacks requires rigorous security and is an ongoing activity. Distributed systems generate huge amounts of data from sensors, devices, and applications in IoT deployments. Effectively managing such huge data, processing, and analyzing them in a way that secures privacy and abides by data protection laws and regulations pose serious challenges to IoT systems. The interoperability and compatibility of various heterogeneous devices and systems within an IoT environment or network raise a challenge. Standardized communication protocols, defined data formats, and correct interfaces are the key to the creation of well-ordered integration and interoperability among the different types of IoT devices and platforms.

### 14.3.3 Working of Distributed Systems in Collaboration with IoT

IoT distributed systems obtain data from sensors, actuators, and other connected devices located in a wide variety of scenarios, including homes, factories, vehicles, and infrastructure. These devices are in continuous surveillance and acquisition of data on their environment, equipment status, and user interactions. Distributed systems will process the collected data at the edge devices or within distributed cloud environments. Edge computing allows data processing tasks to be performed closer to the data source. This will lessen latency and bandwidth usage. Distributed processing algorithms analyze sensor data, detect patterns, and extract actionable insights in real time (Figure 14.2). Distributed storage systems are very useful as it stores large volumes of IoT data in distributed databases or cloud storage environment. In distributed storage, the entire data are replicated or copied across multiple nodes to provide redundancy and fault tolerance and avoid

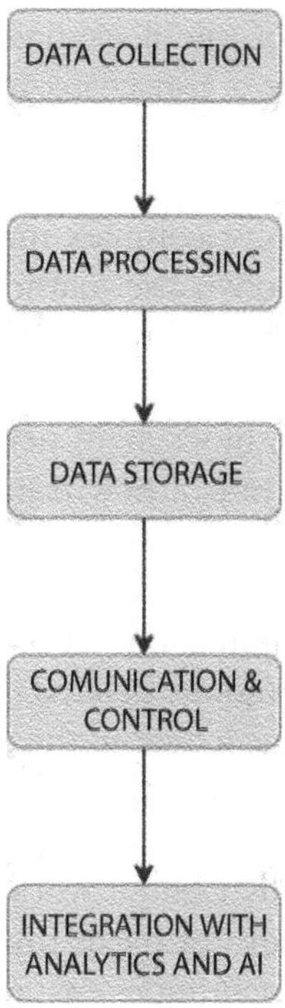


**Figure 14.2** Working of distributed database with IoT. [Source: Created by author using draw.io based on the text included in this chapter].

single point of failure. Distributed storage architectures provide storage for large volumes of IoT data that can be stored in a scalable and reliable manner, which leads to data retention, analysis, and retrieval. Distributed systems initiate communication and control features between IoT devices, edge nodes, and cloud services. Multiple protocols such as MQTT, CoAP, and HTTP provide secure and efficient data transfer between end devices and cloud platforms. The distributed system integrates with analytics and AI platforms in a way that derives insight from IoT data and makes it possible to take intelligent decisions. Machine learning algorithms analyze IoT data that foretell the breakdown of equipment, optimize energy consumption, and increase operational efficiency in numerous IoT applications.

## 14.4 Distributed Systems in Blockchain

Blockchain networks are decentralized networks, which depend on the distributed network of nodes or computers all over the world to validate and record each transaction, which signifies there is no central authority. Since all nodes have a copy of the blockchain, no one entity controls the blockchain. Blockchains have a consensus mechanism. The nodes reach an agreement on the validity of transactions using consensus mechanism. In Bitcoin, for example, proof of work is utilized as a consensus mechanism where a node has to solve complex mathematical puzzles to verify a transaction and whoever solves the mathematical puzzle first tends to validate the transaction and gets Bitcoin in reward. It is after this stage that the transaction will be packaged into blocks and placed on the block chain. Every single node in a blockchain network holds a complete copy of the ledger. As soon as there is a new transaction, it spreads across all copies at once and becomes updated therein concurrently. Such repetitiveness guarantees availability and fault tolerance of data. The very nature of blockchains makes them immutable because they are distributed. When a transaction is recorded, it cannot be deleted or tampered with. Since there are thousands of replicas of the ledger in the network, tampering with one copy would mean tampering with other copies on the network, which is practically impossible. Finally, security is high when it comes to distributed systems since there is distributed work and data storage. In such a case, attacks on one node will not harm the integrity of the system as a whole. Third, cryptographic techniques ensure the integrity of the data and prevent tampering.

### 14.4.1 Working of Distributed Systems in Collaboration with Blockchain

The major backbone in a P2P network consists of a network of distributed systems—this being blockchain technology. In it, connected nodes tend to exchange data with one another using a peer-to-peer (P2P) network protocol. Each node has a full copy of the blockchain ledger and holds the entire record of transactions. Blockchain networks depend on usage of consensus mechanisms to validate transactions that happen in the blockchain network and reach distributed consensus between the different participants in the network. Some of the common mechanisms for reaching consensus and validating any transaction include the following: proof of work (Bitcoin) and proof of stake (Ethereum). Each participant initiates the transactions, and through broadcasting, it goes to the network nodes. According to consensus rules, it is thereafter verified. Valid transactions are then grouped in blocks to be appended to the blockchain in a sequential and immutable manner.

A smart contract, in relation to blockchain technology, is a self-executing agreement where the terms of the contract are encoded into lines of code. These digital contracts or agreements facilitate trustless transactions and are stored on a blockchain and automatically executed once the prespecified conditions are met. Blockchain-aided distributed systems support decentralized applications or platforms that run on the blockchain, for example, Uniswap, which is a DApp and runs on Ethereum blockchain, DApps are software applications based on a decentralized network of computers. DApps leverage blockchain technology to enable P2P interactions, secure data exchange, and transparent governance.

### 14.4.2 Advantages of Distributed Systems in Collaboration with Blockchain

Participants are enabled to have control over their data and therefore can selectively share it with other parties. Records placed within the blockchain are encrypted and available to parties for whom permission has been given; hence, it enhances data privacy and confidentiality. The full proof secure nature of transactions with highest standard of data integrity is enforced in blockchain with the help of implementation of cryptographic techniques such as public-key cryptography, cryptographic hashing, and digital signatures. These cryptographic mechanisms provide tamper-proofing and resistance to unauthorized changes to the transactions. Blockchain keeps an immutable and transparent record of all transactions in a form such that each transaction is cryptographically linked and time-stamped. The transparent and immutable nature promises data integrity and allows transparent audit trails, improving accountability and building trust. Distributed systems with blockchain technology make it possible for decentralized architecture—there is no need for intermediaries. Such decentralization gives strength to the system, reduces single points of failure, and raises trust among the participants.

## 14.5 Distributed Systems in Machine Learning

Machine learning prefers to have as large dataset as possible simply because the more data units it has, the more it can observe, learn, and test upon. Initially, the idea of keeping the dataset on one machine was well received, but as machine learning is a technology and our dependency on it for classification, regression, developing chatbots, generating medical trends, and handling big data increases, we are faced with challenges when sticking with a single machine system. First, there is limited to no parallelism, which slows the machine learning process, triumphing over its advantages. A single machine is not going to have enough space to handle memory requirements when a scalable dataset is introduced. It has limited computational abilities because no matter how hard a machine is pushed, if it is capable of handling 100 data units, we cannot push it to 200 at a time. This led us toward adoption of distributed systems readily for machine learning algorithms because now the data can be stored on different local networks, devices, or even geographical locations, making the handling of a large dataset an easier task. This has an added advantage of increased resource utilization because all the devices now can process different portions of dataset using their local resources, not shared resources, meaning all the devices will be utilizing their capabilities and not be ideal. It also supports parallel processing because different sets of same data are simultaneously being processed, leaving no time wasted. They can then communicate their findings to each other, making it a collaborative effort, and then the combined output can be presented in half the time. When trends and predictions have to be made for airline schedules, stock market, etc., where terabytes of data can be seen, distributed machine learning can open horizons of opportunities to work with such a high velocity and high volume of data. Machine learning in itself is a complex process where we do not have a skilled workforce or resources to compute them effectively without the risk of overfitting and underfitting, and adding on it is the large size of dataset, which is slow in computation; the lack of support from a single machine can only make things worse, which is why the world is heading toward distributed machine learning.

### 14.5.1 Distributed Learning Paradigms

While traditional machine learning trains a model on a single physical location, distributed machine learning suggests taking a large data model and its corresponding dataset and splitting it among different devices. The two approaches toward it are as follows:

#### *14.5.1.1 Data Parallelism*

Data are partitioned into *n* parts for *n* workers of distributed system in the computing cluster. Each of the worker nodes is supplied with a copy of the model, and each worker then trains the dataset portion given with a different subset of data. The training loops are run on the workers, both synchronously or asynchronously, as per the need of the model. Computation of neural networks has become simplified because of this.

#### *14.5.1.2 Model Parallelism*

When the model is also too large, not just the dataset, we turn to use model parallelism, where the model's components are also split across numerous machines, making the larger model's development a lot more feasible. At the end, we combine the output of different units to form a final result.

### 14.5.2 Distributed Machine Learning Algorithms

#### *14.5.2.1 Alternating Least Squares*

It is a matrix factorization algorithm that supports parallelism. It runs its gradient descent parallel to partitions and minimizes two loss functions alternatively. Its main application is in scaling to large datasets with ease, and it has been implemented for large-scale collaborative filtering issues implemented using Apache Spark as well.

#### *14.5.2.2 Stochastic Gradient Descent*

Known for its computational efficiency with larger datasets, it utilizes small clusters of dataset to work upon, reducing the overall cost per iteration, and we do not even have to process the entire dataset. It shuffles the dataset mandatorily so that a random set is created on which we can perform our calculations.

#### *14.5.2.3 MapReduce*

Another one of the algorithms that work effectively with scalable datasets is MapReduce, identified through its increased application in data preprocessing, feature extraction, training models, and data clustering. It processes the dataset using its two functions: map and reduce. *Map* divides the data into smaller parts according to a user-specified function, whereas *reduce* aggregates the key–value pairs generated in the above step.

### 14.5.3 Potential Future Research Areas

#### *14.5.3.1 Edge Computing*

Due to exponential increase in data produced by digital devices, thanks to 4G and 5G networks, IoT devices, AI becoming omnipresent, the data cannot be directly sent to some centralized data center or cloud core because of the bandwidth it will consume and bottlenecks it can cause, not to mention the delay in response to the customers (Figure 14.3). To avoid such situations, we started investing in moving some of the data storage and computation near the end devices so it can be computed where it was produced.

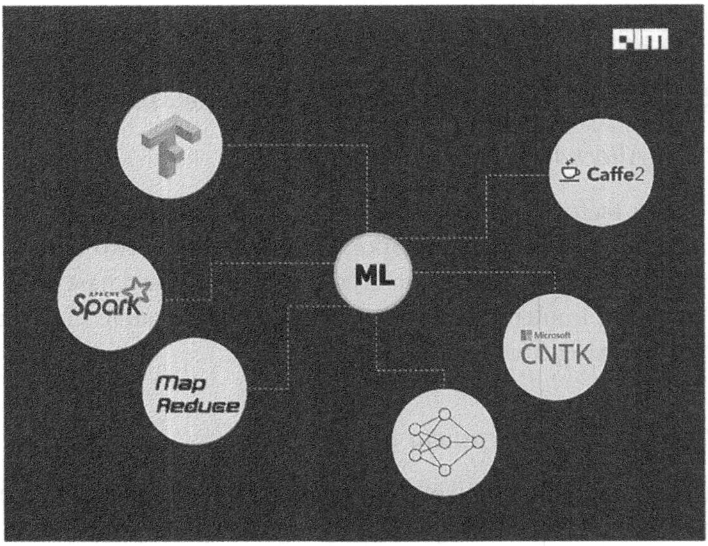


**Figure 14.3** Shows various Machine Learning tools available in the market. Internet of Things access technologies [Infographic]. Adapted from Internet of Things Access Technologies by M.Conran, October 24, 2017, Network Insight. © 2017 Matt Conran.

#### *14.5.3.2 Federated Learning*

It is also a mechanism to train machine learning models without involving the core of the computing architecture. Also termed as collaborative learning, the data from respective devices are taken on the edge devices and computed locally to train models at different locations. It is currently making its way into computer vision domain of AI.

## 14.6 Distributed Systems in AR

AR's architecture involves a lot of implementations on interface distribution so it is easier to work with centralized architecture when we are using AR, but because it needs rapid feedback, it is better if each node is running a synchronized copy of the particular application. To achieve that, several logical objects are shared with each other, and each node replicates it when it receives it. AR's user interface is not one of our regular desktop's user interfaces because it depends on both real-world objects and computer-generated images. When trying to create a distributed system for the same, we need to address these both. Sometimes, the users all might be present in the same real-world scenario, and then, we cannot distribute the real-world objects; we are bound to keep them intact and centralized. Furthermore, ideally, it should capable of creating a world where we cannot distinguish the real from virtual, which is a future goal; thus, while distributing, we have to maintain the standard currently developed to enhance the existing virtual world. AR systems are using distributed application environment by using different distributed languages, one of them being Facile. Now, the distributed components have been isolated, and external views can be used to connect these replications and distributed applications. It can be widely used in gaming and interior and architectural modifications.

### 14.6.1 Application in Medicine

Although we have seen AR and VR being integral in learning, it has found its calling medicine more in the present. AR allows any medical personnel to perform a critical procedure or even the smallest ones without actually risking the life of a patient because it is a simulated environment (Figure 14.4). One of the many research works includes enhancing a

**Figure 14.4** Showcases the use of AR in improving surgical precision with lower risk [12].

person's hand–eye coordination to perform endotracheal intubation (ETI) with AR. To execute this idea, it has been proposed by many to use distributed simulation with 3D deformable models along with dynamic shared state maintenance algorithm.

### 14.6.2 Role of Distributed Systems in AR

Distributed systems ensure that the content created digitally, be it 3D modeled or animated, is delivered in real time with little to manageable latency using content delivery networks (CDNs) and P2P networks. Furthermore, it enhances user experience by simply allowing interaction in real time between multiusers/multiplayers by synchronization techniques, which enables communication irrespective of location. The best example of it is the recent development of games such Valorant, Minecraft, etc. The distributed systems have the option to integrate cloud resources, which can reduce the burden on the central network, if not offload it completely, by taking on some of the tasks such as object recognition. This brings us to our next advantage of using distributed systems with AR because now we can integrate AR with external data sources, paving way for its smooth functioning, with IoT devices and external networks seamlessly making the AR more relevant in our world. Lastly, AR when executed through distributed systems opens the window for platforms where autonomous content can be created, utilized, and profited from, even for autonomous bodies.

### 14.6.3 Working of Distributed Systems in Collaboration with AR

AR means simply adding a layer of computer-generated environment over the real environment. The computer-generated environment can also take inspiration from the real world and generate a virtual world on its blueprint. Once that environment is ready to be used, AR devices with sensors, cameras, etc., are implanted to generate 3D scenes in real time and capture movement of the users involved. These data are processed on the distributed system's worker components. The processed data in the form of 3D models, textures, images, etc., are deployed using P2P or CDNs near the edge of the network, closer to the end users. These data are collaborated with the data generated by other users in the same environment even if it is different cities of the real world. To collaborate and synchronize the data such as user gestures and transfer that smoothly, WebRTC and MQTT are some of the reliable protocols. The tasks can be offloaded from the main network by simply transferring it to remote servers of the cloud, providing low-latency and high-fidelity AR content on devices that may not have enough resources on their own. Since distributed systems work efficiently in collaboration with blockchain, implementing blockchain on distributed AR applications decentralizes the AAA process and allows monetization of digital assets too.

## 14.7 Distributed Systems in Distributed Databases

With the age of digitization, we are currently in thinking that a single machine or centralized database is enough to perform quick query processing, backup, and recovery, and storing large-scale data would be an overestimation of its capabilities. But we can use distributed database to create an illusion of centralized system by implementing location transparency, transaction transparency, local DBMS transparency, schema change transparency, etc. A database manager is the software used to handle query processing and memory allocation within the database, whereas user request interface is how client program sends the request to perform certain actions. This request is received and formatted according to distributed manager understandable form using distributed transaction manager. Since the distributed networks work using communication over the networks, to optimize query processing on high-speed WANs, local processing time and disk's memory access time along with transmitting as concise data as possible are the way to reduce the cost of using distributed databases. Another way of reducing cost and improving performance has been observed as bitmap compression where we ditch the traditional index key–value pair representation with a list and replace it with a bitmap or bit vector. The bitmap indices can reduce I/O when presented with a large amount of data, common AND OR operations can be efficiently performed on the data, and parallelism is increased by executing 32 to 64 bits in parallel. Distributed systems provide a mechanism to maintain a replica of the database on all sites while also ensuring that data that are frequently used on a site are readily available for processing in its local memory without fail. It deploys synchronization techniques such as locks, clock synchronization, etc., which are observed to maintain concurrency of data. Deadlocks, distributed two-phase commit, also ensure that the data are not updated when they are in the middle of a transaction on other sites. To store these data and output generated on different databases, data are fragmented into smaller units, which can be done horizontally, meaning records with all their attributes are present at different locations, or we can do fragmentation by vertically fragmenting the database, that is, by storing attributes with the corresponding records at different locations.

### 14.7.1 Working of Distributed Database

Data partitioning is the simple act of dividing the larger database into smaller subsets, which can be used to distribute data across various nodes of a distributed system for faster performance of the database by reducing the individual load on a node and reducing the response time. Some examples of partitioning include hash partitioning, range partitioning, etc.; once this is done, it is time ensure the network does not have increased dependency over one node, so data are replicated and stored at different nodes. Techniques include Multi-master, Master-Slave, etc., replication. Query processing should be fast to ensure database fulfills the purpose of its creation, which means query processing needs to be optimized by introducing parallel query execution along multiple nodes. After optimization, transaction management ensures database transactions maintain atomicity, consistency, isolation and durability (ACID) properties, and also, it keeps transaction logs for the same. Finally, we implement some recovery procedures to maintain network resiliency (Figure 14.5). Distributed databases ensure a scalable database capable of handling increased volume of data and user interactions, make the network fault-tolerant through replication and recovery, and improve the overall performance through lower latency and consistent communication establishment.

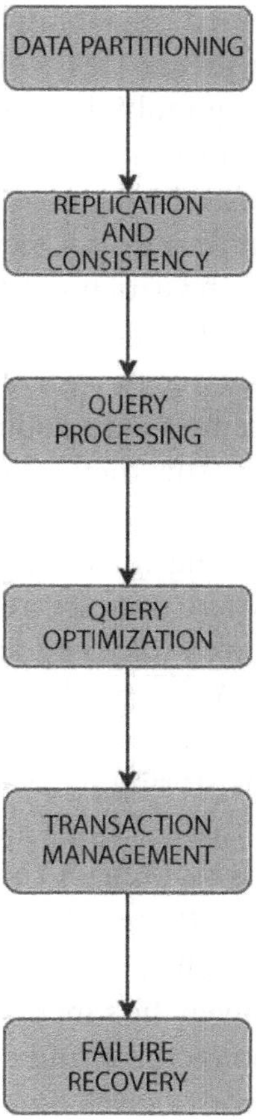


**Figure 14.5** Working of distributed database. [Source: Created by author using draw.io based on the text included in this chapter].

## 14.8 Distributed Systems in Metaverse

Metaverse is the talk of the town and has found its representation in many movies, series, comics such as Snow Crash, etc., to experience it to the fullest; a cohesive environment is required where real-time rendering technologies are available and utilized. Its expansion, as of today, also includes the cloud computing models and edge computing where edge networks with their limited resources can also be less burdened with the help of edge servers. But if we follow the current trend of increase in number of devices, there would soon be a time where edge servers' resources may also seem inefficient due to congestion and lack of dedicated resources for audio and video rendering that metaverse so boasts of. This issue of lack of resources can be overcome with distributed collaborative computing being employed to solve a lot of computation-focused tasks of the metaverse. A large-scale task can be resolved by making multiple mobile networks work in collaboration with each other. This also led to further issues in implementation, called the strangler effect, caused by the weak communication links or lack of individual communication resources. One such example is Roblox outage in 2021, where the cloud infrastructure failed causing an estimated loss of US $1.5 billion. To resolve the effects and create a more fault-tolerant and durable use, metaverse service providers to gather the individual output from various nodes were met with coding techniques to give rise to coded distributed computing. This method of distributed computing has led to improvements in data processing and reduced latency and can be best utilized while implementing interactive services, including gaming services such as Minecraft, where you can create an entire universe of your own, interact with other players on geographically distributed systems, and make real-time changes. Although the efforts to decentralize and distribute computing remain constant, the threat to security remains greater. With more physical locations storing data and its multiples copies being circulated over the network, there is a dire need to prevent data breaches. This is where integration with blockchain comes into use. It can store data securely and provides anonymity, and its immutable ledger removes the requirement for a central controller.

Distributed systems have given the support to accommodate the increasing number of users, their interactions, and curated content that can allow on-demand scaling of resources, as well as giving them decentralized and autonomous ownership and control over the metaverse's economy and right to monetize their intellectual property. The multiple nodes present to compute and store data constantly being produced have made metaverse a fault-tolerant and resilient ecosystem with minimal downtime and multiple backups. Furthermore, distributed systems allowed seamless introduction of concepts of globalization, promoting accessibility, inclusivity, and cross-culture exchanges. However, this does not cover up for the fact that the distributed system's integration has not made unauthorized access, data breaches, and theft of identity a foreign concept to metaverse too. The metaverse ecosystem, being based on blockchain, consumes a significant amount of energy, endangering sustainability and long-term viability of the metaverse. The distributed system is best known for its resource utilization and scalability, but with the amount of data generated at such high velocity, it will be interesting to see how well it can keep up.

### 14.8.1 Working of Metaverse in Collaboration with Distributed Systems

The virtual world is based on distributed system, which is the infrastructure for user interactions, graphics processing, texture identification, etc. The real-time interactions in the metaverse gain support from distributed systems. It further proves its usability by easing the management of digital assets, currencies, non-fungible tokens (NFTs), avatars, etc., through its integration with blockchain simultaneously. All these together help increase the building of a strongly connected network that supports user interactions and socialization of "netizens," as they are called. This is the prime reason for the increase in blockchain-based payments and smooth e-commerce over the metaverse. To strengthen the environment and virtual economies, digital assets and ownership (DAOs), smart contracts, and decentralized governance models are implemented to ensure safe and secure content curation and exchange (Figure 14.6).

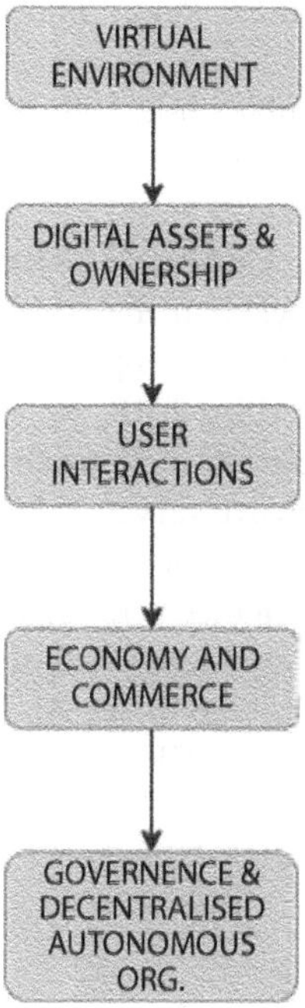


**Figure 14.6** Working of metaverse. [Source: Created by author using draw.io based on the text included in this chapter].

## 14.9 Conclusion

Distributed systems have proven to be extremely effective as in individual technology, as well as an enhancer of other already existing ones. But this should not be the excuse to stop exploring as though distributed systems optimize performance and introduce scalability and security with integration to remote servers and cloud; it also has a long way to go in terms of improving its limits of handling large data, range of application, and contribution to security and privacy. It is an area where scope of development and improvement is not stagnant, and this potential must not be wasted.

## References

1. Tankovic, A Perspective on Distributed Computer Systems. *IEEE Trans. Comput.*, C-33, 12, 1102–1115, Dec. 1984.
2. El-khattam, W. and Salama, M.M.A., Distributed Generation Technologies, Definitions and Benefits. *Electr. Power Syst. Res.*, 71, 301, 2004.
3. Gellings, C.W., Samotyj, M., Howe, B., The Future's Smart Delivery System [Electric Power Supply]. *IEEE Power Energy Mag.*, 2, 5, 302, September-October, 2004.
4. Kumar, S., Tiwari, P., Zymbler, M., Internet of Things is a revolutionary approach for future technology enhancement: a review. *J. Big Data*, 6, 111, 2019.
5. Ryskeldiev, B., Ochiai, Y., Cohen, M., Herder, J., Distributed Metaverse: Creating Decentralized Blockchain-based Model for Peer-to-peer Sharing of Virtual Spaces for Mixed Reality Applications, Association for Computing Machinery, New York, NY, USA, 2018.
6. Dehghani, M. and Yazdanparast, Z., From distributed machine to distributed deep learning: a comprehensive survey. *J. Big Data*, 10, 158, 2023.
7. Chouiten, M., Didier, J.-Y., Mallem, M., Distributed Augmented Reality Systems: How Much Performance is Enough? *IEEE International Conference on Multimedia and Expo Workshops*, Melbourne, VIC, Australia, 2012.
8. Al-Ansi, A.M., Jaboob, M., Garad, A., Al-Ansi, A., Analyzing augmented reality (AR) and virtual reality (VR) recent development in education. *Soc. Sci. Humanit. Open*, 8, 1, 301, 2023.
9. Liu, T.-S. and Zhao, S.-Z., *P2P Distributed Database System*, Science Press, Beijing, 2007.

10. Tripathi, S.L. and Mahmud, M., *Explainable Machine Learning Models and Architecture*, Wiley & Scrivener Publishing LLC, USA, 2023, https://doi.org/10.1002/9781394186570.
11. Kumar Rana, A., Sharma, V., Rana, A., Alam, M., Lata Tripathi, S. (Eds.), *Convergence of Blockchain and Internet of Things in Healthcare*, 1st ed., CRC Press, UK, 2024, https://doi.org/10.1201/9781003466949.
12. Zhou, Z., Siddiquee, M.M.R., Tajbakhsh, N., Liang, J., UNet++: A nested U-Net architecture for medical image segmentation. 2018, arXiv. https://doi.org/10.48550/arXiv.1811.12815.

15

# Power Optimization in 4Bit Comparator Architecture Through Precomputation Technique

**Adarsh Sharma[1], Suman Lata Tripathi[2*], Deepika Ghai[1] and Khilda Afifah[3]**

[1]*School of Electrical and Electronics Engineering, Lovely Professional University, Jalandhar Punjab, India*
[2]*Department of Electronics and Communication Engineering, Symbiosis Institute of Technology (SIT), Symbiosis International (Deemed University), Pune, India*
[3]*School of Electrical Engineering & Management, Telkom University, Bandung, West Java, Indonesia*

## *Abstract*
Efficient power consumption is a critical requirement in modern digital systems, especially for resource-constrained applications. This paper presents an optimized 4-bit comparator design employing the precomputation technique to significantly reduce power dissipation. By precomputing partial results and minimizing unnecessary transitions, the proposed design achieves enhanced power efficiency without compromising performance or accuracy. The methodology involves partitioning the comparison process into smaller, power-efficient stages, reducing dynamic power consumption by mitigating redundant switching activities. Simulation results validate the effectiveness of the approach, demonstrating substantial power savings compared to conventional designs while maintaining competitive delay characteristics. This study underscores the potential of precomputation in advancing low-power digital circuit designs. The circuits were implemented using Cadence Virtuoso Tool using gpdk 90 nm and 45 nm technology node.

***Keywords***: Comparator, precomputation technique, low-power technique, dynamic power, switching activity, Cadence Virtuoso

**Corresponding author*: tri.suman78@gmail.com

Sandhya Avasthi and Suman Lata Tripathi (eds.) Distributed and Parallel Computing, (323–338)

## 15.1 Introduction

The increasing demand for low-power digital circuits has driven significant research in optimizing the power consumption of fundamental building blocks in computing systems. Among these, comparators are critical components widely used in arithmetic units, signal processing, and embedded systems, where power efficiency is paramount. However, conventional comparator designs often suffer from excessive power dissipation due to high switching activity and redundant operations, especially in systems with stringent power constraints. The precomputation technique offers a promising approach to address these challenges. By predicting partial outputs and avoiding unnecessary transitions during the computation process, precomputation significantly reduces dynamic power consumption. This technique not only improves energy efficiency but also maintains the performance and accuracy required in high-speed digital systems. In this paper, we explore the application of precomputation to optimize the power consumption of a 4-bit comparator. The proposed design leverages partitioning strategies and logic-level optimizations to minimize redundant switching, resulting in substantial power savings. Simulation results demonstrate the effectiveness of this approach, showing significant improvements in power efficiency compared to traditional comparator designs.

### 15.1.1 Low-Power Design Techniques

Power optimization plays important role in efficient VLSI (very large scale integration) architecture design. Power consumptions in VLSI circuits are categorized by dynamic power, short circuit power, and leakage power (static power) consumptions. The major contribution in power consumption is due to dynamic power that depends on number switching activities.

$$P = f_{\mathrm{clk}} C_L V_{\mathrm{dd}}^2 + V_{\mathrm{dd}} I_{\mathrm{sc}} + V_{\mathrm{dd}} I_{\mathrm{leakage}} \tag{15.1}$$

where $f_{\mathrm{clk}}$ = clock frequency; $C_{\mathrm{L}}$ = load capacitance; $V_{\mathrm{dd}}$ = suppy voltage, and $I_{\mathrm{leakage}}$ = leakage current.

The low-power techniques include power reduction by reducing supply voltage, switching activity, and reduced clock swing [1].

#### 15.1.1.1 *Reduced Supply Voltage ($V_{dd}$)*

Reduction in $V_{dd}$ reduces power consumption up to a large extent, but it also leads to major drawback of threshold voltage ($V_{th}$) getting closer to $V_{dd.}$ Also, it is very difficult to reduce $V_{th}$ in the same ratio and leads to the leakage current on the higher side.

#### 15.1.1.2 *Reduced Switching Activity*

Dynamic power or switching power depends on the number of binary logic switching from 0 to 1 or 1 to 0; high frequency leads to a higher switching activity, resulting into more power consumption. More than 90% of on-chip power consumption is due to dynamic power.

There are several methods to reduce the number switching activities such signal gating, clock gating, or by addition of precomputation block. In continuous/discrete signal model, the switching frequency *f* is expressed as ½ of the number of transitions activity per unit time:

$$f = \frac{N(T)}{2T} \tag{15.2}$$

By reducing *N* value, one can reduce the overall power consumption as shown in Equation (15.1). Either directly reducing signal frequency or suppressing certain activities will reduce the number of transitions and hence switching power.

#### 15.1.1.3 *Reduced Capacitance*

Capacitances, frequently part of the VLSI circuit, arise due to transistor architecture, interconnects, and load. They affect not only the circuit delay but also the power consumption. So, optimization in node capacitance is important to keep delay and power consumption under limit. Reduced load capacitance directly reduces the dynamic power consumptions.

#### 15.1.1.4 *Reduced Static Current*

Static or leakage current flows even when the transistor is not in operation. Static power is directly dependent on leakage current that can be reduced by reducing the number of leakage path at the transistor and circuit level.

### *15.1.1.5 Parallel and Pipelined Architectures*

At architecture-level design, little addition in hardware and circuit complexity is required to achieve substantial power saving. To improve the computation efficiency, parallel and pipelined architectures were used in complex circuit. Parallel processing effectively increases the throughput compared to a uniprocessing system by performing computations simultaneously without increasing the operating frequency.

$$P_{\text{uniprocessing}} = CV^2f \tag{15.3}$$

where $C$ = average capacitance, and $V$ = operating voltage of uniprocessing system.

Suppose the average switched capacitance in the parallel processing is 2.2C due to change in multiplexing and demultiplexing processes. Parallel processing relaxes in the operating voltage up to 0.6 V at reduced frequency.

The power dissipation parallel processing system:

$$P_{\text{parallel}} = (2.2\text{C})\,(0.6V)^2\,(0.5f) = 0.396\text{P}_{\text{uniprocessing}} \tag{15.4}$$

Power dissipation in pipelined processing of the same architecture:

$$P_{\text{pipelined}} = (1.2\text{C})\,(0.6V)^2\,f = 0.432P_{\text{uni}} \tag{15.5}$$

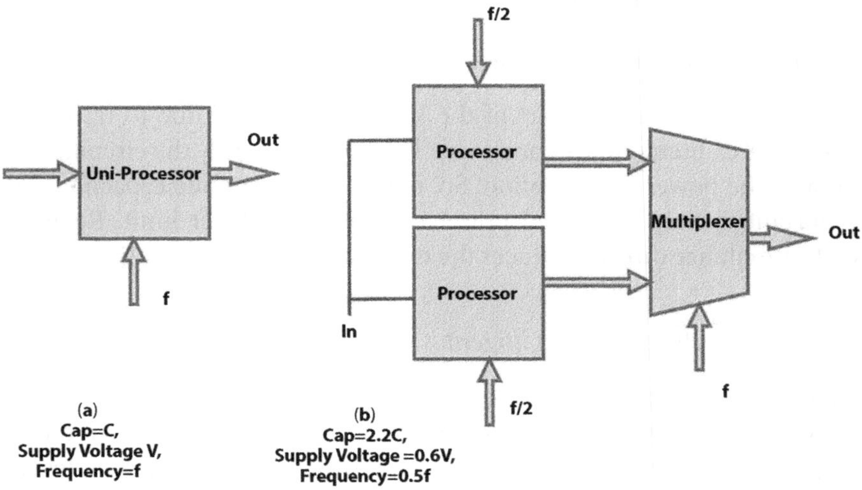


**Figure 15.1** (a) uniprocessing, (b) parallel processing.

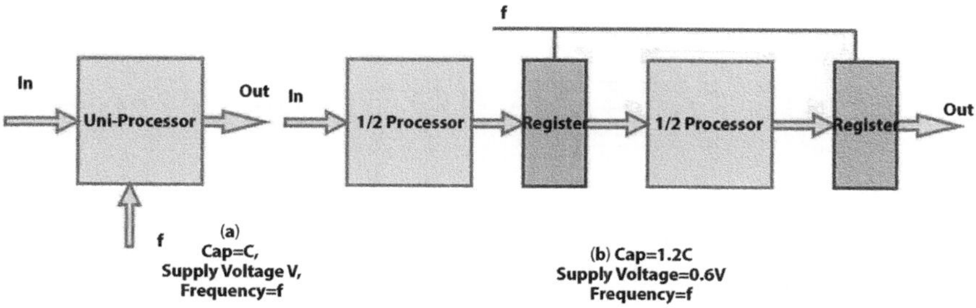


**Figure 15.2** (a) uniprocessing, (b) pipelined processing.

Figure 15.1 a and b show the comparison of architecture of uniprocessing with parallel and pipelined processing architecture. There is compromise in circuit capacitance and frequency in parallel architecture to reduce power consumption. Pipeline processing also improves power but slightly more than parallel processing. Figure 15.2 shows the block diagram of uniprocessing and pipelined processing.

## 15.2 Comparator

A comparator in digital electronics is a circuit or logic device used to compare two binary inputs and determine their relationship. Its primary function is to output signals indicating whether one binary value is equal to, greater than, or less than the other. Comparators are widely used in digital systems, such as arithmetic units, signal processing, sorting networks, and decision-making circuits.

### 15.2.1 4Bit Comparator

A 4-bit comparator is a digital circuit that compares two 4-bit binary numbers and determines their relative magnitudes. The inputs are two 4-bit numbers, $A$ = A3A2A1A0 and $B$ = B3B2B1B0, where $A3$ and $B3$ are the most significant bits (MSB), and $A0$ and $B0$ are the least significant bits (LSBs). Figure 15.3 shows the block diagram of 4-bit comparator.

The comparator produces three outputs:

$A > B$ indicates that $A$ is greater than $B$.
$A < B$ indicates that $A$ is less than $B$.
$A = B$ indicates that $A$ is equal to $B$.

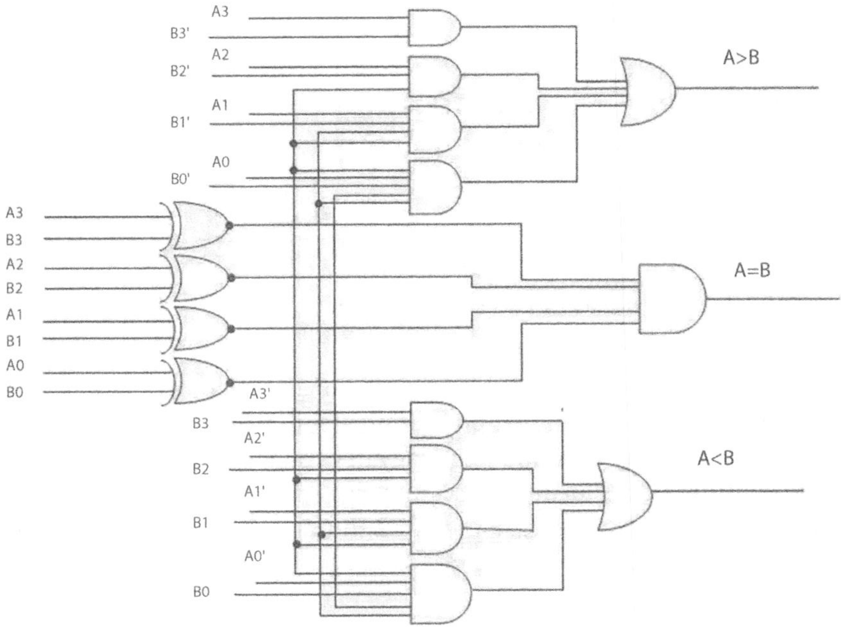


**Figure 15.3** 4-bit comparator.

## 15.3 Precomputation Technique

The precomputation technique is a low-power design strategy used in digital circuits to minimize power consumption by pre-evaluating certain parts of a computation and reducing unnecessary operations during runtime. This technique is especially effective in circuits with repetitive or conditional operations, where the full computation might not always be required.

### 15.3.1 Working Principle

1. **Partial result prediction**: Portions of the computation are performed beforehand based on specific input conditions or patterns. These precomputed results are stored temporarily or used directly to bypass unnecessary operations.
2. **Conditional activation**: Only the parts of the circuit needed for the final output are activated based on the precomputed results. This selective activation reduces switching activity, a major contributor to dynamic power consumption.

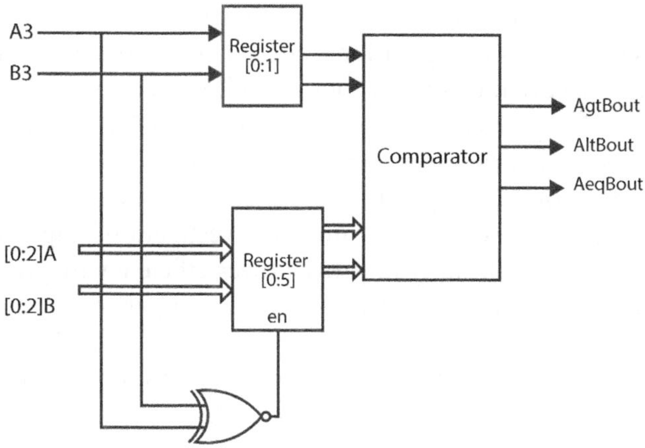


**Figure 15.4** Precomputation technique.

3. **Logic simplification**: Precomputation often simplifies the logic that needs to be evaluated during the operational phase, reducing the overall complexity and power usage.

Figure 15.4 shows the logic diagram of precomputation technique for 4bit comparator. In this design, we have two different registers and one XNOR gate.

## 15.4 Reported Precomputation Circuit

The increasing need for energy-efficient digital circuits has motivated extensive research into low-power design techniques. Comparators, as essential components in digital systems, have been the focus of numerous studies aimed at reducing power consumption while maintaining high performance.

Precomputation techniques to reduce power at the circuit level have been discussed by Sinha and Chander [2]. Decomposition of logic function is to minimize the total power dissipation in the digital circuit. A substantial amount of power can be saved if it is targeted early in the design cycle. Experimentally, it is seen that about 20% to 30% of total power can be saved at the logic level. We have some other techniques to reduce power dissipation in circuits such as clock getting, signal gating, and power gating. Binary decision diagram (BDD)-based logic synthesis and optimization for low-power comparator circuit is discussed by Sinha and Tripathi *et al.* [3]. Precomputation, a widely researched low-power technique, has been applied in various arithmetic circuits such as adders and multipliers to reduce unnecessary operations. For instance, precomputation-based adder designs have demonstrated considerable power savings by predicting carry propagation paths and reducing dynamic activity [4]. These findings suggest that similar principles can be effectively applied to comparators. Power optimization in comparators has been performed using precomputation techniques. However, preliminary investigations suggest that precomputation can significantly improve power efficiency by pre-evaluating critical conditions and selectively enabling comparison operations [5]. Despite its potential, the application of precomputation in comparators remains underexplored, creating an opportunity for innovative designs that balance power savings and performance [6].

## 15.5 Comparator Design with Cadence Virtuoso

### 15.5.1 4Bit Comparator Schematic

Figure 15.5 shows schematic of 4bit comparator circuit. In this, we have input $A$ = A0A1A2A3 and $B$ = B0B1B2B3 and output is $A > B$, $A < B$, and $A = B$. The inputs are two 4-bit numbers, $A$ = A3A2A1A0 and $B$ = B3B2B1B0, where $A3$ and $B3$ are the most significant bits (MSB), and $A0$ and $B0$ are the LSBs [7].

### 15.5.2 4-Bit Comparator Using Precomputation Technique

Figure 15.6 shows 4Bit comparator using precomputation technique. For precomputation technique, we use one 2bit reg, one 6bit reg, and one XNOR gate [8].

Figure 15.7 shows the internal structure of precomputation technique. For designing this, we use d-flipflop as reg.

### 15.5.3 Simulation Results

Figure 15.8 shows the transient response of 4bit comparator. This work is done in Cadence Virtuoso at 45 nm technology node. Here, the output bits are taken as AeB (A=B), AgB (A>B) and ALB (A<B).

Table 15.1 shows the comparison of power and area of 4bit comparator with before using precomputation technique and after using precomputation technique.

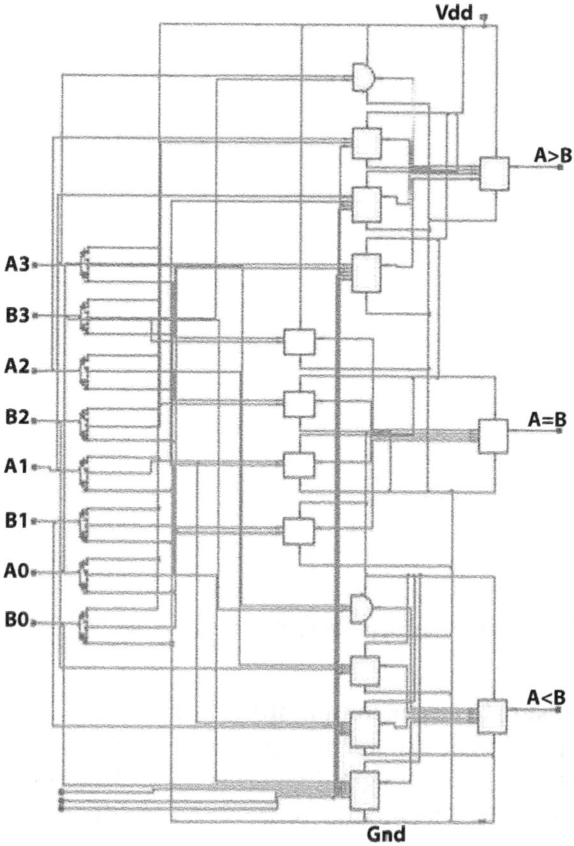


**Figure 15.5** 4Bit comparator schematic.

Figure 15.9 shows a comparison of power and area of 4bit comparator before and after precomputation circuit. A considerable power reduction is observed with slight overhead in IC area using precomputation technique-based comparator than simple comparator.

## 15.6 Future Scopes

The proposed 4-bit comparator design employing the precomputation technique demonstrates significant power optimization; they have several future scopes and development opportunities.

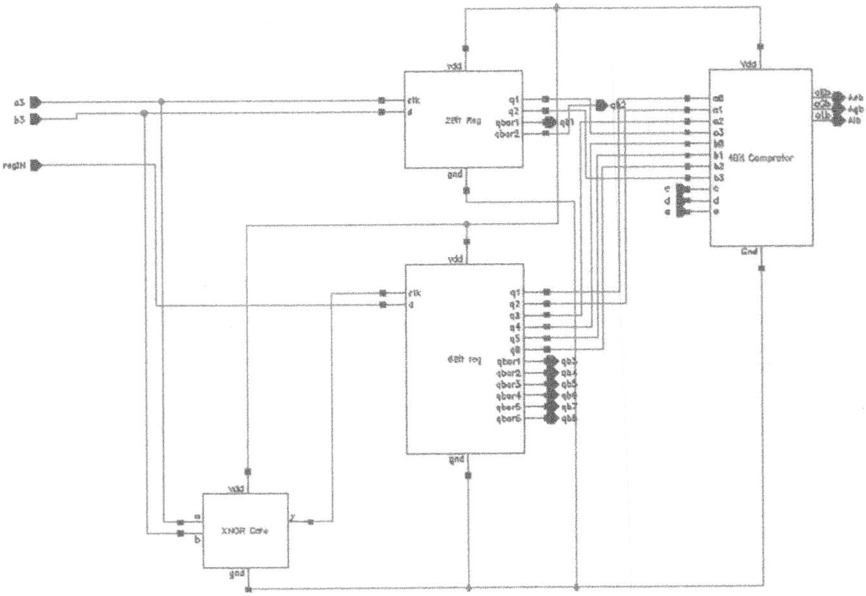


**Figure 15.6** 4Bit comparator using precomputation technique.

1. **Extension to larger comparators**: The principles of precomputation can be extended to higher-bit comparators, such as 8-, 16-, or 32-bit designs. Exploring the scalability and effectiveness of the technique for larger bit widths could lead to its application in more complex systems, such as processors and memory units [9].
2. **Design automation**: Developing automated design tools that incorporate precomputation techniques could enable rapid prototyping of low-power circuits. This would enhance the adoption of such techniques in industry-scale digital design workflows.
3. **Dynamic adaptation techniques**: Implementing adaptive precomputation mechanisms that dynamically adjust based on workload or input patterns could further improve power efficiency, especially in real-time applications [10].
4. **Application in low-power embedded systems**: The optimized comparator can be a key building block in low-power embedded systems for IoT, wearable devices, and mobile computing. These systems often prioritize energy efficiency over computational throughput [11].

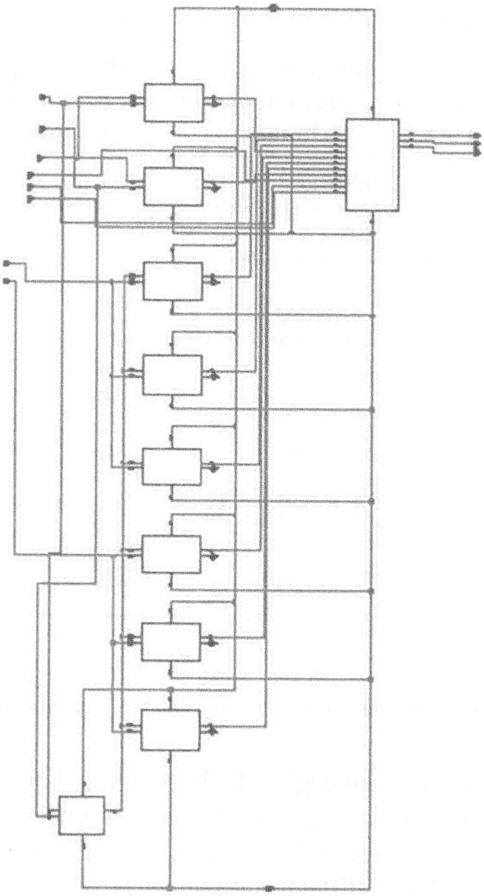

**Figure 15.7** Internal structure of precomputation logic.

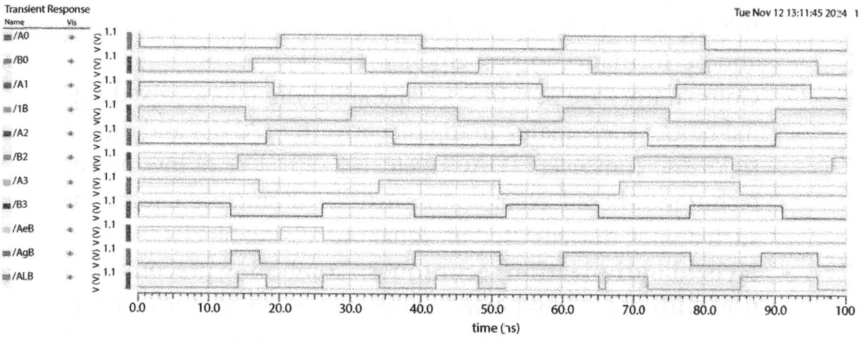


**Figure 15.8** Transient response of 4bit comparator.

**Table 15.1** Comparison of power and area.

| Performance | Before using precomputation technique | After using precomputation technique |
|---|---|---|
| Power (μW) | 400.3E−3 | 321.0E−3 |
| Area ($\mu m^2$) | 408 | 577 |

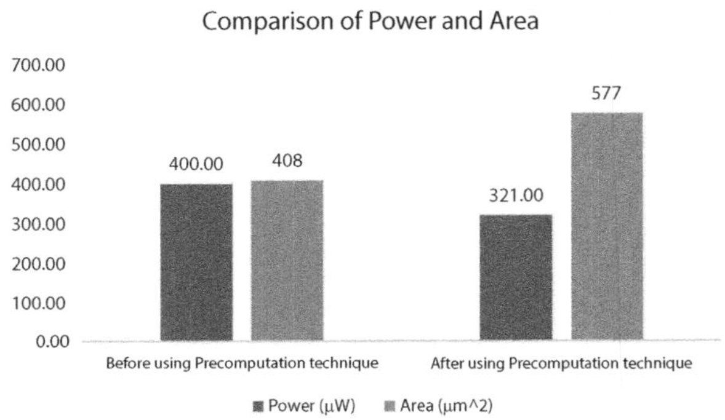


**Figure 15.9** Comparison power and area before and after precomputation circuit.

5. **Exploration of emerging technologies**: Future work can explore the application of precomputation in conjunction with emerging technologies such as FinFETs, tunnel field effect transistors (FETs), and nanoelectronic devices, where power efficiency is a critical design consideration [12–16].
6. **Implementation in field-programmable gate array (FPGA) and application-specific integrated circuit (ASIC) designs**: Investigating the integration of the proposed design in FPGAs and ASICs can demonstrate real-world applicability and performance improvements [17–21].
7. Comparators are part of several analog, digital, or mixed signal blocks such analog to digital converter (ADC) and digital to analog converters (DACs), etc. [22–25]. Use of low-power techniques-based comparators will be a suitable choice for such analog devices used in signal processing blocks.
8. **Hybrid optimization techniques**: Combining precomputation with other low-power techniques, such as clock gating, operand isolation, and dynamic voltage scaling, could result

in even greater power savings and performance improvements [26–28].

## 15.7 Conclusion

In this chapter, various design techniques are discussed for the reduction in dynamic power of VLSI circuit. Reduction in switching activities leads to the reduced dynamic power with addition in the integrated circuit (IC) area. Precomputation circuit is added in the architecture to reduce the switching activity of comparator, resulting in reduced dynamic power. A precomputation circuit-based 4bit comparator is designed with Cadence Virtuoso using complementary metal oxide semiconductor (CMOS) logic techniques to enhance the power efficiency in modern VLSI circuits. This study focused on reducing power consumption while maintaining the performance and stability for low-power applications. By optimizing the trade-offs between power consumption, performance, and area, the proposed precomputation technique designs offer a viable solution for future low-power VLSI systems. In this work, we used precomputation logic technique to power dissipation in 4bit comparator. In precomputation technique, we can reduce the power dissipation, but area will increase because we added some gates. In this, we use D-flipflop and XOR gate in precomputation technique.

## Acknowledgement

The author acknowledges the support provided by VLSI Design LPU, India and Department of ECE, Telkom University Indonesia.

## References

1. Yeap, G.K., *Practical low power digital VLSI design*, Springer Science & Business Media, New York, 2012.
2. Sinha, S.K. and Chander, S., Pre-computation logic for Low Power 4-bit Comparator Circuit. *IEEE 2017 International Conference on Telecommunication, Power Analysis and Computing Techniques (ICTPACT 2017)*, Bharath University, Chennai, 2017.

3. Sinha, S.K. and Tripathi, S.L., BDD Based Logic Synthesis and Optimization for Low Power Comparator Circuit. *2018 International Conference on Intelligent Circuits and Systems (ICICS)*, Phagwara, India, pp. 37–41, 2018.
4. Sharma, M., Gupta, N., Gupta, R., Power Reduction Techniques in VLSI. *Int. J. Eng. Tech. Mgmt. Res.*, 5, 123–129, SE, February 2018.
5. Korah, E. and Vijayan, N., Power Reduction in Logic Circuits Using Power Gating for Deep Sub-Micron CMOS VLSI. *Alliance International Conference on Artificial Intelligence and Machine Learning (AICAAM)*, April 2019.
6. Shi, K. and Howard, D., Sleep Transistor Design and Implementation – Simple Concepts Yet Challenges To Be Optimum. *2006 International Symposium on VLSI Design, Automation, and Test.*
7. Abba, A. and Amarender, K., Improved Power Gating Technique for Leakage Power Reduction. *Res. Inventy Int. J. Eng. Sci.*, 4, 10, 06–10, October 2014.
8. Verma, P., Noor, A., Sharma, A.K., Sampath Kumar, V., Power gating and its repercussions—a review. *2016 IEEE 1st International Conference on Power Electronics, Intelligent Control and Energy Systems.*
9. Anjana, R. and Somkuwar, A.K., Total reduction of leakage power through combined effect of Sleep stack and variable body biasing technique. *2013 International Conference on Information Communication and Embedded Systems (ICICES).*
10. Jiang, H., Marek-Sadowska., M., Nassif, S.R., Benefits and costs of power gating technique. *2005 International Conference on Computer Design.*
11. Chrisjin Gnana Suji, C., Maragatharaj, S., Hemima, R., Performance Analysis of Power Gating designs in Low Power VLSI Circuits. *Proceedings of 2011 International Conference on Signal Processing, Communication, Computing and Networking Technologies (ICSCCN)*, 2011.
12. Tripathi, S.L., Kumar, A., Srinivasa Rao, K., Mudimela, P.R., *Nanodevices for Integrated Circuit Design*, Wiley & Scrivener Publishing LLC, USA, October-2023, DOI:10.1002/9781394186396.
13. Kumar, T.S. and Tripathi, S.L., Process evaluation in FinFET based 7T SRAM cell. *Analog Integr. Circuits Signal Process.*, 109, 545–551, 2021, https://doi.org/10.1007/s10470-021-01938-4.
14. Singh Patel, G., Lata Tripathi, S., Awasthi, S., Performance Enhanced Unsymmetrical FinFET and its Applications. *2018 IEEE Electron Devices Kolkata Conference (EDKCON)*, Kolkata, India, pp. 222–227, 2018, doi: 10.1109/EDKCON.2018.8770411.
15. Tripathi, S.L., Mishra, R., Narendra, V., Mishra, R.A., High performance Bulk FinFET with bottom spacer. *2013 IEEE International Conference on Electronics, Computing and Communication Technologies*, Bangalore, India, pp. 1–5, 2013, doi: 10.1109/CONECCT.2013.6469282.
16. Arora, S. and Tripathi, S.L., A comprehensive analysis of ultra low power GNRFET based 20T hybrid full adder for computing applications. *Phys. Scr.*, 99, 8, 085008, 2024.

17. Kumar, A., Tripathi, S.L., Srinivasa Rao, K., *Machine Learning for VLSI Chip Design*, Wiley Scrivener Publishing LLC, New Jersey, USA, 2023, DOI:10.1002/9781119910497, ISBN 9781119910398.
18. Tripathi, S.L. and Mahmud, M., *Explainable Machine Learning Models and Architecture*, Wiley & Scrivener Publishing LLC, USA, 2023, https://doi.org/10.1002/9781394186570.
19. Raj, B., Tripathi, S.L., Chaudhary, T., Srinivasa Rao, K., Singh, M., *Integrated Devices for Artificial Intelligence and VLSI*, Wiley Scrivener Publishing LLC, USA, 15 August 2024, ISBN:9781394205158, DOI:10.1002/9781394205158.
20. Prasanna, D.L. and Tripathi, S.L., A Review on Tongue Based Assistive Technology, Devices and FPGA Processors Using Machine Learning Module. *Wirel. Pers. Commun.*, 134, 151–170, 2024, https://doi.org/10.1007/s11277-024-10897-8.
21. Tripathi, S.L., Kumar, A., Mahmud, M., FPGA for secured hardware & IP ownership. *2022 IEEE International Conference of Electron Devices Society Kolkata Chapter (EDKCON)*, Kolkata, India, pp. 184–189, 2022, doi: 10.1109/EDKCON56221.2022.10032935.
22. Singh, T. and Tripathi, S.L., Design of low-power SAR ADCs for biomedical applications, in: *Nanoscale Memristor Device and Circuits Design*, pp. 165–179, Elsevier, Amsterdam, Netherlands, 2024, https://doi.org/10.1016/B978-0-323-90793-4.00012-X.
23. Singh, T. and Tripathi, S.L., Design of a 16 bit 500 MS/s SAR ADC for Low Power Application, in: *Electronic Device and Circuits Design Challenges to Implement Biomedical Applications*, Elsevier, Amsterdam, Netherlands, 2021, ISBN: 978-0-323-85172-5 Doi: https://doi.org/10.1016/B978-0-323-85172-5.00021-6.
24. Singh, T. and Tripathi, S.L., An Efficient Approach to Design a Comparator for SAR-ADC. *2022 IEEE VLSI Device Circuit and System (VLSI DCS)*, pp. 116–122, 2022, doi: 10.1109/VLSIDCS53788.2022.9811484.
25. Singh, T., Tripathi, S.L., Mahmud, M., Design of a 16-bit 500 MS/s SAR-ADC at 45 nm for low power and high frequency applications. *Eng. Res. Express*, 6, 015306, 20242024. DOI 10.1088/2631-8695/ad2730.
26. Dinesh Kumar, R., Ramkumar Prabhu, M., Lakshmi Priya, K., Renuga, M., Senthil Kumar, K.S., Vennisa, V., An Investigation of Low Power VLSI Design Techniques. *J. Sci. Comput. Eng. Res. (JSCER)*, 6, 4, 5–9, April 2023.
27. Tripathi, S.L., Saxena, S., Sinha, S.K., Patel, G.S., *Digital VLSI Design Problems and Solution with Verilog*, John Wiley & Sons, Ltd., New Jersey, USA, 2021, DOI:10.1002/9781119778097 ISBN: 978-1-119-77804-2.
28. Tripathi, S.L., Padmanabhan, S., Kumar, D., Raja, P. (Eds.), *Design and Development of Energy Efficient Systems*, Scrivener Publishing, Wiley, USA, 2021, ISBN: 1119761638, 9781119761631 DOI:10.1002/9781119761785.

# Index

# Also of Interest

## By the same editors

*Waste Management and Utilization for a Sustainable Environment,* Edited by Amit Srivastava and Suman Lata Tripathi, ISBN: 9781394292974. Waste Management and Utilization for a Sustainable Environment is an essential guide to understanding how cutting-edge technologies and innovative engineering solutions can transform waste management into a cornerstone of a sustainable future.

*Energy-Efficient Communication Networks,* Edited by Shakti Raj Chopra, Krishan Arora, Suman Lata Tripathi, and Vikram Kumar, ISBN: 9781394271658. *Energy-Efficient Communication Networks* is essential for anyone looking to understand and implement cutting-edge energy optimization strategies for communication systems, ensuring they meet growing energy demands while seamlessly integrating renewable energy sources and enhancing battery life in embedded applications.

*Smart Textiles and Wearables for Health and Fitness,* Edited by Jyotirmoy Pathak, Abhishek Kumar, Suman Lata Tripathi, and Balwinder Raj, ISBN: 9781394302949. *Smart Textiles and Wearables for Health: The Flexible Electronics Revolution* provides an in-depth exploration of how innovative technologies and materials are reshaping healthcare, making it an essential resource for anyone looking to understand the transformative power of smart textiles and wearables in patient monitoring, diagnosis, and rehabilitation.

*Development of 6G Networks and Technology,* Edited by Suman Lata Tripathi, Mufti Mahmood, C. Narmadha, and S. Albert Alexander, ISBN: 9781394230655. *Development of 6G Networks and Technology* provides an in-depth exploration of the potential impact of 6G networks on various industries, including healthcare, agriculture, transport, and national security, making it an essential resource for researchers, scholars, and students working in the field of wireless networks and high-speed data processing systems.

*INTEGRATED DEVICES FOR ARTIFICIAL INTELLIGENCE AND VLSI: VLSI Design, Simulation and Applications,* Edited by Balwinder Raj, Suman Lata Tripathi, Tarun Chaudhary, K. Srinivasa Rao, and Mandeep Singh, ISBN: 9781394204359. With its in-depth exploration of the close connection between microelectronics, AI, and VLSI technology, this book offers valuable insights into the cutting-edge techniques and tools used in VLSI design automation, making it an essential resource for anyone seeking to stay ahead in the rapidly evolving field of VLSI design.

*DECENTRALIZED SYSTEMS AND DISTRIBUTED COMPUTING,* Edited by Sandhya Avasthi, Suman Lata Tripathi, Namrata Dhanda, and Satya Bhushan Verma, ISBN: 978139420436. This book provides a comprehensive exploration of next-generation internet, distributed systems, and distributed computing, offering valuable insights into their impact on society and the future of technology.

*ELECTRIC VEHICLE DESIGN: Design, Simulation and Applications,* Edited by Krishan Arora, Suman Lata Tripathi, and Himashu Sharma, ISBN: 9781394204373. This book will serve as a definitive guide to conceptual and practical knowledge about the design of hybrid electrical vehicles (HEV), battery electrical vehicles (BEV), fuel cell electrical vehicles (FCEV), plug-in hybrid electrical vehicles (PHEV), and efficient EV charging techniques with advanced tools and methodologies for students, engineers, and academics alike.

*INDUSTRIAL CONTROL SYSTEMS,* Edited by Vipin Chandra Pal, Suman Lata Tripathi, and Souvik Ganguli, ISBN: 9781119829256. This volume serves as a comprehensive guide in the journey of industrial control systems with a multidisciplinary approach to the key engineering problems in the 21st century.

*MODERN AUTOMOTIVE ELECTRICAL SYSTEMS: Theory and Applications,* Edited by Pedram Asef, Sanjeevikumar Padmanaban, and Andrew Lapthorn, ISBN: 1119801047. Presenting the concepts and advances of modern automotive electrical systems, this volume, written and edited by a global team of experts, also goes into the practical applications for the engineer, student, and other industry professionals.

*NANODEVICES FOR INTEGRATED CIRCUIT DESIGN,* Edited by Suman Lata Tripathi, Abhishek Kumar, K. Srinivasa Rao, and Prasantha R. Mudimela, ISBN: 9781394185788. Written and edited by a team of experts in the field, this important new volume broadly covers the design of nano-devices and their integrated applications in digital and analog integrated circuits (IC) design.

*EXPLAINABLE MACHINE LEARNING MODELS AND ARCHITECTURES: Real-Time System Implementation,* Edited by Suman Lata Tripathi and Mufti Mahmud, ISBN: 9781394185849. This cutting-edge new volume covers the hardware architecture implementation, the software implementation approach, and the efficient hardware of machine learning applications.

*MACHINE LEARNING TECHNIQUES FOR VLSI CHIP DESIGN,* Edited by Abhishek Kumar, Suman Lata Tripathi, and K. Srinivasa Rao, ISBN: 9781119910398. This cutting-edge new volume covers the hardware architecture implementation, the software implementation approach, and the efficient hardware of machine learning applications with FPGA or CMOS circuits, and many other aspects and applications of machine learning techniques for VLSI chip design.

*INTELLIGENT GREEN TECHNOLOGIES FOR SMART CITIES,* Edited by Suman Lata Tripathi, Souvik Ganguli, Abhishek Kumar, and Tengiz Magradze, ISBN: 9781119816065. Presenting the concepts and fundamentals of smart cities and developing "green" technologies, this volume, written and edited by a global team of experts, also goes into the practical applications that can be utilized across multiple disciplines and industries, for both the engineer and the student.

*DESIGN AND DEVELOPMENT OF EFFICIENT ENERGY SYSTEMS,* Edited by Suman Lata Tripathi, Dushyant Kumar Singh, Sanjeevikumar Padmanaban, and P. Raja, ISBN: 9781119761631. Covering the concepts and fundamentals of efficient energy systems, this volume, written and edited by a global team of experts, also goes into the practical applications that can be utilized across multiple industries, for both the engineer and the student.

*Electrical and Electronic Devices, Circuits, and Materials: Technical Challenges and Solutions*, Edited by Suman Lata Tripathi, Parvej Ahmad Alvi, and Umashankar Subramaniam, ISBN: 9781119750369. Covering every aspect of the design and improvement needed for solid-state electronic devices and circuit and their reliability issues, this new volume also includes overall system design for all kinds of analog and digital applications and developments in power systems.

*Green Energy: Solar Energy, Photovoltaics, and Smart Cities*, Edited by Suman Lata Tripathi and Sanjeevikumar Padmanaban, ISBN: 9781119760764. Covering the concepts and fundamentals of green energy, this volume, written and edited by a global team of experts, also goes into the practical applications that can be utilized across multiple industries, for both the engineer and the student.

**Check out these other related titles from Scrivener Publishing**

*HYDROGEN ELECTRICAL VEHICLES*, Edited by Mehmet Sankir and Nurdan Demirci Sankir, ISBN: 9781394166381. Hydrogen electrical vehicles are an essential component of the "Green New Deal" and this book covers cutting-edge technologies designed for fuel-cell-powered cars.

*PAVEMENT ASSET MANAGEMENT*, By Ralph Haas, W.R. Hudson, and Lynne Cowe Falls, ISBN: 9781119038702. Whether you are new to managing pavement assets or a seasoned practitioner, this book provides the most up-to-date information in the field on the history, technology, practice and look ahead.

Printed and bound by CPI Group (UK) Ltd, Croydon, CR0 4YY
17/09/2026
14964263-0003